# Children's
# Literature
# Review

# Guide to Gale Literary Criticism Series

| For criticism on | Consult these Gale series |
|---|---|
| Authors now living or who died after December 31, 1959 | *CONTEMPORARY LITERARY CRITICISM (CLC)* |
| Authors who died between 1900 and 1959 | *TWENTIETH-CENTURY LITERARY CRITICISM (TCLC)* |
| Authors who died between 1800 and 1899 | *NINETEENTH-CENTURY LITERATURE CRITICISM (NCLC)* |
| Authors who died between 1400 and 1799 | *LITERATURE CRITICISM FROM 1400 TO 1800 (LC)* *SHAKESPEAREAN CRITICISM (SC)* |
| Authors who died before 1400 | *CLASSICAL AND MEDIEVAL LITERATURE CRITICISM (CMLC)* |
| Black writers of the past two hundred years | *BLACK LITERATURE CRITICISM (BLC) AND BLACK LITERATURE CRITICISM SUPPLEMENT (BLCS)* |
| Authors of books for children and young adults | *CHILDREN'S LITERATURE REVIEW (CLR)* |
| Dramatists | *DRAMA CRITICISM (DC)* |
| Hispanic writers of the late nineteenth and twentieth centuries | *HISPANIC LITERATURE CRITICISM (HLC)* |
| Native North American writers and orators of the eighteenth, nineteenth, and twentieth centuries | *NATIVE NORTH AMERICAN LITERATURE (NNAL)* |
| Poets | *POETRY CRITICISM (PC)* |
| Short story writers | *SHORT STORY CRITICISM (SSC)* |
| Major authors from the Renaissance to the present | *WORLD LITERATURE CRITICISM, 1500 TO THE PRESENT (WLC)* |
| Major authors and works from the Bible to the present | *WORLD LITERATURE CRITICISM SUPPLEMENT (WLCS)* |

ISSN 0362-4145

volume 60

# Children's Literature Review

Excerpts from Reviews,
Criticism, and Commentary
on Books for Children
and Young People

**Deborah J. Morad**
Editor

**GALE GROUP**

**Detroit**
**New York**
**San Francisco**
**London**
**Boston**
**Woodbridge, CT**

## STAFF

Deborah J. Morad, *Editor*

Arlene M. Johnson, *Associate Editor*

Sara Constantakis, David Galens, Motoko Fujishiro Huthwaite, Marie Lazzari,
Tom Schoenberg, Erin E. White, *Contributing Editors*

Tim White, *Technical Training Specialist*

Joyce Nakamura, *Managing Editor*

Maria Franklin, *Permissions Manager*
Sarah Tomasek, Edna Hedblad, *Permissions Associates*

Victoria B. Cariappa, *Research Manager*
Corrine A. Boland, *Project Coordinator*
Andrew Guy Malonis, Gary J. Oudersluys, Cheryl D. Warnock, *Research Specialists*
Tamara C. Nott, Tracie A. Richardson, *Research Associates*
Phyllis J. Blackman, Tim Lehnerer, Patricia L. Love, *Research Assistants*

Mary Beth Trimper, *Production Director*
Stacy Melson, *Production Assistant*

Gary Leach, *Graphic Artist*
Randy Bassett, *Image Database Supervisor*
Robert Duncan, Michael Logusz, *Imaging Specialists*
Pamela A. Reed, *Imaging Coordinator*

Library of Congress Catalog Card Number 76-643301
ISBN 0-7876-3225-2
ISSN 0362-4145
Printed in the United States of America

10   9   8   7   6   5   4   3   2   1

# Contents

Preface   vii
Acknowledgments   xi

# Preface

Literature for children and young adults has evolved into both a respected branch of creative writing and a successful industry. Currently, books for young readers are considered among the most popular segments of publishing. Criticism of juvenile literature is instrumental in recording the literary or artistic development of the creators of children's books as well as the trends and controversies that result from changing values or attitudes about young people and their literature. Designed to provide a permanent, accessible record of this ongoing scholarship, *Children's Literature Review (CLR)* presents parents, teachers, and librarians—those responsible for bringing children and books together—with the opportunity to make informed choices when selecting reading materials for the young. In addition, *CLR* provides researchers of children's literature with easy access to a wide variety of critical information from English-language sources in the field. Users will find balanced overviews of the careers of the authors and illustrators of the books that children and young adults are reading; these entries, which contain excerpts from published criticism in books and periodicals, assist users by sparking ideas for papers and assignments and suggesting supplementary and classroom reading. Ann L. Kalkhoff, president and editor of *Children's Book Review Service Inc.*, writes that "*CLR* has filled a gap in the field of children's books, and it is one series that will never lose its validity or importance."

## Scope of the Series

Each volume of *CLR* profiles the careers of a selection of authors and illustrators of books for children and young adults from preschool through high school. Author lists in each volume reflect:

- an international scope.

- representation of authors of all eras.

- the variety of genres covered by children's and/or YA literature: picture books, fiction, nonfiction, poetry, folklore, and drama.

Although the focus of the series is on authors new to *CLR*, entries will be updated as the need arises.

## Organization of This Book

An entry consists of the following elements: author heading, author portrait, author introduction, excerpts of criticism (each preceded by a bibliographical citation), and illustrations, when available.

- The **Author Heading** consists of the author's name followed by birth and death dates. The portion of the name outside the parentheses denotes the form under which the author is most frequently published. If the majority of the author's works for children were written under a pseudonym, the pseudonym will be listed in the author heading and the real name given on the first line of the author introduction. Also located at the beginning of the introduction are any other pseudonyms used by the author in writing for children and any name variations, including transliterated forms for authors whose languages use nonroman alphabets. Uncertainty as to a birth or death date is indicated by question marks.

- An **Author Portrait** is included when available.

- The **Author Introduction** contains information designed to introduce an author to *CLR* users by presenting an overview of the author's themes and styles, biographical facts that relate to the author's literary career or critical responses to the author's works, and information about major awards and prizes the author has received. The introduction begins by identifying the nationality of the author and by listing the genres in which s/he has written for children and young adults. Introductions also list a group of representative titles for which the author or illustrator being profiled is best known; this section, which begins with the words "major works include," follows the genre line of the introduction. For seminal figures, a listing of major works about the author follows when appropriate, highlighting important biographies about the author or illustrator that are not excerpted in the entry. The centered heading "Introduction" announces the body of the text.

- **Criticism** is located in three sections: **Author's Commentary** (when available), **General Commentary** (when available), and **Title Commentary** (commentary on specific titles).

  - The **Author's Commentary** presents background material written by the author or by an interviewer. This commentary may cover a specific work or several works. Author's commentary on more than one work appears after the author introduction, while commentary on an individual book follows the title entry heading.

  - The **General Commentary** consists of critical excerpts that consider more than one work by the author or illustrator being profiled. General commentary is preceded by the critic's name in boldface type or, in the case of unsigned criticism, by the title of the journal. *CLR* also features entries that emphasize general criticism on the oeuvre of an author or illustrator. When appropriate, a selection of reviews is included to supplement the general commentary.

  - The **Title Commentary** begins with the title entry headings, which precede the criticism on a title and cite publication information on the work being reviewed. Title headings list the title of the work as it appeared in its first English-language edition. The first English-language publication date of each work (unless otherwise noted) is listed in parentheses following the title. Differing U.S. and British titles follow the publication date within the parentheses. When a work is written by an individual other than the one being profiled, as is the case when illustrators are featured, the parenthetical material following the title cites the author of the work before listing its publication date.

    Entries in each title commentary section consist of critical excerpts on the author's individual works, arranged chronologically by publication date. The entries generally contain two to seven reviews per title, depending on the stature of the book and the amount of criticism it has generated. The editors select titles that reflect the entire scope of the author's literary contribution, covering each genre and subject. An effort is made to reprint criticism that represents the full range of each title's reception, from the year of its initial publication to current assessments. Thus, the reader is provided with a record of the author's critical history. Publication information (such as publisher names and book prices) and parenthetical numerical references (such as footnotes or page and line references to specific editions of works) have been deleted at the discretion of the editors to provide smoother reading of the text.

- Centered headings introduce each section, in which criticism is arranged chronologically; beginning with Volume 35, each excerpt is preceded by a boldface source heading for easier access by readers. Within the text, titles by authors being profiled are also highlighted in boldface type.

- Selected excerpts are preceded by **Explanatory Annotations,** which provide information on the critic or work of criticism to enhance the reader's understanding of the excerpt.

- A complete **Bibliographical Citation** designed to facilitate the location of the original book or article precedes each piece of criticism.

- Numerous **Illustrations** are featured in *CLR*. For entries on illustrators, an effort has been made to include illustrations that reflect the characteristics discussed in the criticism. Entries on authors who do not illustrate their own works may also include photographs and other illustrative material pertinent to their careers.

## Special Features: Entries on Illustrators

Entries on authors who are also illustrators will occasionally feature commentary on selected works illustrated but not written by the author being profiled. These works are strongly associated with the illustrator and have received critical acclaim for their art. By including critical comment on works of this type, the editors wish to provide a more complete representation of the artist's career. Criticism on these works has been chosen to stress artistic, rather than literary, contributions. Title entry headings for works illustrated by the author being profiled are arranged chronologically within the entry by date of publication and include notes identifying the author of the illustrated work. In order to provide easier access for users, all titles illustrated by the subject of the entry are boldfaced.

*CLR* also includes entries on prominent illustrators who have contributed to the field of children's literature. These entries are designed to represent the development of the illustrator as an artist rather than as a literary stylist. The illustrator's section is organized like that of an author, with two exceptions: the introduction presents an overview of the illustrator's styles and techniques rather than outlining his or her literary background, and the commentary written by the illustrator on his or her works is called "illustrator's commentary" rather than "author's commentary." All titles of books containing illustrations by the artist being profiled are highlighted in boldface type.

## Other Features: Acknowledgments, Indexes

- The **Acknowledgments** section, which immediately follows the preface, lists the sources from which material has been reprinted in the volume. It does not, however, list every book or periodical consulted for the volume.

- The **Cumulative Index to Authors** lists all of the authors who have appeared in *CLR* with cross-references to the biographical, autobiographical, and literary criticism series published by The Gale Group. A full listing of the series titles appears before the first page of the indexes of this volume.

- The **Cumulative Index to Nationalities** lists authors alphabetically under their respective nationalities. Author names are followed by the volume number(s) in which they appear.

- The **Cumulative Index to Titles** lists titles covered in *CLR* followed by the volume and page number where criticism begins.

## A Note to the Reader

*CLR* is one of several critical references sources in the Literature Criticism Series published by The Gale Group. When writing papers, students who quote directly from any volume in the Literature Criticism Series may use the following general forms to footnote reprinted criticism. The first example pertains to material drawn from periodicals, the second to material reprinted from books.

¹T. S. Eliot, "John Donne," *The Nation and the Athenaeum,* 33 (9 June 1923), 321-32; excerpted and reprinted in *Literature Criticism from 1400 to 1800,* Vol. 10, ed. James E. Person, Jr. (Detroit: Gale Research, 1989), pp. 28-9.

¹Henry Brooke, *Leslie Brooke and Johnny Crow* (Frederick Warne, 1982); excerpted and reprinted in *Children's Literature Review,* Vol. 20, ed. Gerard J. Senick (Detroit: Gale Research, 1990), p. 47.

## Suggestions Are Welcome

In response to various suggestions, several features have been added to *CLR* since the beginning of the series, including author entries on retellers of traditional literature as well as those who have been the first to record oral tales and other folklore; entries on prominent illustrators featuring commentary on their styles and techniques; entries on authors whose works are considered controversial; occasional entries devoted to criticism on a single work or a series of works; sections in author introductions that list major works by and about the author or illustrator being profiled; explanatory notes that provide information on the critic or work of criticism to enhance the usefulness of the excerpt; more extensive illustrative material, such as holographs of manuscript pages and photographs of people and places pertinent to the careers of the authors and artists; a cumulative nationality index for easy access to authors by nationality; and occasional guest essays written specifically for *CLR* by prominent critics on subjects of their choice.

Readers who wish to suggest authors to appear in future volumes, or who have other suggestions, are cordially invited to contact the editor. By mail: Editor, *Children's Literature Review,* The Gale Group, 27500 Drake Road, Farmington Hills, MI 48331-3535; by telephone: (800) 347-GALE, (248) 699-4253; by fax: (248) 699-8065.

# Acknowledgments

The editors wish to thank the copyright holders of the excerpted criticism included in this volume and the permissions managers of many book and magazine publishing companies for assisting us in securing reproduction rights. We are also grateful to the staffs of the Detroit Public Library, the Library of Congress, the University of Detroit Mercy Library, Wayne State University Purdy/Kresge Library Complex, and the University of Michigan Libraries for making their resources available to us. Following is a list of the copyright holders who have granted us permission to reproduce material in this volume of **CLR**. Every effort has been made to trace copyright, but if omissions have been made, please let us know.

## COPYRIGHTED EXCERPTS IN *CLR,* VOLUME 60, WERE REPRODUCED FROM THE FOLLOWING PERIODICALS:

*The American Scholar,* v. 22, Autumn, 1953 for "Mr. Eliot, Mr. Trilling, and 'Huckleberry Finn'" by Leo Marx. Copyright © 1953, renewed 1981 by the United Chapters of the Phi Beta Kappa Society. Reproduced by permission of the author.—*The ALAN Review,* v. 19, Spring, 1992. Reproduced by permission.—*Appraisal: Science Books for Young People,* v. 17, Fall, 1984. Copyright © 1984 by the Children's Science Book Review Committee. Reproduced by permission.—*Australian Book Review,* October, 1994; April, 1997. All reproduced by permission.—*Best Sellers,* v. 28, October 1, 1968. Copyright 1968 by the University of Scranton. Reproduced by permission.—*Bookbird,* v. 35, Fall, 1997. Reproduced by permission.—*Booklist,* v. 63, December 1, 1966; v. 67, July 15, 1971; v. 72, February 15, 1976; v. 72, April 1, 1976; v. 74, February 15, 1978; v. 75, November 1, 1978; v. 75, November 15, 1978; v. 76, October 15, 1979; v. 76, December 1, 1979; v. 78, May 1, 1982; v. 79, September 1, 1982; v. 79, January 15, 1983; v. 79, July, 1983; v. 81, December 1, 1984; v. 82, September 1, 1985; v. 83, October 1, 1986; v. 83, April 1, 1987; v. 85, November 15, 1988; v. 85, July, 1989; v. 86, February 1, 1990; v. 87, September 1, 1990; v. 87, January 15, 1991; v. 87, April 15, 1991; v. 88, July, 1991; v. 88, September 15, 1991; v. 88, November 1, 1991; v. 89, September 1, 1992; v. 89, September 15, 1992; v. 89, October 15, 1992; v. 89, December 15, 1992; v. 89, March 1, 1993; v. 89, March 15, 1993; v. 89, May 1, 1993; v. 89, June 1 & June 15, 1993; v. 90, September 15, 1993; v. 90, January 15, 1994; v. 90, February 15, 1994; v. 90, May 15, 1994; v. 91, October 1, 1994; v. 91, December 15, 1994; v. 91, April 1, 1995; v. 91, June 1, 1995; v. 92, March 1, 1996; v. 93, September 15, 1996; v. 94, September 15, 1997; v. 94, October 15, 1997; v. 94, February 15, 1998; v. 94, August, 1998; v. 95, March 15, 1999. Copyright © 1966, 1971, 1976, 1978, 1979, 1982, 1983, 1984, 1985, 1986, 1987, 1988, 1989, 1990, 1991, 1992, 1993, 1994, 1995, 1996, 1997, 1998, 1999 by the American Library Association. All reproduced by permission.—*Books for Keeps,* n. 52, September, 1988; n. 58, September, 1989; n. 60, January, 1990; n. 74, May, 1992; n. 81, July, 1993; n. 93, July, 1995; n. 98, May, 1996; n. 112, September 1998. © School Bookshop Association 1988, 1989, 1990, 1992, 1993, 1995, 1996, 1998. All reproduced by permission.—*Books for Young People,* v. 1, February, 1987 for "Another Swift, Sure Novel from Monica Hughes" by Patty Lawlor. Reproduced by permission.—*Books in Canada,* v. 15, December, 1986 for a review of "Blaine's Way" by Mary Ainslie Smith; v. 16, August-September, 1987 for a review of "Log Jam" by Mary Ainslie Smith; v. 26, March, 1997 for "Strength from Solitude" by Frieda Wishinsky. All reproduced by permission of the respective authors./ v. 22, September, 1993 for a review of "A Handful of Seeds" by Elizabeth Anthony; v. 25, May, 1996 for a review of "Castle Tourmandyne" by Alison Sutherland; v. 27, June, 1998 for a review of "The Faces of Fear" by Katherine Matthews. All reproduced by permission of the publisher.—*Boy's Life,* v. LXXXIV, August, 1994 for "My Life's Work: Oceanographer" by Mark Henricks. Reproduced by permission of the publisher, the Boy Scouts of America, and the author.—*Bulletin for the Center for Children's Books,* v. 20, December, 1966; v. 21, April, 1968; v. 25, September, 1971; v. 25, June, 1972; v. 26, January, 1973; v. 29, December, 1975; v. 29, March, 1976; v. 30, September, 1976; v. 31, July-August, 1978; v. 32, January, 1979; v. 32, March, 1979; v. 32, April, 1979; v. 33, January, 1980; v. 35, December, 1981; v. 36, June, 1982; v. 36, October, 1982; v. 38, September, 1984; v. 38, December, 1984; v. 39, November, 1985; v. 40, July-August, 1987; v. 42, May, 1989; v. 43, October, 1989; v. 43, May, 1990; v. 44, October, 1990; v. 45, October, 1991; v. 45, May, 1992. Copyright © 1966, 1968, 1971, 1972, 1973, 1975, 1976, 1978, 1979, 1980, 1981, 1982, 1984, 1985, 1987, 1989, 1990, 1991, 1992 by The University of Chicago. All reproduced by permission./ v. 46, September, 1992; v. 47, November, 1993; v. 48, January, 1994; v. 48, July-August, 1994; v. 48, February, 1995; v. 48, March, 1995; v. 49, October, 1995; v. 49, March, 1996; v. 49, June, 1996; v. 52, September, 1998. Copyright © 1992, 1993, 1994, 1995, 1996, 1998 by The Board of Trustees of the University of Illinois. All reproduced by permission./ v. 14, May, 1961. Copyright © 1961, renewed 1989 by The University of Chicago. Reproduced by permission.—*Canadian Book Review Annual,* 1995; 1996; 1997. All reproduced by permission.—*Canadian Children's Literature,* n. 46, 1987; v. 20, Spring, 1994; v. 22, Summer, 1996. Copyright © 1987, 1994, 1996 Canadian Children's Press. All reproduced by permission.—*Canadian Literature,* n. 116, Spring, 1988 for a review of "Blaine's Way" by David W. Atkinson; n. 117, Summer, 1988 for a review of "Log Jam" by Roderick McGillis. Both reproduced by permission of the respective authors.—*Children's Literature,* v. 19, 1991. © 1991 by The Children's Literature Foundation, Inc.

## COPYRIGHTED EXCERPTS IN *CLR*, VOLUME 60, WERE REPRODUCED FROM THE FOLLOWING BOOKS:

# Children's Literature Review

# Robert D(uane) Ballard

## 1942-

American author of nonfiction and fiction; oceanographer, geologist, and explorer.

Major works include *Exploring Our Living Planet* (1983), *Exploring the Titanic* (edited by Patrick Crean, 1988), *The Lost Wreck of the Isis* (with Rick Archbold, 1990), *Exploring the Bismarck* (with Rick Archbold, 1991), *Lost Liners: From the Titanic to the Andrea Doria, the Ocean Floor Reveals the Greatest Lost Ships* (with Rick Archbold, 1997).

## INTRODUCTION

Credited with the discovery and photography of the most publicized shipwreck of the twentieth century, the *Titanic,* Ballard is a world-renowned scientist and explorer who is also a recognized pioneer of deep-sea exploration. A veteran of almost one hundred deep-sea expeditions, Ballard has years of experience searching the mysterious ocean floors of the world. In addition to the *Titanic,* Ballard has also uncovered the "unsinkable" German battleship *Bismarck* and has examined the sunken luxury liner *Lusitania,* the ill-fated warships of the Battle of Guadalcanal, and a collection of ancient Roman vessels sunk in the Mediterranean Sea. Ballard has shared these discoveries as well as his vast experience in his fiction and nonfiction for an audience ranging from elementary to adult readers. In addition, he has written nonfiction focusing on such scientific topics as plate tectonics, and has published a suspense thriller for young adults and adults titled, *Bright Shark* (1992), on which he collaborated with Tony Chiu. Ballard's most widely read work for children, *Exploring the Titanic,* has been highly recommended by critics for its unique combination of history and modern scientific exploration and technology. Ballard adopts this formula in many of his nonfiction writings about submerged and lost ships, including *Exploring the Bismarck* and *Exploring the Lusitania,* two works aimed at audiences in grades five through eight. He uses the wrecks as focal points to educate his audience about the ocean, its fluctuations and life forms, and the historical and social events surrounding the passengers and crew of each ship. While reviewers have praised Ballard's engaging adventures, his vivid descriptions of events and atmosphere, and the revealing evidence of his accounts, the scientific community was additionally excited by Ballard's deployment of new and highly advanced technology during his expeditions. These included a small research submarine coined the *Argo,* an underwater research robot known as the *Angus,* a camera sled, and innovative methods for exploring and photographing deep-sea events, artifacts, and life forms.

For Ballard, his writings have become an efficient way

of "getting the word out," as he was quoted in *Something about the Author* (*SATA*). He added, "Since all of my writings deal with expeditions I am conducting in the deep sea, the writing process has become part of an epic journey which now seems incomplete unless I return from an important expedition to report its findings not only in scientific journals for my colleagues, but to the general public whose tax dollars paid for the expeditions." Ballard's revealing prose, considerable detail, and his carefully chosen and illustrative photographs bring history to life, drawing young readers into his journeys beneath the ocean depths. In his review of *Exploring the Titanic,* Robert Hull summed up: "Ballard, in short, is that relative rarity among writers of non-fiction for children, a narrator of firsthand experience who is deeply enthusiastic and effortlessly knowledgeable."

### Biographical Information

Born in Wichita, Kansas, Ballard was raised in southern California, where his family moved during World War II while his father worked as a flight engineer at the aircraft testing grounds in the Mojave Desert. Born three days after the *U.S.S. Yorktown* was sunk, Ballard grew up listening to stories about the war at sea. The pier and beaches near his home were his playground, and he spent his free time swimming in the ocean and exploring the tidal pools, plants, and creatures along the shore. He enjoyed reading about Osa and Martin Johnson, who led photographic expeditions to the South Pacific and Africa, and of Captain Nemo. The adventurous Ballard drew his greatest inspirations, however, from his family, particularly his father. He told *Oceanus,* "It was my father who taught me to take charge of my life." His father, a former cowhand, was a self-taught scientist who had a long, successful career, eventually becoming chief engineer of the Minuteman missile program.

Ballard attended college at the University of California in Santa Barbara, receiving a Bachelor of Science degree in chemistry and geology in 1965. The following year he married his first wife; the couple had two children, but later divorced. While studying geophysics as a graduate student at the University of Hawaii, he supported himself by taking care of two trained porpoises at a marine park, a job he claims made him a better parent. He continued his graduate work at the University of Southern California, served in the U.S. Army from 1965 to 1967, and then joined the navy. As a lieutenant he was assigned as a liaison officer between the Office of Naval Research in Boston, Massachusetts, and the Woods Hole Oceanographic Institute in Woods Hole on Cape Cod. When his naval appointment ended in 1969, Ballard stayed on as a research associate in ocean engineering and, after earning a Ph.D. in marine geology and geophysics from the University of Rhode Island in 1974, was promoted through the ranks, eventually becoming a senior scientist at Woods Hole.

Ballard has led an exceptionally busy and innovative career. During the 1970s and 1980s, he made several underwater discoveries that scientists rank among the most important of the twentieth century. These include his 1985 discovery of the wreck of the *Titanic* lying on the floor of the North Atlantic, as well as the *Bismarck* two years later. His dissertation focused on plate tectonics, a revolutionary theory suggesting that segments of the earth's outer crust were in constant motion. Although previously dismissed by many scientists, the plate tectonics theory has become widely accepted among scholars today. In a similar vein, Ballard uncovered hydrothermal vents off the coast of Ecuador and collected an astonishing number of photographs showing colonies of previously unknown creatures feeding on the sulfur and minerals emitted from these vents. During the 1980s he also concentrated on engineering technology that would enable unmanned exploration of the ocean depths. He spearheaded the development of the *Argo-Jason,* a technological system propelled by a remotely controlled aquatic robot and using video cameras to photograph the underwater environment. This technology was instrumental in finding *Titanic* and other deep sea wrecks. Ballard published his first nonfiction work for adults, *Photographic Atlas of the Mid-Atlantic Ridge*

*Rift Valley,* in 1977; ten years later, he wrote *Exploring the Titanic* for a child audience. In 1991, he married his second wife, and the couple had one child.

One of Ballard's most cherished innovations, the JASON Project, brings the excitement of science and hunger for learning into junior high school classrooms. In a press release about the initiative, Ballard noted, "I believe that all children are born scientists, the first question they ask is why. We just need to build on their natural curiosity." Recognized as one of the world's most comprehensive and interactive distance-learning programs, the JASON Project broadcasts live from research centers in remote areas directly to classrooms via satellite broadcasts and the Internet. Ballard's most recent undertaking has been with the Mystic Aquarium in Mystic, Connecticut, where he has founded the Institute for Exploration and Sea Research. In an interview with *Insight,* Ballard remarked, "I've come to realize that the deep sea is a preserver of human history. There is more history preserved in the deep sea than in all the museums of the world combined."

## Major Works

Ballard's first major work of nonfiction, *Exploring Our Living Planet,* reflects his early interest in plate tectonics. Produced by the National Geographic Society, *Exploring Our Living Planet* features paintings, photos, maps, and graphics that help explain plate movements and thermal vents and how they create volcanic eruptions, tropical storms, and earthquakes above the sea. The work extensively explores prehistoric geology and the development of modern plate tectonics, the spreading of the sea floor, hot spots, and the movement of the crustal plates. A *School Library Journal* reviewer noted the book as "highly illuminating, clearly written, and beautifully designed," and called it a "work of art." Ballard's *Exploring the Titanic* covers one of the most fascinating disasters of the twentieth century. The compelling and sympathetic account of the maiden and last voyage of the first-class ocean liner has been highly praised by critics for its factuality, evocative atmosphere, and searing portrait of the stratified society of the ship represents. *Exploring the Titanic* was followed by *The Discovery of the Titanic* (1989), written in collaboration with Rick Archbold for young adults and adults. In both works, Ballard shares his personal adventure of searching for the *Titanic,* clearly describes the technology he employed to uncover its remains, and concludes with a plea to leave the sunken vessel undisturbed as a memorial to the dead. Critics further commended the book's straightforward, well-paced and non-condescending prose, as well as its attractive presentation and eye-catching illustrations. Roger Burford Mason noted Ballard's understanding of young people's interest in the subject, praising the author's imaginative and respectful presentation, which draws readers into their "own exciting adventure." Mason also noted, "Ballard is very good on atmosphere—the excitement and anticipation of the passengers; the glamour, glitter, and novelty; the bustle and noise—and in capturing it all, he intensifies our sympathy for the victims who drowned in the icy seas on [April 15], 1912."

The technology Ballard used to locate the *Titanic* enabled him to detect and photograph other ocean liners lost at sea. Ballard and his crew excavated artifacts from an ancient Roman shipwreck they named the *Isis*. The excavation took place before the eyes of thousands of school children in the U.S. and Canada who witnessed the recovery as part of the JASON project. Ballard documented the expedition in *The Lost Wreck of the Isis*, a work targeting children in grades five through eight. For this title, however, Ballard interspersed his account of the exploration with a fictional, first person narrative told by Antonius, a 14-year-old Roman boy who is aboard the *Isis* when she sinks in the second century A.D. Leone McDermott noted, "Adventure lovers will find this an engrossing read, as will those interested in history or scientific exploration."

Ballard also uncovered World War II German warship, the *Bismarck,* and communicated his research and findings in *Exploring the Bismarck*. Uniting history and modern science and technology, this nonfiction account tells of the sea battle and the ensuing tragedy through the eyes of four young German sailors on board and then recounts how Ballard and his crew discovered the wreck a half-century later. Although some critics thought the book's technology-oriented descriptions lacked the depth of Ballard's previous titles, most reviewers praised Ballard's formula—the lucid historical accounts combined with his scientific exploits—and found the illustrations both engaging and functional. Ballard continued to explore great shipwrecks in several works in which he collaborated with Rick Archbold, including *The Lost Ships of Guadalcanal* (1993), *Lost Liners: From the Titanic to the Andrea Doria, the Ocean Floor Reveals the Greatest Lost Ships, Ghost Liners: Exploring the World's Greatest Lost Ships* (1998) and his most recent title, *Return to Midway: The Quest to Find the Lost Ships from the Greatest Battle of the Pacific War* (1999). In *Lost Liners*, Ballard tells the stories of several ill-fated ocean liners such as the *Lusitania, Britannic, Empress of Ireland,* and the *Andrea Doria,* then takes readers to the ocean floor to view their remains. In the final chapter, he appeals to the public to help preserve the wrecks as underwater marine museums. Typical of Ballard's nonfiction, *Lost Liners* is lavishly illustrated with photographs, paintings, and drawings of history and of the scientist's recent discoveries.

## Awards

Ballard has won many science awards. Among these are the Centennial Award from the National Geographic Society in 1988, the Westinghouse Award from the American Association for the Advancement of Science in 1990, and the first annual Science Service/Science News Award for Contributions to Science, Youth, and Explorations in 1994 by the Explorers Club in New York for outstanding and unselfish devotion to assisting students in furthering their understanding of science and its importance to society and the world's well-being.

---

## AUTHOR'S COMMENTARY

**Eli Lehrer with Robert Ballard**

SOURCE: "Deep-Sea Explorer Brings History to Life," in *Insight on the News,* Vol. 15, No. 16, May 3, 1999, p. 21.

Insight: You were born in Kansas. How did you become fascinated with the sea?

Robert Ballard: During World War II, my father moved to the West Coast, to San Diego. I was born three days after the *Yorktown* was sunk and, for the most part, I grew up on stories of the war. I was weaned on Crusade in the Pacific and Victory at Sea. That is how I got interested in going out to find the *Yorktown*. If you know anything about the history of California, you'll know that during the war San Diego was a Navy town. All my childhood was in the Navy and, to me, going to sea was the most natural thing in the world. When I opened my eyes, I didn't see amber waves of grain, I saw the sea. My house was one block away from a pier and, growing up, that pier was my playground.

Insight: Your National Geographic documentary describes the search for the *Yorktown* as an almost impossible one. What made it so hard?

RB: It was one of our toughest ever. Midway is aptly named: It is midway between nowhere and nowhere. Despite all of our technology, ships still go 10 to 12 miles an hour, so it took forever to get our research ship from San Diego to way out in the middle of the Pacific. It's also very deep out there. We had to work 17,400 feet down. The search area was larger than that for *Titanic* and *Bismarck* put together. Mixed into that real estate then were some very tall volcanic mountains—places where you easily could hide an aircraft carrier. An aircraft carrier is big, but so are the features at the bottom of the sea. There are places that it could have gone down where we probably never would have found it.

Then we blew up our [deep-submergence explorer] vehicle.

There we were with this delicate piece of machinery, all of our delicate instruments, damaged like two sticks of dynamite had exploded right there. It should have knocked us out of the game.

Any one of these problems would have been bad, and we had all of them. Looking for the carrier was sort of like the battle itself. We found it partly through luck, and we won our battle in the last 20 minutes.

Insight: What is it like to find a ship such as the *Yorktown?*

RB: It's always a complicated set of emotions. We are coming in on this thing, we've got it on sonar, we're zooming on it—and there's a tremendous amount of excitement. At the same time, sitting next to me are the survivors. What's going through their minds? They are very emotional, and I've found that all of these survivors have a tremendous sense of guilt. They wonder why they were the ones to live. When they see the ship for the first time, they cry.

I've had to become conscious of this; I'm very excited myself and I want to celebrate, but sitting next to me is someone who is crying. I have this complicated feeling: On one hand, I'm excited; on the other, I realize that we are, in effect, at a grave site.

Insight: Why look for the more recently sunken ships? What do we gain by finding ships like *Titanic* and *Yorktown?*

RB: The searches for these ships really have to be separated from archaeological expeditions. The idea in those searches is to retell history—to take a very, very good moment in human history and, by going out and finding the physical pieces, get people to watch and think about it. We take out survivors, show how things happened and allow viewers to share a cathartic experience. Through all this, we are doing more than remaking a movie on Midway; we really are bringing history to life. You want it to be a documentary, not some sort of dramatic production.

And if you don't study history, you may be doomed to repeat it. Look at our National Geographic special: Half of it is about the Battle of Midway itself. That's history, and by finding the *Yorktown,* we teach people about it. Meanwhile, I am committed to create museums in the deep sea.

The United States has just created 12 marine sanctuaries—the Yellow stones of the future. They are not meant for scuba diving; not everyone can do that. But already, every year, we take 600,000 or 700,000 children to places all over the world where scientists are doing good, exciting work. Already, a child in a school can have a complete heads-up display from a robot 3,000 or 4,000 miles away and 9,000 feet under the sea. This is not science fiction; this is science fact. We are seeing the beginning of real electronic travel. People will be able to travel without leaving their homes. They will be able to visit the battlefield and the *Yorktown* the same way you might visit the battle field at Gettysburg.

So far, we've just scratched the surface of what is possible. We're already setting up a site in the Florida Keys, and that's just the beginning. Right now, we don't have the bandwidth to bring this archaeological adventure directly into people's houses, but in a few years anybody will be able to sit down at home and travel in this way.

Insight: A recent court ruling has opened the *Titanic* to tourist dives despite the objections of the company that has salvage rights to the ship. What are your thoughts on this?

RB: I'm very happy about that court decision. I strongly believe in the concept of visitation, and it's a perfect way to monitor what the salvager is doing. The ship should be a sanctuary, a museum.

Insight: You've been going to sea regularly for more than a quarter of a century. What draws you back time and again?

RB: Through the 33 years I've been going to sea, I've been able to change the venue every 10 or 15 years. All my career, I've been in deep submergence in one way or another. For the early years, my work was in plate tectonics. I was mapping the deep ocean ridge, and I was one of the first to explore those interesting parts of the oceans. In 1983, during the waning years of the Cold War, I was asked to survey two nuclear submarines that we had lost at sea. I went down there and was amazed at how well preserved the submarine's parts were. It was a revelation.

Then, I entered a new phase in my career, focusing on contemporary history, and that's when I found *Titanic.* I've come to realize that the deep sea is a preserver of human history, that there is more history preserved in the deep than in all the museums of the world combined. That's why I built this new institute in Connecticut. My mission is to bring together oceanography with archaeology and create a new field of deep-water archaeology. Until we went ahead, no ship of antiquity ever had been discovered in a depth greater than 200 feet. Now we are opening up all kinds of new fields. We are looking at evidence of the biblical flood, and we are working with a Phoenician ship from the Iron Age.

Insight: Through all your career as an explorer, you've located ships covering a great part of human history. Where are the important deep-water archaeology sites left to be investigated?

RB: I'm interested in trying to find the Sea People, "a mysterious group of ancients who invaded Egypt during the dynastic period. On this, I'm working with Dr. Laurence Stager at the Semitic Museum at Harvard University who is the co-chief scientist for that project. Dr. Stager is convinced that these sea people were the Philistines and that they established a port at a place called Ashqelon. Statistically, we think, it's likely they would have lost a ship in that area, so we are going there to try to find out.

One other place that we're doing work is the Black Sea.

It is the largest anoxic body in the world. In the absence of oxygen you can't have wood-boring organisms and, as a result, some of the best mummified wood ships from antiquity should be there. We know that people were going there 7,000 years ago. We couldn't get into the area during the Cold War, but we are going to be doing a major expedition there next summer. There's still an enormous amount to be found.

---

# GENERAL COMMENTARY

**Mark Henricks**

SOURCE: "My Life's Work: Oceanographer," in *Boy's Life,* Vol. LXXXIV, No. 8, August, 1994, pp. 28-30.

American and French scientists huddled inside the bathyscaphe *Archimede.* They had slowly dived 9,000 feet beneath the Atlantic Ocean. With lights and cameras, they were probing an underwater mountain range.

Suddenly, a fire broke out. Smoke filled the craft. The men scrambled for oxygen masks.

When Robert Ballard inhaled through his mask, he got nothing. The frantic American cried for help. But the Frenchmen near him did not understand English. "I was not panicking," he remembers. "I was dying."

Finally, one of the Frenchmen saw the problem. He turned on Ballard's oxygen and said, *"Pardon."*

Danger is part of Robert Ballard's job. He is an oceanographer, a kind of deep-sea science detective. He hunts for clues to solve the mysteries of the sea.

Ballard specializes in exploring shipwrecks and the sea floor. "I mount expeditions, learn from them, and publish the results," he says.

Using high-tech equipment, he and his team set out in 1985 to find the *Titanic.* On her maiden voyage in 1912, the British ocean liner had struck an iceberg and sunk in the Atlantic on her way to New York.

Ballard's hunt lasted for months. His team bounced sound waves off the ocean floor and scanned with remote-control cameras.

Finally, a camera focused on a piece of wreckage. It led the explorers to the 46,328-ton *Titanic* that lay broken in two in 12,500 feet of water. Photographs of the ship amazed the world—and made Robert Ballard famous.

Ballard has discovered other famous shipwrecks. He found the *Bismarck,* a big, German battleship sunk during World War II. It was nearly 16,000 feet down.

In the Mediterranean Sea, he found the remains of ancient Roman boats. He explored the *Lusitania,* a British ship torpedoed in the Atlantic during World War I.

Plenty of danger lurks beneath the waves. Once, as Ballard studied an extinct underwater volcano, his submersible craft crashed into a mountain. Shaken but unharmed, Ballard piloted the damaged craft to the surface.

No wonder Ballard prefers to use remote-control robots to explore the deepest, most dangerous water. They bring back information without risking lives. He says, "You get to go, but you don't die."

Ballard is based at the Woods Hole Oceanographic Institution in Woods Hole, Mass., an ocean research lab. His work has led to important scientific discoveries.

Ballard made the first dives to the Mid-Ocean Ridge, the world's longest mountain range. It runs 36,000 miles across the floors of the Atlantic, Pacific and Indian oceans.

His biggest scientific find came in 1977 near the Pacific's Galapagos Islands. He discovered seabed cracks called "hydrothermal vents." Hot mineral water spewed from the cracks. Giant worms and clams fed on the minerals in the hot water.

Scientists were amazed that creatures could live in darkness 8,000 feet below the sea. Ballard says, "We discovered a complete life system we didn't even know existed." . . .

Diving beneath the sea or steering underwater robots takes up only a small part of Ballard's time. Underwater expeditions require months of planning and office work. He must raise money, design experiments and prepare for the voyage.

When he returns, he shares his discoveries with the world. He writes books and produces television shows. He analyzes experiments and writes reports for other scientists.

In 1989 Ballard began the Jason Project. Each year thousands of kids watch special live broadcasts of scientific explorations. Satellites allow kids to ask questions and even operate a remote-control underwater probe.

Ballard also runs a company that designs underwater robots. And he serves as scientific consultant for the television series "SeaQuest DSV." The program follows the adventures of a submarine crew in the next century.

"There are very few shows on TV where scientists and engineers are heroes," he says. "They're generally nerds."

There is nothing nerdy about exploring the ocean. And it is unlikely that oceanographers will run out of adventures. The earth's surface is 71 percent water. But less than 1 percent of that area has been studied.

Robert Ballard calls the oceans of the world "the true frontier for the next several generations." He and other oceanographers will keep searching for secrets of the deep.

---

# TITLE COMMENTARY

## EXPLORING OUR LIVING PLANET (1983)

**Arrolyn Vernon**

SOURCE: A review of *Exploring Our Living Planet,* in *School Library Journal,* Vol. 30, No. 5, January, 1984, p. 93.

On both the grand and the human scales, here is a tour of the earth, as plate tectonic geology interprets it and as the resources of the National Geographic Society portray it: folio size, color paintings and photos, maps, clarifying block diagrams. Ballard, a marine geologist, concentrates on processes that most clearly evidence crustal plate movements (sea-floor spreading) or whose mechanisms are now explained by plate movements (earthquakes, volcanoes) or are being studied most intensely in light of the theory ("hot spots," mountain building). His text is generous, clear and popular but authoritative. Human adventures of discovery and survival are interwoven. There is good material here for beginning earth science reports on earthquakes, volcanoes, tsunamis. These explorations and theorizings can explain heretofore puzzling phenomena: mineral formation, mineral salts in the water cycle and rifting on land (Iceland and Afar) but other land-forming processes are not treated. Plate tectonic geology is a grand synthesis but a fine book like this complements, rather than supersedes, fine earlier titles which deal with wind and water action, wave erosion, etc. . . .

**William D. Romey**

SOURCE: A review of *Exploring Our Living Planet,* in *Science Books & Films,* Vol. 19, No. 4, March-April, 1984, p. 199.

In its overall presentation and brilliantly elegant photography, *Exploring Our Living Planet* upholds the National Geographic Society's reputation for quality publications. Unfortunately, several faults mar the beginning of the book. The first chapter, "Discovery of the Earth," which should begin with "Once upon a time" is an inadequate repetition of overly familiar and oversimplified conjecture. Some of the classic plate tectonic models used are now under criticism, suggesting greater complexity than this book admits. Double-page drawings

of scenes from the geologic past detract from the book, giving the beginning an unfortunate, textbook-like quality. From chapter two on, however, the book improves, and the author and editors provide a clear, exciting, and elegant text that is supported by splendid photographs. A few "throw-away" assertions presented in the guise of "facts" continue to mislead, but most of the data are accurately presented. Inaccuracies—perhaps results of artistic license—mar some maps and diagrams, but the illustrations are mainly informative and useful. Computer-drawn block diagrams in several chapters provide brilliant vehicles for visual presentation of complex information on earth structures. This is a stunningly attractive book.

*School Library Journal*

SOURCE: A review of *Exploring Our Living Planet,* in *School Library Journal,* Vol. 30, No. 9, May, 1984, pp. 23-4.

Highly illuminating, clearly written, and beautifully designed, this work of art is suitable for sixth graders and up for science research and for browsing.

The book is divided into five sections: the first covers prehistoric geological history and the development of modern plate tectonics; other sections cover the spreading, hotspots, slipping, and collision of crustal plates. Almost every page glows with high-quality color photographs, paintings, relief maps, or diagrams—all extending the impact of the text.

Coverage of the subject is extensive; it is both global and historical and current, including recent scientific theory and discoveries. The effect on people of the earth's living crust is also thoroughly examined. Full credit is given to contributors such as illustrators, photographers, scientists and consultants. There is also a foreword by Walter Cronkite, a glossary, a bibliography, and an index.

**Deborah Robinson**

SOURCE: A review of *Exploring Our Living Planet,* in *Appraisal: Science Books for Young People,* Vol. 17, No. 3, Fall, 1984, p. 18.

Alfred Wegener, a German meteorologist, died in 1930 in a Greenland blizzard, his controversial ideas about "drifting" continents widely discredited. Only a few years later the dramatic discovery of the 46,000 mile Mid-Ocean Ridge coupled with enhanced understanding of the magnetic field vindicated Wegener. Plate tectonics has become the backbone of modern geology in the same sense as evolution is central to modern biology. A marvelously clear, succinct explanation of how the continents actually move and why we may marvel at earthquakes, hotspots, volcanoes, and other natural phenomenon are equally central to this clearly written text. The work is current (Galapagos Rift highlighted), cosmopolitan in coverage for contemporary as well as historical events, and the information provided spans early history. The color illustrations and photographs are more than worth the purchase price. Glossary, a simple and quite nice geological time chart, index, and bibliography complete the book. Do buy it if you have not already.

**Peter Stowe**

SOURCE: A review of *Exploring Our Living Planet,* in *Appraisal: Science Books for Young People,* Vol. 17, No. 3, Fall, 1984, pp. 18-9.

The National Geographic's recently published book, **Exploring Our Living Planet** is in the usual Geographic tradition of excellence. This 366 page book is centered around the Earth as a constantly changing planet where nothing is stable for long, and there are constant shiftings of its crust, a shifting of the plates that make up its surface. All of this is evidenced by the number of volcanoes, tidal waves, faults, and water level changes in the various parts of the world. A good deal of the book's content also focuses on some of the old and recent explorations such as those done by the *Alvin, Trieste* and such research vessels as the *Glomar Challenger.* The eight chapters fairly clearly point up the subject matter with titles like "Birth of an African Ocean," "The Mountains of the Sea," "Earth's Fountains of Heat," and so forth.

The book also contains a very helpful glossary and index and is saturated by Geographic's usual excellent color photography and artistry. The excellent publication is ideal as a resource for a research paper or just interesting reading, and would be a real asset to any library.

## 📖 *EXPLORING THE TITANIC* (edited by Patrick Crean, 1988)

**Roger Burford Mason**

SOURCE: "*Titanic* Myth Probed," in *Books for Young People,* Vol. 2, No. 5, October, 1988, p. 11.

The *Titanic,* like the Wall Street crash and Marilyn Monroe, is one of the enduring images of the 20th century. Children have always been fascinated by the story of the *Titanic,* and Robert D. Ballard's **Exploring the Titanic** satisfies youthful curiosity about the subject as no previous treatment could have done.

The basic facts are simple and well known, but Ballard covers them again clearly and with affecting sympathy. He understands young people's love of odd and impressing facts, and that is what he gives them: the *Titanic* was taller than the tallest skyscraper, carried enough food to feed a town the size of Brantford, Ontario, for six months, and its swimming pool was the first shipboard pool in the world. Ruth Becker, one of the survivors, recalled, "Our cabin was just like a hotel room.

The dining room was beautiful—the linens, all the bright, polished silver . . . ," and Ballard notes the thick carpets, wooden paneling, marble sinks, curved staircases, glass domes, millionaires, and socialites—all of which made the *Titanic* the *dernier cri.*

Of course, the *Titanic* was also an apt metaphor for the society that launched it, and Ballard does well to show how tightly stratified the classes were, from the richest, quite literally at the top (which is why they survived in disproportionate numbers), to the poor emigrants who travelled in the hot, noisy bowels of the ship. He points out that while the wealthy were devouring caviar and champagne, the poorly paid stokers would have had to work most of their lives in the hellish conditions of the boiler rooms just to buy a first-class ticket. He shows, chillingly, that when the ship began to sink, the tightly packed passengers travelling third-class had to break through locked doors into the forbidden first-class areas to reach the decks and the possibility of survival.

Ballard is very good on atmosphere—the excitement and anticipation of the passengers; the glamour, glitter, and novelty; the bustle and noise—and in capturing it all, he intensifies our sympathy for the victims who drowned in the icy seas on [April 15], 1912.

Ballard deals imaginatively and respectfully with the disaster, but he also draws the reader into his own exciting adventure, the triumphant search for the lost wreck in the previously inaccessible depths of the north Atlantic. Haunted by the story of the ship from boyhood, Ballard pursued his ambition to hunt down and explore what remained of it to illuminate its myth and tragedy.

Two expeditions were necessary. The first, in 1985, using the latest sophisticated underwater techniques, eventually found the wreck and took video pictures of the huge boilers before the onset of winter forced the team to return to base. The following year a new team relocated the wreck and explored it by video and still photography and, most excitingly of all, by naked eye from an ingenious deep-water submarine.

Ballard's description of the search is well paced, and his discoveries are brought to life in simple, direct language that doesn't patronize. A remote-control camera went deep inside the stricken behemoth as it lay in 60 feet of mud nearly eight miles down, and the photographs sent out from below decks are haunting: a beautiful china doll's head, startlingly white and entirely preserved; a stoker's tin mug, still standing on the boiler where he set it down just as the ship foundered; a statue, undefiled by time and the sea; and, most affectingly, numberless shoes lying in pairs where drowned bodies had come to rest.

Ballard's team took nothing from the wreckage except these telling and poignant pictures—silent and powerful testimony to the scale and pathos of the tragedy. These images from the sea bed, as well as those in Ballard's writing, are marvellously evocative of that doomed, lost age destroyed forever by the subsequent war.

The book's layout and design are pleasing in scale and clean and attractive in execution. The cover reverses to become an eye-catching wall poster of the ship, while the diagrams and charts inspire the appropriate sense of superlative size and dramatic consequence. Also included are an interesting and useful glossary of nautical terms and a list of books for further reading. Maritime artist Ken Marschall's painted portraits of the great ship, both afloat in its prime and wrecked on the sea floor, give imaginative substance to Ballard's words and inhabit the mind long after the book is shut.

Icarus aspired to the glory of flight but was doomed by human limitations, and perhaps this is the secret of the *Titanic*'s continuing hold on the imagination. Sinking into the dark Atlantic, glittering with lights, the *Titanic* became another symbol of mankind's vaunting imagination and unavoidable mortality. **Exploring the Titanic** is a compelling publication and a valuable addition to nonfiction materials for young readers.

### Ann Welton

SOURCE: A review of *Exploring the Titanic,* in *School Library Journal,* Vol. 35, No. 3, November, 1988, p. 116.

In straightforward prose, complemented by excellent illustrations, the story of the *Titanic*'s first and final voyage as well as that of her rediscovery and exploration is told. The text captures the drama of both the night of the sinking as well as that of the discovery of the great ship on the ocean floor. The technically accurate and lucid explanations are greatly enhanced by Marschall's stunning paintings, as well as by diagrams and current and period photographs. Giving a wealth of detail on both the *Titanic*'s sinking and the exploration of the wreck 74 years later, this is the title of choice for both report writing and browsing on this topic. Although the glossary is good, it does not cover all unfamiliar words. "Funnel," for example, is not defined and may confuse readers who do not realize that this refers to the smokestack. This is a minor quibble, however, given the general excellence of the work.

### Kirkus Reviews

SOURCE: A review of *Exploring the Titanic,* in *Kirkus Reviews,* Vol. LVI, No. 22, November 15, 1988, p. 1670.

A riveting account of the author's successful search for the *Titanic* and his subsequent examination of the remains.

Not just a digest of Ballard's **Discovery of the Titanic,** this is a new, heavily illustrated version with a text

aimed at younger readers. After a moving summary of the ship's first and only voyage, Ballard describes his own exhausting search and dramatic, last-minute sighting in September 1985. The following year, he returned with a small submarine to explore the wreck and the debris-field around it. The immediacy of his narrative is bolstered by a combination of well-chosen photographs, both new and old, and Marschall's crystal-clear paintings—giving the book stunning visual impact; this is not only an exciting, well-told story but a browsing item *extra ordinaire.* For various reasons, Ballard took no artifacts from the site (he deplores the fact that a later, French expedition did), but—with this—he brought back treasure nonetheless.

### Margery Fisher

SOURCE: A review of *Exploring the Titanic,* in *Growing Point,* Vol. 27, No. 6, March, 1989, p. 5134.

After the location of the wreck of the *Titanic* in 1985 the author joined a joint French and American exploratory expedition in the following year; this was followed by a later Swiss/French/American investigation which brought up various items from the doomed liner. An American statute forbade the selling of 'souvenirs' or memorabilia from the ship and the solemnity of this account is intensified by a description of the lowering of a memorial plaque on to the wreck. There is a brief outline of the 1912 disaster and sadly impressive notes on two children, Ruth Becker and Jack Thayer, who survived. The technical aids used in the exploration and the photographic views of parts of the liner commend the book to young readers from ten or so who can hardly fail to be interested in this remarkable return to the scene of a major tragedy of our century.

### Victor Neuburg

SOURCE: A review of *Exploring the Titanic,* in *The School Librarian,* Vol. 37, No. 2, May, 1989, p. 79.

The sinking of the *Titanic* in 1912 was a tragic event which has fascinated both young and old ever since. Interest in the tragedy seems never to have dwindled, and when Dr. Ballard discovered the wreck after a long underwater search, lying on the ocean floor at a depth of 13,000 feet, the event became headline news. This was in September 1985, and he subsequently explored the ship, photographing her in considerable detail. The result of his investigations was published and became a bestseller. Now he has produced a version for young readers, and it is a marvellous book. The copious illustrations, mostly in colour, are moving and vivid; the narrative is equally so and always readable. There is no sense at all of condescending to his audience. At the end of the book there is a glossary and a 'time-line' which runs from 1907, when plans to build the *Titanic* were laid, right down to 1987 when the US Congress moved to make the ship a national monument. Many young readers from about ten to fourteen or fifteen will, surely, find this book as enthralling as I did.

**Robert Hull**

SOURCE: A review of *Exploring the Titanic,* in *Books for Keeps,* No. 58, September, 1989, p. 15.

The secret of Robert D Ballard's book is not that it's on a fascinating subject. It is that Ballard the writer is Ballard the insider, the explorer and experiencer of everything (sinking apart) that he recounts. He led the French-American expedition which discovered the *Titanic* in 1985, and round that story are woven others: his original interest in the *Titanic,* his exploration of the ship in 1986, and the sinking itself.

The whole book is compellingly written. His descriptions of descents to the wreck are dramatic, and his account of the sinking is done with a telling realism which has much to do with relying on survivors' anecdotes and details of radio messages—seven iceberg warnings in that one day. Ballard has a feel for atmosphere and character, and a novelist's respect for minutiae. We are given the flavour of the actual, odd fragments of revealing evidence like the third-class passengers playing with bits of ice that had fallen from the iceberg onto the deck.

Carefully chosen photographs and contemporary drawings of the ship help the young reader imagine exactly what he's talking about. Look at the photograph of a team of twenty horses pulling an anchor, or the two spreads' length of drawing showing the length of the ship in cut-away, which gives a remarkable impression of its size and organisational complexity. The visuals in general are informative and revealing, and beautifully integrated with the text, though some photographs of parts of the wreck are smaller than they might be.

Ballard, in short, is that relative rarity among writers of non-fiction for children, a narrator of firsthand experience who is deeply enthusiastic and effortlessly knowledgeable. The only problem with this book might be that the children will want to read it right through and not stop to get on with their *Titanic* topic.

## 📖 *THE LOST WRECK OF THE ISIS* (with Rick Archbold, 1990)

**Don Reaber**

SOURCE: A review of *The Lost Wreck of the Isis,* in *School Library Journal,* Vol. 37, No. 1, January, 1991, p. 98.

The importance of science is underlined in this undersea archeological adventure that discovers and explores an ancient Roman ship. In addition to the romance of an archeological search and the adventure of ships and storms at sea, Ballard shows how the principles of science are used to design and create state-of-the-art searching tools such as robot systems and fiber-optic cables. The story is narrated by Ballard, discoverer of the *Titanic* and *Bismarck* wrecks. Beautiful full-color photographs illustrate scenes and action; clear, colorful diagrams explain ideas and concepts. This contemporary account is interspersed with imaginative sections that tell the story of Roman shipping in the second century A.D. from the point of view of Antonius, a 14-year-old Roman boy who is aboard the *Isis* when she sinks. A book that will be popular for reading aloud in the lower grades, and useful as well as interesting for older readers.

**Leone McDermott**

SOURCE: A review of *The Lost Wreck of the Isis,* in *Booklist,* Vol. 87, No. 10, January 15, 1991, p. 1055.

In the spring of 1989, marine geologist Robert Ballard (best known for his 1985 discovery of the *Titanic*) launched an innovative project combining deep-sea exploration and telecommunications. Using a camera-equipped underwater robot named JASON, Ballard and his crew excavated artifacts from an ancient Roman shipwreck (nicknamed the *Isis*) and simultaneously beamed live images of the process to 12 museums and 250,000 students in the U.S. and Canada. In a fascinating account of the *Isis* project, Ballard does a fine job of taking the reader along for the ride. The book alternates documentary chapters with historical fiction and includes many sidebars on Roman history, archaeology, and the science of underwater exploration. Ballard's first-person narrative has a conversational "you are there" quality that draws the reader in and allows a great deal of information to be imparted without ever seeming dry. The fictional sections bring fact to life with a hypothetical account of the people and events of the *Isis*'s fatal voyage. Photographs, maps, diagrams, and artwork [by Wesley Lowe] are plentiful throughout, and there is an extensive glossary. Adventure lovers will find this an engrossing read, as will those interested in history or scientific exploration.

**D. A. Young**

SOURCE: A review of *The Lost Wreck of the Isis,* in *The Junior Bookshelf,* Vol. 55, No. 2, April, 1991, p. 64.

Dr. Ballard discovered the wreck of the *Titanic* in 1985 with *Argo* the underwater deep-towed vehicle whose video cameras transmitted such fascinating pictures of what remains of that giant liner.

With a more sophisticated version of the *Argo* aptly named *Jason* Dr. Ballard and his team began the search for a wreck from Roman times in the Tyrrhenian Sea. He planned a television link-up with science museums in America so that young audiences could share the excitement of his discoveries as they came to light.

How all this was achieved forms half of the present volume. The sea-bed revealed a collection of amphora and other objects undoubtedly the remains of a ship's cargo much of which has been subsequently raised to the surface for further investigation. The ship itself became the *Isis*. In the other half of the book Dr. Ballard gives an account in story form of the last voyage of the *Isis* from Ostia: its cargo, passengers and crew: its successful sales in Carthage: its re-loading in Carthage: the sailing into the storm that wrecked the *Isis*. The narrative is well fleshed out with detail almost to the extent of providing an excellent guide to everyday life in Ostia and Carthage in AD 355. What an absolutely marvellous way of bringing history to life!

**Kathryn R. Downs**

SOURCE: A review of *The Lost Wreck of the Isis*, in *Language Arts*, Vol. 69, No. 4, April, 1992, p. 302.

**The Lost Wreck of the Isis** is a wonderful and exciting book! Robert Ballard and his team set out on their boat called the *Starella*. They are on a very special voyage. They are after the remains of the ancient Roman ship, the *Isis*. Using Jason, the underwater robot, they managed to find it. The book tells two stories. One, the story of Ballard's search to find the *Isis;* and the other, the story of the original trading ship *Isis*. Ballard's story is illustrated with photographs, maps, and diagrams. The story of the ancient *Isis* is illustrated with spectacular paintings. If you study ancient civilization, this book would really give a lot of information.

### EXPLORING THE BISMARCK (with Rick Archbold, 1991)

**Miriam Martinez and Marcia F. Nash**

SOURCE: A review of *Exploring the Bismarck*, in *Language Arts*, Vol. 68, No. 6, October, 1991, p. 498.

Over 50 years ago the mighty German warship *Bismarck* set out to sink British ships in the North Atlantic. By doing so, the Germans hoped to cut off Great Britain's supply line and thus hasten their invasion of that country. The *Bismarck* was pursued and eventually sunk by a determined British Navy. This book tells the story of that famous sea battle through the eyes of four of the young German sailors who were on the *Bismarck*, as well as the story of the search for and discovery of the wreck a half-century later. Paintings, photographs, maps, and diagrams help to tell this fascinating story that brings together history and modern scientific exploration.

*Kirkus Reviews*

SOURCE: A review of *Exploring the Bismarck*, in *Kirkus Reviews*, Vol. LIX, No. 20, October 15, 1991, p. 1339.

The author's **Discovery of the Bismarck** in a young readers' version, featuring plenty of well-chosen color photos and dramatic military paintings plus a view of the Nazi battleship's brief career through the eyes of four crew members. Ballard has searched out other wrecks with his remote-control deep-sea camera sled, most notably the *Titanic;* here, he once again re-creates the weary hours watching the video screen, capped by the thrill of discovery as a vague undersea shadow suddenly takes a shape not found in nature. A fine account, enhanced both by the striking illustrations and by a description of how the survivors were rescued and treated by their British captors. Glossary; chronology; brief bibliography.

**Julie Cosaro**

SOURCE: A review of *Exploring the Bismarck*, in *Booklist*, Vol. 88, No. 5, November 1, 1991, p. 511.

Ballard describes the destruction of Hitler's indestructible battleship in 1941 and the young men aboard ("only 115 out of a crew of 2,206 survived") as well as the ship's discovery on the ocean floor in 1989. Ironically, he dedicates his book to his 20-year-old son Todd, pilot of the Argo underwater search robot, who died in a car accident shortly after the expedition. As in his previous books about shipwrecks, Ballard uses the early chapters to provide a lucid description of the ship's structure and function, as well as a riveting account of its famous chase-and-destroy scene, based upon eyewitness accounts ("One man whose arms had been blown off was trying to grab a line in his teeth"). The second section details the hard work, boredom, and exhilaration of the discovery and exploration of the ship's ruins. As usual in the Time Quest Books, the text is complemented by paintings, diagrams, and photographs, many taken from German archives. . . . [T]his will, undoubtedly, attract fans of World War II thrillers and weapons books.

**Jerome Williams**

SOURCE: A review of *Exploring the Bismarck*, in *Science Books & Films*, Vol. 28, No. 2, March, 1992, p. 55.

The *Bismarck*, Germany's largest battleship, was launched on February 14, 1939, and sank into the North Atlantic on May 27, 1941, only nine days into its first wartime mission. The battered hulk was found on the ocean bottom by the underwater camera sled *Argo* on June 8, 1989. This book tells two stories: one, which occupies over two-thirds of the total pages, deals with the *Bismarck* from its launch to its loss at sea; and the other describes the successful search for the sunken vessel by Ballard's group. To the science or technology-oriented reader, this book is a disappointment. No clearly defined scientific objective for the expedition is given, and no attempt is made to explain why severe time limits were in force when resupply ports in Britain were not far away. Nor do we ever get to really understand the gear carried by the ship or the maneuvering capabilities of the underwater camera sled *Argos*. Also, the illustrations are beautiful, but no attempt is made to clearly distinguish between the actual underwater video pictures taken by *Argos* and the drawings produced by imaginative artists. In summary, this is a pretty good history book, but not a very good science book.

 *BRIGHT SHARK* (with Tony Chiu, 1992)

### Kirkus Reviews

SOURCE: A review of *Bright Shark,* in *Kirkus Reviews,* Vol. LX, No. 3, February 1, 1992, p. 126.

Verisimilitude is a not unexpected virtue in this deep-sea thriller centered around the search for a long-lost Israeli submarine, given that Ballard is a renowned oceanographer credited with discovering the *Titanic.* Still, he and coauthor Chiu offset that advantage for the most part with a slow-paced story marred by excessive and often unnecessary scene-shifting.

Navy Lt. Edna J. Haddix is in charge of what is seemingly a civilian research ship operating in the Mediterranean off the shores of Crete in the spring of 1988, but her real purpose is to deploy the vessel's underwater robot vehicles to find and explore the wreckage of the *Dakar,* which was lost 20 years earlier. The US hopes to find evidence that will verify the smuggling of nuclear materials to the Israelis in 1968, but there are far darker secrets aboard the doomed sub-secrets that will reveal a decades-old pact between right-wing Israelis and their counterparts in the Soviet Union. The action is spread over six days as elements around the world try to aid or hinder the search. In Washington, Department of Energy official Clifford Zeman dispatches old friend Wendell Trent to aid Haddix and fends off the bureaucratic and political forces who want to shut down the operation. In Israel, aging hero Leon Rose is willing to do anything, including sink the American ship, to preserve the veil of the past. His allies in Russia give him unsanctioned help in the form of a new undersea missile, as everything moves inevitably to a frightening confrontation at sea.

In the end, Ballard and Chiu salvage their story with a slam-bang finish and the clever postponement—until the closing pages—of the final, horrifying secret of *Dakar.*

### Publishers Weekly

SOURCE: A review of *Bright Shark,* in *Publishers Weekly,* Vol. 239, No. 7, February 3, 1992, p. 64.

It is 1988, and the American research vessel *Fanning II* is conducting underwater tests off the coast of Greece when it discovers traces of the *Dakar,* an Israeli submarine lost in 1967. The *Dakar* so concerns U.S. intelli-

gence that a file, code-named Bright Shark, remains open after 20 years. Nor is America the only interested party. As Navy lieutenant Edna Haddix and Department of Energy troubleshooter Wendell Trent seek to solve the *Dakar*'s mystery, Israel and the U.S.S.R. join forces to preserve the submarine's secret—at the price of direct confrontation with the U.S. Oceanographer Ballard and journalist/novelist Chiu produce a page-turning narrative plausible in its context and convincing in its details. The descriptions of modern undersea exploration with remote-controlled probes are no less exciting than the unfolding of the top-secret back-channel Soviet-Israeli relationship. The authors cleverly eschew sexual and romantic episodes for vignettes filling in the chinks in recent history; readers will particularly enjoy the barbed treatments of the 1988 Moscow summit and of Greece's Papandreou regime in its final stages. This breathless novel establishes the abundant potential of the near past as a setting for the techno-thriller.

### Diane Goheen

SOURCE: A review of *Bright Shark,* in *School Library Journal,* Vol. 38, No. 10, October, 1992, p. 150.

Ballard draws on his experiences in the discovery of the *Titanic* and joins with journalist Chiu to weave an intriguing novel. Navy Lieutenant Edna Haddix is sent to oversee underwater tests in the Mediterranean, should the civilian vessel *Fanning II* discover anything of interest in what is slated as an expedition concerning the continental drift. Discover they do, and Haddix assumes control of what is to become a dangerous mission of great international interest. The team has located a sunken submarine, whose top secret cargo, if discovered, will hold serious ramifications for Israel, the former Soviet Union, and the United States. As the tale unfolds, readers gain insight into the world of oceanography and international relations. Although lengthy, **Bright Shark** should hold the interest of many YAs.

 *LOST LINERS: FROM THE TITANIC TO THE ANDREA DORIA, THE OCEAN FLOOR REVEALS THE GREATEST LOST SHIPS* (with Rich Archbold, 1997)

### Brad Hooper

SOURCE: A review of *Lost Liners: From the Titanic to the Andrea Doria, the Ocean Floor Reveals the Greatest Lost Ships,* in *Booklist,* Vol. 94, No. 4, October 15, 1997, pp. 380-81.

A lovely book that—ironically—is about tragedies! In large format, the authors (one of whom, Ballard, discovered the *Titanic* wreckage) take the reader on the voyages of a handful of ill-fated ocean liners of the past and then down to the sea floor to view their remains. In an arrestingly illustrated introduction that chronicles the history of the transatlantic ocean liner (a history that, unfortunately for the romantics among us, is past), the authors affirm that the "truly 'lost' liners that sank at sea form the real legacy of this vanished age." Then the authors profile the major ocean queens that sank (among them, the *Lusitania,* the *Titanic,* and the *Andrea Doria*) and show what is left of them below the waves. The final chapter is a plea for protecting historically significant shipwrecks, illustrations include specially commissioned paintings by Ken Marschall, illustrator of the magnificently rendered *Titanic: An Illustrated History* (1992). A shining addition to the travel and technology collections.

### Publishers Weekly

SOURCE: A review of *Lost Liners: From the Titanic to the Andrea Doria, the Ocean Floor Reveals the Greatest Lost Ships,* in *Publishers Weekly,* Vol. 244, No. 43, October 20, 1997, pp. 66-7.

The technologies that enabled Ballard to locate and photograph the *Titanic* have led to the discovery of other notable lost liners. The *Lusitania, Britannic, Empress of Ireland, Andrea Doria* and others have all been tracked to their watery crypts and brought back to these pages. Coauthors of **The Discovery of the Titanic,** Ballard and Archbold give a full account of the circumstances that sent the ships to their doom, going beyond shipwrecks to a nostalgic portrait of the glory days of North Atlantic liners and the competition for speed (a contributing factor to the loss of the *Titanic* and *Andrea Doria*). The *Lusitania* and *Britannic* were victims of wars, *the Empress of Ireland,* of a collision in dense fog; the *Normandie* burned and foundered while in port in New York. Much of the material is familiar, but recent ocean-floor discoveries via exploratory robots are intriguing. Ballard strongly advocates leaving the ships alone to serve as underwater marine museums. But until the technology exists for us all to visit, the book's 400 lavish period photographs, color photos of the sea floor and paintings by Ken Marschall, whose work was featured in *Titanic: An Illustrated History,* will have to serve.

 ### GHOST LINERS: EXPLORING THE WORLD'S GREATEST LOST SHIPS (with Rich Archbold, 1998)

### Carolyn Phelan

SOURCE: A review of *Ghost Liners: Exploring the World's Greatest Lost Ships,* in *Booklist,* Vol. 94, No. 22, August, 1998, p. 1992.

Best known for the undersea discovery of the *Titanic,* Ballard introduces readers to that shipwreck and four others of the twentieth century: *the Empress of Ireland, the Lusitania,* the *Britannic,* and the *Andrea Doria,* which collided with the *Stockholm.* Each chapter describes the exploration of one of the wrecks and offers information about the ship's origins, amenities, importance, and why

it sank. In each chapter, one passenger is profiled in a sidebar, giving readers a personal story and a photograph to bring the experience more sharply into focus. Exceptionally detailed dramatic paintings by Ken Marschall, show the ships as they appeared on the water, while sinking, and beneath the sea. Many period photos, posters, and sketches set the scene; photographs of undersea exploration show the ships and their artifacts as they appear today. The large, attractive format and informative text combine to make this an appealing book on a subject that continues to fascinate young people.

### Elizabeth Bush

SOURCE: A review of *Ghost Liners: Exploring the World's Greatest Lost Ships,* in *Bulletin of the Center for Children's Books,* Vol. 52, No. 1, September, 1998, pp. 6-7.

Readers afflicted with *Titanic* fever can not only plumb the remains of the reigning queen of shipwrecks, but also of four of her nearly-as-famous sisters in disaster. And who better to serve as tour guide than Ballard, discoverer of the *Titanic*'s resting site? Opening with comments on how underwater exploration has evolved over the decade since the three-man *Alvin* first probed the *Titanic,* Ballard plunges into the main event—discussion of the sinkings and current states of the *Titanic, Empress of Ireland, Lusitania, Britannic,* and *Andrea Doria.* Each chapter begins with a recap of the disaster and eyewitness testimony; Ballard then discusses the peculiar challenges in investigating each wreck, and speculation regarding any lingering mysteries (he favors, for example, the probability of ignited coal dust as the agent in the *Lusitania*'s "second explosion"). Heavily illustrated with color underwater photos of creditable clarity and Marschall's detailed paintings, this title will attract browsers like barnacles to a sunken hull; to rely on the pictures, though, is to miss an equally dramatic and immediate narration: "Effortlessly we rose up the side of that famous bow, now weeping great tears of rust, past the huge anchor and up over the rail." A glossary is included to help sort out some rudimentary nautical terms, as is a list for further reading.

### Ann G. Brouse

SOURCE: A review of *Ghost Liners: Exploring the World's Greatest Lost Ships,* in *School Library Journal,* Vol. 44, No. 9, September, 1998, pp. 212-3.

The discoverer of this century's most sought after ship wreckage recounts his exploration of the *Titanic.* Photographs taken during those dangerous dives plus eerily realistic artwork support the awe and reverence Ballard reveals in his text. In additional chapters he examines other, equally sensational ship disasters of the 20th century. He tells of the *Lusitania,* the *Britannic,* the *Andrea Doria*'s collision with the *Stockholm,* and the *Empress of Ireland*'s sinking in the St. Lawrence River. Each story is accompanied by black-and-white and full-color archival and contemporary photographs, diagrams, and magnificent full-color illustrations. Photographs of the sunken ships and artifacts on the ocean floor and riverbeds add notes of sobering reality to seemingly mythic tales. A few well-chosen quotes from passengers and crew about their experiences add a measure of poignancy. Careful observation of the destroyed ships and historical records reveal the often preventable causes of these accidents. Ballard's *Exploring the Titanic* details his development as an undersea explorer, the drama of the sinking, and the thrill of viewing the ship 70 years after her disappearance. Given the strength of *Titanic* fever that has gripped public imagination, the stories in *Ghost Liners* will be devoured by students, history buffs, and all who are fascinated by human tragedy.

---

**Additional coverage of Ballard's life and career is contained in the following sources published by The Gale Group:** *Contemporary Authors,* **Vol. 112 and** *Something about the Author,* **Vol. 85.**

---

# Floyd Cooper

## 1956-

African-American author and illustrator of picture books, poetry, and nonfiction.

Major works include *Grandpa's Face* (written by Eloise Greenfield, 1988), *Laura Charlotte* (written by Kathryn O. Galbraith, 1990), *Brown Honey in Broomwheat Tea: Poems* (written by Joyce Carol Thomas, 1993), *Coming Home: From the Life of Langston Hughes* (1994), *Meet Danitra Brown* (written by Nikki Grimes, 1994), *Mandela: From the Life of the South African Statesman* (1996).

## INTRODUCTION

Cooper has illuminated hundreds of years of the African-American experience through his artwork for a variety of songs, stories, and poems that he has authored or that have been written by others. Hailed by critics for what a *Publishers Weekly* reviewer called his "painterly, sun-drenched portraits," Cooper captures the warmth of intergenerational love in his eloquent and inspirational illustrations for such books as Eloise Greenfield's *Grandpa's Face,* Patricia C. McKissack's *Ma Dear's Aprons,* and Sandra Belton's *From Miss Ida's Porch.* Whether he uses oil-wash or watercolors, his art has been described as "glowing," not only evoking mood but revealing "keen observations of people and neighborhood," noted Lois F. Anderson. In a HarperCollins Listserv Interview, Cooper commented that his ability to visually feel the stories he illustrates was due to his mother having read to him daily as a child. "The key is to visualize a scene that is true to a particular text, but also different (with more details perhaps), so as to EXPAND the story as much as possible." Rendering young and old faces with soft, muted colors, Cooper often employs family members as models for his characters. Using erasers to help create his images, the artist has been developing a technique that can be found in all of his books.

Cooper has written and illustrated two biographies, one about the poet Langston Hughes, and the other on the renowned South African statesman, Nelson Mandela. In these works, Cooper concentrated on the childhood and adolescence of these prominent African-Americans to create strong, appealing portraits of two black heroes. In a departure from his picture books about black families, he has also illustrated a twelfth-century Japanese tale of court life called *The Girl Who Loved Caterpillars.* Cooper has used his art and writing to heighten awareness, not only of the contributions of his people, but to stress the beauty and truth in all peoples, as his multicultural works attest.

## Biographical Information

Born in 1956 in Tulsa, Oklahoma, Cooper was raised there with his younger brother and two younger sisters, but spent summers with his grandparents in Muskogee. An avid drawer since he was three years old, young Cooper dreamed about moving to New York; however, a four-year state scholarship led him to the University of Oklahoma, where he received a bachelor of fine arts degree in 1980. While in college, Cooper did some freelance illustration work and, after graduation, worked for Hallmark Co. in Kansas City, Missouri. In 1984, he finally moved to New York City, where he accepted a position as an advertising and corporate illustrator. Interested in illustrating children's books and, despite contrary advice from his mentor, Cooper produced the artwork for *Grandpa's Face*, which a *Kirkus Reviews* critic noted as "an outstanding debut." In *Seventh Book of Junior Authors and Illustrators*, Cooper is quoted as saying, "I feel children are at the frontline in improving society. . . . This might sound a little heavy, but it's true. I feel children's picture books play a role in counteracting all the violence and other negative images conveyed in the media." Cooper once explained that illustrating is "a lifelong process," and concluded: "I would illustrate and draw even if I weren't paid to do it."

## Major Works

*Grandpa's Face*, written by Eloise Greenfield, is the sensitive portrait of Tamika and her grandpa. One day, Tamika sees her grandpa's expression become cold and harsh; unaware that he is practicing for the part of an angry character in a play, she grows worried that he may someday become so angry with her as to look at her with that same expression. Illustrating the work in pastel tones of gold and rich warm brown, Cooper's work was praised by a *Publishers Weekly* critic for "reinforc[ing] in the pictures the feelings of warmth and affection that exist between generations." Such feelings were also kindled in his artwork for Kathryn Galbraith's *Laura Charlotte,* as a young girl's fear of the dark at bedtime is diminished with the story of how her favorite stuffed animal—an elephant who once belonged to her mother—came to be. Cooper's grainy, "somber-toned illustrations envelop the reader in their warmth as they capture the mood of summer nights and cozy bedrooms," noted a *Publishers Weekly* commentator.

Cooper has illustrated several collections of poetry for younger children, including three volumes by Joyce Carol Thomas. Thomas's first collection, *Brown Honey in Broomwheat Tea*, features watercolor illustrations that a

*Publishers Weekly* reviewer characterized as "essentially realistic but enveloped in a haze of light," and that *Booklist* contributor Janice M. Del Negro noted "invite the viewer to participate in the family gatherings and ritual tea brewing that take place."

In 1994, Cooper published his first work as both author and illustrator: *Coming Home: From the Life of Langston Hughes.* Focusing on the poet's lonely childhood and, with his parents' extended absences, his search for a stable home, Cooper's biography tells of the writer's early years "in a warm and intimate tone that conveys both the deprivations and sources of strength" in Hughes's youth. A reviewer for *Publishers Weekly* noted that the book portrayed "warmly lit oil portraits, so atmospheric that the sounds of daily life seem to emanate from them," while Hazel Rochman declared, "Like Hughes's poetry, the power of Cooper's story is that it confronts the sadness even as it transcends it."

*Meet Danitra Brown*, by Nikki Grimes, is a picture book collection of poems about friendship and self-knowledge. Through the eyes of her best friend, the reader is introduced to the self-possessed Danitra Brown, who always wears the color of royalty—purple—and has no time for boys who cannot see inner beauty and strength. Coo-

per's hazy, muted illustrations capture the spirit of Danitra and the neighborhood.

Continuing to pursue an interest in biography, Cooper wrote and illustrated *Mandela: From the Life of the South African Statesman.* Retaining a focus on his subject's youth, Cooper illuminates the South-African leader's philosophical origins as a child growing up in a Transkai village and outlines Mandela's ability to withstand personal difficulties—including an almost thirty-year prison term—during the decades of fighting apartheid in his homeland. Hazel Rochman commented, "The writing is reverential and exclamatory . . . [and] the handsome double-spread oil-wash paintings in soft, warm shades of brown capture the rural landscape and the individual people." Praising Cooper's artwork, A *Publishers Weekly* critic deemed the book "a forceful, credible picture of a strong and deeply devoted statesman," while *The New York Times* declared, "Mr. Cooper's glowing illustrations convey character with particular eloquence."

## Awards

Cooper has received the Coretta Scott King Honor Book

Award for Illustration for *Brown Honey and Broom-wheat Tea* in 1994, *Meet Danitra Brown* in 1995, and *I Have Heard of a Land* in 1999. *Grandpa's Face*, written by Eloise Greenfield, was an American Library Association Notable Book selection, and *Laura Charlotte* received a Parents' Choice Award in 1990.

---

# TITLE COMMENTARY

📖 *GRANDPA'S FACE* (written by Eloise Greenfield, 1988)

### Kirkus Reviews

SOURCE: A review of *Grandpa's Face,* in *Kirkus Reviews,* Vol. LVI, No. 21, November 1, 1988, p. 1604.

"Grandpa's face told everything about him . . . even when he was mad with Tamika, his face was a good face, and the look of his mouth and eyes told her that he loved her." But Grandpa is an actor, and one day Tamika sees him privately practicing a face with "a tight mouth and cold, cold eyes . . . that could never love her or anyone." Dismayed, she acts out her fear at the dinner table, slopping food about and distressing her parents; it's Grandpa who realizes that her uncharacteristic behavior comes from some hidden trouble, who draws her out and then helps her to understand that the fearsome face was just pretend and could never be aimed at her.

Poet Greenfield tells this warm family story with tenderness and grace; and Cooper makes an outstanding debut. The realistic, full-color double spreads are rich in earth tones and vibrant colors; the faces—especially the crucial expressions on Grandpa's mobile visage—are well characterized and convey emotion with subtlety and precision (also, Tamika's body-language after her trauma is especially poignant). The well-composed backgrounds develop a strong sense of place—a city street of well-kept brownstones, a lovely park touched by the setting sun.

### Denise M. Wilms

SOURCE: A review of *Grandpa's Face,* in *Booklist,* Vol. 85, No. 6, November 15, 1988, p. 576.

Tamika loves her grandfather's face. Its expressiveness intrigues her, and even when she's done something wrong, she's reassured by the deep caring she sees in his eyes. One day, when Grandpa is privately rehearsing a role he has in a play, Tamika is shocked at the hard, cold, face he displays. Could her treasured Grandpa turn that face on her one day? The prospect upsets Tamika so much she misbehaves at the dinner table and then fearfully watches her grandfather's reaction. But love is still apparent in his face, and when the two talk afterwards (Tamika confesses her fear), Grandpa reassures her that he could never regard her with anything but love. Cooper's illustrations underscore the story's emotional warmth. Though his faces are of uneven quality (some secondary characters appear stiff), the scenes are full of the closeness that exists between Tamika and her grandfather. The close-knit family here is black, the young-old connection so vibrantly portrayed universal.

### Hanna B. Zeiger

SOURCE: A review of *Grandpa's Face,* in *The Horn Book Magazine,* Vol. LXV, No. 2, March-April, 1989, p. 197.

Tamika and her grandpa have a very loving relationship; she spends a great deal of time with him, listening to his stories and going for "talk-walks" to the park or around the neighborhood. Tamika has learned to watch his face for changing feelings, knowing that even when he is angry, his eyes still say he loves her, and she can kiss "the sturdy brown of his face." Grandpa is an actor with a theater group, and often Tamika goes to see him perform. One day, opening the door to his room to ask for a story, Tamika sees him reading his lines in front of a mirror. As she watches, his face changes and becomes hard, cold, and hating. Frightened that her beloved grandpa might look at her that way, she is unable to tell anyone about her fear. At the dinner table she mopes and plays with her food, making her parents angry and, finally, upsetting a glass of water onto Grandpa's shirt. Wisely, Grandpa takes Tamika off to the park for one of their walks and is able to comfort her and assure her of his love. Floyd Cooper's illustrations are done in deep, dark pastels with gold and honeyed browns predominating. The extreme close-ups of the faces of the grandfather and the little girl add a special dimension to the story.

### Donnarae MacCann and Olga Richard

SOURCE: A review of *Grandpa's Face,* in *Wilson Library Bulletin,* Vol. 63, No. 8, April, 1989, p. 92.

Eloise Greenfield's text in **Grandpa's Face** contains no ethnic tags, yet it is similarly anchored in the reality of a specific place and situation. Greenfield sustains a strong focus throughout—namely, the inner conflict that develops when a child's imagination must deal with an alien expression on a familiar face.

Tamika has a grandfather who is a professional actor and she is, therefore, accustomed to the roles he assumes. But when he rehearses the emotions of a fiercely angry character, the child becomes frightened. Only after Tamika and her Grandpa have one of their "talk-walks" is she able to overcome the fear.

I could point out the storytelling features of the "talk-walk" as characteristic of African American family life, but I think it is more important to emphasize the universality of relationships within this narrative. The exchanges between the two leading characters represent children and grandparents in a plausible interaction. They also highlight the difficulty that a youngster may have in separating the real from the fanciful. Tamika knows all about acting from direct family experience, yet the immediacy of what looks like a personality change overwhelms her completely.

Greenfield deflects here the notion that ethnic literature must be social rather than personal. Grandpa is a universal grandfather figure, not a surrogate father who is replacing a missing parent.

Floyd Cooper's cityscapes are also affirmative, helping us appreciate old brownstone buildings rather than associate them with neighborhood disintegration and blight.

## M. Hobbs

SOURCE: A review of *Grandpa's Face,* in *The Junior Bookshelf,* Vol. 54, No. 2, April, 1990, p. 72.

Floyd Cooper's richly textured illustrations of black subjects are wonderfully true to life, and the close-ups here of little Tamika and her actor-grandfather are immediate and beautiful. Moreover, Tamika becomes any very young girl who is troubled and becomes unaccountably fractious: her behaviour at table and the expressions of the grown-ups as they attempt to diagnose the trouble belong to every race and nation. Eloise Greenfield's story-line is perhaps less satisfactory, however, because it is not a situation into which young children will readily imagine themselves. Tamika sees her adored grandfather in his dressing room pulling a terrible face

*From* The Girl Who Loved Caterpillars: A Twelfth-Century Tale from Japan, *adapted by Jean Merrill. Illustrated by Floyd Cooper.*

(presumably rehearsing the part he is to play), and her subsequent naughtiness is because she is afraid one day he may look like that at her; he satisfies her that he will not. The somewhat sombre reds, yellows and blues of the softer but detailed backgrounds are most attractive.

## LAURA CHARLOTTE (written by Kathryn Galbraith, 1990)

### Ilene Cooper

SOURCE: A review of *Laura Charlotte,* in *Booklist,* Vol. 86, No. 11, February 1, 1990, p. 1091.

Laura can't fall asleep, so she asks her mother to tell her a story, one that Laura has heard before and loves. When Mama was a little girl, her grandmother gave her an elephant made of gray flannel and pink gingham, and she gave it the prettiest name in the world—Charlotte. They share everything until Charlotte is lost outside, and her ear gets chewed off by a cat. Fortunately, Grandmother is there to sew a new one. When Mama grows up, she gives the elephant to her own little girl, Laura Charlotte, "Laura after her grandmother, and Charlotte because it's the prettiest name in the world." While this fictional reminiscence may have more emotional pull for adults than children, youngsters should still bask in the warmth of a shared experience. Certainly, everyone will enjoy Cooper's luminous paintings. As he did in *Chita's Christmas Tree,* Cooper draws a young heroine whose innocence and joie de vivre are a delight to behold. His use of soft focus and glowing colors are especially appropriate for this evocative story.

### Kirkus Reviews

SOURCE: A review of *Laura Charlotte,* in *Kirkus Reviews,* Vol. LVIII, No. 4, February 15, 1990, p. 263.

In a bedtime story about a bedtime story, Laura's mother tells her about the birthday long ago when she received a toy elephant—handmade by Laura's great-grandmother—and named it Charlotte. Mama tells how she treasured Charlotte and took such care of her that Charlotte eventually became the favorite of her own little girl, whom she named Laura Charlotte. Glowing with love and security, this marks a strong debut for its author. Cooper's rich, lucent art—in the style he used so successfully for Howard's *Chita's Christmas Tree*—is a perfect complement to the affectionate story. Just right for storytime as well as bedtime.

### Karen Litton

SOURCE: A review of *Laura Charlotte,* in *School Library Journal,* Vol. 36, No. 4, April, 1990, p. 90.

A warm, family-history story, temperamentally akin to Ehrlich's *Zeek Silver Moon* or Jarrell's exquisite *The*

*Knee-Baby.* Laura, still awake in bed, asks her mother to tell her again the story of Charlotte, the stuffed elephant who links Mama's childhood with her own. Mama complies with pleasure, reliving her early life with Charlotte and her quiet joy in passing on a gift of love to her daughter. Laura knows just how the story goes, and prompts her mother with the telling, from Charlotte's first arrival as a birthday gift, through Mama's nighttime rescue of her lost elephant, to Laura's own welcome arrival and Charlotte's new place in her life. The story's simple declarations and sure details draw readers into an authentic shared familiarity. Cooper's pictures are endearing, filling the pages with photograph-like re-creations of Mama's past and of the story's present. The twilight colors, rendered with high graininess, perfectly suit the moods of bedtime and of reminiscence. The conversations and the time shifts, while smoothly integrated, make this most comfortable for one-on-one sharing, but with the right reader, it would work well for story times, too.

## Roger Sutton

SOURCE: A review of *Laura Charlotte,* in *Bulletin of the Center for Children's Books,* Vol. 43, No. 9, May 1990, pp. 213-14.

Laura can't sleep, so Mama comes in to tell the story of Charlotte, even though Laura has "heard it a million times before." Charlotte was Mama's closest companion, a stuffed elephant she had received for her fifth birthday from her grandmother. And now a handed-down Charlotte is Laura's "best friend." Where, then, is Charlotte when Laura can't sleep? Why is great-grandmother suddenly around to restitch an injured Charlotte? What can it possibly mean to Laura when her mother says, "but one day I was too old to play with Charlotte"? The generalized sentimentality (grandma, birthday, stuffed toy) and lack of any real story mark this as a book for nostalgic adults rather than for children, who invest their toys with far more spirit than Charlotte possesses. The illustrations, including a saccharine cover portrait of Laura and Charlotte, are likewise sentimentally lit and gaudily colored, with a grainy "time-ago" patina that fails to obscure the awkwardly drafted figures who only occasionally resemble themselves from page to page. This one's a greeting card. . . .

## Trevelyn Jones & Luanne Toth

SOURCE: A review of *Laura Charlotte,* in *School Library Journal,* Vol. 36, No. 12, December, 1990, p. 22.

A little girl begs her mother for the oft-told tale of her gray flannel elephant and how it was made by her grandmother for her mother and passed down to her. With its strong sense of intergenerational love and luminous paintings touched with nostalgia, this will transport readers back in time and completely enchant them.

## THE GIRL WHO LOVED CATERPILLARS: A TWELFTH-CENTURY TALE FROM JAPAN (written by Jean Merrill, 1992)

## Ilene Cooper

SOURCE: A review of *The Girl Who Loved Caterpillars: A Twelfth-Century Tale from Japan,* in *Booklist,* Vol. 89, No. 1, September 1, 1992, p. 54.

Twelfth-century Japan was hardly an era of feminism, but this story retells a tale, found on a scroll, of a strong girl with ideas of her own. Izumi's parents have high hopes for her—perhaps she will become a lady-in-waiting at the Emperor's court. But unlike the exquisite noblewoman who lives next door, Izumi has no interest in butterflies, or lute playing, or writing poetry. Her attention is focused on the creepy crawlies, especially caterpillars, from which others recoil. So Izumi spends her time playing with scruffy common boys who bring her the creatures, following her passion for nature and being the object of the neighbors' gossip. Even though she does not blacken her teeth, as is the fashion, or trim her bushy eyebrows, she attracts the attention of the Captain of the Stables. Their correspondence ends, however, when he responds to the mores of his time and writes Izumi that her world is too strange for him. Izumi resumes feeding her caterpillars. In an afterword, Merrill reports that the original account had a traditional ending, "What happened next will be found in the second chapter," but the chapter has been lost. The drama of the story is stunningly captured by Cooper's soft oil-wash paintings. Edging the narrow bands of text, the artwork takes center stage. With medieval Japan in the background, Izumi, her friends, and her caterpillars are the focus of scenes that pulse with life and beauty. Izumi herself almost takes the reader's breath away, so real is she; her life-affirming determination electrifies every page. Truly, a timeless story.

## Joanne Schott

SOURCE: A review of *The Girl Who Loved Caterpillars: A Twelfth-Century Tale from Japan,* in *Quill & Quire,* Vol. 58, No. 9, September 9, 1992, p. 78.

The unusual and tantalizing source for this book is a 12th-century Japanese story about court life whose promised second chapter—which may contain the conclusion to the heroine's tale—has either been lost or was never written.

Izumi's father hoped she might marry a nobleman, but she dashes these hopes and embarrasses her parents with her thorough nonconformity. She refuses to pluck her eyebrows or dress her hair, and makes friends with the rough boys who deliver the caterpillars and other insects she loves to study. The Captain of the Stables is intrigued nevertheless, and he watches Izumi from outside her window. The two exchange notes, but his final correspondence—to which Izumi does not reply—claims that "no man exists sensitive and brave enough to tune his life" to a girl who loves caterpillars.

Merrill's prose is dignified and suits the story, contrasting Izumi's way of life with the expectations of the court, and revealing a delightful, original, and very likeable heroine. Cooper's sensitive paintings are beautifully executed in warm and subtle colours, full of detail in costume and setting. He introduces a note of poignancy to the Captain and his portrayal of Izumi is as richly individual as the text demands.

## Kate McClelland

SOURCE: A review of *The Girl Who Loved Caterpillars: A Twelfth-Century Tale from Japan,* in *School Library Journal,* Vol. 38, No. 9, September 9, 1992, p. 269.

A retelling of a Japanese story believed to date from the 12th century. Izumi is the privileged and pretty daughter of a provincial inspector in the emperor's court; she refuses to conform to standards of beauty and decorum. Preoccupied with the study of "the original nature of things," Izumi particularly loves caterpillars, and most enjoys the company, not of noblemen, but of low class boys who supply her with caterpillars to study. She attracts the admiration of a young nobleman who concludes he is not good enough for her; the story thus ends abruptly for, as an author's note explains, the rest of it has been lost. The retelling of this curious fragment is graceful and competent. Cooper's warm, beautiful oil wash paintings are in his familiar, appealing style, but they are flawed by inaccuracy of detail in both costume and setting, reflecting a period hundreds of years later than the story's setting. Still, this unusual piece will find use in classrooms; literally unfinished, it is a natural for creative writing assignments and, teamed with Cole's *Dragon in the Cliff,* could lead to discussion of the difficulties faced by women with a passion for science.

## Kirkus Reviews

SOURCE: A review of *The Girl Who Loved Caterpillars: A Twelfth-Century Tale from Japan,* in *Kirkus Reviews,* Vol. LX, No. 18, September 15, 1992, p. 1191.

A 12th-century Japanese story, adapted from three credited translations, about a young woman of respectable rank who defies convention by refusing to pluck her eyebrows or blacken her teeth; more significantly—unlike "the Perfect Lady" next door, who collects butterflies and flowers—she's fascinated by small creatures like insects and frogs. Ragged boys who bring her insects are Izumi's friends. She also has an admirer who values her true worth; he sends her an ingenious mechanical snake, and they exchange some subtle verse, but he goes on his way, "amused and wondering." Perhaps, Merrill suggests, what followed has been lost.

What remains is an intriguing glimpse of an independent-minded woman, deplored but not thwarted by her family. Merrill's adaptation is dignified and energetic, with touches of humor. Cooper's three-quarter-spread paintings (the text is nicely accommodated at one side) feature subtle, beautifully modeled portraits and exquisite fabrics against impressionistic, elegantly composed backgrounds in glowing, mellow earth tones. A lovely, unusual book.

## *FROM MISS IDA'S FRONT PORCH* (written by Sandra Belton, 1993)

### Kirkus Reviews

SOURCE: A review of *From Miss Ida's Front Porch,* in *Kirkus Reviews,* Vol. LXI, No. 17, September 1, 1993, p. 1140.

"You can know where you're going in this world only if you know where you've been!" Addressing adults as much as children, the narrator fondly recalls the sights and sounds of her neighborhood, especially Miss Ida's porch, a "telling place" where one summer night she heard old Mr. Fisher recall the time Duke Ellington himself came to stay because no hotel in town would have him. Another neighbor remembers hearing Marian Anderson sing at the Lincoln Memorial; a third, her farewell concert at Constitution Hall 25 years later. The author works earnestly and effectively to establish a sense of historical continuity; her strong purpose is buffered by some eloquent writing, and also by Cooper's soft-focus paintings, in which past and present mingle in warm medleys of brown and gold.

## Elizabeth Hanson

SOURCE: A review of *From Miss Ida's Front Porch,* in *School Library Journal,* Vol. 39, No. 11, November, 1993, p. 76.

Miss Ida's porch is a meeting place for the residents of Church Street, particularly for the in-between kids who are "old enough to stay up through the twilight time, but not quite old enough to want to hang out and look at boys." The neighbors are lured there by the long, easy evenings of storytelling and sharing. Belton's prose is lyrical and loving as this strong sense of place and African-American history is revealed in the neighbors' stories. Expert mixing of fictional characters with their accounts of such events as Marian Anderson being banned from singing at Constitution Hall are at the heart of this substantive work. This book is outstanding in its depth of emotion and evocative depiction of poignant historical moments. Wonderfully complementing it are Cooper's beautiful illustrations that are tenderly wrought in oil washes on board. The pictures add to the warmth and sense of community. The bibliography includes books, sound recordings, and videotapes. This is Belton's first book for children, and is a powerful debut.

## MEET DANITRA BROWN (written by Nikki Grimes, 1994)

### Hazel Rochman

SOURCE: A review of *Meet Danitra Brown,* in *Booklist,* Vol. 90, No. 12, February 15, 1994, p. 1085.

A series of simple poems tells a friendship story in the voice of Zuri Jackson, who admires her spirited buddy, Danitra Brown. Their relationship is upbeat but unsentimental. They have lots of fun together riding bikes and jumping rope, and they help each other out with chores and problems. Zuri is sorry one time when she betrays her friend's secret, but they make up, and Danitra comforts Zuri when she feels bad that she has no dad around. Zuri loves the way her friend ignores the neighborhood taunts about her thick coke-bottle glasses; in fact, Danitra's proud example helps Zuri when the kids tease her about her very dark skin (her Mom tells her to say, "The blacker the berry, the sweeter the juice"). Cooper's double-page spread oil-wash illustrations in rich shades of brown and purple are reminiscent of those he did for the poetry anthology **Pass It On.** He sets the individual portraits within a lively city neighborhood, in changing seasons, indoors and out. We feel the girls' energy and their bond, in joyful games and in quiet times together.

### *Publishers Weekly*

SOURCE: A review of *Meet Danitra Brown,* in *Publishers Weekly,* Vol. 241, No. 15, April 11, 1994, p. 65.

In a series of poems, an African-American girl sings the praises of her best friend and their special relationship. According to Zuri, the speaker here, Danitra is "the most splendiferous girl in town." Zuri respects Danitra's quirks (she wears only purple clothing) and admires her ability to walk away from boys who taunt her about her glasses. Zuri is, moreover, grateful that "Danitra knows just what to say to make me glad." Grimes's poetry has a very deliberate rhyme scheme, but it also smoothly describes a number of vignettes and links them with consistent themes and characterizations. Issues of race, feminism and family structure are delicately incorporated, and successfully build an emotional connection for the reader. Cooper's misty oil paints depict two proud, happy kids in an often grim urban landscape. Splashes of green leaves and storefront fruit and flower displays further brighten the sidewalks and apartment-building stoops. Though the selection may be especially touching for African Americans, anyone who has a best friend can relate to this realistic but bubbly volume.

### *Kirkus Reviews*

SOURCE: A review of *Meet Danitra Brown,* in *Kirkus Reviews,* Vol. LXI, No. 8, April 15, 1994, p. 557.

In a lively cycle of 13 poems by the author of *Somethin' on My Mind* (1978), Zuri Jackson celebrates her vibrant best friend Danitra: "the most splendiferous girl in town . . . She's not afraid to take a dare. / If something's hard, she doesn't care. / She'll try her best, no matter what." Danitra shares work, play, and confidences with equal verve, knows how to defuse a mean tease or comfort a friend, and loves to wear purple. In expansive double spreads, Cooper visualizes the girls' city neighborhood in glowing impressionistic pastels while focusing on subtly modeled close-ups of them in their many moods. The joyous portrayal will appeal to a broad age range. . . .

### Betsy Hearne

SOURCE: A review of *Meet Danitra Brown,* in *Bulletin of the Center for Children's Books,* Vol. 47, No. 11, July-August, 1994, p. 357.

With a smooth, scatterbrush effect in browns and russet reds, Cooper offers a filmy artistic backdrop for these thirteen poems, all about narrator Zuri's best friend Danitra. The girls are African American, and the neighborhood is inner city, but the friendship will seem familiar to a broad spectrum of readers: Zuri admires Danitra, gains support and protection from her company, and sometimes fights with her. The verse is naive and tuned to tell a story, the rhyming determined but rarely strained: "Danitra's scared of pigeons. I promised not to tell, / then I opened my big mouth and out the secret fell." Zuri's few shadowy moments and flashes of insecurity are as natural as the dense hues of the illustration; yet in total effect, the illustration is as upbeat as the poetry, with skillful drafting especially evident in facial expression and body postures. While some kids may get impatient with Danitra's idealized persona, for many children—especially those afraid of more formal or lyrically complex poetry—this book will prove a satisfying introduction and sturdy friend.

## COMING HOME: FROM THE LIFE OF LANGSTON HUGHES (1994)

### *Publishers Weekly*

SOURCE: A review of *Coming Home: From the Life of Langston Hughes,* in *Publishers Weekly,* Vol. 241, No. 28, July 11, 1994, p. 79.

This insightful picture book illuminates, in both words and art, moments from the childhood of poet Langston Hughes (1902-1967). Facing difficult times with his parents because of segregation and other forms of racism, Hughes spent many of his early years in the care of his grandmother in Lawrence, Kansas. As told by Cooper in the first book he has written as well as illustrated, the wide-open Midwest offers Langston plenty of space to dream, but staying with poor and aging Grandma proves mostly sad and lonely. An eventual move to the home of

*From* Coming Home: From the Life of Langston Hughes, *written and illustrated by Floyd Cooper.*

family friends ushers in a rosy period of love and care that encourages Hughes's burgeoning writing career. Young readers may not understand how Hughes's childhood shaped his adult work, but they are likely to enjoy this story in and of itself. Warmly lit oil portraits, so atmospheric that the sounds of daily life seem to emanate from them, are almost sure to prompt questions about the era, while a muted palette of browns, golds and pinks establishes a comfortable mood. A fine tribute.

**Lois F. Anderson**

SOURCE: A review of *Coming Home: From the Life of Langston Hughes,* in *The Horn Book Magazine,* Vol. LXX, No. 5, September-October, 1994, pp. 604-05.

This brief portrait of Langston Hughes is Floyd Cooper's first picturebook text; lovingly written, the biography highlights pivotal events in Hughes's life, emphasizing his loneliness as a child and his development as a poet. The book opens with Hughes's poem "Hope," setting the tone for Cooper's simple narrative. "Some-

times when I'm lonely, / Don't know why, / Keep thinkin' I won't be lonely, / By and by." Hughes lived in many places, even as a child, and, according to Cooper, finally found a home in Harlem, where he became a prominent writer of the Harlem Renaissance. Cooper's hazy illustrations in gold, brown, and sepia tones reveal keen observations of people and neighborhood. The text and art combine to create a fine tribute and introduction to the writer's life.

**Hazel Rochman**

SOURCE: A review of *Coming Home: From the Life of Langston Hughes,* in *Booklist,* Vol. 91, No. 3, October 1, 1994, p. 321.

The lonely child's search for home is the center of this touching picture book about Langston Hughes. In the first book that artist Cooper has written as well as illustrated, he combines large, soft-textured, earth-tone paintings with a warm, immediate storytelling voice. Dreamy words and pictures express the boy's yearning for a "home with his ma and pa. A home he would never have to leave." There are close-ups of his strong grandmother (who told him family stories of pride and glory) as well as views of his loving foster home and of the streets of Kansas City, where the child heard the "jazzy old blues music that drifted down the alleys and tickled his soul." Like Hughes's poetry, the power of Cooper's story is that it confronts the sadness even as it transcends it. Children like Hughes who dream of a "real home" will take heart from the story of the boy who found community and grew up to write astonishing poetry about it. Some of that poetry has recently been reissued in *The Dream Keeper*

### Louise L. Sherman

SOURCE: A review of *Coming Home: From the Life of Langston Hughes,* in *School Library Journal,* Vol. 40, No. 11, November, 1994, pp. 95-6.

Langston Hughes's lonely boyhood is presented with empathy in this picture-book biography. Cooper recounts how Hughes was raised by his grandmother, whose vivid stories of black heroism fueled his imagination, until she, with age, retreated into silence. His mostly absent parents appeared briefly but were unable to offer him a real parental relationship. When he moved in with family friends, he felt for the first time what it was like to have a home. Cooper's writing proves equal to his artwork in highlighting elements that convey the emotion and important events from his subject's youth. His earthtoned, hazy paintings have little detail but expressively depict moments and people. This does not attempt to be a complete biography. Rather, it focuses on those aspects of Hughes's childhood that relate to the central theme of finding a home. Teachers looking for a good way to introduce youngsters to this prominent poet will find this book to be an excellent accompaniment to his work.

### Roger Sutton

SOURCE: A review of *Coming Home: From the Life of Langston Hughes,* in *Bulletin of the Center for Children's Books,* Vol. 48, No. 5, January, 1995, p. 162.

Smoothly linked vignettes form a somewhat impressionistic biography of Langston Hughes . . . Cooper chronicles Hughes's childhood in a warm and intimate tone that conveys both the deprivations and sources of strength in the poet's early life, but the thematic emphasis on Langston's looking for "home" never quite sinks into the story. When Cooper writes, "Langston never had a home like most people," he is speaking metaphorically, but kids who have just read how Langston, after separations from his parents and grandmother, finally found a home with loving neighbors, will be confused. There is also no mention in the text (although it is stated in an author's note) that when he was thirteen Langston moved to Nebraska to live with his mother: was that "home" or

not? It's not a very straightforward account but it does have an emotional appeal; grainily realistic paintings have warm golden colors but are marred by perplexing expressions on characters' faces.

### Joanne Schott

SOURCE: A review of *Coming Home: From the Life of Langston Hughes,* in *Quill & Quire,* Vol. 61, No. 3, March, 1995, p. 79.

In his debut as a writer, Floyd Cooper has drawn from the incidents of Langston Hughes's life to create a sympathetic portrait of the poet's childhood. Growing up with his grandmother, separated from his parents, Hughes led a solitary life in which his own dreams and observations assumed great importance. Although it was a childhood of poverty, it was rich in experience. His heritage was a rich one, too, and his grandmother made sure he heard the stories that connected him to that heritage and to the heroes in his own family. She herself had worked on the Underground Railroad and her first husband rode with John Brown.

Cooper's illustrations emphasize the individuality of all the characters he shows us. Even background ones, caught in moments of action, have life and reality. His emphasis on warm tones and his soft-edged style suggest the appearance of old photographs and successfully create an image of an earlier time.

Hughes's poems are readily accessible to young readers. Cooper reveals the person behind that poetry and lets the reader discover the continuity of Hughes's background, his childhood experiences, and his art.

### *JAGUARUNDI* (written by Virginia Hamilton, 1995)

### Karen K. Radtke

SOURCE: A review of *Jaguarundi,* in *School Library Journal,* Vol. 40, No. 12, December, 1994, p. 75.

An original fantasy that "introduces young readers to a variety of real rain forest animals." As the ecosystem is gradually being tamed by humans who clear the land to build homes, ranches, and farms, Rundi Jaguarundi decides to move north where the great Rio Bravo flows and the forest canopy is still said to exist. He invites Coatimundia and other animals to accompany him. Big Brown Bat decides to stay, advising the others to learn to adapt, because there will always be danger, always be change. Jaguar announces he will not give up *his* hunting ground—it's him or them. Only Coatimundi decides to go with his friend. When they reach the Rio Bravo, it, too, has been claimed by man, so they continue on separately. Eventually Rundi settles down to raise a family. A picture glossary lists and defines the common animals found in Central and South America. Cooper's paintings convey the misty heat of the tropical habitat. The animals are realistically depicted, but the story and pictures do take liberties with the animal groupings—prey and predator stand together. The strength of this book is in its smooth presentation of cogent reasons for preserving the rain forest and its dwellers. A valuable curriculum item, which will fill many needs.

### Hazel Rochman

SOURCE: A review of *Jaguarundi* in *Booklist,* Vol. 91, No. 8, December 15, 1994, p. 753.

This compelling picture book is an animal fantasy rooted in physical reality. A jaguarundi (wildcat) tries to persuade the endangered animals of the rain forest to run north across the river to freedom, but one by one the other animals give their reasons for staying where they are. "Adapt," says the bat. "I'll never flee nor change my ways," gloats a powerful predator. Only the raccoonlike coati joins the jaguarundi on the perilous journey north. This isn't a formula story: the two emigrants find no paradise. The Promised Land has also been fenced and stripped by settlers. But the travelers adapt, and they survive in their new place. Hamilton says in a note that "the story parallels humans who escape their homelands in search of better, safer lives." The facts about the real animals are as powerful as the metaphor, and Cooper's glowing paintings capture the elusive beauty of each wild creature in its habitat. We feel the strength and the fragility as we try to know more. The book ends with small paintings and brief factual paragraphs about each of the 17 species mentioned in the story: where they live, how they behave, how endangered they are.

### Susan Dove Lempke

SOURCE: A review of *Jaguarundi,* in *Bulletin of the Center for Children's Books,* Vol. 48, No. 6, February, 1995, pp. 198-9.

Since the land where he lives is being cleared and settled, Rundi Jaguarundi decides to head north to the Rio Bravo in search of a forest canopy. Coati Coatimundi agrees that this is a good plan, and they spread the word to the other animals to meet and discuss it in the Great Pineapple Field of the Fallen Timber. Kit Fox, Howler Monkey, and several other rare or endangered animals join them, but the other animals decide against heading north. Big Brown Bat advises them that adapting to the changing environment is the best way, while Jaguar roars his defiance, saying, "I'll never flee, nor change my ways." Once Rundi and Coati have crossed the river, they are disappointed to find more settlers, but, being too tired to continue, decide to follow Big Brown Bat's advice and adapt. There is little action or conflict in this book, and the language is slow and stately, but children often feel so deeply for the plight of animals that the dignified pace won't discourage their interest. Cooper's

paintings are darkly mysterious, with animal faces gleaming out from the background of shadowy plants and rocks. His cats are particularly successfully drawn, although the occasionally odd use of perspective makes other animals difficult to see in their entirety. This might be a little too quiet for story hour but could prove a boon for primary-grades discussion of animal endangerment in the face of diminishing resources, and a closing section gives information on the animals shown in the story.

## PAPA TELLS CHITA A STORY (written by Elizabeth Fitzgerald Howard, 1995)

### Ilene Cooper

SOURCE: A review of *Papa Tells Chita a Story,* in *Booklist,* Vol. 91, No. 15, April 1, 1995, p. 1427.

What a treat for readers—a chance to renew their acquaintance with Chita, last seen in *Chita's Christmas Tree* (1989). Here, Chita sits on her father's lap as he tells the story of his experiences in the Spanish-American War. Part truth, part tall tale, Papa's story begins when he volunteers to carry a secret message through the swamps, beating off snakes, alligators, even a bird of prey. Chita, the little African-American child growing up in turn-of-the-century Baltimore, is based on Howard's cousin; the incidents of the book also are based on fact. In an author's note that will interest adults, Howard amplifies the story as she explains how black citizens bravely served in the Spanish-American War, though "fighting for their country did not lead to glory." Cooper's softly focused paintings, rendered in oil wash on board, are a nice fit with the tall-tale aspects of the story. Chita may have grown up long ago, but the love and fun between father and daughter transcends the decades.

### Ruth Semrau

SOURCE: A review of *Papa Tells Chita a Story,* in *School Library Journal,* Vol. 41, No. 6, June, 1995, p. 87.

After the supper dishes are washed and put away, Chita sits with her father and helps him reminisce about his army days. During the Spanish-American War, Papa delivered a secret message to the troops across the island of Cuba, through the dangers of snakes, alligators, predatory birds, thorns, and brambles. As they recount the events, each peril grows to monstrous proportions in Chita's imagination and Cooper's darkling images, but the message is delivered and Papa earned a medal to prove it. Oil-wash illustrations seem to arise from a smoky past and evoke action scenes of derring-do and quick thinking. Teachers who are encouraging student writing will enjoy this model of a common theme in family stories—"what Daddy (or mayhap Mommy) did in the war." Students will likewise enjoy this engaging tall tale for what it is, and perhaps retell some of their own family stories.

## 📖 ONE APRIL MORNING: CHILDREN REMEMBER THE OKLAHOMA CITY BOMBING (written by Nancy Lamb, 1996)

### Roger Sutton

SOURCE: A review of *One April Morning: Children Remember the Oklahoma City Bombing,* in *The Horn Book Guide,* Vol. VII, No. 2, January-June, 1996, p. 387.

Written by the children of Oklahoma City. A straightforward account of the events of the 1995 bombing is interspersed with quotes from children that echo the horror, grief, and confusion of the tragedy and offer simple suggestions for coping. Written in collaboration with teachers, clergy, and counselors, the book may be useful but is repetitive and sentimental. Cooper's gentle illustrations show adults and children grieving and healing.

### Betsy Hearne

SOURCE: A review of *One April Morning: Children Remember the Oklahoma City Bombing,* in *Bulletin of the Center for Children's Books,* Vol. 49, No. 10, June, 1996, pp. 342-43.

Like Ross and Myers's *Dear Oklahoma City, Get Well Soon,* this is a book aimed at both children and adults, with limited success in shaping the material for either audience. The first three pages, clearly meant to reassure adults, offer a formidably black-framed note from the author and two messages from experts, one "A Letter to Parents and Teachers" and the other about "The Journey of Healing." The next page, "Before," describes the explosion at the Oklahoma City Federal Building, and each of the succeeding pages is divided between adult descriptions and children's reiterations: "Along with the buildings, along with the lives of innocent people and the hopes and dreams of survivors, the explosion also destroyed the sense of security the children had always lived with. 'Anything can happen to anyone, anytime, anywhere,' said Emili. 'There could be a bomb right here,' said Abby. 'At my school, at my house, even in my car.' 'You can't really control what happens,' said Cicely." The last double spread, "After," returns to a straightforward description of the rescue efforts, cleanup, and national outpouring of aid. Cooper's rough-textured, soft-edged illustrations on mottled backgrounds show an ethnically varied cast of children, their peers, and their families in various stages of grief or recovery. The figures are capably drafted; the scenes seem suspended in time. Children may find the text both repetitious and amorphous, but the overall tone is not so sentimentalized as *Dear Oklahoma,* and an adult who connects with the book could render it a cohesive experience by storytelling between the lines.

### Jody McCoy

SOURCE: A review of *One April Morning: Children Remember the Oklahoma City Bombing,* in *School Library Journal,* Vol. 42, No. 7, July, 1996, p. 92.

Trauma, therapy, and healing are the intensely personal experiences that Lamb hopes to reach into with this book. She interviewed 50 Oklahoma City children, ages 3-15, to create a verbal collage of their thoughts and feelings following the April 1995 bombing, woven with her own sensitive narrative. No doubt the process was healing for the author and the children—but whether the book itself will heal remains to be seen. Compassion is clearly evident in the quotes and in Cooper's exquisitely warm, gentle, and hug-filled illustrations. Contrary to its visual appearance, this is not a book for young children, though the pictures and carefully chosen quotes could be shared with them. It is a valuable addition to libraries serving older children and adults who may well find it supportive to research on this historically significant event. This is a strong companion to *Dear Oklahoma City, Get Well Soon,* which combines letters from children outside Oklahoma City and comments from adults involved, and Clive Irving's *In Their Name,* a far more detailed account of the event and the lives lost. **One April Morning** is, however, a labor of love, a thing of beauty, deeply evocative, and a beneficent memorial.

## 📖 MANDELA: FROM THE LIFE OF THE SOUTH AFRICAN STATESMAN (1996)

### Cyrisse Jaffee

SOURCE: A review of *Mandela: From the Life of the South African Statesman,* in *The Horn Book Guide,* Vol. VIII, No. 1, July-December, 1996, p. 156.

This admiring picture-book biography is illustrated with Cooper's characteristic muted colors and impressionistic style. The portrait provides a lyrical and informative look at the statesman's life, focusing on his childhood and young adult years. The emphasis is on his development, not on his twenty-seven years in prison or his recent accomplishments. A valuable introduction to a modern hero. A pronunciation guide is included.

### *Kirkus Reviews*

SOURCE: A review of *Mandela: From the Life of the South African Statesman,* in *Kirkus Reviews,* Vol. LXIV, No. 15, August 1, 1996, pp. 1148-9.

A biography of Nelson Mandela, subtitled "From the Life of the South African Statesman." Cooper sets out a nearly impossible task, and in condensing a 78-year-old life, leaves out descriptions of torture, terror, and murder; of Mandela's wide-ranging and sometimes controversial talks with world leaders after his release from prison; and of—except in the author's note—the Nobel

Peace Prize he shared in 1993. This ambitious attempt focuses on where Mandela came from and how his character was formed, his stubbornness and desire to "stand firm" for what he believes. Key events in Mandela's youth are used to illustrate his development; he marries, divorces, and remarries within one sentence; readers get a short lesson on apartheid without being shown the absurdity of the principle of minority rule; the 27 years Mandela spent in prison are treated only briefly.

With stunning paintings of village scenes and reverential treatment of Mandela as determined student and eventual leader, this book will leave readers wanting more; without understanding or knowing about the disturbing violence of the policies Mandela fought, readers won't appreciate him or this tame depiction of his times. The author's note supplies a few crucial biographical details but repeats information and dates.

### Publishers Weekly

SOURCE: A review of *Mandela: From the Life of the South African Statesman,* in *Publishers Weekly,* Vol. 243, No. 35, August 26, 1996, p. 98.

Cooper's poetic portrait of Nelson Mandela emphasizes the leader's lifelong commitment to "stand[ing] firm for what he believed was fair and right." Appropriately for his audience, the author focuses more closely on Mandela's boyhood and schooling than on his adulthood as an antiapartheid activist or his ascension to the presidency of South Africa. Lyrically linking Mandela's Thembu heritage with his education in modern subjects, Cooper describes the young Mandela's relationship to Thembu elders, such as Old Chief Joyi, "[who] with his wrinkled blue-black skin and dry, dusty voice, had lived and seen much from the days of forever before." This dextrous attention to Thembu traditions paves the way to a stronger appreciation of the adult Mandela's commitment to freedom for all of South Africa's peoples. Striking an appealing balance between the representational and the symbolic, Cooper's intentionally grainy oil washes present impressive likenesses of Mandela throughout the stages of his life. Skillful design accommodates a lengthy text by setting it in relatively small type and superimposing it over sweeping, two-page spreads. A forceful, credible picture of a strong and deeply devoted statesman.

### Hazel Rochman

SOURCE: A review of *Mandela: From the Life of the South African Statesman,* in *Booklist,* Vol. 93, No. 2, September 15, 1996, p. 243.

Most children's biographies of Mandela are about his political life as an adult, and they are illustrated with dramatic documentary photographs. This picture book about the South African leader focuses on his happy childhood and youth as the son of a chief in the hills of the Transkei. The writing is reverential and exclamatory, which keeps the hero at a distance, but the handsome double-spread oil-wash paintings in soft, warm shades of brown capture the rural landscape and the individual people. The last third of the book, about Mandela's life in the city, includes a powerful close-up scene of a policeman demanding to see people's "pass books," a scene that shows what apartheid was like in daily life. At the back, a long author's note fills in the biographical details (including Mandela's 27 years in prison and his triumphant release); there is also a pronunciation key and a brief bibliography of good adult books.

### Carolyn Noah

SOURCE: A review of *Mandela: From the Life of the South African Statesman,* in *School Library Journal,* Vol. 42, No. 11, November, 1996, pp. 96-7.

Readers are introduced to the formation and growth of the young Nelson Mandela. Rolihlahla, known to his family as Buti, came from a royal Thembu family and was taught the ways of leadership early in his life. This brief account traces his days as a school boy, where he is assigned the name Nelson; as a college man; and as the first black to open (with his partner) a Johannesburg law office. It touches even more briefly on his work with the ANC, his two marriages and families, and his prison years. The text conveys the timelessness of the African traditions and landscape: "Always, the wind had blown mightily through the valley that cradled his village. Sunsets had forever before kissed the hills . . ." Most importantly, it sketches the lessons through which Mandela learned to hold fast to his beliefs. Wind is an important image in the narrative, often as a reminder of strength. Cooper's oil paintings are infused with golden light. Elegant composition and subtle shifts in perspective add emotional value to the carefully focused account. The author's obvious reverence for his subject shines through in this thoughtfully crafted, beautiful book.

### Journal of Adolescent & Adult Literacy

SOURCE: A review of *Mandela: From the Life of the South African Statesman,* in *Journal of Adolescent & Adult Literacy,* Vol. 40, No. 7, April, 1997, pp. 587-88.

Recognizing that many middle school and high school students prefer nonfiction to fiction, teachers constantly search for great nonfiction. Remembering that most reluctant readers prefer texts with illustrations to help them visualize keeps teachers looking for picture books that appeal to older readers. Consequently, nonfiction picture books like . . . *Mandela* are winners with these readers. . . .

[S]tudents interested in world leaders, Africa, civil rights, or apartheid will want to read **Mandela: From the Life of the South African Statesman.** Cooper's story begins with Rolihlahla Mandela's birth in 1918. Nicknamed Buti,

Mandela was later named Nelson when he entered an English school. All Buti's life, he remembered his father telling him to "stand firm for what he believed was fair and right." Buti does that as he seeks an education, attends law school, flees from an arranged marriage, and later goes to prison for life for questioning South Africa's apartheid. After 27 years in prison, his commitment to standing firm is rewarded as he is released and made president of the new government in South Africa.

[The biography] . . . entertain[s] and inform[s], use[s] beautiful art to extend the texts, and serve[s] as [a] model . . . of lucid and compelling writing for our students.

## 📖 *MIZ BERLIN WALKS* (written by Jane Yolen, 1997)

### Publishers Weekly

SOURCE: A review of *Miz Berlin Walks,* in *Publishers Weekly,* Vol. 244, No. 22, June 2, 1997, p. 71.

Yolen is pitch-perfect in her delivery of this tender tale of the friendship that blossoms between an elderly white woman and an African-American girl. Miz Berlin is well known in her neighborhood for the long and slow walks she takes around the block each evening. Mary Louise can't help wondering about the odd lady, who seems to be talking to herself as she passes by. One day Mary Louise's curiosity impels her to accompany Miz Berlin for a short stretch of the walk, and to her delight she discovers Miz Berlin's talent for spinning stories. The two form a poignant bond that sustains Mary Louise

even when Miz Berlin's walking days come to an end. Dedicating her story to her real-life grandmother, Fanny Berlin, Yolen adopts first the voice of the grown Mary Louise, who narrates the tale in flashback, and then interpolates the voice of Miz Berlin. Her mellifluous text, occasionally peppered with Southern dialect, has the easygoing pace of her heroine's strolls. Atmospheric descriptions of wind that "whispers kindly through the tall sycamores" and "the time it rained feathers" provide Cooper with choice imagery for his subtle, grainy paintings soaked in Virginia sunlight. He pairs lively portraits of Miz Berlin and Mary Louise with scenes of Mary Louise imagining herself in Miz Berlin's adventures, progressively involving the reader and strengthening the implied message that storytelling has a reality of its own.

### Susan Dove Lempke

SOURCE: A review of *Miz Berlin Walks,* in *Booklist,* Vol. 94, No. 2, September 15, 1997, p. 243.

Miz Berlin, an elderly white woman, goes for a walk every evening with her black umbrella, her blue button coat, or her paper fan, depending on the weather. A young African American girl watches her and, one night, can't resist following her down the block, fully expecting Miz Berlin to yell at her. Instead, Miz Berlin, without even acknowledging her presence, starts telling a story: "Well, child, I recall the time it rained feathers in Newport News." She keeps talking to the end of the block, where Mary Louise must turn back, but the next night she continues the tale, and it becomes their routine. The stories vary, one night a folk tale, another the

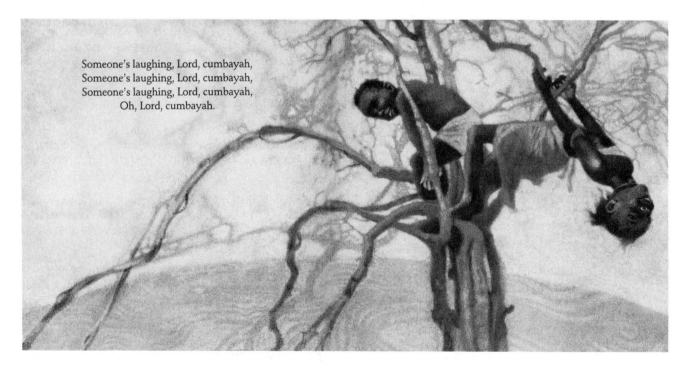

Someone's laughing, Lord, cumbayah,
Someone's laughing, Lord, cumbayah,
Someone's laughing, Lord, cumbayah,
Oh, Lord, cumbayah.

*From* Cumbayah, *adapted and illustrated by Floyd Cooper.*

story of when she was born, and Mary Louise goes home and repeats them to her doll "in order to keep ahold of them." The words are narrated by Mary Louise as an adult, and Yolen focuses tightly on her point of view. Cooper's luscious oil-wash paintings maintain Yolen's vision perfectly, as he portrays the luminous young Mary Louise listening to the stories and imagining herself right there with Miz Berlin. This poignant book conveys through simple words the power of stories to build bridges between two very different people, and it reminds us that the stories are left behind after the people are gone.

### 📖 *CUMBAYAH* (1998)

**Lolly Robinson**

SOURCE: A review of *Cumbayah,* in *The Horn Book Guide,* Vol. IX, No. 2, January-June, 1998, p. 399.

The well-known folk song has been illustrated in Cooper's unique pastel style with contemporary scenes set in different countries. While the book has a message rather than a story, Cooper pulls it off because no one is better at faces. His compassionate eye shows the beauty of individuals and seems to hint at a story behind each face. A note explains the origins of the song, and piano and guitar music appear on the endpapers.

**Susan Dove Lempke**

SOURCE: A review of *Cumbayah,* in *Booklist,* Vol. 94, No. 12, February 15, 1998, p. 1014.

In an introductory note giving background to the familiar folk song, Cooper explains that the term cumbayah means "come by here" in Gullah dialect, though the exact origins of the song are unknown. After inviting children to add their own words, he sets down some verses ("Someone's working, Lord, cumbayah"; "Someone's crying, Lord, cumbayah"), using large, luminous pictures depicting people of diverse races and ethnicities, individually and in multiracial groups, to create a message of harmony and common bonds. It's a warm, inviting book, complete with musical notation, including harmonies and guitar chords, on the endpapers.

*Publishers Weekly*

SOURCE: A review of *Cumbayah,* in *Publishers Weekly,* Vol. 245, No. 12, March 23, 1998, p. 94.

The inspirational folk song resonates with new meaning in Cooper's picture book rendition. The author and artist expands on the classic lyrics with his own original verses and his signature soft, luminous oil paintings of contemporary children, which bring home its modern implications; "Someone needs You, Lord, cumbayah, . . . / Oh, Lord, cumbayah" accompanies a scene of a home-

less mother and son huddled on a city street corner as a crowd of people hustle by. A fascinating foreword explains the origin of cumbayah (or "come by here"), its migration and historical import. This volume will be welcomed by religious instructors, music teachers and families alike.

**Jane Marino**

SOURCE: A review of *Cumbayah,* in *School Library Journal,* Vol. 44, No. 5, May, 1998, pp. 130-1.

This book combines the simple verses of this well-known spiritual with Cooper's glowing illustrations to tell a global tale far beyond the words. The pictures, oil wash on illustration board, begin with a circle of children sitting cross legged, joining hands, and singing the first verse. Each subsequent stanza is illustrated with page-encompassing paintings that show children and adults from around the world. (However, none of these places are identified in the book.) Youngsters are shown sleeping under trees; fishermen work throwing their nets; for the verse, "Someone's hurting, Lord" a child is shown covering his face as he crouches in hiding while bombs fly in the background; and a seemingly homeless pair sit in a doorway, illustrating the words, "Someone needs you, Lord." Many of the pictures have a circular flow to them as objects curve around the characters: a fishing net hovers in a semicircle over the fishermen. Children sleep beside trees whose trunks curve around them. The final line, "Oh Lord, Cumbayah" shows another group of children raising colorful banners above their heads. The book concludes with the words and music for the song. Although beautifully done, this is a message-laden book that will be useful, to be sure, for adults to teach children about tolerance and differences among peoples as well as similarities.

### 📖 *TREE OF HOPE* (1999)

*Kirkus Reviews*

SOURCE: A review of *Tree of Hope,* in *Kirkus Reviews,* Vol. LXVII, No. 18, October 15, 1999, p. 1646.

Through Florrie's eyes readers experience the despair and hopelessness of talented actors who were forced to leave the stage to find other work when the Lafayette Theatre closed its doors; the golden days of the Harlem Renaissance of the 1920s have disappeared into the Great Depression of the 1930s, and Florrie's father, once an actor, toils at the Allnight Bakery. Florrie's greatest dream is for her father to be able to leave his job and return to the stage, and so she makes a wish on a tree that grows next to the Lafayette Theatre; it has become a symbol of endurance for black actors, a tree of hope. A director, Mr. Welles, arrives when President Roosevelt orders that the doors of the theatre be opened; there is to be a staging of *Macbeth,* and Florrie's father gets a part. An author's note attests to the veracity of events in the story, when Orson Welles directed African-Americans in roles from which they were once excluded. Cooper's lavish oil-wash, full-page paintings pay mute tribute to the loss of luster and its regeneration in Harlem, in scenes in which the footlights cast a glow, and in which the faces tell a story that hardly needs words.

---

**Additional coverage of Cooper's life and career is contained in the following sources published by The Gale Group:** *Contemporary Authors,* **Vol. 161 and** *Something about the Author,* **Vol. 96.**

# Florence Parry Heide

## 1919-

(Also writes as Alex B. Allen and Jamie McDonald) American author of fiction, picture books, and poetry.

Major works include *Sound of Sunshine, Sound of Rain* (1970), *The Shrinking of Treehorn* (1971), *When the Sad One Comes to Stay* (1975), *Growing Anyway Up* (1976), *The Problem with Pulcifer* (1982).

## INTRODUCTION

With more than seventy-five works to her credit, including picture books, juvenile novels, mysteries, short stories, songs, and poems, Heide has fashioned her personal childhood experiences into wacky, imaginative tales that encourage primary- and middle-graders, as well as young adults, to recognize their own strengths and take charge of their lives. The lesson she learned as a child—to take command of her own attitude and actions—resonates in the cheerful tone and underlying messages of her works. Typically told from a young person's point of view, Heide's stories are marked with a strong sense of love, hope, and comedy, as well as the insecurities involved in adapting to circumstances beyond our control. Adept at finding the fun in most situations, Heide is also regarded for her light didactic touch and subtle moralizing. Thematically, she looks for humor in child-parent struggles and emphasizes the need to have a cheerful spirit while confronting life's challenges. Her best-known works are three Treehorn picture books that juxtapose youthful wonder with the rigidity of adult order. Critics have celebrated her exuberant, if sometimes irreverent wit in *The Shrinking of Treehorn*, in which a young boy is somewhat ignored by the inflexible structure of the adult world around him. *Treehorn's Treasure,* written ten years later, follows the same basic premise as its predecessor and evokes fun as well as pain. The third in the series, *Treehorn's Wish,* was written three years later and was found to be as enjoyable as the previous two stories.

In addition to her comic and whimsical picture books, Heide has also collaborated on two mystery series with her friend and partner, Sylvia Van Clief, and later, with Heide's daughter Roxanne and her son David. Her mysteries have attracted reluctant readers with their easy, intriguing, and fast-paced plots. One series features the Spotlight Club, while the other is set at Brillstone Apartments. Although reviewers have argued that the stories contain too many coincidences, digressions, and easily concocted solutions, most have found these books to be action-oriented and entertaining. Despite her characteristically lighthearted tone, Heide has not hesitated in her young adult fiction to delve into such painful subjects as self-absorbed parents, blindness, mental illness, and adolescent alienation. Some reviewers have criticized her

work for its lack of direction and plot development, and for conclusions that sometimes end abruptly or just "trail off." Heide, however, is respected for her strong characterizations and her keen perception of the excitement, as well as the difficulties and frustrations of growing up. Overall, Heide recognizes herself as an enthusiastic storyteller. She once commented in *Major Authors and Illustrators for Children and Young Adults,* "Writing for children was an unexpected delight: I could reach my child-self (never long away or far from me) and I could reach the selves of other children like me. . . . Ideas flew into my head, I couldn't write fast enough to accommodate them."

### Biographical Information

Born in Pittsburgh to a banker and an actress, Heide felt she was an ordinary child with shortcomings. Her father died when she was three, and, shortly after, her young, widowed mother stopped acting and began a new venture as a columnist and drama critic in Pittsburgh. The young Heide spent a lot of time with her extended family in her grandparents' house in Punxsutawney, Pennsylvania, where her mother came to visit on weekends. At the large home, Heide became entrenched in the bustle of family life, with grandparents, aunts, uncles, and cousins always close at hand. Eventually, when Heide's mother was financially able, she brought her children to live with her in the city, where Heide became very shy, awkward and unsure of herself because of the unfamiliar surroundings and new people. Throughout her childhood, however, Hiede maintained her belief in the power of a cheerful spirit, a strength she attributes largely to her mother, who so courageously faced the unexpected disaster of her husband's death. With her mother busy working, Heide spent much time reading books, playing with her dolls, and inventing magic tricks with her brother. Her mother always encouraged her to write, but being a wife and mother was always Heide's first choice for a career.

Heide later attended the University of California, Los Angeles, where she received a Bachelor of Arts degree in English in 1939. She moved to New York to work and, after a few years, moved back to Pittsburgh. Shortly thereafter, she met Donald Heide, and the couple was married in 1943; they had five children. A self-proclaimed "late bloomer," Heide began writing stories while her children were in school. In 1967, she published her first work for children, *Maximilian,* written with her friend Silvia Van Clief, with whom Heide would collaborate on numerous titles for young people. While enjoying a successful second career as an author, Heide has credited her mother with helping her appreciate what writing involves, including the demands, rewards, and expression of ideas. She stated in *Contemporary Authors,* "Writing has brought me scores of new friends, has opened many doors, inside and out, has created for me a life within my life. It's the best of all worlds!"

## Major Works

*Sound of Sunshine, Sound of Rain*, the story of a blind black boy, explores what it might be like to be blind. The young boy listens for "weather signals" and likes to hear "sunshine sounds" so that he may go to the nearby park for the day. "The text, though perceptively written, is too long for the picture-book crowd and too quiet and introspective for most children. But special readers will find much to enlighten them about how it feels to be handicapped by blindness," stated Barbara S. Miller. Although Zena Sutherland called this book an "unusual story," she further remarked that it could "be used as a basis for discussion and an avenue to understanding" about blindness.

Heide's most acclaimed book, *The Shrinking of Treehorn*, explores the rigidity of the grown-up world through the eyes of a young boy. In *Something about the Author Autobiography Series* (*SAAS*), Heide said she "wanted to write a story about a boy to whom something extraordinary happens and no one notices." Treehorn feels that he is shrinking and receives no help from the adults in his life. His teacher tells him to "see that it's taken care of before tomorrow. We don't shrink in this class." His

mother disregards him with, "Heaven knows I have tried to be a good mother." The problem is solved by Treehorn when he plays a game he finds under his bed called "The Big Game for Kids to Grow." Zena Sutherland found this book a "tongue-in-cheek story with a fanciful plot and meaningful dialogue," and added that it "comes off as a piquant ploy." John Donovan commented, "The book is delicious. It doesn't attack adults, but it certainly observes them closely and to their detriment." In *Treehorn's Treasure* (1981), the sequel to *The Shrinking of Treehorn*, Treehorn, once again ignored by adults, discovers that the tree in his yard is growing dollar bills. Being ignored works to Treehorn's advantage as he is able to buy comic books and candy; however, he becomes so preoccupied with his comics that he begins to treat the adults the same way they have been treating him. "It's the same joke, but *Treehorn's Treasure* is as sharp and tart as Heide's . . . first deadpan classic," stated Pamela D. Pollack, while Zena Sutherland concluded, "This is Heide at her best."

Heide has written numerous books for adolescents that directly confront pain and alienation. *When the Sad One Comes to Stay*, Heide's first novel, is the story of Sara, whose ambitious and rather insensitive politician mother has taken her daughter away from her home with her kindhearted and warm father, deemed a "lazy, slow, stupid ox" by her mother. Sara befriends a lonely old woman named Maisie who teaches Sara ways to keep the "Sad One" away and never allow loneliness to take over. When a choice must be made between her mother and Maisie, Sara casts her lot with her mother—and with probable loneliness as well.

"Perhaps Heide is romanticizing the poverty of Sara's father or the deep understanding of Maisie, but the story has compelling psychological truth," Matilda Kornfeld commented. Zena Sutherland deemed the book a "sensitive and convincing study of a child who—torn between two value systems–responds to pressure and example."

*Growing Anyway Up* tells of a young girl named Florence who is overcome with guilt and grief over her father's sudden death during a business trip. She hides behind protective rituals and "nervous tics" that she believes will make her safe, such as never making eye contact and repeating "dangerous" things backwards, word by word or letter by letter. Her widowed mother decides to move them to Pennsylvania to be closer to her sister-in-law, Nina. Florence's compulsions increase when her mother becomes involved with a man that she eventually marries. Aunt Nina helps Florence deal with her emotions, including the guilt she feels for not giving her father a good luck kiss when he left on his trip. The last chapter jumps ahead to a time when Florence is doing well in boarding school.

Anita Silvey noted, "Although the ending seems a bit truncated and Florence's problems are much too neatly wrapped up, the novel is remarkable for its humor, its lean, intense prose, and its strong characterization of a girl who finds herself an outsider." Zena Sutherland opined that "the adult characters are convincing enough but not explored in depth," but "Florence is," and concluded that Florence's "fears, her compulsive patterns of behavior . . . her self-denigration are depicted with sharp perception."

*The Problem with Pulcifer* is a humorous look at television addicts through the eyes of a young boy named Pulcifer who doesn't want to watch television and would much rather read books. The adults in his life, including the librarian, his teachers, and his parents are very concerned about Pulcifer's problem.

When a psychiatrist tells Pulcifer that he was able to break the same habit when he was a child, Pulcifer's parents let him know that they still love him and leave him alone with his stack of library books while they go off to watch television. Ilene Cooper observed that Heide's "joke goes on too long, but for the most part it is a good one." Zena Sutherland maintained, "Heide makes her point with humor, deriding not television but television addiction in a clever story."

Written in collaboration with her daughter Judith Heide Gilliland, *The Day of Ahmed's Secret* (1990) takes young readers to Egypt where a young boy named Ahmed has become old enough to help his father deliver bottled gas for customers' cook stoves. Proud that he is strong enough to contribute to the family's income, Ahmed is also excited because he has learned to write his name and wants to share this surprise with his family. Marcus Crouch pointed out, "The ideas in this beautiful book may be beyond the immediate grasp of children attracted to a picture-book, but they surely must be touched by its vitality." "Perceptive readers will be left to contemplate what life must be like for a young boy who works hard all day, has no schooling, and for whom learning to write his name is a singular accomplishment . . . A quiet book that nevertheless projects a powerful presence, this will push both browsers and students to broaden their world view," commented Denise M. Wilms.

## Awards

*Sound of Sunshine, Sound of Rain* received the Children's Book of the Year award from the Child Study Association of America in 1970; *My Castle* received the Children's Book of the Year award in 1972. *The Shrinking of Treehorn* was chosen as a Children's Book Showcase selection in 1972 and received the Judenbuchpreis for best children's book in Germany in 1977. It also received an American Library Association notable book citation and a *School Library Journal* Best of the Best Books 1966-78 citation in 1978. *When the Sad One Comes to Stay* was selected as a notable trade book in the field of social studies by the Social Studies—Children's Book Council in 1975. *Growing Anyway Up* was named a Golden Kite honor book by the Society for Children's Book Writers in 1976. The following works received an American Library Association notable book citation: *Banana Twist* in 1978; *Treehorn's Treasure* in 1981; *Time's Up!* in 1982; and *The Day of Ahmed's Secret* in 1990. In addition,

*Banana Twist* won the Charlie May Simon award in 1980 and *The Day of Ahmed's Secret* was recognized as a *School Library Journal* Best Book in 1990. Heide received the Golden Archer award in 1976 for her entire body of work.

---

# TITLE COMMENTARY

📖 *MAXIMILIAN* (with Sylvia W. Van Clief, 1967)

## Polly Goodwin

SOURCE: A review of *Maximilian,* in *Washington Post Book World,* December 31, 1967, p. 10.

Maximilian hated being a mouse. He didn't like to squeak or scamper or eat cheese. He wanted to be a bird. So he climbed into a nest and stayed there, uncomfortably hot, until all the eggs hatched and the little birds began to fly. Only Maximilian couldn't. In fact, it wasn't long at all before he had second thoughts and was happy to be a squeaking, scampering mouse. No child is going to resent the obvious moral: It's always better to be oneself. Not when a story is as funny as this one or has such hilarious illustrations [by Ed Renfro]. A perfect "Fun and Frolic" book.

## Zena Sutherland

SOURCE: A review of *Maximilian,* in *Bulletin of the Center for Children's Books,* Vol. 21, No. 6, April, 1968, p. 128.

The idea of an animal wanting to be something other than what he is is not a new idea in picture books, but it has seldom been more amusingly handled. Maximilian's mother takes it calmly when he announces that he wants to be a bird instead of a mouse. He doesn't like squeaking or scampering or crouching; Maximilian wants to fly. He stows away in a nest and pretends to be one of the nestlings; Mother Bird (who has been offended when one of her friends said that one of the children looked like a mouse) reluctantly admits that this one can't fly. Indeed, that it's a mouse. Thankfully, Maximilian gives up the whole project. The style is light and humorous, the scratchy illustrations full of vitality.

📖 *GIANTS ARE VERY BRAVE PEOPLE* (1970)

## Kirkus Reviews

SOURCE: A review of *Giants Are Very Brave People,* in *Kirkus Reviews,* Vol. XXXVIII, No. 10, May 15, 1970, p. 549.

To minuscule Mrs. Pimberly timid Bigelow is a giant, and "Giants are very brave people." So girded, and saying *Fee Fi Fo Fum,* he manages to eat the soup part of alphabet soup (the letters might spell a magic word and turn him into a mushroom) and negotiate his bath (not, however, without his rubbers and raincoat and a residual fear of melting). He's "a little braver, after all" and treating Mr. P. to a ride in his toy train takes his mind off his troubles. There it ends, not very bravely, and though there's a little progress there's very little application.

## 📖 SOUND OF SUNSHINE, SOUND OF RAIN (1970)

### Barbara S. Miller

SOURCE: A review of *Sound of Sunshine, Sound of Rain,* in *School Library Journal,* Vol. 17, No. 8, April, 1971, p. 96

Large libraries and those with special collections will want to acquire this poignant, first-person story depicting a blind, black boy's feelings about and reactions to the world around him. The youngster, always listening for "weather signals," is delighted when he hears the "sunshine sounds" for they mean he may go to the nearby park to spend the day alone. The two such days covered by the story bring the boy unexpected pleasure for he discovers a friend, the ice-cream vendor, who opens new vistas for him as he shares his ability to see beauty in the things around them and introduces him to the idea of color: "colors are just like sounds" but they are also only "on the outside"—there is no best color. The book is greatly enhanced by vividly colored illustrations [by Kenneth Longtemps] which appear on all but a few pages. The text, though perceptively written, is too long for the picture-book crowd and too quiet and introspective for most children. But special readers will find much to enlighten them about how it feels to be handicapped by blindness.

### Zena Sutherland

SOURCE: A review of *Sound of Sunshine, Sound of Rain,* in *Bulletin of the Center for Children's Books,* Vol. 25, No. 1, September, 1971, p. 8.

An unusual story, the speaker a blind black child whose comments are fraught with poignant acceptance. The static quality of the book may limit its appeal, but the situation of the child can be used as a basis for discussion and an avenue to understanding. The child wakes in the morning and feels for his clothes; he listens to his mother's gentle voice and his sister's sharp impatience. The sister takes him to a park to sit in the sun while she is in school, and an ice cream seller sits down to talk. His sister has told the boy how bleak and dirty the park is. No, says his new friend, there is beauty in it for those who can see beauty: what you see is inside yourself. Later, his sister asks the boy if the man is black, but he cannot tell. "I wish every one in the whole world was blind," she cries. The next day it rains: no park. Tomorrow, the blind boy thinks. While there is no false cheeriness, the book has a vague conclusion that stresses the hopelessness of the child's burden, and the story has an

unfinished quality that is disappointing—yet it may serve a purpose in making sighted readers aware of the limited horizons of the blind.

## 📖 THE KEY (1971)

### Georgess McHargue

SOURCE: A review of *The Key,* in *The New York Times Book Review,* May 30, 1971, p. 8.

The three stories in Florence Parry Heide's **The Key** possess the same characteristic of making demands on the reader, without the slightest danger of slackening attention. These children find themselves in situations so cut off from all surface ordinariness that reality becomes distorted for us as well as for them. Here it is sometimes what the characters *do not know* for which we must allow, the terrible unknowingness that comes from poverty of experience. At other times what is demanded seems more like an act of faith. In the title story we find a young boy whose only rule of behavior is a harsh piece of street wisdom: "If anybody notices you, you're dead. You gotta keep outta the way." Numbed by the breakup of the only stability he knows, he runs away from a foster home, desperately seeking a day when the key he wears around his neck (which *mustn't* be just an ordinary skate key) will open the door to "a special place. . . . a place where no one could see you." It will be a hardy reader who can enter the world of **The Key,** a world of the trapped, the lost, and the damaged, without flinching. But it will be a lazy or insensitive one who comes out untouched.

### Sally C. Estes and Elinor Walker

SOURCE: A review *The Key,* in *The Booklist,* Vol. 67, No. 22, July 15, 1971, p. 951.

Three compelling short stories of nameless children caught in circumstances they cannot change or fully understand. In "Wild bird," an Indian boy walks the hot streets of a city with his grandfather who repeatedly tries to convey how life was in "the other time." In "The key," a boy's rule of survival in his hostile city world is to keep himself small and unnoticed when bad things happen. "Let down your golden hair" tells of a girl who cares for her retarded sister until her drunken mother signs "the blob" away to the "paper people." Despite their seeming simplicity, the stories will be most meaningful to perceptive readers.

## 📖 THE SHRINKING OF TREEHORN (1971)

### Sidney D. Long

SOURCE: A review of *The Shrinking of Treehorn,* in *The Horn Book Magazine,* Vol. XLVIII, No. 1, February, 1972, p. 45.

Treehorn was shrinking. He could no longer reach the

shelf where his candy bars were hidden. His shirtsleeves were too long, and he tripped on his trousers. "'I think I must be shrinking or something,'" he tells his parents, who are perplexed and annoyed by his predicament. Although Treehorn is stoical about his dilemma, most of the people he has to deal with feel that he is trying to create a deliberate inconvenience. Treehorn, himself, is inconvenienced; finally he is so small that in order to play "THE BIG GAME FOR KIDS TO GROW ON," he must kick the spinner and even carry a game piece from space to space. (The game, of course, provides the solution to his problem.) A comedy of the suburban bizarre, illustrated by an artist [Edward Gorey] who understands—and is able to define meticulously—the Gothic aspects of Treehorn's tidy world.

### Zena Sutherland

SOURCE: A review of *The Shrinking of Treehorn,* in *Bulletin of the Center for Children's Books,* Vol. 25, No. 10, June, 1972, pp. 156-57.

Edward Gorey's sophisticated drawings are exactly right for this tongue-in-cheek story with a fanciful plot and meaningful dialogue, especially amusing for readers with a dry sense of humor. Treehorn is a boy and his shrinking is literal. He gets smaller and smaller, trips on his own clothes, cannot reach things, and is almost entirely disregarded by his parents. ("I wonder if he's doing it on purpose. Just to be different.") His teacher says, "Nursery school is down the hall, honey," but when she realizes that the tot is indeed a shrunken Treehorn, she says firmly, " . . . see that it's taken care of before tomorrow. We don't shrink in this class." Perhaps meant as an acid comment on the failure of communications between generations or even between individuals, the book comes off as a piquant ploy.

### Margery Fisher

SOURCE: A review of *The Shrinking of Treehorn,* in *Growing Point,* Vol. 14, No. 4, October, 1975, p. 2721.

To the young, adults are apt to seem inattentive, unsympathetic and unaccountably reluctant to let them join the ranks: to adults, a child's turbulent desire to grow up to equal terms is as difficult to understand or to accept. *The Shrinking of Treehorn* encapsulates the junior generation-gap in a superb alliance of words and pictures. When small Treehorn finds he is becoming even smaller, he tries in vain to convince his parents of the seriousness of the case. Preoccupied with, respectively, business and house-wifery, his father vaguely commiserates and his mother gives him a cushion to sit on at table. Treehorn cures himself, eventually, by intelligently using an old game he finds under the bed called "The Big Game for Kids to Grow"; and when he notices that he is turning green, he utters the pay-off line, "If I don't say anything they won't notice"—which, as the last page clearly shows, is only too true. Edward Gorey's drawings, the narrow,

weasel-like faces of the characters and the simple line with which he activates parents and small boy, enforce the somewhat bleak and terse humour of this cautionary tale.

### J. Russell

SOURCE: A review of *The Shrinking of Treehorn,* in *The Junior Bookshelf,* Vol. 40, No. 2, April, 1976, p. 92.

Another of those crazy stories you either love or hate. "We don't shrink in this class", said Treehorn's teacher firmly, but Treehorn was shrinking. Another story where child triumphs over adults. "Heaven knows I've tried to be a good mother", sniffed Treehorn's mother, and paid no more attention. Do not be put off by the title (why on earth did they give the boy the name of Treehorn)—think of it as "The shrinking of Fred". A funny book for adults and children alike in which Edward Gorey's pen and ink drawings match wittily the text of this altogether satisfying book.

### John Donovan

SOURCE: "American Dispatch," in *The Signal Approach to Children's Books,* edited by Nancy Chambers, Scarecrow Press, 1980, pp. 184-85.

A book sure to be on anyone's approved list in the children's rights area would be Florence Parry Heide's *The Shrinking of Treehorn,* illustrated by that genius Edward Gorey. "Something very strange was happening to Treehorn," it begins. "The first thing he noticed was that he couldn't reach the shelf in his closet that he had always been able to reach before, the one where he hid his candy bars and bubble gum." Then Treehorn discovers that his clothes are getting too big and that he's tripping on them. "'Too bad, dear'" says his mother. At dinner, as Treehorn shrinks below the tabletop, his father urges him to sit up. "'I can hardly see your head,'" his father says. Arguments ensue. Treehorn insists he is shrinking. "'Don't argue with your mother, Treehorn,'" his father says. "'Nobody shrinks.'" Treehorn continues to shrink; he can't post a letter in the mail box; he can't climb onto the school bus; he can't reach the water fountain in the corridor at school; the principal at school thinks Treehorn is shirking, not shrinking. Well, Treehorn finally gets back his size but it's not because anyone helped him! The book is delicious. It doesn't attack adults, but it certainly observes them closely and to their detriment.

## 📖 *MY CASTLE* (1972)

### Michael J. Bandler

SOURCE: "Then to Read," in *The Washington Post Book World,* November 5, 1972, p. 1.

The lonely, diminutive hero of *My Castle* is a Puerto Rican tenement dweller whose life revolves around the fire escape he visualizes as a magical world fit for a king. He's familiar with the day's routine, but every so often, something unexpected—perhaps a blue butterfly or a spider—penetrates the imaginary kingdom. Florence Parry Heide has given us a poignant, unvarnished story of ghetto life, and Symeon Shimin's brown-tinted drawings add to the book's realism.

## Zena Sutherland

SOURCE: A review of *My Castle,* in *Bulletin of the Center for Children's Books,* Vol. 26, No. 5, January, 1973, p. 77.

The castle is a fire-escape landing, the speaker a child (no name) who sleeps there and spends much of his time alone, watching people below. Mother works, he watches for her at the end of the day. They have a sandwich, sitting in the castle. Soon it is time to bring the mattress out, to see if Mr. and Mrs. Rodriguez are in *their* castle (the landing below) yet. There is a certain wistful quality to the text, echoed in the handsome but repetitive pictures, but there is no plot and seemingly no direction to the book—it simply describes a small child's lonely day.

## WHEN THE SAD ONE COMES TO STAY (1975)

### *Publishers Weekly*

SOURCE: A review of *When the Sad One Comes to Stay,* in *Publisher's Weekly,* Vol. 208, No. 8, August 25, 1975, p. 293.

Ms. Heide has created a devastating world in an artfully constructed story of conflicting values. Sara is a young girl whose "upwardly mobile" mother, Sally, has deserted home and husband. After a long absence, while Sara has been poor but happy with her unambitious father, Sally returns to take the girl into a posh neighborhood and to give her social advantages. While Sally pursues her career, Sara is friendless and lonely until she meets an elderly woman, Maisie Best. The two outcasts form a bond, with Maisie giving the girl hints on how to outwit "the sad one," the evil that destroys hope. A crisis of conscience, betrayal and a new Sara bring the unforgettable novel to a shocking but inevitable close.

## Matilda R. Kornfeld

SOURCE: A review of *When the Sad One Comes to Stay,* in *School Library Journal,* Vol. 22, No. 2, October, 1975, p. 99.

A shattering story, told by a girl torn between warm memories of her loving "no-good" father and the bright future her smart, success-oriented mother is urging upon her. Living with Sally, who is "in politics," Sara's only friend is a lonely old woman who treats Sara as if she

were the granddaughter she has never seen. Maisie is full of folk wisdom and knows many ways of keeping the "Sad One" at bay, of never allowing loneliness to take over. To Maisie Sara talks about the good times she remembers with her father and stepbrother, Bigun. When Sally has to go to New York, an invitation to spend a few days with one of the stylish girls in her new neighborhood quickly replaces Sara's plan to stay with Maisie. As Sara finds herself making fun of "Crazy Maisie," she feels the "Sad One" move in. The story poses a problem without solution: Sally has learned the lessons of upward mobility too well and is dedicated to seeing that Sara leaves the baggage of poverty behind. But Sara's father who has love, warmth, fun and imagination to offer has not kept Bigun from getting into trouble. Perhaps Heide is romanticizing the poverty of Sara's father or the deep understanding of Maisie, but the story has compelling psychological truth.

## Zena Sutherland

SOURCE: A review of *When the Sad One Comes to Stay,* in *Bulletin of the Center for Children's Books,* Vol. 29, No. 7, March, 1976, p. 111.

It is usually the male who is depicted in our literature as the ruthless person whose successful career has been built on a calculated program of taking care of Number One. In this poignant story told by Sara, it is her shrewd and beautiful mother, Sally, whose goals in the political arena are meant to be achieved by the perfect setting and the right people. And for Sara that means separation from a father deemed "a lazy, slow, stupid ox" by Sally. But her father was love, warmth, laughter, and security to Sara; she finds a substitute adult in Maisie, an old woman who is sloppy and loving. Sally doesn't know about Maisie; they've just moved to a new home where Sara can go to a "good" school, meet the "right" girls, and help bolster Sally's perfectionist image. In a poignant dénouement, Sara not only rejects Maisie but derides her when she must choose between defending the friendship or jeering at it to cement a bond with the "right" girls her mother has arranged an acquaintance with. Sara's careful comments on her mother and her acceptance of Sally's materialistic values are beautifully contrasted with the freedom she enjoys with Maisie and the remembrances of the gaiety and affection in her relationship with her father. Subtle, and perhaps not for every reader, this is a sensitive and convincing study of a child who—torn between two value systems—responds to pressure and example, and chooses the expedient.

##  THE TENNIS MENACE (under pseudonym Alex B. Allen, with son David Heide, 1975)

### Zena Sutherland

SOURCE: A review of *The Tennis Menace,* in *Bulletin of the Center for Children's Books,* Vol. 29, No. 4, December, 1975, p. 57.

Most of his friends are playing baseball, most of the tennis courts are occupied by older children, and Andy can't find a partner or a court to practice his tennis game for the tournament. Sheila, next door, likes to play, but Andy finds her complaints and bad manners irritating. A new subscriber on his paper route provides Andy with a court and a partner (his visiting grandchild, Tracy) who is pleasant and capable. Andy and Tracy help each other improve; the story ends with the two paired in the tournament and Andy winning. The plot isn't strong and the characterization is minimal, but the writing style is adequate, the message about sportsman- or womanship clear, and the book should be welcomed by all players who've bemoaned the lack of tennis stories—although the text includes explanations of scoring for the nonplayer.

## 📖 MYSTERY OF THE VANISHING VISITOR (with daughter Roxanne Heide, 1975)

### Judith Goldberger

SOURCE: A review of *Mystery of the Vanishing Visitor,* in *The Booklist,* Vol. 72, No. 12, February 15, 1976, p. 859.

Cindy, Jay, and Dexter discover a mysterious prowler at the home of a knick-knack-collecting neighbor for whom they are house-sitting. The prowler, it seems, is after hidden money, and the three children do their best to outwit him. They catch on just in time to prevent a very jolly traveling dictionary salesman from making off with the cash, which they hand over to its owner, an antique dealer. The story has some suspenseful moments, and the flamboyant dictionary man adds humorous commentary along the way. One point sticks in the throat: why doesn't the antique dealer prosecute that thief? No one even tries to get him arrested! Perhaps crime almost pays. . . .

## 📖 GROWING ANYWAY UP (1976)

### Barbara Elleman

SOURCE: A review of *Growing Anyway Up,* in *The Booklist,* Vol. 72, No. 15, April 1, 1976, p. 1113.

Florence, feeling guilty about her father's sudden death, hides herself behind complicated protective rituals designed to make things "safe." She "does her eyes" (looks up, down, right, and left a certain number of times); repeats "dangerous" things backwards, word for word, or letter for letter; and never, ever makes eye contact. Convinced no one likes her, especially her mother, she silently criticizes everybody and feels persecuted in return. When vivacious Aunt Nina enters her life with a spontaneous hug and a genuine interest in her, Florence begins to realize another dimension to her life. The final chapter jumps ahead, and Florence is now in boarding school coping with life. Her newfound insight is somewhat abrupt, and Heide's message comes on a bit heavy, but readers with similar feelings—though possibly not so

intense—will relate to this unusual story of a girl's emotional upheaval.

### *Kirkus Reviews*

SOURCE: A review of *Growing Anyway Up,* in *Kirkus Reviews,* Vol. XLIV, No. 9, May 1, 1976, p. 535.

Bright but strangely silent, with a "nervous tic," Florence Stirkel is forever "doing" every new thing and person with her eyes to make them "safe" for her. And the compulsion gets worse when she and her widowed mother move from a Florida house to a city apartment and her mother takes up with George B-for-boring Hawthorne, who carries around huge "lumps of silence" which he throws into his incessant monologues. Enter then father's sister Nina who makes everything okay, if not perfect—and who even helps Florence connect her "tics" with her guilt over withholding a good luck kiss when her father left on that last business trip. We're not as taken as Florence is with Aunt Nina's childish gaiety, but we're willing to go along with the niece—as her observations throughout have had more wit and point than those of most such bright young commentators on the domestic front.

### Anita Silvey

SOURCE: A review of *Growing Anyway Up,* in *The Horn Book Magazine,* Vol. LII, No. 3, June, 1976, pp. 288-89.

Florence Stirkel isn't particularly pleased that she was named after the city where her parents honeymooned, but she feels she "should be glad they didn't go to Niagara Falls." An intense, private person, she has developed a peculiar set of rituals that she goes through when she meets people, and these nervous mannerisms interfere with her relationships with schoolmates and with grown-ups. She has always been totally excluded by both groups until she encounters her Aunt Nina, who makes it possible for Florence to express herself to another person. And eventually Aunt Nina helps bring about an emotional catharsis that allows Florence to face her deep-seated guilt about her father's death and to begin to get along with people. The first-person narrative contains many sharp, psychologically probing portraits of the various characters; for instance, George, her stepfather, "carries big lumps and clumps of silence around with him and throws one in every few minutes." Although the ending seems a bit truncated and Florence's problems are much too neatly wrapped up, the novel is remarkable for its humor, its lean, intense prose, and its strong characterization of a girl who finds herself an outsider.

### Zena Sutherland

SOURCE: A review of *Growing Anyway Up,* in *Bulletin of the Center for Children's Books,* Vol. 30, No. 1, September, 1976, pp. 10-11.

Florence Stirkel, who tells the story, is a withdrawn and disturbed child whose undemonstrative mother, a widow, decides to move to Pennsylvania to be near her sister-in-law, Nina. Florence dislikes the private school in which she has been enrolled, and she dislikes the man who courts and later marries her mother. Only Aunt Nina, volatile and affectionate, awakens Florence's interest and gives her self-confidence. Nina, in fact, is Florence's bridge to a stability that is only beginning to be evident by the end of the book. The adult characters are convincing enough but not explored in depth; Florence is. Her fears, her compulsive patterns of behavior (saying words backwards, feeling unsafe unless she looks in certain directions in a certain way a certain number of times) her self-denigration, are depicted with sharp perception.

##  MYSTERY OF THE MIDNIGHT MESSAGE (with daughter Roxanne Heide, 1977)

### Judith Goldberger

SOURCE: A review of *Mystery of the Midnight Message,* in *Booklist,* Vol. 74, No. 12, February 15, 1978, p. 1013.

The three young members of the Spotlight Club become involved in a fast-moving if somewhat implausible escapade complete with mysterious maps, safe combinations, and murderous thug. Cindy, Jay, and Dexter manage to pull their own weight through it all, without being impossibly clever. The logistics are silly if readers demand common sense in characters, but the story moves along and will catch and hold some.

### Cynthia Percak Infantino

SOURCE: A review of *Mystery of the Midnight Message,* in *School Library Journal,* Vol. 24, No. 8, April, 1978, p. 84.

While basically a formula mystery in a familiar series, this has enough fast-paced excitement to keep young armchair detectives on the edge of their seats. Cindy, Jay, and Dexter (members of the Spotlight Club) eventually avert an attempted robbery in a posh suburb—but not before a series of near-dangerous encounters with the criminals. The story, though full of incredible coincidences, loose ends in the plot, stereotyped thugs ("'Otherwise, I'da gone straight for good, honest,' whined Buzzy.") and cliches, is perfect for whiling away a rainy afternoon.

## FABLES YOU SHOULDN'T PAY ANY ATTENTION TO (with Sylvia W. Van Clief, 1978)

### *Publishers Weekly*

SOURCE: A review of *Fables You Shouldn't Pay Any Attention To,* in *Publishers Weekly,* Vol. 213, No. 5, January 30, 1978, p. 129.

If the authors don't win a prize for their spiffy nonsense, there is no justice. Each racy piece in their book is the antithesis of a cautionary tale, with the absurdities compounded by [Victoria] Chess's comic-horror depictions. "Genevieve" is a careless child who ruins or loses her clothes, her toys, all her possessions. The other kids in the family take extremely good care of their things. When Christmas comes, their parents conclude that Genevieve is the only kid who needs anything. While she gets all new clothes and toys, her siblings wind up with very little. "Cyril" the mean squirrel proves that selfishness pays. In the other rib ticklers, readers find how other vices pay off. Pay no attention to the moral, but enjoy.

### Mary M. Burns

SOURCE: A review of *Fables You Shouldn't Pay Any Attention To,* in *The Horn Book Magazine,* Vol. LIV, No. 3, June, 1978, pp. 271-72.

In a manner reminiscent of Saki's "The Storyteller," the authors have constructed a deliciously irreverent collection of fractured fables in which the smugly virtuous do not always triumph over their slovenly, tardy, selfish, or greedy companions. Not that the latter are particularly charming; rather they survive or win simply because they have the ability to maintain their independence and assert their individuality. Some children have rationalized that if the early bird catches the worm—the lazy worm, conversely, doesn't get caught; and they will revel in these anti-aphorisms. From Gretchen the fish—whose gluttony at the table and lack of manners enabled her to avoid baited hooks while her self-congratulating companions nibbled their way to oblivion—to Genevieve, the destructive child who needed more gifts than did her tidy relatives, the characters are a remarkable gathering of nonconformists. Their manipulative personalities are deftly captured in the slightly ghoulish ink-and-wash illustrations.

### Zena Sutherland

SOURCE: A review of *Fables You Shouldn't Pay Any Attention To,* in *Bulletin of the Center for Children's Books,* Vol. 31, No. 11, July-August, 1978, p. 178.

Although repetitive in pattern, these seven short fables have a bland humor that should appeal to children, for they are the reverse of moral tales. All the other children are careful with their clothes and toys, but careless Genevieve gets all the loot at Christmas because her parents see that the others don't need new belongings. All the other fish eat moderately, but greedy Gretchen says "It pays to be greedy," because the hungry fish pursue worms and are caught. Muriel, a discontented cow, strays over to where the grass looks greener, on the other side of the fence, and it *is* greener, and the farmer's wife gives Muriel a diamond collar. And so on, blithe fables given added zest by the slightly macabre Chess drawings.

## 📖 *BANANA TWIST* (1978)

### Barbara Elleman

SOURCE: A review of *Banana Twist*, in *Booklist,* Vol. 75, No. 5, November 1, 1978, p. 479.

Jonah D. Krock's initial meeting with Goober Grube is fraught with comical misunderstanding—Goober thinks Jonah has a banana fixation and Jonah thinks Goober is a fish-happy creep. The only thing they have in common, it seems, is an inordinate love for banana splits. Determined to avoid Goober, despite the fact that they both live on the fourteenth floor, Jonah concocts flagrant lies (his family is so large they take turns sleeping in the elevator) and develops complicated means to avoid the boy. Goober, on the other hand, stalks the hallways seeking Jonah out, especially when his aquarium is leaking or his fish need special attention. When filling out an admittance form for a private school, which he longs to attend to escape the daily diet and television restrictions enforced by his health-nut mother and athletic father, Jonah borrows Goober's opinions and hobbies only to find that it lands him the computer-chosen perfect roommate—none other than Goober Grube. Told with sparkling ease, this whacky story oozes funny situations at every turn of the page.

### *Kirkus Reviews*

SOURCE: A review of *Banana Twist*, in *Kirkus Reviews,* Vol. XLVI, No. 23, December 1, 1978, p. 1307.

Jonah Krock is one of those kids who thrive on TV and chocolate bars—much to the chagrin of his health-food-and-fitness parents; and this summer he's filling out an application for boarding school, writing high-falutin' nonsense in hopes of a fall admission—each boy gets his own refrigerator and TV. He's also trying to avoid Goober, a new neighbor who misinterprets a momentary confusion and thinks Jonah's fixated on bananas. Jonah mischievously compounds the error—and the interest—by pretending to be the janitor's son, and Goober, another fast-talker with oddball tendencies, goes on and on about Jonah's "flagrant symptoms" and different-wave-length sensibility. Although the humor will leap right over many kids' heads, the story is brisk, cute, and given a boost by the total twist of an ending.

### Karen M. Klocker

SOURCE: A review of *Banana Twist*, in *The Horn Book Magazine,* Vol. LV, No. 1, February, 1979, p. 61.

The author has demonstrated her versatility in a wide range of books. The present one is brimming with zany characters and hilarious situations, but unfortunately the ending seems pat and anticlimactic. Jonah B. Krock is applying for admission to the Fairlee School, where he would have a television set and a refrigerator in his room. For a boy whose parents have denied him television during the school year and whose mother is a nutrition fanatic, such conditions seem irresistible. The narrative interweaves two threads: Jonah's efforts to appear a perfect student on the Fairless application and his equally arduous efforts to avoid Goober Grube, who lives in the apartment down the hall. Goober is constantly trying to make a friend of Jonah—and to psychoanalyze him at the same time. The author maintains the child's point of view throughout, never trivializing problems that may seem insignificant to the adult. The relationship between children and adults is as distant and uncomprehending as the one depicted in *The Shrinking of Treehorn.*

### Zena Sutherland

SOURCE: A review of *Banana Twist*, in *Bulletin of the Center for Children's Books,* Vol. 32, No. 8, April, 1979, pp. 137-8.

Because his parents prefer health foods and decry television, Jonah looks forward to being admitted to Fairlee, a private school for boys; he knows, although his parents don't, that each room at Fairlee has a refrigerator and a television set. Throughout the story he pauses to record some section of the questionnaire he's answering, piously framing his comments in hopes of admission. The burden of the story is Jonah's series of encounters with Goober, an eccentric boy who lives in the same apartment building and who is just as convinced that Jonah's eccentric—a conclusion that's not surprising, since Jonah tells horrendous lies about himself. Jonah tries unsuccessfully to avoid Goober, but the book ends with his discovery that not only has Goober been accepted at Fairlee but also that they will be roommates. There is some fun in the story, but it suffers from heavy-handedness, not usually a facet of Heide's writing. Too much coincidence, too much contrivance, and not enough balance of other aspects of Jonah's life weaken the book.

## 📖 *SECRET DREAMER, SECRET DREAMS* (1978)

### *Kirkus Reviews*

SOURCE: A review of *Secret Dreamer, Secret Dreams,* in *Kirkus Reviews,* Vol. XLVI, No. 21, November 1, 1978, p. 1193.

"Which words should I choose to . . . clothe her silent, uncommunicated thoughts?" asks 13-year-old Caroline's teacher as she embarks on this story of a "special" child who cannot read or write and only occasionally utters a word. Unfortunately the words she does choose—sustenance, destiny, immobile, shatteringly ecstatic—express her own overrefined literary pretentions, not the confused gropings of a child vainly seeking clues and signals everywhere: in the eyes of her classmates, the shapes of plates on the dinner table, her own cells ("moving, dividing within me"), her dog (does he catch "the scent of the past with its stores of messages, of memories?"), and in books, read to her by her ever-patient father, with their "beckoning words . . . that are locked, unspeaking, in the silent pages." Occasionally note is taken of Caroline's behavior—pounding her head against glass at the aquarium, dashing around the classroom in tears—which, in the context of her thoughts, effectively reminds us that she has her reasons, which no one else can remotely guess. But then it's back to the stale and fancy phrases, betokening a mind whose alienation from the world is in quite a different direction from Caroline's.

### Booklist

SOURCE: A review of *Secret Dreamer, Secret Dreams,* in *Booklist,* Vol. 75, No. 6, November 15, 1978, p. 547.

Thirteen-year-old Caroline is an emotionally disturbed adolescent who cannot speak. Her story, communicated as if in the first person, is conveyed through a series of incidents, wanderings, feelings, and observations that incrementally offer a sense of her reality. Some incidents stop abruptly as Caroline's mind wanders or as she finds the people or situations too intense, too hurtful, too hurried, or too condescending. Other incidents are highly charged with activity, an outlet for emotions she cannot, frustratingly, verbalize. Her family (mother, father, and sister), classmates, and teacher (in a special-ed classroom) speak only as Caroline hears them, interacting with others and with her only as she observes them. Thus each reader is able to see the potential effect of his or her verbal and nonverbal behavior in the presence of a person with problems similar to Caroline's. Whether or not this fictionalized case study is the way it really seems for children like Caroline is impossible to know, but Heide succeeds in making it *feel* right for the reader through skillful use of structure and perceptive character development.

### Virginia Haviland

SOURCE: A review of *Secret Dreamer, Secret Dreams,* in *The Horn Book Magazine,* Vol. LIV, No. 6, December, 1978, p. 645.

The author of **The Shrinking of Treehorn** and of novels for older children has created with the intensity of poetry a picture of the inner world of mute, thirteen-year-old Caroline—a private world full of longing, with "the hugeness" of words weighing down her tongue, clogging her throat, and choking her. The child, with her frustrations, sudden apparent joys, and occasional hopes, is surrounded by her tender father and impatient mother; her sometimes mean, sometimes kind older sister; the dog that Caroline joyfully finds and names Brumm (one of her rare spoken words, uttered with difficulty); and her classmates in a special school. The prologue, supposedly written by a caseworker, states that the girl is unforgettable: "I speak for myself, out of my own need," she says; "no one can speak for her." The story is also unforgettable.

### Zena Sutherland

SOURCE: A review of *Secret Dreamer, Secret Dreams,* in *Bulletin of the Center for Children's Books,* Vol. 32, No. 7, March, 1979, pp. 117-8.

Caroline's teacher introduces her in a few pages—after that it is Caroline's story. She is thirteen, a special child who cannot read, write, or speak, save for an occasional word, and the author, expressing Caroline's feelings about herself and her world, gives her a full vocabulary for that expression. If one can accept this device, the book becomes believable, for Caroline "writes" with perception and anguish about her frustration. She listens to others, when she wants to listen, and she often expresses her anger and despair through hostile acts. The story can help readers understand the plight of someone so handicapped, and it draws a vivid picture of the complex attitudes and emotions of the members of a family with whom such a special child lives. The book ends on a poignant note, as Caroline speaks of her dog, " . . . Brumm barks helplessly, his voice as unintelligible as my own, his message and mine forever undelivered."

### FEAR AT BRILLSTONE (with daughter Roxanne Heide, 1978)

### School Library Journal

SOURCE: A review of *Fear at Brillstone,* in *School Library Journal,* Vol. 25, No. 4, December, 1978, p. 68.

[*Fear at Brillstone*] is the follow up [of] their **Brillstone Break-In.** Logan Forrest has just landed a delivery job for the Cosmos Courier Service, located in the same building as the theft-plagued Tradewinds Import Company. Logan learns the details of the robberies from elevator operator Barney Olds, but it is Logan's photography hobby which inadvertently gets him into the case. While teaching his friend Liza Webster how to use a zoom lens, the two teenagers take a series of photos of the office building. It becomes obvious that someone is after the film, which reveals the identity of the thief. It turns out to be the owner of the Tradewinds, stealing his merchandise for the insurance by hiding valuable items in a statue on the building's balcony. Although the characters are not well developed they prove to be a colorful lot that fit well into the authors' slick plotting. But the premise of this formula story is shaky and its wrap up terribly sudden.

### Zena Sutherland

SOURCE: A review of *Fear at Brillstone,* in *Bulletin of the Center for Children's Books,* Vol. 32, No. 5, January, 1979, pp. 81-2.

Logan gets a summer job as a messenger for a courier service and is interested both in the fact that the building is condemned and that a third robbery of an antique store in the building has taken place. He and his friend Liza just happen to take some pictures, and later Logan finds someone is trying to steal the film. It is Liza who spots a clue in one picture, and it is she whose absence leads Logan to her rescue when she's trapped by the thief. The story is liberally sprinkled with suspicious characters, a device that accounts for a certain amount of padding in a mystery story that has little natural narrative flow although it has a good deal of action and adequate writing style.

## MYSTERY OF THE MUMMY'S MASK (with daughter Roxanne Heide, 1979)

### Booklist

SOURCE: A review of *Mystery of the Mummy's Mask,* in *Booklist,* Vol. 76, No. 4, October 15, 1979, pp. 359-60

This particular Spotlight Club mystery pokes the merest tip of its head above the mass of its companions. Yes, it stars those indestructible three children who seem so utterly unencumbered by protective parents, and yes, all the pieces get discovered at the right time and fit neatly together without floppy edges. But it's not as silly as the others, and it moves along without digressing much onto things its readers don't care about.

## TREEHORN'S TREASURE (1981)

### Publishers Weekly

SOURCE: A review of *Treehorn's Treasure,* in *Publishers Weekly,* Vol. 220, No. 5, July 31, 1981, p. 59.

It's been 10 years since Heide and [Edward] Gorey made news with **The Shrinking of Treehorn,** and this sequel has been promised and eagerly awaited since. A virtually guaranteed bestseller, the story begins with Treehorn—ignored as usual by parents, other relatives, even workmen at his house—making a remarkable discovery. Dollar bills are growing on the tree in his yard. Treehorn picks a few to invest in comic books and candy bars and tries to tell his great news to family and friends but all answer with Heide's inspired nonsequiturs. What happens finally is a terrific twist to a cunningly built story, marvelously matched by Gorey's drawings with their dynamic admixture of stateliness and the eldritch.

### Pamela D. Pollack

SOURCE: A review of *Treehorn's Treasure,* in *School Library Journal,* Vol. 28, No. 3, November, 1981, p. 76

It's the same joke, but **Treehorn's Treasure** is as sharp and tart as Heide and Gorey's first deadpan classic, **The Shrinking of Treehorn;** and the get-rich fantasy it embodies is even more satisfying to kids. Treehorn, as ever, is

the stoic victim of benign neglect from all the adults in his world. But this time—at least for a while—never being taken seriously works to his advantage. It's how, despite parental exhortations to thrift, he gets away with spending wads of dollar bills from a backyard "money tree" (the result of a coupon for "Instant Magic" Treehorn innocently stashes in the trunk). The magic is as innocently undone, but by then Treehorn has a stockpile of comics and gum. In this sequel comic-book-addict Treehorn, always lost in the comics' larger-than-life fantasies, has grown as impervious to his parents as they are to him (and to each other). That's the dark side of Heide's satire, but it doesn't dominate. Treehorn, in his trenchcoat (worn, rain or shine, for the pockets) is a true eccentric of the kind Gorey draws best, and the horror comics Treehorn reads gives Gorey full range for his macabre talents.

### Zena Sutherland

SOURCE: A review of *Treehorn's Treasure,* in *Bulletin of the Center for Children's Books,* Vol. 35, No. 4, December, 1981, p. 69.

Macabre and elegant, Gorey's sophisticated line drawings are perfectly suited to the dry wit of the story, a pointed commentary on the manifold imperfections of human communication, particularly on those adults who hear children but don't really listen. It's true that in the course of the story there is one fanciful fact that listeners dismiss whenever Treehorn tries to tell them that the leaves on a tree in his yard are turning into dollar bills, but that's the crux of the story. This is Heide at her best.

### Kirkus Reviews

SOURCE: A review of *Treehorn's Treasure,* in *Kirkus Reviews,* Vol. L, No. 1, January 1, 1982, p. 6.

An equally inspired sequel to **The Shrinking of Treehorn.** There, the small boy's preoccupied parents were oblivious to the fact that he was growing smaller. Here, his mother is so wrapped up in spending money and his father in saving it that neither registers Treehorn's repeated announcements that the leaves on the backyard maple tree are turning to dollar bills. Treehorn, who has already adapted to the prevailing climate by taking refuge in comic books, considerably enlarges his collection with the first ripe $26.00 he harvests from the tree. But just when "probably thousands" of leaves have turned, Treehorn's father decides that the original dollar bill he gave Treehorn to save and which Treehorn then stashed in the tree, enclosed in an envelope addressed to the Instant Magic Company—should be placed in a bank to draw interest. Whereupon, of course, George Washington's many faces rapidly fade away. Once again, poor Treehorn's lonely plight is pictured in scenes at once poignant and hilarious—as when he navigates, flashlight in hand, through an elegant dark restaurant where his mother never notices that he hasn't had a chance to eat or order. And once more Treehorn comes through on his own, handling both the indifferent adults and the villains of his horror-comic fantasies with similar aplomb.

## Ethel L. Heins

SOURCE: A review of *Treehorn's Treasure,* in *The Horn Book Magazine,* Vol. LVIII, No. 1, February, 1982, pp. 42-3.

A decade after **The Shrinking of Treehorn,** author and illustrator have accomplished a sequel, almost identical in format and outward appearance. While the diminutive, deadpan boy is concerned about receiving his overdue allowance so he can buy more comics and send for some things advertised in them—such as a "strong-man kit"— his mother is preoccupied with redecorating the house. But "'money doesn't grow on trees,'" says his father; and that very day out in the yard Treehorn discovers the leaves of a tree turning into green dollar bills. Of course, none of the grownups pays the slightest attention to what he says, so he picks twenty-six of the dollars and spends them on comics, bubble gum, soda pop, and candy bars— some of which come in handy that evening when he accompanies his mother and his Aunt Bertha to a chic, dimly lit restaurant. Once again the child lives in his own self-contained world while the responses of the adults run on as a dissonant counterpoint. And once again the line drawings with their incisive, peculiarly Goreyesque wit make their own emphatic comments. But the story is more wordy than the first one and lacks some of its bite, pungency, and bizarre originality.

## TIME'S UP! (1982)

### Ilene Cooper

SOURCE: A review of *Time's Up!,* in *Booklist,* Vol. 78, No. 17, May 1, 1982, p. 1160.

Noah has been plunked down in a new neighborhood because of his father's job; he's lonely, his mother is frantically studying for tests, and his father keeps him busy doing chores. Life is bleak until a girl named Bib, her shy little brother, and a house painter, Bruce Dooster, appear on the scene. A madcap mix-up in which Noah's father's boss gets mistaken for a vacuum cleaner salesman is the highlight of the book. Writing with broad strokes, Heide sometimes goes overboard with her spoofery. The father, "an efficiency nut" with no redeeming qualities, is such a caricature that he engenders real dislike, but [Marylin] Hafner's pencil illustrations boost the story's farcical mood.

### Zena Sutherland

SOURCE: A review of *Time's Up!,* in *Bulletin of the Center for Children's Books,* Vol. 36, No. 4, June, 1982, p. 188.

Noah and his parents have just moved to the country and he despairs of ever making friends. He also despairs of

his parents: his mother is amicable but feckless, always with ear plugs to shut out the world while she works on her thesis, and his father is a fanatic about efficiency, always timing Noah and giving him elaborate instructions for Noah's many chores. The plot, like the style, is loose and breezy, so that the character exaggeration is almost always tongue-in-cheek and always humorous. The story is told by Noah, and it's primarily a tale of adapting to a new environment and making new friends, but when the crunch comes (they have barely adjusted when Dad announces they're moving again) Mom is disenchanted, in part because of her studies and in part because she is pregnant. Noah saves the day because he's never mailed the letter accepting the new job, so they don't have to move. The course of action is related to the characters, exaggerated though they may be; things don't just happen by contrivance. A sunny and often witty book.

## Carolyn Noah

SOURCE: A review of *Time's Up!,* in *School Library Journal,* Vol. 28, No. 10, August, 1982, p. 117

Noah, an insecure "nonely" (an-only) child, inhabits a loveless home driven by his father's obsession with efficiency and nearly abandoned by his mother's preoccupation with study. New in town and friendless, Noah is unable to accept friendship from neighbor Bib nor to offer it to preschooler Gabriel. In fact, though desperately lonely, the boy's energies are absorbed by comic books and longing for a bicycle. In 100 pages, the characters all attain a remarkable lack of dimension. Then, in the following 18, plot and personality coalesce to tie up everyone's loose ends. Here Dad loses a job cheerfully; he and Mom show signs of humanity. Noah makes friends with the neighbors and gets his bike. The final scene, in which everyone (including Noah's teacher-cum-painter-cum-pizza man and Dad's rotten boss) collides, is great fun and written with the facility that Heide often displays. But pouring lots of energy into the last few pages is not enough fuel to make the vehicle fly.

## THE PROBLEM WITH PULCIFER (1982)

### Ilene Cooper

SOURCE: A review of *The Problem with Pulcifer,* in *Booklist,* Vol. 79, No. 1, September 1, 1982, p. 43.

His problem? He doesn't want to watch television. His hand-wringing parents must deal with the fact that their son—horrors!—prefers books. Despite their buying nice new remote-control TVs and setting a good example by watching lots of TV themselves, nothing seems to turn their son on to television. Even a trip to a psychiatrist proves futile, and Pulcifer's parents must face the fact that their son is TV-impaired; he simply settles down to enjoy a stack of library books. The obvious joke will amuse readers, but some of the more subtle nuances, such as using a form of aversion therapy to recondition Pulcifer, miss the mark. A plus is the simple but effective pencil drawing [by Judy Glasser] that features a deadpan Pulcifer and a group of the homeliest adults around. The joke goes on too long, but for the most part it's a good one.

## Zena Sutherland

SOURCE: A review of *The Problem with Pulcifer*, in *Bulletin of the Center for Children's Books*, Vol. 36, No. 2, October, 1982, p. 27.

Heide pokes fun at television addicts, conformity, and certain adult-child relations in a very funny book that is written with acidulated exaggeration but that has a strong unstated message. Everybody worries about Pulcifer, who refuses to watch television as all normal people do; instead he reads books. Shameful! Frustrating to the teachers, to his parents, to a psychiatrist who points out that he read as a child and understands, but *he* broke the habit. Even the school librarian worries when Pulcifer checks out books instead of the AV equipment that dominates the shelves. *Everybody* watches television but Pulcifer. He's not motivated, the psychiatrist explains; Pulcifer's parents tell him the fact that everyone else watches should be motivation enough. Not a good reason, Pulcifer says. Sadly his parents tell him they love him anyway; they go off to watch television and Pulcifer settles happily into an armchair with his stack of new library books. Heide makes her point with humor, deriding not television but television addiction in a clever story illustrated with cartoon style drawings, angular, stiff, and spare.

## Michael Cart

SOURCE: A review of *The Problem with Pulcifer*, in *School Library Journal*, Vol. 29, No. 2, October, 1982, p. 152.

The problem with young Pulcifer is that he doesn't watch television. Instead he (shudder, gasp!) reads books. If you smell a satire here, you have good scents, although it's true that Florence Parry Heide, author of the Treehorn books, isn't exactly Jonathan Swift. But her cautionary story is diverting and the stratagems Pulcifer's parents and the other tube-addict adults use to cure the boy of his reading habit are amusing—especially sending him to a remedial class at school where the books bear a loony resemblance to television programs. Judy Glasser's illustrations, which look like the unlikely offspring of a marriage between Lois Lenski and *New Yorker* cartoonist Ton Smits, complement the author's deadpan style very nicely.

## 📖 *TIME BOMB AT BRILLSTONE* (with daughter Roxanne Heide, 1982)

### Denise M. Wilms

SOURCE: A review of *Time Bomb at Brillstone*, in *Booklist*, Vol. 79, No. 10, January 15, 1983, p. 681.

Liza doesn't trust smooth-talking Randy the first time she meets him, and it's not long before she suspects that he wants to blow up the garage he's just taken over from his father to collect insurance money. She wants to talk over her fears with her good friend Logan, but he seems too occupied with their mutual friend, Elaine. Liza gathers enough circumstantial evidence to convince her of Randy's nasty plan, but how to convince others and then put a stop to it is a problem she's not sure how to handle. The Heide's mystery thriller is weakened by contrived circumstances and pedestrian characterizations, but its easy suspense will sustain nondemanding readers.

## 📖 *BANANA BLITZ* (1983)

### Publishers Weekly

SOURCE: A review of *Banana Blitz*, in *Publishers Weekly*, Vol. 223, No. 17, April 29, 1983, p. 50.

A whiz at inventing humorous stories, Heide gives her fans a sequel to *Banana Twist*, in which the miniature Machiavelli, Jonah Krock, is up to new tricks. Anticipating the luxury of Fairlee School, with a refrigerator and TV in every room, Jonah groans when he finds his smarmy neighbor, Lewis Trane (Goober), from Manhattan is his roommate. Jonah's dreams of devoting a year to gluttony—feasting on the refrigerator full of candy bars—and sloth—absorbing all the TV shows—are dashed. Goober insists on improving Jonah's mind and body, stocking health food and handing out lessons on being a good student. The rivalry between the boys is the base of a funny, fast-moving adventure that peaks with a "banana twist," Jonah's scheme to win big bucks by keeping count of commercials mentioning the fruit.

### Kirkus Reviews

SOURCE: A review of *Banana Blitz*, in *Kirkus Reviews*, Vol. LI, No. 11, June 1, 1983, p. 619.

You can close Heide's *Banana Twist*, which ends with obnoxious new neighbor Goober's acceptance to the very boarding school narrator Jonah hopes to attend, and slide right into *Banana Blitz*, where Jonah, looking forward to the promised TV and refrigerator in every room, walks into his room to find Goober already installed. Pimply, sanctimonious Goober, who looks like "something from under a rock" when Jonah wakes up to his white-ointment face, stinks up Jonah's junk food with the fish he keeps in the fridge and assaults his ears with mnemonic devices for rote learning. Alas for Goober, he mixes up his "I before e" sentence with his "Boston Tea Party" ditty on the surprise history quiz, whereas Jonah remembers Goober's ditty and gets an "A." And all the time that Goober is studying and pontificating, Jonah is watching banana commercials, hoping to win a thousand-dollar contest by counting the number of times the word "banana" is used. And just when he thinks he has missed the last program, it turns out that Goober, "rearranging his priorities," has cut class, caught the commercial, and completed Jonah's chart to win him the contest. This last news comes to their room in the form of a man-sized banana (a messenger from the Banana Institute) that Jonah is sure must be the hallucination Goober accuses him of having. Which makes a hilarious end to a story that snaps and crackles with kid-sized wit.

### Barbara Elleman

SOURCE: A review of *Banana Blitz,* in *Booklist,* Vol. 79, No. 21, July, 1983, p. 1401.

In the follow-up to Heide's funny **Banana Twist,** Jonah arrives at his new boarding school dreaming of freedom to enjoy his in-room refrigerator and television. What he finds, however, is his old antagonist, Goober, who has taken over the entire space with his health foods and skin ointments. Financing his own candy-bar addiction is a problem to Jonah until he hears about the $1,000 offered by the American Banana Institute for counting the number of times the word *banana* is used in a series of commercials. Watching the TV commercials is necessary to winning, and the manipulations Jonah goes through and the problems Goober gives him are just part of the fun that Heide concocts in this lightweight, breezy story. Underneath lies a subtle message on how two people with different ideas *can* come to terms.

### 📖 *TREEHORN'S WISH* (1984)

#### Publishers Weekly

SOURCE: A review of *Treehorn's Wish,* in *Publishers Weekly,* Vol. 225, No. 17, February 17, 1984, p. 89.

**The Shrinking of Treehorn** and **Treehorn's Treasure** imprinted the hapless child in the memories of millions of readers. In their third book, Heide's understated telling and [Edward] Gorey's macabre, stately drawings sharpen the satire and deepen sympathy for Treehorn. On his birthday, his worldly parents are still ignoring their son but he trusts they'll give him plenty of gifts since he had received nothing worth mentioning the year before. When he finds a genie in a jar, Treehorn is even more sanguine but rather wastes his first two wishes. His mother takes him shopping—for *her* new hat—and Treehorn thinks seriously about ensuring that his third wish will bring him something worthwhile. Back home, the boy's final conference with the genie compels a hope that author Heide will do better by Treehorn, next time.

### Ethel R. Twichell

SOURCE: A review of *Treehorn's Wish,* in *The Horn Book Magazine,* Vol. LX, No. 3, June, 1984, pp. 328-29.

Once again Treehorn's parents are so maddeningly preoccupied with their own doings that his concern with his upcoming birthday is virtually unnoticed. Full of anticipation, Treehorn prepares space in his room for lavish presents and diffidently suggests his hopes for a birthday cake. Gorey's elegantly spare and witty drawings echo Treehorn's isolation, as his mother, with only the barest recognition of his existence, obsessively cleans her refrigerator and his father pontificates on the virtues of hard work. In this emotional desert it is doubly fortuitous that Treehorn discovers a genie-filled jug and avails himself of the usual three wishes. Poor Treehorn. The genie, like the other adults, is bored with him and his wishes, only wanting to return to his jug for another snooze. Diversions, such as Mom's shopping and a visit from the meter reader, tend to dilute the focus on childlike anxieties and on the absurdities of the adult world, which were so sharply defined in **The Shrinking of Treehorn.** Yet the wry humor of both drawings and text nicely prepare for the bittersweet ending. Treehorn's only present is a larger version of last year's birthday sweater. Thanks to the genie, he does have his cake but sits down to eat it—alone.

### Zena Sutherland

SOURCE: A review of *Treehorn's Wish,* in *Bulletin of the Center for Children's Books,* Vol. 38, No. 1, September, 1984, p. 6.

Treehorn fans will welcome this third blandly written story that is filled with sharp observation and witty comments on parent-child relations and particularly on the way in which adults fail to listen to what children are saying. Gorey's lean, stylish line drawings are just right for this tale of a bored genie who wants nothing more than to crawl back into his jug and of the ingenuous boy, Treehorn, who has to choose the usual three wishes. Although the primary audience for the book is the middle-grades reader, many older readers and even some adults may relish the nuance and humor of the story.

### Margery Fisher

SOURCE: A review of *Treehorn's Wish,* in *Growing Point,* Vol. 25, No. 2, July, 1986, p. 4646

The small boy called Treehorn whose diminutive size left his parents astonishingly uncaring is seen in a third adventure, **Treehorn's Wish,** starting this time when he finds a dirty jug in a hole in the garden. Being an unflappable child, he spends a little time wondering whether the strangely dressed man who appears is in fact a genie or only the meter reader. Even when his wishes begin to come true his rationalist parents spoil the fun; 'Work is its own reward' is his father's comment when his son explains about the useful being who has saved him so much trouble, while his mother remains preoccupied with decisions about supper and a new hat. The full sharpness of the wit is really for adults to see and perhaps even to profit by; the incredible blindness of parents is only too clear after Treehorn's mother has pulled the cork out of the jug, where the genie has been taking a rest before arranging for the third wish:

> There was a puff of smoke, and the genie stood in the kitchen. Treehorn's mother opened the refrigerator.
>
> "All right, what's your wish?" said the genie crossly. "Hurry up. I haven't got all day".
>
> Treehorn wished he had more time to decide. He said "I wish my name was on my birthday cake".
>
> "It is", said the genie. "Now I have to find another jug. Tiresome, but that's the rule".
>
> There was another puff of smoke, and the genie was gone.
>
> "I do wish your friends wouldn't come over at meal times, dear", said Treehorn's mother.

Edward Gorey's drawings add their own comment on the appalling lack of contact between the sadly acquiescent child and his incredibly insensitive parents.

## TIME FLIES! (1984)

### Zena Sutherland

SOURCE: A review of *Time Flies*, in *Bulletin of the Center for Children's Books*, Vol. 38, No. 4, December, 1984, p. 66.

There's a bit of off-beat Treehorn-type humor in this amusing story told by Noah, who's busy evading chores set by his time-expert father, who adjusts to the burden of a noisy new sibling, who gains confidence as one after another of his ideas (deliberately or accidentally) proves fruitful. Heide's at her best when she writes with a light, wry touch, and in this book that's maintained throughout. The scribbly line drawings [by Marylin Hafner] pick up the note of casual, cheerful muddle very nicely.

### Ilene Cooper

SOURCE: A review of *Time Flies*, in *Booklist*, Vol. 81, No. 7, December 1, 1984, p. 523.

Noah Langren, who was introduced in *Time's Up!*, now must deal with a new baby sister and the consequences of fouling up an ad his father has written for the *New York Times*. In a sequel funnier than the first book, Heide has also humanized the character of Mr. Langren, an uptight, unlikable sort. This is written in a breezy style that kids will appreciate, and the varied supporting characters, especially one engaging teacher, will make up for any remaining flaws in the father. Once again, Hafner's humorous pencil illustrations enliven the text.

## TALES FOR THE PERFECT CHILD (1985)

### Zena Sutherland

SOURCE: A review of *Tales for the Perfect Child*, in *Bulletin of the Center for Children's Books*, Vol. 39, No. 3, November, 1985, p. 48.

Seven very short stories are written in so direct and simple a style that they can be used for children in the primary grades as well as for the middle grades, but it is the latter group that should respond the more appreciatively to the bland, sly humor that is Heide at her best. The amicably ghoulish illustrations [by Victoria Chess] are just right for the tales of a procession of children who are sloppy, lazy, deceitful, parent-manipulative, self-indulgent, and iron-willed in avoiding cleanliness, responsibility, and other conforming traits. The style is nicely honed, and while the author's tongue may be in her cheek, the fact that her protagonists prevail over fate and mothers will undoubtedly win readers.

### Publishers Weekly

SOURCE: A review of *Tales for the Perfect Child*, in *Publishers Weekly*, Vol. 228, No. 24, December 13, 1985, p. 53.

Chess's pictures of anthropomorphic bears, imaginatively attired, do justice to these stories, among the most fiendish inventions by the author of the Treehorn epics. Heide soberly recites trenchant stories of the ways adopted by boys and girls beside whom even really rotten children would seem perfect. Harriet, for instance, assiduously practices whining and proves unbeatable at the art. "A good whiner sticks to one subject . . . never gives up." Harriet wears her mother down and gets her way, no matter how long it takes. Then she rests, stops whining, until it's time for another match. Irving likes to wear disgraceful clothes and loll about the house. When his mother orders Irving to dress in his best and pay a social call with her, he obeys. Then he gets so dirty, accidentally, that he has to stay home. The other kids in the book are equally ingenious at evil and good for laughs.

### Jill Bennett

SOURCE: A review of *Tales for the Perfect Child*, in *Books for Keeps*, No. 52, September, 1988, p. 10.

Think twice before putting this subversive book in your classroom, for here are seven easy lessons on how to get your own way while seeming to be perfectly well behaved. Ruby, for instance, wants to visit a friend but mother insists she 'watches' younger brother Clyde while she takes a bath. So Ruby does just that as he wreaks havoc right through the house. The likes of Arthur, Bertha and Harriet similarly get the better of their parents. These 'perfect' children are thinly disguised (or rather fatly) as furry animals—rather evil-looking ones—by Victoria Chess whose illustrations on every page are the 'perfect' complement to the deadpan tales.

## 📖 *THE DAY OF AHMED'S SECRET* (with daughter Judith Heide Gilliland, 1990)

### Denise Wilms

SOURCE: A review of *The Day of Ahmed's Secret,* in *Booklist,* Vol. 87, No. 1, September 1, 1990, p. 58.

This exceptionally vivid picture book is as noteworthy for what it implies as for what it says. Set in Egypt, it introduces a young boy named Ahmed, whose job is to deliver canisters of bottled gas to customers for their cook stoves. He's proud that he is now strong enough to do the work, thus relieving some of his father's labors and contributing to the family income. Ahmed's narrative describes the sights and sounds of Cairo as he makes his rounds with his donkey and cart. He's excited today, for he has a special secret to tell his family. At the book's end, readers see him proudly show his family that he can write his name: [Ted] Lewin's watercolor illustrations are a tour de force in their depiction of busy, light-drenched streets, dim interiors, and riveting faces. They extend the sensory images of Ahmed's narrative to create an exotic, bustling world where poverty is taken for granted but dignity remains. Perceptive readers will be left to contemplate what life must be like for a young boy who works hard all day, has no schooling, and for whom learning to write his name is a singular accomplishment. Yet the text betrays no condescension toward its subject; the slice of life displayed here speaks matter-of-factly for itself. A quiet book that projects a powerful presence.

### Zena Sutherland

SOURCE: A review of *The Day of Ahmed's Secret,* in *Bulletin of the Center for Children's Books,* Vol. 44, No. 2, October, 1990, p. 30.

Ted Lewin's wonderfully detailed watercolor paintings of Cairo streets or equally impressive portraits of the speaker, Ahmed, and his family, are nicely integrated with the direct, simple text. Independent readers will get a vivid impression of the bustle and color of the city, the read-aloud audience will share in the suspense of Ahmed's references to the secret he is saving to tell his family at the end of his work day (delivering containers of fuel), and readers-aloud will be equally touched by Ahmed's sense of responsibility, his appreciation of his city, and his joy in his "secret": the achievement of having learned to write his name.

### Marcus Crouch

SOURCE: A review of *The Day of Ahmed's Secret,* in *The Junior Bookshelf,* Vol. 55, No. 6, December, 1991, pp. 242-43.

Unless they think hard about it children may be disap-

pointed with Ahmed's secret when it is at last disclosed, but I hope that will not prevent them from enjoying a vivid and convincing picture of everyday life in the streets of Cairo. Ahmed goes about his daily business of delivering 'butagaz', hauling the heavy metal 'bottles' cheerfully up flights of stairs and along narrow alleys, his eyes alert to friends and customers and to the colourful traffic of the city, donkey carts and camels as well as sleek cars. Then he goes home to show the family his secret, believing that what he can now do may last 'like the old buildings in the city, a thousand years'. The ideas in this beautiful book may be beyond the immediate grasp of children attracted to a picture-book, but they must surely be touched by its vitality.

## 📖 *SAMI AND THE TIME OF THE TROUBLES* (with daughter Judith Heide Gilliland, 1992)

### Betsy Hearne

SOURCE: A review of *Sami and the Time of the Troubles,* in *Bulletin of the Center for Children's Books,* Vol. 45, No. 9, May, 1992, p. 239.

"My name is Sami, and I live in the time of the troubles. It is a time of guns and bombs. It is a time that has lasted all my life, and I am ten years old." The narrator goes on to describe his daily life in the family's makeshift basement artillery shelter, which Sami's mother has decorated with exquisite carpets and a brass wedding vase to remind them of their former life (before Sami's father was killed by a car bomb in the market). While the story is moving, it is neither focused enough on a selective incident (which would allow fuller development) nor informative enough in context to be read aloud without considerable adult explanation. Young listeners do not learn where or when the action is set (the jacket copy mentions Beirut), which is important because the implications of the action are more serious than in this team's previous picture book about the Middle East, *The Day of Ahmed's Secret.* [Ted] Lewin's watercolors are rich, even glowing, in picking up the rugs' ruddy hues and the ashen scenes of a war-torn street. In spite of insufficient background, the strongly anti-war message will provide opportunities for discussion between children and informed adults.

### *Publishers Weekly*

SOURCE: A review of *Sami and the Time of the Troubles,* in *Publishers Weekly,* Vol. 239, No. 21, May 4, 1992, p. 56.

With a child's frankness, Sami tells of life in war-torn Beirut—an existence spent between the relative safety of Grandfather's cellar hearing gunshots and falling bombs, and brief sojourns into the city's rubble to experience life above ground. Sami's poignant and appealing narrative is imbued with a wisdom far beyond his years. Left fatherless by a bomb blast, he has boyish yearnings to play at soldiers and build a sandcastle, but these are tempered by ever-present reality. He understands that the future depends on his generation, and the text picks up moments of relaxation—the discovery of a luscious peach on sale, memories of a day at the beach. Lewin's brooding watercolors dramatically depict the contrast between cellar-bound days and rare moments of eye-squinting sunshine. And while his studies do not portray the worst horrors of living in a war zone, they exude a brave optimism. This uncommon picture book, valuable for its portrait of children caught in modern-day conflicts, is sure to lead to thought-provoking discussions.

## Ellen Fader

SOURCE: A review of *Sami and the Time of the Troubles,* in *The Horn Book Magazine,* Vol. LXVIII, No. 4, July-August, 1992, pp. 445-46.

Sami is a ten-year-old boy who lives with his family in Beirut, and his time of troubles, which has lasted his entire life, is the war raging in the streets of his city. Narrated in the first person, Sami's story is one of constant fear, memories of his father lost to the violence, and a few treasured days of peace. During these quiet times, he shares a picnic at the beach with his family, marvels at the goods for sale in the market, and watches a wedding party in the street. Sami takes encouragement from the stories he has heard about "the day the children marched," when hundreds of young people marched with placards demanding an end to the fighting, and he decides that it is time to stage another protest. While the physical and emotional desolation of Sami's world is painfully felt, children will be left with a sense of hope that Sami and the other young people of the city will be able to make a difference and stop the war. Lewin's graceful watercolor paintings are among his best in recent years and recall the complexity of his work in *The Day of Ahmed's Secret.* The coziness of the family's shadowy basement hideout, full of richly patterned rugs, contrasts sharply with the ruins of burned-out buildings and the litter of cars destroyed by bombs. Especially intriguing are the emotions—anger, fear, sadness, and hope—visible on all the characters' faces. Sami's story recalls the suffering of innocent people during other military conflicts, and older children will be able to make apt comparisons between this terror-filled time and the situations in, for example, Northern Ireland and during the Second World War. Despite the story's universality, a note summarizing the conflicts raging in Lebanon would have greatly increased this remarkable book's usefulness.

## 📖 *GRIM AND GHASTLY GOINGS-ON* (1992)

### *Publishers Weekly*

SOURCE: A review of *Grim and Ghastly Goings-On,* in *Publishers Weekly,* Vol. 239, No. 34, July 27, 1992, p. 64.

Unsavory beings of all types inhabit this wickedly funny collection from the team responsible for *Tales for the Perfect Child.* Poems and art dramatize and wildly exaggerate universal fears—thereby offering some comic relief. Monsters, naturally enough, predominate: monsters in your closet, under your bed, *in* your bed; monsters who eat children, monsters banished by children, monster mothers bragging about their babies, as mothers will ("Mine is ugly." / "Mine is mean." / "Mine is turning / nice and green"). Snappy and rhythmic, typically closing with a satisfying twist, Heide's verses find their match in [Victoria] Chess's colorful, elaborately patterned illustrations, which spare no wart nor fang and masterfully convey the spine-tingling sense that something creepy is just a breath away. With such good-humored verses and cheerful, stylish ghouls, the shivers inspired are delicious indeed.

## Deborah Stevenson

SOURCE: A review of *Grim and Ghastly Goings-On,* in *Bulletin of the Center for Children's Books,* Vol. 46, No. 1, September, 1992, pp. 12-13.

Heide and Chess, collaborators on *Tales for the Perfect Child,* team up again for a gleefully gross and ghoulish collection of poetry. These poems generally revolve around food ("What You Don't Know about Food" deserves to become a classic) or monsters of fearsome orality and appetite (notably the fascinatingly repellent "Hungry Jake"—"one day by some mistake / he ate himself"), subjects guaranteed to keep young readers' interest. The verses achieve a controlled frightfulness paralleled by Chess' lividly colored and meticulously drawn grotesqueries, who grimace cheerfully next to each poem. These could also be read aloud to younger monster fans—anybody fond of Silverstein's "The Slithergadee" is a good candidate. Besides, where else are you going to learn about the evil secret mission of rubber bands, or how monster mothers brag about their offspring?

## Hazel Rochman

SOURCE: A review of *Grim and Ghastly Goings-On,* in *Booklist,* Vol. 89, No. 2, September 15, 1992, p. 144.

From Mother Goose to the supermarket tabloids, the combination of the lurid and the mundane fascinates: What if . . . ? Heide and Chess once again indulge kids' delicious fear of monsters, especially those lurking in daily life—under the bed, in the closet, on your plate. That slimy, gross spinach might slither and grow and eat you. Rubber bands appear useful, but at night they creep and ooze and suck your blood. The noise on the basement stairs is Mr. Glump bumping with his buckets of bones, bunches of bones. Hungry Jake has such an appetite he eats everything in sight, even himself (can that be his own ear he's putting in his mouth?). Not all the verses and pictures are as astonishing. Most are disarming, taking kids' ordinary fears to ridiculous extremes and containing them in sing-song nonsense rhymes and pale watercolor grotesques, yet they leave that shiver of uncertainty: What if the armchair you're sitting in grabbed you tight?

## *TIMOTHY TWINGE* (with daughter Roxanne Heide Pierce, 1993)

### Janice Del Negro

SOURCE: A review of *Timothy Twinge,* in *Booklist,* Vol. 90, No. 2, September 15, 1993, p. 157.

Timothy worries about everything, from sharks surrounding his house to the raisins (or are they?) in his toast. He hates going out; he hates staying in; he hates books, television, and setting the table; and he won't get a snack before bedtime because who knows what's in the refrigerator. "The worst of all was still ahead. It was time at last to go to bed. Only at night did aliens fly . . . " Finally, one of Tim's fears materializes—aliens come to visit and insist they want to be friends. Tim has such a great imagination that they make him "the full-time ruler of the Galaxy," after which "Tim got to be brave—oh very, very! He got to be extraordinary." [Barbara] Lehman's bright cartoon-style watercolors will have plenty of appeal for children, and although adults may tire of the relentlessly rhyming text, kids will be busy enjoying the results of Tim's excessive "worry warting."

### Jacqueline Elsner

SOURCE: A review of *Timothy Twinge,* in *School Library Journal,* Vol. 39, No. 11, November, 1993, p. 82.

This story in rhyme covers many—maybe most—childhood fears. You name it, Timothy Twinge is afraid of it. He imagines that he has lost body parts during the night, that he will fry like an egg in the sun, and that he will literally get "lost" in a book. Setting the table, eating, and watching TV are all scary things for him. Adults do not try to allay his fears. At bedtime, he imagines the worst of aliens flying in through his window. They do come, but they speak politely to the boy and say, "This is cause for celebration / A human with imagination! / We've watched your thoughts go to and fro. / You're really braver than you know." Reassured, he readies himself for a raisin toast binge, a previously feared food. Lehman's bright watercolors are done in intense hues. . . . Unlike many picture book characters, *Timothy Twinge* is allowed to solve his problems without parental involvement.

## *THE BIGNESS CONTEST* (1994)

### Lynn Cockett

SOURCE: A review of *The Bigness Contest,* in *School Library Journal,* Vol. 40, No. 5, May, 1994, p. 95.

The author of *The Shrinking of Treehorn* has shifted gears to create Beasley, a hippopotamus whose aim is to grow as large as possible. Disappointed that he never wins anything, he is encouraged by Aunt Emerald, who says, "'you can always find something that you can do well.'" She holds a "Bigness Contest" and he is declared the winner . . . until his huge cousin Borofil, who was too lazy to enter the competition, comes out of the water. All ends well, though, when a second contest declares Beasley the laziest of all. Beasley is a lovable character with a sincere heart. The excellent, detailed watercolors complement the humorous, polished prose and portray happy, well-adjusted characters. The setting's jungle greens predominate and are highlighted by the watermelon-pink underbellies of the hippos. The hero's determination coupled with [Victoria] Chess's unequaled illustrations make this a story-time crowd pleaser. No contest.

### Hazel Rochman

SOURCE: A review of *The Bigness Contest,* in *Booklist,* Vol. 90, No. 14, May 15, 1994, p. 1372.

Role models and positive thinking are the but of Heide and Chess' latest wicked parody. Hippopotamus Beasley worries that he's too big to be good at anything. He desperately wants to win first prize and get a blue ribbon, but he's too clumsy for the gymnastics contests, and everything's too small for him in the costume competition. His gracious Aunt Emerald encourages him to try; there's always something one can do well, "that's what contests are for." They decide on a Bigness Contest; he gives up trying to diet and exercise; he eats and eats—and wins. "So what?" says his cousin Borofil, who just sits all day in the river. Beasley decides to follow his cousin's example and practice being lazy. He gets so good at it that he even beats Borofil. Chess's garish illustrations of a tropical paradise with bright green palm trees and cavorting pink hippos bring out the general foolishness of all the striving. The Best Costume contest is won by a hippo dressed as a fairy queen, and the huge mournful faces of the losers will remind kids of the beauty pageant and wrestling ring. Silly humor can do a lot for self-image.

### Deborah Stevenson

SOURCE: A review of *The Bigness Contest,* in *Bulletin of the Center for Children's Books,* Vol. 47, No. 11, July-August, 1994, p. 359.

Poor Beasley. Even though his aunt Emerald points out that "hippopotamuses are supposed to be big," he thinks he's too big to be good at anything. And he doesn't fare well in the Running Contest, the High Jump Contest, the Jump Rope Contest, the Somersault Contest, or even the Best Costume Contest. He wins the Aunt-Emerald-sponsored Bigness Contest—until his even bigger cousin Borofil turns up. Beasley then decides to devote his life to sitting lazily in the river with Borofil; he finally wins Aunt Emerald's Laziness Contest, and he and Borofil are "very, very big" and "very, very happy, but they are too lazy to smile." It's an entertainingly silly story, and the aristocratically named hippopotami make appealing dramatis personae, but the plot doesn't quite have the strength of its characters. The offhand Laziness Contest after the big-deal Bigness Contest is rather anticlimactic, and it's not clear why Beasley would beat out long-time sitter Borofil for laziness. They're still a fun crew to contemplate: Victoria Chess—who else?—has a gift for making her gimlet-eyed hippos slightly disgusting even as she renders them pinkly attractive (and Aunt Emerald, in her verdant muumuu and Lady Bracknell-ish accoutrements of lorgnette and fan, is a daffy and determined dowager). Kids may wish Beasley had won both contests, but you could use this to coax them into making revolting hippo noises or to trick them into inaction with a laziness contest of your own.

📖 *OH, GROW UP!: POEMS TO HELP YOU SURVIVE PARENTS, CHORES, SCHOOL AND OTHER AFFLICTIONS* (with daughter Roxanne Heide Pierce, 1996)

### Kirkus Reviews

SOURCE: A review of *Oh, Grow Up!: Poems to Help You Survive Parents, Chores, School and Other Afflictions*, in *Kirkus Reviews*, Vol. LXIV, No. 3, February 1, 1996, p. 227.

Twenty-nine funny poems about the everyday indignities of childhood, from braces and hand-me-downs to the rigors of family and school life: "Could anything be drearier/than the food in the school cafeteria?" [Nadine Bernard] Westcott's bright, zany ink-and-watercolor illustrations and hand-lettered titles get right into the poems, sometimes encasing lines in dialogue balloons, sometimes adding an extra element to the drama, as in **"Danger: Overload,"** in which a busy mother fires a list of chores at her daughter, who then gets them hopelessly mixed up. The illustration of this debacle shows that the daughter has been wearing headphones and listening to music the whole time: "No wonder that I got confused—my mother, though, is not amused." Fans of Shel Silverstein and Jack Prelutsky will find plenty to like in these mother/daughter collaborations.

### Publishers Weekly

SOURCE: A review of *Oh, Grow Up!: Poems to Help You Survive Parents, Chores, School and Other Afflictions*, in *Publishers Weekly*, Vol. 243, No. 6, February 5, 1996, p. 90.

Dealing with annoying circumstances can try the patience of even a saintly child, but this droll collection from Heide and her daughter is bound to fortify young readers suffering the slings and arrows of outrageous childhood. "I only have one life to live," laments the narrator of a poem titled "Advice," but "my parents want to live it." Another says, "I used to *hate* sharing./ Now it seems good./ I share my chores—/ I think everyone should." Wescott's waggish, detailed watercolors provide more than half the book's amusement. As fit punishment for a sister who hogs the bathroom plucking her eyebrows, Westcott depicts the younger brother camping out in the bathtub in full snorkeling regalia. Although the poems' rhythms and rhymes are sometimes uneven, both text and art focus on children of good humor and high energy who cleverly cope with familiar ordeals. Whether these narrators are being grounded or outnumbered, their complaints are earnest rather than churlish, heartfelt rather than whiny, and always full of fun.

### Elizabeth Bush

SOURCE: A review of *Oh, Grow Up!: Poems to Help You Survive Parents, Chores, School and Other Afflictions*, in *Bulletin of the Center for Children's Books*, Vol. 49, No. 7, March, 1996, p. 229.

The Heides take on a host of childhood annoyances, trials, and miseries from bullies and brats to cafeteria cuisine, allowances and hand-me-downs to the dread principal's office. While not uniformly hilarious, most poems nonetheless elicit empathetic chuckles or groans. It's kid-2; parents-0 in **"Doubles"** ("'I need my allowance, Mom,' / I say. / 'I really need it bad!' / 'All right,' says Mom, 'then here it is.' / And now I'll go ask Dad.") **"Dinner at a Fancy Restaurant,"** in which a young diner deflates a pompous waiter with his order **"I Weesh La Peanut Butter,"** may strike a chord among readers not to the manor born, and **"Grounded"** ("I said a bad word and I'm grounded./ I just wanted to hear how it sounded") has universal appeal.

### Carolyn Phelan

SOURCE: A review of *Oh, Grow Up!: Poems to Help You Survive Parents, Chores, School and Other Afflictions*, in *Booklist*, Vol. 92, No. 13, March 1, 1996, p. 1185.

Brothers, sisters, braces, hand-me-downs, fancy restaurants, parental advice, school cafeteria food, and other facets of growing up are viewed from a child's perspective. Most of these humorous rhymes end with a clever twist, or a bit of irony. After a boy details all the faults his little sister finds with her lunch, the poem ends with this stanza: "The Popsicle is too ice-cold, she whined and sulked and cried. I put it in the microwave— / she's *still* not satisfied." Fresh, lively, and wildly colorful, Westcott's line-and-watercolor artwork illustrates the book with pictures as bright and buoyant as the verse.

 *TÍO ARMANDO* (with daughter Roxanne Heide Pierce, 1998)

### Kirkus Reviews

SOURCE: A review of *Tío Armando*, in *Kirkus Reviews*, Vol. LXVI, No. 5, March 1, 1998, p. 339.

A graceful chronicle of the last year in a beloved great-uncle's life, relayed month by month in the first-person narration of a Mexican-American girl.

Tío Armando moves in with Lucitita's family after the death of his wife, Amalia. A connection is drawn between the elderly man and Lucitita and the year is filled with thoughtful exchanges between the two as she puzzles out his serene reaction to losing his wife. Readers begin to sense that Tío Armando is preparing Lucitita for his own passing. "I will never leave you," he promises, and she realizes, after his death, that she understands. The lengthy prose is unusually well-crafted, quiet and subdued yet filled with authentic details of life in this household. Tío Armando is a unique person, visiting strangers in the hospital and spreading kindness wherever he goes. [Ann] Grifalconi's gentle watercolors group people together in intimate moments and in larger groups that convey familial bonds.

## Ann Welton

SOURCE: A review of *Tío Armando,* in *School Library Journal,* Vol. 44, No. 5, May, 1998, pp. 116-17.

Lucitita loves her *Tío Armando.* He is really her great-uncle, and even though he is old, he knows how to enjoy life, a gift he shares abundantly with the younger members of his family. Lucitita observes that since her *tío* came to live with them " . . . everything and everyone is joined together." The oversized double-page spreads are arranged chronologically, from one May to the next, by which time the man has died. There is just enough foreshadowing in the flowing, evocative text to keep readers wanting to see what will happen next. Grifalconi's soft watercolor and pencil illustrations are soothing, doing a creditable job of setting a mood of gentleness, connection, and love.

## *IT'S ABOUT TIME* (1999)

### Kathleen Squires

SOURCE: A review of *It's about Time,* in *Booklist,* Vol. 95, No. 14, March 15, 1999, p. 1344.

A blue-haired pixie leads readers through 14 easy-to-read poems that demystify the concept of time. Concrete examples creatively interpret time, even making light of its elusiveness: "In Syracuse it's four o'clock / it's half past two in Delhi. / It's ten in Rome and three at home—but what time is it really?" Time is cut into slices of eternity, personified as a fleeting runner, and shown in the relative context of growth to make the overwhelming, indefinable quality more accessible and tangible. The verses, which outshine the retro illustrations [by Cathryn Falwell], are fun to read aloud and a good teaching tool for language skills and abstract thinking.

## *THE HOUSE OF WISDOM* (with daughter Judith Heide Gilliland, 1999)

### Publishers Weekly

SOURCE: A review of *The House of Wisdom,* in *Publishers Weekly,* Vol. 246, No. 34, August 23, 1999, p. 58.

The inspiration for Heide and Gilliland's ambitious tale is the landmark learning institution built in Baghdad in 830 A.D. by the Caliph al-Ma'mun. Told from the perspective of a boy, Ishaq, who lives in the House of Wisdom with his scholar father, the narrative transports readers to the Islamic Empire, at a time of dramatic academic and cultural growth. Ishaq aspires to the scholarly heights of his father, but finds his studies slow-going, unlike the sports he enjoys—"Then the time flew!" He simply does not share his father's "fire" for learning. But when the Caliph one day chooses Ishaq to lead an expedition in search of ancient manuscripts, Ishaq discovers for himself the truth of his father's words—that the scholars of history are "like the leaves of the same tree, separated by many autumns." The book's lofty subject and weighty text may make it best suited to those who have already been exposed to history's great thinkers, but all readers can appreciate the authentic feeling of the time and setting. Ishaq's character remains intangible, but the House of Wisdom's contribution to modern civilization comes through loudly and clearly. [Mary] Grandpré's lushly colored pastels detail the ornate patterns of the Baghdad rooftops as easily as they convey the sweltering heat of a caravan of camels. A fitting homage to the quest for knowledge.

---

# Monica (Ince) Hughes

## 1925-

English-born Canadian author of fiction.

Major works include *The Keeper of the Isis Light* (1980), *Hunter in the Dark* (1982), *The Dream Catcher* (1986), *The Crystal Drop* (1992), *A Handful of* Seeds (1993).

For information on Hughes's career prior to 1985, see *CLR*, Vol. 9.

## INTRODUCTION

Generally considered to be one of Canada's foremost writers for elementary- and middle-graders and young adults, Hughes is best known for her stimulating and masterful science fiction through which she examines the challenges faced by contemporary youth and ways to handle them. A respected author of realistic and historical fiction as well, Hughes grapples not only with current and past social and cultural issues, but with broader environmental concerns, drawing on her considerable scientific background and eclectic interests, including adaptation to alien cultures and climates, erosion of energy and food sources, and the power of computers. Most of her works are set in Canada or a very similar, yet alien world. By being forced to make moral judgements within conflicting cultures, her protagonists move from being ordinary self-centered individuals to responsible but still credible young adults. The prolific Hughes is praised for her vigorous plotting, three-dimensional characterizations, and perceptive insight into moral questions. Thematically, her fiction focuses on isolation and the search for identity. Critics laud her readable style and technological expertise, as well as the tenderness and hope that permeate her writings. Sarah Ellis extolled Hughes's work by concluding, "Hers is a major contribution to the fields of Canadian writing for children and juvenile science fiction."

### Biographical Information

Hughes was born in Liverpool, England in 1925 to Edward Lindsay and Phyllis (Fry) Ince. Shortly after her birth, the family moved to Egypt where Hughes's father, a mathematics professor, had accepted a position at the University of Cairo. Her family remained there until 1931, when they returned to England so Monica and her sister could be educated at English schools. In school, the young Hughes was read the Norse sagas, and was later influenced by the writings of Arthur Ransome and E. Nesbit. While living in London, Hughes visited museums, libraries, and art galleries, from which she developed a fascination for history, art, and the written word. When Hughes was nine, her family moved again,

this time to Scotland. Her father taught her about the stars, her mother told her stories of comets, and both stressed the importance of reading. Interested in quality rather than genre, her father introduced her to a wide variety of literary classics. Hughes recollected, "I discovered science fiction in the works of Jules Verne. A world not only of might-have-been, but of might-be-in-the-future. . . . The science fiction bug had bitten me."

Hughes attended Edinburgh University from 1942 to 1943, then joined the Royal Navy as soon as she turned eighteen, working on codes in London and as a meteorologist in Scotland and Belfast. Discharged in 1946, she moved to Southern Rhodesia, where she worked for two years as a dress designer and then as a bank clerk. She returned briefly to London and then, in 1952, set out for Canada with plans of eventually traveling to Australia.

In Canada, Hughes worked in Ottawa, Ontario, as a laboratory technician for the National Research Council, where she spent many long hours discussing the mysteries of space with her coworkers—further igniting her passion for scientific fact and fiction. In 1957 Monica married Glen Hughes, a civil servant, and made Canada her permanent home. Eventually, the Hughes family moved to Edmonton, Alberta. While writing had always been a favorite hobby as a child, it was only after her youngest child began school that Hughes turned to writing as a career possibility. "I decided that I would spend a year attempting to write professionally—as opposed to playing at writing, which I had done all my life," Hughes explained in *Something about the Author Autobiography Series (SAAS)*. "I promised myself that I would write uninterruptedly for four hours every weekday for a year and see what came of it." In the beginning, Hughes wrote with an adult audience in mind. However, after she was commissioned to compose a historical novella for grade-school use, *Gold-Fever Trail: A Klondike Adventure* (1974), Hughes concentrated on writing almost exclusively for children and young adults. In 1974, her first science-fiction tale about a colony of people who lived under the sea, *Crisis on Conshelf Ten*, was published, inspired by a program about Jacques Cousteau. *The Keeper of the Isis Light* was based on a newspaper article about a boy who was forced to live in isolation due to a medical condition. Similarly, *Hunter in the Dark* was inspired by her son, who skipped school to go deer hunting the last day of the hunting season. When Hughes asked her son why, his reply was "because." Although the answer bothered the mother in her, the writer was intrigued. In each case she asked, "what if . . . ," "what would it be like if . . . ," or "why." Hughes shared her philosophy of writing for children in *Canadian Children's Literature*: "I think one of the functions of a good writer for children (besides, obviously, being entertaining) is to help them explore the world and the future. And to find acceptable answers to the Big Questions: 'What's life about?' 'What is it like to be human?' . . . [T]hose are the questions that demand completely truthful answers, not part ones. So I think my chief criterion . . . is that one should write as truthfully as possible, even if it isn't easy or painless. . . . But always . . . always there must come hope."

**Major Works**

Hughes's most ambitious and acclaimed work is the *Isis* trilogy: *The Keeper of the Isis Light*, *The Guardian of Isis* (1981), and *The Isis Pedlar* (1982). The trilogy embodies many of its author's favorite themes, including moral growth through struggle, survival in alien environments, and the integration of cultures. Set on an isolated planet, the series examines the sociological evolution of a colony over three generations and introduces one of Hughes's most endearing characters, Olwen Pendennis, a human orphan who has been raised in seclusion by a benevolent robot who altered her body to withstand atmospheric conditions.

At the opening of *The Keeper of the Isis Light*, the planet is inhabited only by sixteen-year-old Olwen and the robot, the Guardian. Because the Guardian has erased her memories to protect her, Olwen has no recollection of her life before the age of five, when her parents were killed. When a new party of settlers arrives, Olwen must struggle through many trials and adversities that test her personal courage and moral fiber. As Olwen tries to understand why the new settlers are repulsed by her leathery green-gold skin and huge nostrils, she is confronted with the fact that the changes made to her body make her physically different from the people of Earth. Olwen wants acceptance and love from these people, but chooses to live in isolation rather than change her appearance to fit in. She accepts herself for what and who she is.

Hughes continues to probe themes of isolation and identity in her realistic and historical fiction as well. Perhaps her most impressive work is *Hunter in the Dark*, which relates how Mike, a teenage boy suffering from leukemia, stalks a deer and in the process comes to terms with his own approaching death. *The Dream Catcher*, the sequel to *Devil on My Back* (1984), is also set in the future. Society has been forced to live in arks with no communication between the different arks. Eventually, a group from Ark 3 is sent out to explore. Among the members of the exploration team is a young girl named Ruth, different from the others, who is trying to find her place in society. Tony O'Sullivan commented, "Monica Hughes creates a world without villains. Every character is seen with sympathy and understanding. The central tension in the book comes from the clash of Mind and Machine." O'Sullivan concluded by describing the novel as "part of a longer series in which problems of individual freedom and social good are explored with a degree of freshness."

A survival story set in the year 2011, *The Crystal Drop* tells of orphaned siblings, teenage Megan and her younger brother Ian, who leave their barren farm to search for their uncle some fifty miles away in the Canadian Rockies. The Canadian prairies have become a burning desert through global warming and a hole in the ozone layer, with no government help or media communication available. Critics have noted that the adventures of the children as they struggle to survive and deal with the dangers of the road are so vivid that *The Crystal Drop* reads more like realistic than science fiction. Endorsed by UNICEF and illustrated by Nicaraguan-born Luis Gray, *A Handful of Seeds* teaches the young about the problem of global poverty. Concepción, a street child in a Central American barrio, has brought with her the only legacy from her dead grandmother: a handful of bean, corn, and chili seeds, as well as the motto to save enough to plant and share. By planting the seeds, she teaches the other barrio children how to survive without stealing and develop self-reliance. As Ronald Jobe stated, "No reader closes a novel by Monica Hughes without being changed in some way. The richness of characterisation stimulates us to a greater awareness of the issues involved in our lives, an appreciation of the power of landscape over human activity and to get to know ourselves by being alone with characters who are struggling with the life challenges put in front of them."

## Awards

Hughes has received several awards for her contributions to children's literature, including the Vicky Metcalf Award from the Canadian Authors Association in 1981 for her body of work and for a short story in 1983. *Hunter in the Dark* received the Alberta Culture Juvenile Novel Award and the Bay's Beaver Award, both in 1981; won the Canada Council prize for children's literature in 1982; and was named a best book for young adults by the American Library Association and received the Young Adult Canadian Book Award, both in 1983.

Hughes won the Canada Council prize for children's literature for *The Guardian of Isis*, while *The Keeper of the Isis Light* was named a best book for young adults by the American Library Association, both in 1981. *The Keeper of the Isis Light* was also named to the International Board on Books for Young People's honor list in 1982. *Ring-Rise, Ring-Set* (1982) was the Guardian Award runner-up in 1983. Hughes also won the Alberta R. Ross Annett Award from the Writers Guild of Alberta in 1983, 1984, and 1986, and received a Hans Christian Andersen Award nomination in 1984.

---

## AUTHOR'S COMMENTARY

### Monica Hughes

SOURCE: "Science Fiction as Myth and Metaphor," in *ALAN Review,* Vol. 19, No. 3, Spring, 1992, pp. 2-5.

"I never read science fiction," a group of Grande Prairie librarians confessed to me years ago. I still occasionally hear, "I've always disliked science fiction," but happily this is usually mitigated by, "But I read **Keeper of the Isis Light,** and I loved it."

Where does this prejudice spring from, and why is **Isis** okay? When I look back on my childhood reading, I can't remember even considering science fiction as any different from mainstream fiction. I do remember that my father's choices for Sunday afternoon reading aloud were most eclectic. After *Lorna Doone* he might give us Poe's *Tales of Mystery and Imagination.* After *Treasure Island* maybe the weird surrealism of G. K. Chesterton's *The Man Who Was Thursday* or *The Napoleon of Notting Hill.* Or perhaps H. G. Well's *The Invisible Man.* The touchstone was always a great story line; whether it took place in the past, the present or the future was immaterial to him.

My own taste was formed by good luck. In the classroom of the school I first attended was a shelf of books by E. Nesbit. For the first time I discovered magic. I discovered in *The Enchanted Castle* that:

There is a curtain, thin as gossamer, clear as glass, strong as iron, that hangs forever between the world of magic and the world that seems to us to be real. And when once people have found one of the little weak spots in that curtain—which are marked by magic rings and amulets and the like—almost anything may happen.

Such enticing words: "Almost anything can happen." They have the same ring as "What if?" which is the springboard for all science fiction. In fact some of E. Nesbit's work could as easily be defined as science fiction. "What would happen if you discovered an ancient Egyptian amulet which enabled you to travel into the past?" There was a wonderfully spell-binding authenticity in Nesbit's description of Atlantis—not surprising, as I discovered years later when I read Plato's *Republic* and discovered where Nesbit had got her material. When we lived in Edinburgh I used to search the jumbled trays of oddments in second-hand stores, hoping against hope that I too might find a magic amulet. After all, why not?

Before my lack of success blighted me entirely, my father gave me James Jean's *The Mysterious Universe,* a very odd book to give a twelve-year-old. But it was the perfect gift for me, in that moment when I was beginning to suspect that I would never find that magic amulet. I reread James recently and was amazed at how far from today's understanding of the genesis of planets his writing was. Enlarging on the then popular theory that planets were formed as a result of the near collision of wandering stars, he postulated that this was a rare and almost miraculous event, as follows:

The total number of stars in the universe is probably something like the total number of grains of sand on all the seashores of the world. Such is the littleness of our home in space when measured up against the total substance of the universe. This vast multitude of stars is wandering about in space. A few form solitary groups which journey in company, but the majority are solitary travellers. And they travel through a universe so spacious that it is an event of almost unimaginable rarity for a star to come anywhere near another star. For the most part each voyages in splendid isolation, like a ship upon an empty ocean.

Specifically false, maybe, but there is an underlying poetic truth in his words. I used to look up at the night sky and try to comprehend the magnitude of the distances of which Jean spoke, and begin to ask myself: "What if?"

In the old Carnegie Library close to our home in Edinburgh I discovered the nineteenth and early twentieth century writers of adventure stories, and among them was Jules Verne. His stories were to me no less real than the adventures of the Scarlet Pimpernel or the Three Musketeers or the Prisoner of Zenda. I had never been exposed to popular science fiction magazines or early 'space opera,' and I thought of science fiction as a branch of literature as legitimate as historical fiction.

And why not? It has the honourable beginnings in the writing of Plato, whose *Republic* was a forerunner of More's *Utopia* and Butler's *Erewhon,* and in Lucian, who took an imaginative journey to the Moon in the second century A.D., and whose satiric writings were to become an archetype of fantastic journeys such as Gulliver's.

But the prejudice still lurks. Perhaps it has something to do with the position of Science Fiction on the shelves of chain bookstores, squeezed in between Romance and Westerns. But, luckily for me, I was unaware of this prejudice, and I had not yet met the Grande Prairie librarians when I began writing, and I fell into the science fiction genre quite by chance.

Reading voraciously and longing to write like Rosemary Sutcliffe or Alan Garner does not, unfortunately, automatically produce a publishable book, and I was struggling with unconvincing adventure stories when I happened to see a TV program by Jacques Cousteau in which he talked about an undersea habitat, which he called Conshelf One, that he had designed and was testing on the continental shelf of the Red Sea, to find out human reactions to living beneath the sea at pressures of three to four atmospheres for a week or so.

As I watched, I thought that it was a waste that they would all go back to France at the end of the experiment, leaving the little house empty. What would it be like to live under the sea? What would it be like to be a *child* growing up under the sea?

As soon as these thoughts whizzed through my head I knew that I *had* to write about them and find out the answers to my questions. Almost at once I realized that I could turn to no 'expert' for advice, nor was I likely to find a book on 'living under the sea.' I was writing about the future! It took major research, but was a lot of fun as well as hard work, and it set me on the path I have followed since, that of juvenile Science Fiction writer, beginning with **Crisis on Conshelf Ten.**

It took me more questions, a few more books about possible futures, to realize the power of science fiction for the writer as well as for the reader and teacher. It can be a positive tool to help us think clearly and creatively in new modes. How will humans cope in a polluted world? How will we overcome the effects of global warming? Mythic stories can give us new hope for tomorrow and reflect, in a nonthreatening way, on the social, economic and ecological problems of the late twentieth century.

Simple ideas can lead to fascinating conclusions. For instance, in 1974 I read a wire-service story in the Edmonton *Journal* about David, aged three, apparently condemned to spend the rest of his life isolated from true human contact, because of a fatal genetic flaw in his immune system. The story moved me deeply, and I cut it out and filed it in my "Ideas" file, where I place every thought, chance news story, passing event or char-

acter that I feel may one day be a story. Each time I finished writing another book I would reread this story about David, but I didn't know how I wanted to handle it.

Five years later, having read this cutting and worried about it at least ten times, I realized that what I wanted was an answer to the question: "David, are you lonely?" How to find the answer? Obviously not by researching the 'real' David, a horrible invasion of his privacy, but perhaps by finding a character in a situation *similar* to David's, putting this person in a story and then asking him this question.

First, I considered isolated places on Earth—such as light houses; only they are not so very isolated nowadays. It was then that I began to realize the strength of science fiction—that by taking my character to a planet far away from Earth, *alone,* I would achieve a real isolation.

Of course this had to be done *logically,* and the working out of this logic gave me my initial plot development, of Olwen, alone on Isis after the death of her parents, alone except for Guardian. It also led me to the character-driven, rather than the plot-driven story, and I began to realize that perhaps some of the 'bad press' about science fiction is due to the fact that much of it is plot-driven almost to the exclusion of believable and likeable characters. In order to answer my initial question: "David, are you lonely?" I *had* to develop a character—the David paradigm—who could talk to me and tell me how she felt.

To my amazement and delight Olwen also developed physically into a woman different from anything I had anticipated when I began. Because of her physical difference from the colonists, I had Guardian design for her a body-suit, modelled on Guardian's memory of typical Earth beauty, that would hide her bizarre physical appearance from the colonists. As Olwen became aware of her difference, she asked Guardian to make a mirror so she could see herself. In an unexpectedly triumphant moment of personal growth, she looked at herself, liked what she saw and determined never to wear that concealing, lying, suit again. It wasn't until **Keeper of the Isis Light** was finished, much of it consisting of the words and actions that Olwen had dictated to me, that I realized that indeed the bodysuit was a metaphor for the Jungian masks which we all, at some time or another, wear and the discarding of which is one of the triumphs of 'growing up.'

The writing of science fiction is full of magic moments like this, when the writer discovers more in her work than she believed she had put into it. They happen at the subconscious level, perhaps more readily in science fiction and fantasy because the setting and situations therein are removed from the mundane to the more mythical, containing elements that echo the folk tales and legends of the past.

As Jane Yolen has pointed out in *Touch Magic,* many

children today are illiterate in their own mythology and, like feral children unable to understand or communicate, have lost touch with the past, the knowledge of which is so necessary if we are to build a stable present and lay the foundations for a less precarious future. Levi-Strauss tells us that the old mythologies were developed to explicate the terrors of an environment which seemed irrational and random in its actions to preliterate peoples. Despite—or perhaps in part because of—scientific advances, the world our young people have inherited is also a rather terrifying place. I believe that science fiction can at least fill the gap left by the loss of the old mythologies, that it can help explicate today's world and tomorrow's possibilities for young people.

Which all sounds pretty grandiose, but it is my defense to those librarians and teachers who still distrust Science Fiction as a genre. I do believe that all really good fiction for young people works at three levels, the top level being the story line, with a theme of universal application beneath and, somewhere lurking beneath that level, like mist, like the iridescent colour of bubbles, the mythic level. When one finds it, it enriches a story wonderfully, makes it resonate at many different levels, so that it can be read with pleasure over and over again. Natalie Babbit's *Tuck Everlasting* and Ursula LeGuin's *The Tomb of Atuan* jump to the mind. I believe that, of their nature, Science Fiction and Fantasy are genres where one is especially likely to find this mythic level.

Having said that, I must say that I don't design a story with three levels and look for a suitable 'message' for my young reader. It would destroy my excitement in the discovery of story, and it certainly wouldn't work anyway. I write, with concentration and total selfishness, to try and answer for the child within me the myriad questions that come crowding into my head. From that first story, **Crisis on Conshelf Ten** which answered to my satisfaction the question: What would it be like to be a young person growing up under the sea? through its sequel *Earthdark,* about life on the Moon, to all the others, such as two very different books in which I look at possible climate changes and their effect on society.

Back in 1980 the ecological question was: Is Earth heating up due to the greenhouse effect, or cooling down as a result of particulate pollution actually reflecting the sun's energy? Living on the prairies, I felt at that time that the Ice Age scenario had more drama—had I lived close to the sea, I'm sure I would have tackled the other possibility, with the threat of coastal city flooding.

The coming of another Ice Age would obviously take an enormously long time and require a story with generations of protagonists. Was there some possibility of 'speeding up' this disaster? I found the answer in an issue of *Nature:* the suggestion, now well known, that the 34-million-year event and the 56-million-year event, each of which appear to have wiped whole species of fauna, were due to catastrophic collisions with either a very large meteor or a comet.

With the passage of Halley's Comet in mind, I developed this scenario. At first I intended the action to take place in and around the underground city where the scientists lived and worked. But, feeling that Nature as antagonist was not quite strong enough from a juvenile story, I thought of the Ekoes, imagined descendants of the Inuit people, living with Nature, rather than against her, as a metaphor antagonistic to the work of scientists. Once I had developed this idea, the story took on a life of its own. Liza met Namonnie, and at the end I found myself, to my surprise, facing the dilemma of the rights of technological society. At the time of writing the story I was involved in the church group, Project North, which was working with the findings of the Berger Commission on behalf of native peoples against the immediate development of the Norman Wells pipe line; out of my subconscious had come the ultimate reason for the story. Inadvertently, Science Fiction had become parable, and out of parable comes questions. Whose rights should prevail? Is there another solution other than the weakest going to the wall? Questions of today, but presented as a parable of the future. Recognition of these elements in science fiction writing can make for challenging classroom discussion.

Much more consciously, I worked for a couple of years on a story to do with Global Warming, now considered the more likely future. Its immediacy was made clear to me in several years of frightening droughts in the southern regions of the Prairie provinces. The very clarity of the 'message' made this book extremely difficult to write. I did not want it to be a diatribe. It was only after a couple of events, one involving the folklore of the 'Dirty Thirties' and the other the opening of the UNESCO World Site at Head-Smashed-In Buffalo Jump in Southern Alberta, that I was able to find a way of distancing my anger and frustration from the story I wanted to tell. This story, **The Crystal Drop,** is science fiction only in the sense that it is about the next century, for it is not a future of technological marvels, nor of space wars or laser guns. It is the story, on the one hand, of human greed in the face of diminishing water supplies, and on the other hand, of a transcendent hope that we can heal our damaged Earth.

Sometimes a passing conversation, such as the one I held with a librarian from Liverpool, northern England, is enough to start a story. The plight of young people there, leaving school with no hope of work, youths who have seen their jobless parents collecting their unemployment money for as many years as they can remember, was something that bothered her. It began to bother me too. What would become of a society, I wondered, in which there was absolutely no employment for the eager, imaginative young people leaving school? How could society contain all that wasted energy? What solutions would they come up with? Out of these questions, based on the reality of today's economic structures, came **Invitation to the Game,** which begins in a world not much different form ours, but then turns, at its conclusion, to a definitely science fiction solution.

The *what ifs* of science fiction can lead to stimulating classroom discussion, discussion that draws from the futuristic metaphor back home to rootlessness, loneliness, prejudice, anger, to the problems of broken homes or blended families, as well as, hopefully, keeping that magic I first discovered on my classroom shelf in the novels of E. Nesbit.

# GENERAL COMMENTARY

## J. R. Wytenbroek

SOURCE: "The Debate Continues: Technology or Nature—A Study of Monica Hughes's Science Fiction Novels," in *Science Fiction for Young Readers,* edited by C. W. Sullivan III, Greenwood Press, 1993, pp. 145-55.

> Once again we see the theme which Monica [Hughes] hammers home again and again with great gusto and invention: the necessity of knowing the interface between the wilderness and civilization, between our past and our future, of knowing the interface and establishing intercourse across that border at all cost however inviolate that border may seem to be. [Tim Wynne-Jones in "An Eye for Thresholds"]

For some years, discussions have continued regarding the problems, even dangers, inherent in anti-technological, "back-to-nature" science fiction for adolescents. Perry Nodelman argues, in his article "Out There in Children's Science Fiction: Forward into the Past" and again in his rebuttal to Jill May's response to his paper, that this anti-technological stance is, in fact, regressive. He states that such young adult science fiction novels "all hide a retrogressive vision under their theoretically revolutionary fervor."

Whether one agrees with the substance of Nodelman's arguments in these two articles or not, his accusation that "at the . . . heart of [these] novels" lies an "anti-technological and even anti-evolutionary bias" that is an expression of a "clear prejudice against scientific knowledge" that cause the characters to embark upon a "curious descent into complacency" is frequently heard, although it is more usually leveled against pastoral fantasies than science fiction. On one level, the criticism is valid. Many science fiction novels for young adults, including those set in postnuclear holocaust times, indicate that the only way to either save the world from its current path of destruction or ensure that destruction does not recur in the future is to retreat to a un- or even anti-technological state in which humanity once more moves in tune with its natural environment, an environment so often at risk or already destroyed in these novels.

Of course, the argument that humanity does indeed need to move back into a more balanced relationship with the natural world before we damage it irrevocably and, in so doing, destroy ourselves is also valid. This argument is gaining strength as we come to recognize the precarious situation our environment is now in after centuries of general abuse and decades of the intensive abuse of modern industry and technology. But do we, in fact, have to discard all technology to restore what we have almost destroyed and to save ourselves?

Monica Hughes's science fiction for young adults addresses this question again and again. Her central argument is that we must return to a more conscious and balanced relationship with the natural world if we are going to survive, not only on a physical level but, perhaps more important, on an emotional and spiritual level. However, she is equally adamant that it would be most difficult, maybe even impossible, for us now to survive on a physical level without technology: She argues clearly through her novels that technology used properly and wisely can enhance our lives and free us to explore the richness of our human heritage on the emotional, spiritual, and cultural levels.

Most of Hughes's science fiction novels deal with this issue in one way or another. In her early novel, *The Tomorrow City* (1978), Hughes explores the concept of a city computer, named C-Three, that, once unwittingly programmed by Caro, the teenaged daughter of its inventor, slowly takes control of the city it was meant to serve and improve. As it does, C-Three simply and literally eliminates the city's "undesirable" or unproductive elements, such as winos, the elderly, and pets, while programming the remaining citizens to accept and indeed desire the changes it brings. Refusing to watch the TV programs with their subliminal brain-washing messages, Caro and her friend Dave Sullivan eventually find a way to stop the computer, although both pay a great price. David loses his beloved dog in an early and abortive attempt to unplug Caro's family TV set, and Caro loses her eyesight when they finally and successfully manage to stop the computer altogether.

Two elements that appear again and again in Hughes's science fiction works surface in this early novel. One is the dehumanizing effect of technology run rampant, technology that takes control of its human masters. The loss of emotional concern and involvement with others is an immediate side effect of such control in most of the novels. For example, in *The Tomorrow City,* Caro's father, usually a caring and sensitive person, completely accepts the "necessity" of the city's driving David's grandmother out of her lifelong home so a playground can be built for the children, the "future" of the city that C-Three has been programmed to protect. Already under the influence of the subliminal messages, Mr. Henderson sees the old woman's house only as an impediment to the "progress" the computer envisions and refuses to help Caro and David try to save her home. The other citizens are in equally bad shape emotionally, and all relationships become distant and formal as C-Three programs people for efficiency and optimal performance to ensure its mandate, which it can fulfill on only the most superficial levels—the happiness and well-being of the children.

The other major theme that appears in this novel and that will recur is the theme of personal cost. Hughes is uncompromisingly realistic in her science fiction novels. She implies throughout them all that we cannot reduce our destructive overuse of technology without paying a price; the young people in her novels who confront tyrannical computers or overly technologically oriented societies must pay a price for their freedom, sometimes a heavy price, as David does with his dog and Caro does with her eyesight.

However, in this early novel we do not get a "back-to-nature" theme as a counterbalance to the tyranny of technology. Instead we get a "back-to-humanity" theme, which, given the setting of an ordinary twentieth-century city, works well. Here, where Hughes has not quite balanced the equation of technology and nature, she is neither excessive nor retrogressive in her vision. The Tomorrow City will become a city of today once more, and control of the city will return to the people who will then proceed to progress in their own way at their own pace, evolving naturally as opposed to evolving in the artificial fashion induced by C-Three. And Caro recognizes that the city's people may still not be mature enough as a whole to recognize the value of the gift that she and David have returned to them at the end of the novel:

> Everyone in the city was still asleep, unaware of their new and hard-won freedom. Would they understand? Would they be grateful? Or would they just be angry because it wasn't going to be easy any more?

It is through this technologically induced trance that Hughes presents complacency, not in the more humane solution to it.

*The Tomorrow City* is, however, the only one of Hughes's science fiction novels that does not include the third theme—that of the importance of the environment. In *Beyond the Dark River* (1981), Hughes presents a post-nuclear world, in which the cities in Alberta, Canada, as elsewhere, have been destroyed, but both native Indians and the exclusive religious communities of the Hutterites have survived. In their search for a cure for a mysterious plague that is killing all the children of one Hutterite community, a Hutterite boy and a native girl travel through the nearby city, looking for information that will help them save the children. They find nothing there of help, only the evidence of decay and devastation, which has reduced the few remaining city people to diseased and decadent cannibals. They realize they must rebuild their world themselves, that there is and can be no help from the self-destroyed technological society.

But the Hutterites have also paid a price for their lack of technology, although not as heavy a one as the technological society they have spurned. They have no protection against such plagues, as they have not developed any advanced medical systems to deal with emergencies such as the one they face now, considering such illness simply "the will of God." They have kept no records of their own history through writing or song, and thus they cannot help the native healer when she discovers that the generation before her friend's one was wiped out by a similar plague. They have some technology, such as windmills, but no longer know how to create such things. And their loss of contact with the commercial center of the city has further deprived them of the few things they used to purchase that rendered their lives slightly easier and more comfortable. However, this theme is not explored fully in this novel, as the interdependence of the two young people and the need for additional interaction between the two cultures is more central.

Even in her earliest, seemingly anti-technological writing, Hughes is never against technology itself. She is against the control of technology over humanity. She is also against the use of technology to make a profit at the expense of other people or as a tool for the exploitation of others. The ecologically sound environment being engineered on the Moon in the early novel *Earthdark* (1977), for example, utilizes technology to its fullest extent in the force fields, airtight domes, and other technologies needed to make the Moon a more inhabitable environment for its colonists. Even the people in the undersea communities in *Crisis on Conshelf Ten* (1975) utilize the latest available technology so that they can live permanently and comfortably deep under the ocean while also using technology to help feed Earth's starving population and to reoxygenate Earth's oxygen-depleted air, depleted through decades of uncontrolled pollution. In both novels, technology itself is not evil. But Hughes all too realistically points out the flaws in human nature that make people misuse technology, thereby creating a monster. The multinational corporations in both novels are the ones misusing technology to exploit people. Their chief concern is profit at any cost, and human life is as expendable as the environment in their one-eyed search for more and more profit. These corporations use extensive technology in their quest for profit, using it to rape both the Moon and the oceans. Through a twist in *Earthdark*, however, Hughes shows that the technology being used to exploit the Moon and its colonists was, in fact, first invented by those colonists to ensure their survival on the hostile satellite. Thus, she clearly establishes from the earliest novels that it is *how* humanity uses technology, not technology itself, that can be so negative and have such devastating results.

Despite the appearance of these themes in the earliest novels, *Ring-Rise, Ring-Set* (1982) is the first science fiction novel in which Hughes really explores all three themes mentioned earlier: the dehumanizing effect of an overuse of technology, the price to be paid for freedom from this enslavement, and the need for a closer relationship between humanity and nature. *Ring-Rise, Ring-Set* is set on a future Earth that is just entering a second ice-age caused by sun-blocking rings left around the Earth by a disintegrated meteorite. In this novel, the importance of both the technological and the ecologically holistic perspectives is bought out very clearly. The scientific community that has been established just below the encroaching ice fields, along with other scientific communities of the same nature all over the world, is the only hope for the world. Without technological intervention, Earth is doomed to a second, possibly permanent Ice Age that will destroy everything outside of a narrow belt at the equator. Yet this scientific community has become a cold, emotionless group, in which women have been subjugated to purely domestic roles, children are raised in communal, nonfamilial units with little parental contact and no affection; the slightest deviation from the accepted norm is treated with open suspicion and hostility, and knowledge of a purely scientific nature flourishes at the expense of art, literature, and music, which have become dying luxuries, little mourned by this cold, rational community committed to survival at any cost.

Liza, a young adult in the community, refuses to accept her role as subservient, emotionless, and domestic; and through a series of misadventures, finds herself out in the frozen wastes near the ice field in winter, where she is rescued by a group of Ekoes (Eskimos) who have assumed that she is a long lost relative. This second community in which she initially stays for many months has the humanity that her city lacks. Love, compassion, sorrow, and anger are deeply felt and openly expressed. For the first time in her life Liza *feels* loved, welcomed, wanted. She becomes part of a community where all work equally hard and in very similar ways for the survival of the whole group, without a hierarchy of male intelligentsia and female servants. But theirs is a harsh life, and there has been little time for the development of art and music here, either, although they do have a rich oral tradition. Also the Ekoes, while emotionally and spiritually wealthy, are totally at the mercy of their deteriorating environment; although they have adapted naturally to it with remarkable success, unless the Ring is removed, the caribou will eventually perish—and once the caribou are gone, the Ekoes will die. Therefore, they need the technocrats to preserve their very lives. But the technocrats, who come up with one solution to part of the problem near the end of the novel, are now so dehumanized by their total reliance on technological solutions and a technologically based life-style that they are willing to sacrifice the lives or culture of the Ekoes to advance their solution to the problem rather than look for a less deadly alternative.

In this novel, then, Hughes shows once more the importance of the interdependence of peoples. The technocrats may be able to save the world from certain destruction. They may be able to save the Ekoes from more immediate destruction if they want to. But they need an infusion of the humanity still so alive among the Ekoes before they care enough to save the Ekoes and, also, to save themselves as human beings. Neither can really survive without the other. Each has something essential to offer the whole of humanity. But here, as in *Beyond the Dark River,* Hughes reveals clearly that the superior culture is the one that maintains its deepest human val-

ues, that remains both emotionally and spiritually engaged with its own humanity. At the end of the novel, by refusing to go into the protection of the city and embrace the technological life-style, the Ekoes choose their humanity and possible death over dehumanization and probable survival. Hughes explicitly indicates that the former choice is the better choice of the two. Furthermore, there is a great potential cost to Liza, who opts at the end to share the fate of the Ekoes rather than return to the safety of the city. But Hughes further implies that, by choosing humanity over survival, Liza touches the buried humanity of the city's scientists, one of whom is her own father, which causes them to find an alternative method of combating the ice *without* destroying the Ekoes, and Liza along with them. . . .

As with *Ring-Rise, Ring-Set,* Hughes's other novels usually end with hope. There is hope in the sweet rain that falls on Caro's blinded face at the end of *The Tomorrow City.* There is hope offered for the isolated community at the end of *The Guardian of Isis* and, particularly strongly, at the end of *The Isis Pedlar.* Hope for two communities, if not so much for the individual who sacrifices himself for those communities, is strong at the end of *Devil on My Back.* And hope is like a beacon by the end of the otherwise horrifyingly bleak *Invitation to the Game.* But these endings of hope do not support Nodelman's complaint regarding the "retrogressive vision" and "descent into complacency" in young adult science fiction. The hope in Hughes's novels is hard won through individual sacrifice and loss. And the hope depends on balance, on some kind of contact or bridging between the technological societies and environmentally based societies frequently set in opposition in the novels. Hughes attests that this hope arises from her deep conviction that "over all, pattern will emerge out of chaos." This hope, however, like all her themes, is founded firmly on realistic principles. "True hope is . . . rooted in the hard facts of the past and the present, but it desires to transform—not to replace, nor merely rearrange, but to transform—their undesirable patterns."

The Isis books pursue this theme of hope and the balance essential to hope in a somewhat different way than does most of Hughes's other young adult science fiction. Beginning in *The Keeper of the Isis Light* (1980), Hughes shows the dangers that beset a community that starts off balanced with technological advantages that help them settle with ease into their chosen agricultural lifestyle on their new planet and then abruptly abandons all technology. In a study of human nature that is superb on many different planes, Hughes shows the potential devastation when a society deliberately turns its back on even basic technological aids in a hostile environment, which the planet Isis can be. By refusing all technology and labelling it as "evil," the human community on Isis becomes self-defeating, almost being destroyed by a series of natural calamities the people no longer have the capabilities to deal with in the second novel of the trilogy, *The Guardian of Isis* (1981). They are also almost destroyed again by purported "magic," which is simply forgotten technology, in the third novel, *The Isis Pedlar* (1982). Both times they are saved by the high technology of the robot guardian of Isis. Here technology is shown to be necessary for survival, as it was in getting the settlers from Earth to Isis in the first place, years before. But narrow-mindedness, prejudice, and fear have deprived most of the settlers of all the advantages of technology, causing them to become as imprisoned in their "simple" life as the people were mentally imprisoned by C-Three in *The Tomorrow City* and as the people are imprisoned on many levels in the sterile cities of *Ring-Rise, Ring-Set* and *Devil on My Back.*

The people of Isis do not lose their humanity to the extent that the city dwellers do in any of the three books above, but their narrowness sets up prejudices, suspicions, fears, and hostility among them that finally erupt into attempted lynchings, the first physical violence that has ever manifested itself in the society, near the end of *The Isis Pedlar,* The ones most free of these negative qualities, and thereby the freest creatures in general on Isis, are Olwen, the keeper of the Isis light, David and Jody N'Kumo, from the settlers' community, and the guardian of Isis, a very human robot. These four, all physically or emotionally rejected by society at one time or another, are the ones who save the community during its times of greatest danger, and they are also the only ones who can accept the importance and necessity of technology. Here Hughes is showing that prisons of mind and soul are not the exclusive problem of the sterile technological society, but that any society can become dehumanized if it is self-isolated and allows itself to become unbalanced. Technology is presented primarily as a good thing throughout the trilogy, something that is helping save the people of Earth and that could greatly enhance the chances of survival and the development of the Isis community, at least in its early stages. By the end of *The Isis Pedlar,* however, it is too late for advanced technological aids, and the community must learn a new humanity within its chosen course; thus, it still has the chance to break free from the self-imposed prison of fear, prejudice, and hostility, opening the possibility for technological development again in the future.

Like the early community on Isis, the forest community of free slaves in *Devil on My Back* (1985) depends for survival on higher levels of technology than it currently enjoys. However, unlike the people of Isis, the free slaves have not refused technology but rather have not had an option. Escapees from the inhuman, tyrannical, and totally computerized city of ArcOne, they left with what little they could take, which over the years has amounted to only one axe, one saw, and one knife. On the other hand, ArcOne has too much technology so that its people, like those of *The Tomorrow City,* are completely controlled by the computer, at least all except the slaves and the Overlord. But unlike *The Tomorrow City,* the people of ArcOne have not wrenched themselves free of the computer's oppression, and the computer has become a tyrant, dictating every aspect of every person's life, either directly or indirectly. Here the computer is the ultimate Overlord, beyond all but the most

cursory control of the human overlord. There is no freedom of any kind in ArcOne, and the social structure of lords, workers, soldiers, and slaves accentuates the total dehumanization of the people in the city.

The bridge between the two communities is Tomi, son of the Overlord, who is ejected by mistake from the city during a slave riot. He eventually finds his way to the community of free slaves who help him find his personal freedom, including his own identity as a human being. Once he finds true freedom, he elects to go back into prison, into ArcOne, so that he can smuggle out to the forest community the tools and seeds they so desperately need, as they are unable to forge new tools for themselves from the depleted resources of an Earth raped and pillaged for centuries for her mineral wealth. Tomi pays a great price for the survival of the forest community, exchanging his new found freedom for captivity and for the community's continuing freedom. However, in the process, he finds a new and unexpected freedom for himself. As he begins to help his friends achieve the needed balance, he finds a totally unpredicted chance to work toward the freedom of tyrannized ArcOne. At the end of the novel, ArcOne remains the cold, emotionally and spiritually sterile place it had been before Tomi's accident, but once again the humanizing force of Tomi and, unexpectedly, his Overlord father, begins immediately to affect, to counter, and (we are left with every reason to believe) to eventually undermine the dehumanization of this society, bringing it freedom, humanity, and a new, more balanced relationship with nature, as does indeed happen at the end of the novel's sequel, *The Dream Catcher.*

A much more frightening type of dehumanization takes place in Hughes's most recent novel, *Invitation to the Game* (1990). This time, she does not use the tyranny of the uncontrolled computer, or even the threat of extinction to dehumanize, but rather the novel is based on the simple human weakness for an easy life, an important theme in *The Tomorrow City,* as well. Hughes also reverses a pattern evident in both young adult and adult science fiction that Margaret Esmonde discusses in her article "From Little Buddy to Big Brother: The Icon of the Robot in Children's Science Fiction." Esmonde argues that "the negative aspect of the computer in children's science fiction exists in sharp contrast to the benevolent icon of the robot." She goes on to say that "whereas in the robot stories the mechanical character is almost certain to be benevolent, in computer stories, the machine without exception poses a serious threat to man's free will and even his life." She concludes that

> one may speculate that the robot's anthropomorphic appearance somehow reassures us of some common bond while the impersonality of the computer banks with their flashing lights, or the repulsive, disembodied brain, both sealed in a sterile, protective environment, accents the differences between man and machine.

Hughes herself has followed this pattern before with her

negative computers and her benevolent robot guardian of the Isis novels. However Hughes has set *Invitation to the Game* on a post-pollution-crisis Earth, where, after most of the human population was wiped out by a pollution-based cataclysm, the remaining people created benevolent robots to help them reconstruct their world. But the efficiency of the robots has rendered them vital to the survival of a humanity afraid of returning to its old destructive patterns, and as the population increases, there are increasingly few jobs for humans. Vast slums are created in the cities for the huge number of unemployed, where most students end up upon graduation from the government-run boarding schools. In this novel, the robots themselves have not taken over. They have simply, as in many adult science fiction stories, become so indispensable that people are losing their own function in their society and are, in the process, becoming dehumanized.

The city Hughes depicts in *Invitation to the Game* is more frightening than those in any of the previous novels, for it is the city of nightmare, of gray, broken slums housing broken people who try to keep the tatters of their humanity together by living with dignity and true supportive community within this ugly world. Other inhabitants of this broken world cannot even maintain that much of their threatened humanity, sinking into gang violence, anesthetizing themselves with drugs or alcohol or both, or living for the wildly colored nightlife. The most frightening thing about the city in this novel is that, unlike any city in Hughes's other novels, it is already here, at least in part. One need only watch TV or walk some of the streets in larger North American cities to see the same numb despair on the faces of people in the tenements and listen to the news of the violence and substance abuse in such places to know that the nightmare has already begun, and we do not even have the excuse that the controlling powers do in *Invitation to the Game.* In other words, the more young adult science fiction she writes, the more realistic Hughes gets on many levels, and therefore the more frightening.

But hope is equally as strong as despair in this powerful novel. Through a lengthy process that is never explained to them, the members of the newly graduated group on which the novel focuses find themselves on a new, previously unpopulated planet, a completely pastoral planet, where they have the chance to begin again. They are not forewarned that they will be sent there, and they are given nothing with which to begin life on this new planet, except the advantage of their particular skills and training and having explored their area of the planet through induced dream states in which they were given realistic "tours" of their region where they found what growing things could be safely eaten, where there was water, and what dangers lurked.

The novel, then, seems to be one of Nodelman's "retrogressive visions," with the first ten Adams and Eves left in an idyllic paradise to simplistically regain what all humanity lost when it moved from its supposedly idyllic prehistory past, before the first technology—

simple tools—changed the course of humanity forever. However, a closer reading shows quite the opposite. All the members of the team were highly trained before they left school and were more than competent in a field that will aid the survival of the team. One is a trained doctor, another a biologist, another a chemist, another a woodworker, and so on. Their technological society has given them all the skills needed for survival, as it has, in varying combinations, the other groups "seeded" on the new world at the same time as this group. As Lisse, the protagonist, states near the end of the novel, while she is making the first writing paper for the new colony, "we have been reliving the discoveries and inventions of our remote ancestors only speeded up enormously, so that we will move from the Stone Age to the Bronze in less than five years." She goes on to

> wonder how far we will go. Iron Age. And what then? Our memories hold all the discoveries of humankind: coal, gas, oil, electricity, fission power. Pollution. The end of the line. Pollution caused the sudden drop in fertility that nearly destroyed human life on Earth. It was only the robots that saved us, becoming our hands and feet and brains when there weren't enough humans left. Then we recovered and couldn't get rid of them. The Government was faced with a choice: get rid of the robots—or get rid of the young people. It's ironic that is was easier to get rid of the young people. It all has to do with the use of power. We hope we won't make the same mistakes. We are careful and we talk a lot about what went wrong on Earth.

This is not a "retrogressive vision." This group has enough vision to desire a more advanced future, but also the wisdom born of bitter experience to know that there must be limits to technological advance. These young people have recovered their full humanity, at great cost, and have learned the importance of a true and good balance between technology and a natural life-style.

Through these novels, Monica Hughes offers young people and us all a chance, maybe a last chance, to see the necessity of this balance, to see the importance of preserving our own humanity by moving closer to a more natural life-style that will help protect and maintain our environment while utilizing the real benefits of humanized technology, a technology that works for us all, not one that controls or imprisons us on any level of our beings or that is used by some to exploit others. In all these novels, she presents the importance of human emotions, culture, and spirituality to help us keep that precious and precarious balance, so that we will not find ourselves, like Lisse and her friends, citizens of a nightmare reality come true, and come to stay.

**Ronald Jobe**

SOURCE: "Know the Author," in *Magpies,* Vol. 11, No. 2, May, 1996, pp. 22-4.

Do you know Olwen? Mike Rankin? Tome? Megan and

her brother Ian? All these are notable individuals for Canadian youngsters, at least in the literary sense. Teens instinctively recognise them as friends, having vicariously experienced their exploits.

Monica Hughes, nationally acclaimed award winner, is renowned for her strength of characterisation, the result of a lifelong exploration of the inner emotions, tensions and desires of individuals. She is fascinated by news clippings revealing unique situations that allow her to speculate . . . What if . . . Monica is fascinated by the effect of an often hostile environment, with its strong sense of isolation, on the characters in her books. Equally at home in settings, with similarities to both Australia and Canada, she relishes speculating about the future of our planet, especially the issues that will impact on the lives of young people in her books. She is fascinated by the impact of the past—can it indeed become the future?

Monica is perhaps best known as a science fiction writer, a genre aptly suited to share her concern for our dwindling resources, uncertain influence of computers to run our lives, survival in alien worlds and conflicting views between technology and environmental issues. Yet not all of her books are future focused. Several relate to young people today who are facing issues of self identity, interpersonal communication and, in some cases, their own death.

Monica Hughes, born in Liverpool, England, gained a sense of wonder and a love of astronomy and space from her mathematics professor father. As her first six years were spent in Cairo, it is not surprising that images of sand, heat-waves and scarcity of water make an impact in her novels. Returning to school in England, Monica, a voracious reader, was immersed in the myths, legends and Norse sagas as well as the fantasy of Enid Nesbit. Later, at the age of seventeen, she became a weather operator with the Women's Royal Naval Service. After the war she travelled to Southern Rhodesia (now Zimbabwe) for two years but decided not to stay. She then turned to Canada, where she worked as a lab assistant in Ottawa, until she met and married her husband Glen and they ventured west to Edmonton.

Monica knew she wanted to be an author. 'I dreamed of being a writer from when I was about ten. I tried to write short stories and poems and articles and things all the way through my teens; then I wrote adult stories and articles and attempted to break into the commercial market in my 20s and 30s with total failure a hundred per cent failure, until I discovered that my voice was in children's novels.' At this point she realised it was requisite for her to undertake a comprehensive reading program to gain a knowledge of what was being written for young people. She gained a respect for the powerful influence the landscape has on the actions and emotions of the individuals in a story.

Monica Hughes is concerned about challenging readers and making them question their options for the future.

Regardless of genre; whether it be science fiction, realism, fantasy or future landscapes; the issues of survival, friendship, role of women, voices of minorities, power vs. control and alone vs. lonely are explored in the following five thematic types.

Canadian teachers often say that they do not like reading science fiction! Yet almost instantly they add—but I loved *Keeper of the Isis Light* (1980). This book has become one of the turning points in Canadian literature for young people.

'Simple ideas can lead to a fascinating conclusion. For instance in 1974 I read a wire-service story in the Edmonton *Journal* about David, aged three, apparently condemned to spend the rest of his life isolated from true human contact, because of a fatal genetic flaw in his immune system. The story moved me deeply and I cut it out and filed it in my "ideas" file, where I placed every thought, chance news story, passing event or character that I feel may one day be a story. Each time I finished writing another book, I would re-read this story about David, but I didn't know how I wanted to handle it.

Five years later, having read this cutting and worried about it at least ten times, I realised that what I wanted was an answer to the question: "David, are you lonely?" How to find the answer? Obviously not by researching the "real" David, a horrible invasion of his privacy, but perhaps by finding a character in a situation similar to David's, putting this person in a story and then asking him this question.'

The resulting *Keeper of the Isis Light* (1980) introduces Olwen, a sixteen-year-old girl (by Isis time) living with her Guardian on a remote planet. They are in charge of sending a signal back to earth. Life is peaceful for them until they are informed that settlers are to arrive. Guardian makes a body suit and mask for Olwen, supposedly to protect her from any germs the settlers may have brought. Despite uncertainty about her acceptance, she goes to extend a welcome and invites the son of the leader to visit her. It is only when we witness Mark's shocked reaction to her unmasked face, stepping backwards off a cliff, that we realise Guardian has made significant changes to Olwen's body. Readers will want to re-read this novel, becoming aware of the embedded clues, before reading more about Olwen and Mark in *The Guardian of Isis* (1981) and *The Isis Pedlar* (1991).

'It wasn't until *Keeper of the Isis Light* was finished, much of it consisting of the words and actions Olwen had dictated to me, that I realised that indeed the body-suit was a metaphor for the Jungian masks which we all, at some time or another, wear and the discarding of which is one of the triumphs of "growing up".'

*The Golden Aquarians* (1994) is once again set on a distant planet in the year 2092. Colonel Angus Elliot has summoned his son Walt, to the watery planet of Aqua.

His father wants him to be part of his research team which has once again been given the challenge to 'terraform' the planet into an environment for growing an oil-plant crop to supplement Earth's dwindling resources. Huge machines are levelling the small hills and creating dikes to drain the marshes. It is Walt the Aquarians, amphibian-like creatures who have telepathic abilities, warn of a massive tidal wave due in six days which will eradicate the surface of the planet. At loggerheads with his father who can Walt convince to help?

Another powerful novel with a harsh landscape is set in Southern Alberta west of Fort Macleod. *The Crystal Drop* (1992). Megan and her brother experience the effect of a terrible long-lasting drought in the beginning of the 21st Century. After their mother has died in child-birth, their only chance of survival is to head west where they know their Uncle Greg lives. Tortuous days of heat, no shade and near exhaustion follow. When they do try to get some water from fenced-in farms, the owners turn dogs on them or shoot at them.

Another pair of novels, feature images of shifting sands in an endless desert setting which evoke an air of mystery and isolation. Princess Antia, herself accustomed to the luxuriant life, finds herself forced to go to the island desert of Roshan, to become engaged to Jodril, the chief's heir. She does not go willingly and acts accordingly. In one episode, despite a coming sandstorm, she storms out into the desert where she is rescued by the mysterious lady of the sands—*Sandwriter* (1985). Sandwriter knows about Antia, and knows that it will be Anita and Jodril's daughter who will replace her as wise woman. When their daughter, Rania, has her tenth birthday, a young boy brings her a gift as well as a message from Sandwriter—it is time to honour the promise made by her parents before she was born. She must go into the desert to begin her training—*The Promise* (1989).

For fourteen-year-old Tomi, this is the beginning of a grand few days—he is to receive his full 'infopak' to wear on his back, given to boys deemed capable of leadership and containing the accumulated wisdom of the people. He lives in a class-structured society under a massive dome of ArcOne, which protects its inhabitants from the hostile world outside—*Devil on My Back* (1984). Instead he is caught in the middle of a revolt and flushed down a chute into the river below. His survival and eventual realisation of freedom is helped by a band of individuals who themselves had escaped. Tomi returns to ArcOne so that in *The Dream Catcher* (1988) he might be able to drop seeds, tools and supplies into the river to assist his friends in their survival.

Monica once said, in a talk, that writers need to look inside themselves and search their own loneliness to find people and bring them out. One of the most powerful of Monica's character portrayals is sixteen-year-old Mike Rankin—*Hunter in the Dark* (1982). He has life going for him: friends, affluent loving parents and talent as a basketball player. All that changes when he begins to feel ill and his parents make the decision not to tell him the seriousness of his disease. But Mike knows something is not right. Hughes constructs a realistic and compelling narrative of Mike's struggle to rationalise his impending death from leukemia. She approaches the topic in a very touching and sobering manner, yet one that is honest and free of maudlin sympathy for Mike. The sustained allegory of the deer hunt to Mike's search for his own raison d'etre and his eventual comfort in the 'dark' of his own understanding is particularly effective. Suspense on the trip rises until he actually faces the deer—will he pull the trigger?

Self identity is important—and so is gaining a new one Moving to Edmonton with her single mum is no fun for Paula Herman in *My Name Is Paula Popowich!* (1982), until she discovers the photograph of a handsome man and starts to ask questions. In the process she discovers her Ukrainian/Canadian grandmother, a father who died six years before, and a mother who is really a caring loving individual. How joyous it is to be introduced to your culture.

Monica's recent novels have given her an opportunity to explore a time dimension to her writing. *Castle Tourmandyne* (1995) explores the relationship between two cousins. Marg has been given an exquisite antique doll's house along with the warning to assemble it with love, yet her cousin Peggy takes charge. Only when she realises the influence of the doll's house on her cousin's life, does she enter the house as a character herself to try to reverse the events.

Time travel is a very appealing genre for Canadian writers, yet Monica places a unique twist on her *Where Have You Been, Billy Boy?* (1995). The year is 1908 and a young orphan, Billy, is helping an old man to run a carousel at a local carnival in a large eastern American city. The carousel has the special feature that if you place the gears in the right position, you can go fast enough to go forward in time. What temptation! Billy does . . . to the amazement of Susan who discovers him coming out of an old barn on her family's ranch in Alberta. He can't believe it is 1993! But how to get back? With the help of her older brother and a neighbour, the old shabby carousel, after years of neglect, is made to work one last time—back Billy goes! With loving care the kids restore the carousel, so that on July 4th, 1995 it is unveiled with great celebration. At that time a visitor arrives to bring greetings—her grandfather Billy wanted to be remembered to them! Truly . . . can the past communicate with the present?

No reader closes a novel by Monica Hughes without being changed in some way. The richness of characterisation stimulates us to a greater awareness of the issues involved in our lives, an appreciation of the power of landscape over human activity and to get to know ourselves by being alone with characters who are struggling with the life challenges put in front of them.

# TITLE COMMENTARY

## 📖 SANDWRITER (1985)

### Margery Fisher

SOURCE: A review of *Sandwriter,* in *Growing Point,* Vol. 24, No. 2, July, 1985, p. 4471.

The plot of this tale of a secondary world is relevant to our times; the greed of the rich continent Kamalant threatens the marginal, ascetic desert land of Roshan with its one treasure. The theme is wider, though, for behind the desire for material gain is the universal jealousy of superficial minds confronted with the confidence reposed in deeper values. The story of sheltered Antia, whose adolescent love for her tutor is disturbed by suspicion of his loyalty to her royal parents, is brought to life, as these imagined lands are also by a magnificent background of contrasted landscapes and a sharp portraiture of the people of the two lands, with the silent, mysterious figure of the Sandwriter as the unifying element. Of all Monica Hughes's invented worlds this one may well be the most potent and the most stirring so far.

### Robin Barlow

SOURCE: A review of *Sandwriter,* in *The School Librarian,* Vol. 33, No. 3, September, 1985, p. 256.

Antia is a young princess, brought up on the twin continents of Komilant and Kamalant. She lives a pampered and cosseted life until she is ordered across the Small Sea to the island of Roshan to be betrothed to Jodril, heir to the chief. Antia is unwilling to go until her tutor, Eskoril, persuades her to act as his spy. Roshan is a simple community, the antithesis of sophisticated Kamilant. Antia detests every minute of her visit, and is constantly bickering with Jodril. We gradually learn that Roshan harbours an ancient mystery and secret wealth, which Eskoril is determined to discover. As events unfold, Antia changes her allegiances, reneges on Eskoril, and finally becomes betrothed to Jodril.

Monica Hughes has established a reputation as a popular science fiction writer, notably with *Ring Rise, Ring Set.* However, *Sandwriter* does not have quite the same depth or originality; it seeks to create a world of mysticism and supernatural power which never quite comes off.

### M. Hobbs

SOURCE: A review of *Sandwriter,* in *The Junior Bookshelf,* Vol. 49, No. 5, October, 1985, p. 227.

Interestingly, though *The Hero and the Crown* [by Robin McKinley] is (as befits the winner of the 1985 Newbery Medal) a book of much greater depth and reso-nance, Monica Hughes's *Sandwriter* is more consistently well-written, within its own smaller limits. Moreover, though the latter at first works within fairytale conventions—the pampered Princess Antia sent to be betrothed to the prince of a distant country and grumbling at its more primitive lifestyle—there is authentic detail in the desert life she encounters and, though wisely not spelt out, a serious presentation of the moral dangers to a country's people of discovering rich resources like oil. The ancient Sandwriter, a hereditary sibyl, whose existence is a jealously guarded secret of the desert tribes, accepts Antia (after she has learnt some hard lessons) as a kindred spirit. She helps her defeat the greedy tutor who has tried to use her as a means of access to the desert's black treasure, and to whom she has unwittingly betrayed those whose values she comes to adopt. In a nicely developed little love story, she accepts at the end her prince, in the presence of Sandwriter.

### Diana Manuel

SOURCE: A review of *Sandwriter,* in *The Christian Science Monitor,* Vol. 80, No. 114, May 9, 1988, p. 24.

*Sandwriter,* by Monica Hughes, introduces a similarly unfamiliar land—the desert island state of Roshan—that comes complete with heroic prince and princess, oases, mirages, and hooded figures flitting in and out of threatening sandstorms.

The author works hard to duplicate the kinds of believable settings and characters that made her Isis trilogy so popular, but keeps falling into one pretentious trap after another.

Declarations, such as "The first step in wisdom is being aware that one knows nothing," have a hollow ring, and it's difficult to visualize the monstrous kroklyns and shabby lemas that comprise Roshan's beastly population Still, this is a suspenseful tale.

### Jean Kaufman

SOURCE: A review of *Sandwriter,* in *Voice of Youth Advocates,* Vol. 11, No. 3, August, 1988, pp. 138-39.

Princess Antia, a spoiled, childish young lady, consents to visit the barren desert island of Roshan only because her attractive tutor, Eskoril, asks her to spy for him. Roshan has none of the luxuries that Antia is used to and Antia is teased by Prince Jodril whom it is hoped she will marry. While on a trip to the outback, Antia learns of Roshan's secret from its mysterious guardian, Sandwriter. Antia is caught between her growing admiration for Roshan and the people who live there and her promise to spy for Eskoril. When Antia finally admits to Jodril that she has been spying, she promises to help protect Roshan's secret. Eskoril tries to find the secret but with the combined efforts of Antia, Jodril and Sandwriter he is driven off. The ending hints of further adventures to come.

I enjoyed *Sandwriter.* The characters are interesting, the plot developed clearly and there is enough mystery surrounding Sandwriter to create interest in a sequel. However, I do have reservations as well. It does not have the same quality of Hughes's *Keeper of the Isis Light.* Antia matures too easily and is forgiven too quickly and the other characters do not have sufficient depth. This is an interesting, light weight fantasy that I recommend for fantasy fans and fans of Monica Hughes.

 *THE DREAM CATCHER* (1986; U.S. edition, 1987)

### E. Cowell

SOURCE: A review of *The Dream Catcher,* in *The Junior Bookshelf,* Vol. 50, No. 3, June, 1986, pp. 115-16.

A sequel to the author's *Devil on My Back.* After the Age of Confusion, several Arks are set up in different parts of the world but with no communication between them. Ark One, for instance, collects and stores knowledge, particularly technological information. The story of Ark One is told in *Devil on My Back.* In Ark Three, a perfect thought pattern called the Web has been developed in which *all* minds are linked together by psychic means. By means of these protected colonies, it is hoped that one day civilisation can be re-established in the world.

*The Dream Catcher* is the story of a girl, Ruth, who seems a misfit in Ark Three, for at the age of fifteen, she has no vocation as a Healer, an Esper, a Communicator or a Teacher. She could be a danger to the Web. She alone is receiving messages from outside the Ark. Can there be other Arks, other people?

A party is sent out to find Ark One, but when they reach it all the group, except Ruth, are made prisoners. The society here is a very different one, a rigid hierarchy in a computer society. There is a privileged class who possess all knowledge and are set apart from the soldiers and slaves. It is only by the power of the Web that Luke, the leader, is able to enter the vital computer and travel along the circuits, changing what must be changed to reform the society.

The author is expert at this kind of speculative fantasy but she has a sound scientific basis as well as a social conscience. The result is a readable exciting story which is convincing and gives ground for thought.

### Margery Fisher

SOURCE: A review of *The Dream Catcher,* in *Growing Point,* Vol. 25, No. 4, November, 1986, pp. 4704-708.

*The Dream Catcher* is a sequel to the compelling futur-

ist tale, *Devil on my Back.* In the first book we were introduced to the survival construct known as Ark I, where the original attempt to retain a modicum of civilisation after the 'time of confusion' in the twenty-second century has degenerated into a divisive class system of scholars, soldiers and slaves. Now we move to Ark 3, a truly democratic example of the five enclaves projected after the disaster. Here several young people are approaching the time when they will be selected for their function in the adult world. One of them, Ruth, is unhappy about being different from her peers but her instructors, finding her to be a true kinetic, help her to develop her gift and include her in a group sent to try to make contact with Ark I. Her recurring dreams of a red-haired girl and a song about the Freedom Man help to locate the enclave but they find it guarded by barbed wire and ruled by a wholly tyrannous system. Both plot and setting become metaphors for the universal struggle between freedom and oppression, as Ruth and Tomi, the 'Freedom Man' of her dreams and centre of the earlier book, make a bold attempt to change the situation. Technology in the shape of governing computers, psychology in the effect of kinetic power and its control, are merged in a story giving full scope to the development of character in action and in argument.

### Kirkus Reviews

SOURCE: A review of *The Dream Catcher,* in *Kirkus Reviews,* Vol. LV, No. 1, January 1, 1987, pp. 59-60.

After the End of Oil, the universities established protected enclaves to preserve humanity. Ruth's enclave has stressed philosophy and empathy to create a mind-linked web for support of all. However, Ruth, 14, has rare talents which set her apart from her comrades and put her in contact with another faraway enclave. There, science and technology have become perverted, resulting in a slave society with the masters surrendering control to the computer. Ruth leads a party to the twisted enclave, where, with Luke, who also has special powers, they subdue the computer and free the slaves.

An example of anti-science fiction, where technology gone wrong is the villain. Although the story is well-paced and holds interest, the adults are too conveniently altruistic, and things go too smoothly to build much dramatic tension. A sequel to the author's *Devil on My Back,* with echoes of an earlier love story between escaped slave Rowan and Lord Tomi of the enclave, this book stands alone but would benefit from knowledge of the earlier book. Slight but passable fare.

### Tony O'Sullivan

SOURCE: A review of *The Dream Catcher,* in *The School Librarian,* Vol. 35, No. 1, February, 1987, pp. 62, 64.

*The Dream Catcher* follows *Devil on My Back* in the sequence describing the world of Arks following the End of Oil. Ruth suffers ostracism from the Group, for her dreams place her outside the Web. The powers of perception are ultimately acknowledged and with the help of Luke, she sets off Outside to discover Ark One. Images of Lord Tomi and Rowan are her loadstones. Telekinesis and telepathy are the weapons at their disposal. Monica Hughes creates a world without villains. Every character is seen with sympathy and understanding. The central tension in the book comes from the clash of Mind and Machine. The two most exciting scenes are the connecting of the rope across the swollen river and the reprogramming of the computer where Luke and Ruth's telepathic powers are strained to the highest pitch.

This is a quietly absorbing and reflective novel which sees itself as part of a longer series in which problems of individual freedom and social good are explored with a degree of freshness.

### Carolyn Phelan

SOURCE: A review of *The Dream Catcher,* in *Booklist,* Vol. 83, No. 15, April 1, 1987, p. 1206.

A science-fiction adventure set in a future culture with a disturbingly plausible pseudohistory, this novel supposes that the only vestiges of civilization left after "the Age of Confusion that followed the End of Oil" are certain domed cities. Called Arks, they were built by a university and the inhabitants were kept separated in the hope that each city would develop its own strengths and that one, at least, would survive. Founded by the humanities faculty and dedicated to communication and understanding, Ark Three has developed a civilization in which each member is linked to the whole community by reaching out psychically to form a cooperative "Web" that is mutually supportive of its members. Ruth is a 14-year-old misfit whose tremendous psychic powers make it difficult for her to mesh with the Web; she actually begins to receive strong signals in the form of vivid dreams from a source outside Ark Three. Ruth and a group of companions set out on a difficult journey beyond their sheltering dome. This is a companion piece to *Devil on My Back,* which takes place in Ark One, a rigid hierarchical society. The messages Ruth has been receiving emanate from Tomi, the hero of the earlier book, and the two protagonists join forces near the end of this novel. Although the pace of *The Dream Catcher* is uneven and the plot development not wholly satisfying, the central characters and ideas are sufficiently involving to hold readers' interest. The unusual use of color in the dust-jacket illustration creates a suitably otherworldly quality. Recommended for libraries with a demand for science fiction or for books with Canadian authorship.

### Zena Sutherland

SOURCE: A review of *The Dream Catcher,* in *Bulletin of the Center for Children's Books,* Vol. 40, No. 11, July-August, 1987, p. 211

In a sequel to *Devil on My Back* an adolescent girl, who feels a misfit in her domed community of the future, runs away. Ruth is caught and learns that the authorities consider her a rare and valuable member of Ark Three (the home dome) and a useful guide, because of her psychic powers, to the culture of Ark One and the rebels who have escaped from its harsh rule. The concept is one familiar to science fantasy buffs: the remnants of our self-destroyed world try again. This meshes nicely with the first book but stands firmly on its own, a compelling narrative with strong characters and a plot that has good structure and momentum.

## 📖 *BLAINE'S WAY* (1986)

### Mary Ainslie Smith

SOURCE: A review of *Blaine's Way,* in *Books in Canada,* Vol. 15, No. 9, December, 1986, p. 18.

*Blaine's Way,* by Monica Hughes, is an ambitious departure for this well-established children's writer, probably best known for her science fiction. This novel spans Blaine's life from early childhood on his parents' unsuccessful farm in Southern Ontario during the Depression of the 1930s through his growing up on his grandparents' farm after he has lost his own home. The climax of the story takes place on the beaches of Normandy where Blaine, having lied his way into the army at the age of 16, finds himself part of the horrors of Dieppe.

Throughout the book, the connecting symbol is the train. The New York Central races past his parents' poor farm bringing to his mother, and thus to Blaine, dreams of escape from poverty and drudgery to the bright lights and excitement of the cities. When Blaine moves to his grandparents' farm, there is only the "Toonerville Trolley," the slow-moving milk run that links the towns and cities in Southern Ontario.

But it moves so relentlessly along its track, rarely bothering to slow down or even whistle for crossings, that it often leaves tragedy behind. As Blaine's grandfather explains, two or three people a year in their area are killed by this train, which has also been nicknamed "The Grim Reaper." Blaine learns many lessons as he grows up about the inexorability of death and disaster, first of all in a rural community and then, more dramatically, in war.

When Blaine finally gets to ride on a train himself, it is to a basic training camp away from what he eventually realizes he loves and values more than bright lights and adventure. Blaine is seriously injured at Dieppe, and in his delirium recalls an accident at home with the old Toonerville Trolley where canning tomatoes were spread like blood all along the line.

One last train brings Blaine back home, damaged but hopeful that he can reestablish a natural order to his life. Hughes's characters seem very real, and her sympathetic writing provides a glimpse of a past that many of her readers can explore further just by asking older relatives and friends.

## Mary Pritchard

SOURCE: A review of *Blaine's Way,* in *Canadian Children's Literature,* No. 46, 1987, pp. 66-7.

*Blaine's Way* is a visit to southwestern Ontario as it was during the Great Depression and World War II. Monica Hughes's award-winning ability to evoke the ambiance of a bygone era plants the reader firmly in narrator Blaine Williams' shoes to experience being both victim and beneficiary of these great historical events. This is not the kind of historical novel in which the author fictionalizes the life of a prominent political decision maker or creates a fictional character who lives within earshot of the great. It is, rather, social history at its best, demonstrating the effects of historical events on the daily lives of those who suffer them, far from the corridors of power.

The central theme of the story, supported by the recurring image of the passing train, is the desire for escape from the oppressive poverty, back-breaking labour, and claustrophobic parochialism. Freedom is realized only ironically in the horrors of Dieppe and in the hero's willing and permanent return to his roots. At this level, *Blaine's Way* is the story of a generation of young rural Canadians who grew up during the Depression, saw the war as a means of escape, and, if they survived, returned to take up their old lives, albeit in a new world.

At age six, when the story begins, Blaine has already been indoctrinated with the notion of escape by his dreaming mother, who is caught between grinding poverty exacerbated by her husband's ineptitude and romantic dreams of a better life in the big cities to which one might escape on the great New York Central trains that daily pass the profitless farm. The first third of the novel is punctuated by the quarrelling of Blaine's parents as his mother progresses from dreams of escape to threats and retractions—"It's all right, Blaine. I didn't mean it. I won't ever leave you"—to the day when she makes good the choric threats and trudges off alone, not to the great train, but to a bus that carries her off to Toronto, never to be heard from again.

If all this sounds depressing, it is, from the crumpled frame of a cheap Christmas sled to the boarding of the windows of the farmhouse on 'Auction Saturday' and Blaine's recognition that "the trains would never stop for the likes of us, for life's failures." Throughout the farm days, the family lives so near the edge of disaster that every event seems to contain the seed of ultimate defeat or death. Even when the potentiality is comic, as when Blaine collapses on the first day of school because his circulation has been cut off by overly-tight garters, the event becomes traumatic, partly because the doctor's fee exhausts the family finances, but also because the

debilitating power of the Depression leaves little of such resources as humour.

The final straw for Blaine's mother, the move to Tillsonburg to live once more dependent upon her parents, brings distinct improvements for Blaine. The extended family revolves around his gentle, generous grandmother (one of the most evocative scenes is her kindness to the vacuum-cleaner salesman) and his tough, realistic grandfather. From this point on, we see Blaine growing through the tribulations of school, the difficulty of assessing his moral responsibility in the death of a friend, the drifting away of his father, and the loss of his dog, to the determination that "I'm going to live, even if it hurts."

In the tobacco fields that have brought new prosperity to the region, Blaine slaves to save the money to get away. Yet, at the same time, he is unwittingly strengthening the ties that will bring him back, relinquishing some of his hard-earned money to help rebuild the barn after a fire, building a solid relationship with his friend Nancy, even seeing the train that carries the Royal Tour of 1937 as "travelling across Ontario, stitching together all the little communities into a single patchwork." His triumphant "I've made it. I'm on the train" as he goes off to war is negated, finally, in the recognition that his escape from home is really an affirmation of it. The "right train", then, is the train that brings him back, wounded but wiser, to where he belongs.

There is a residual sadness in the story. The wound Blaine carries is emotional as well as physical, so while he progresses throughout the novel in understanding his father, his mother remains forever identified with the dream of escape, which for the present-day Blaine has shrunk to a single word—"greed."

## Sarah Ellis

SOURCE: A review of *Blaine's Way,* in *CM: A Reviewing Journal of Canadian Materials for Young People,* Vol. 16, No. 1, January, 1988, pp. 4-5.

In *Blaine's Way* Monica Hughes does something quite innovative in a young adult novel, something I'll wager gave the marketing department at Irwin a few sticky moments. She tells the story of a boy from age six to manhood and even, by using the framework of a flashback, of him as an old man. I think this framework of reminiscence is what makes the book work so well. An author cannot afford to be nostalgic. Nostalgia saps a story of immediacy. But an old man, telling his life story into a tape recorder for his newborn great-grandson, is going to sound nostalgic. And his memories of a boyhood in the dirty thirties, of running away to war, and of coming home disabled are going to be rambling and slightly romantic. Through the device of the flashback Monica Hughes also manages to do something a young adult author can almost never do. She can give advice. Here is Blaine at the end of his life:

Just don't forget that greed leads to suffering; . . . But there's always freedom to change. And now it's yours, my grandchildren, and yours, young Blaine, the first of the next generation. It's in your hands to make this a better world.

In current young adult writing it seems that we are often so concerned with stylishness that we don't risk things like actually imparting wisdom any more. Hughes takes this risk and succeeds.

## David W. Atkinson

SOURCE: A review of *Blaine's Way,* in *Canadian Literature,* No. 116, Spring, 1988, pp. 143-45.

Hughes's novel is a retrospective journey through the childhood and teenage years of her protagonist, Blaine Williams, and centres on the need to temper youthful dreams with the difficult lessons of experience. . . .

*Blaine's Way* also focuses on how growth demands experience in the world. Presented with a tape recorder and a set of empty tapes, an elderly Blaine Williams is asked to provide an account of his boyhood for his first great-grandchild. As a young boy, Blaine is mesmerized by the trains that rush by the northern boundary of his parents' southern Ontario farm: they represent an escape to a world of excitement and riches far removed from the threadbare existence of his parents. At the outset of the novel, Blaine promises himself that he will eventually leave to "find the real world, the world where dreams come true." What Blaine learns is that the real world of dreams is not necessarily better than what he already has.

This lesson is a difficult one to learn, and most certainly Blaine experiences his share of adversity. First, Blaine's mother flees to the big city to pursue her own dreams, and then his father leaves to work in town, no longer able to face constant reminders of his failure as a farmer and a husband. Blaine must come to grips with these losses, although it is not a matter of him having to struggle alone. Throughout, Blaine is supported and comforted by his loving grandparents and good friends, one of whom he discovers means far more to him than just being a friend. Always, however, Blaine retains his insatiable appetite for the beyond, which romantic novels and trips to the Canadian National Exhibition will not satisfy.

When war comes, it presents the opportunity for which Blaine has long been waiting. Lying about his age, Blaine enlists in the Canadian Army, which, he discovers, is drearier in many ways than anything he has yet known. He also experiences the deaths of friends, and, when his own day of glory finally comes at Dieppe, the romance of dreams is shattered by the pain and ugliness of war. Home becomes the place of dreams, and, as one of the few survivors, Blaine is fortunate to have his dream become a reality. . . .

[However] Hughes's book is not so focused, although her message is still unmistakable: the bigger and better things in life are not necessarily the goals for which one should strive, and too often we fail to realize what is valuable until we are in danger of losing it. Commonplace though these ideals might be, they have particular significance for a generation of young people enjoying a standard of living which Hughes's young protagonist would never dream possible. . . .

[Also] *Blaine's Way,* . . . sometimes suffers from a sentimentality incongruous with its realism, although this sentimentality might be forgiven in that the narrator is an elderly man looking back over his life. And the final page of the novel is just too obtrusive, as Blaine talks of the "Grim Reaper," and provides some last-minute preaching for his great-grandson.

## LOG JAM (1987; British edition as *Spirit River,* 1988)

## Patty Lawlor

SOURCE: "Another Swift, Sure Novel from Monica Hughes," in *Books for Young People,* Vol. 1, No. 1, February, 1987, p. 4.

A new Monica Hughes book is always a ray of bright light. Not only does it guarantee a good, thoughtful read but, for a moment, it answers the questions that recur at the end of each of her books. What will her *next* book be like? Will the action take place in this world or another world? Will it be set in the past, the present, or the future?

*Log Jam,* Hughes's latest book, is consistent with her overall body of work. Her empathy with young people, her belief in the rights, strengths, and inherent goodness of individuals, and her passion for nature in general and the western Canadian wilderness in particular are strongly evident. While it does not break new ground in terms of either plot or setting, *Log Jam* returns to themes explored in her earlier contemporary titles, such as *The Ghost Dance Caper, Hunter in the Dark,* and *My Name Is Paula Popowich!*

*Log Jam* has a dual story-line. In alternating chapters, Isaac Manyfeathers and Lenora Rydz, young people in vastly different circumstances, both struggle with the issues of freedom and choice in their lives. Isaac is a 17-year-old native boy on the run from a medium-security prison where he has been serving time for his unwitting participation in a warehouse break-in. On his own and down on his luck, Isaac looks to his roots for a second chance. He sets off into the wilderness on a twofold quest: to return to his grandmother, with whom he spent his first five years, and to seek his spirit in the ways of his ancestors.

Lenora, by contrast, is a 14-year-old Torontonian newly arrived in Alberta and also, in her own way, on the run from a situation: she must accept a stepfather and two older stepbrothers into her life. Feeling alienated in the midst of her new family, Lenora's unhappiness is further aggravated by their close living quarters and their overexposure to one another on a camping trip.

The two story threads are woven together in the novel's three final chapters. Lenora is involved in a canoeing accident and is rescued by Isaac. But Isaac's motive is neither heroic nor altruistic. Disoriented from fasting for several days, he perceives Lenora as a spirit sent to him in answer to his quest. Once she regains consciousness, Lenora realizes that her rescuer is none other than the escaped convict that her family had been warned about by the forest wardens. When she convinces Isaac that she is not a "sun child," she is even more horrified to discover he is unwilling to let her go, since she can lead the authorities to him.

In the long term and as a result of their encounter, both Isaac and Lenora take stock of themselves. Both see clearly the extent to which they can take control of certain aspects of their lives and how important it is to deal responsibly with the choices available to them. The log jam of the title is significant not only as the physical obstruction encountered by Lenora's canoe but also as an emblem of psychological blockage.

Hughes's style is swift and sure, with descriptive passages deftly interwoven with the story's action. The account of Lenora's canoe trip down the river with her stepbrother, Denis, is full of excitement. An earlier incident dealing with Lenora's first attempts at fly-fishing is briefer but no less vivid in the telling. Particularly enjoyable are Hughes's wry comments, which so aptly depict a teenager's perspective. At the Rocky Mountain House Historical Site, for example: "They parked in the neat parking lot, went correctly through the orientation centre, and stared at models of what would be there when the archaeologists got around to finding it."

Both Isaac and Lenora are well-developed and sympathetic individuals. With Lenora's help, it is clear that stepbrother Denis will shape up, but big brother Brian, an overbearing know-it-all, is likely beyond redemption. The characters of Lenora's mother and stepfather are not nearly so successful as those of the young people, and their reactions at the story's conclusion are unsatisfying. But these are minor complaints about a high-calibre new work from a writer of considerable stature.

## Mary Ainslie Smith

SOURCE: A review of *Log Jam*, in *Books in Canada*, Vol. 16, No. 6, August-September, 1987, pp. 34-6.

In *Log Jam* the two main characters start out on their journeys separately and then come together, the fate of each depending on the other. Isaac Manyfeathers, a 17-

year-old, convicted of aiding in a robbery, has escaped from his detention centre into the Alberta foothills.

Convinced that he should deprive himself of food and drink like his ancestors on a spirit quest, he plans to travel back to his grandmother's isolated home, where he spent his early childhood before his mother took him away to the city and the loneliness of the white man's world.

At the same time, 14-year-old Leonora is having the most miserable time of her life on a camping trip with her mother, her stepfather of a few weeks, and her two new stepbrothers. A yearly camping trip has been a tradition for the three males, and Leonora and her mother are along on sufferance and very clearly in the way. Leonora enlists the younger brother, Denis, as an ally and the two of them sneak away from the others and attempt a white-water canoe trip with disastrous results. When a hallucinating Isaac finds and rescues the injured, half-drowned Leonora, he believes that she is the Sun Child, the answer to his spirit quest. The transition back to their real, contemporary world is not easy for either of them. . . .

Hughes shows up clearly as [an] experienced and polished writer. She is an expert at setting up tensions among her characters and creating in a few lines of dialogue all the complex levels of rivalry, frustration, love, and hate that can exist within a family. Her parallel plots develop surely until the two protagonists, Leonora and Isaac, come together in what we feel is an entirely believable and inevitable fashion.

## Marcus Crouch

SOURCE: A review of *Spirit River*, in *The Junior Bookshelf*, Vol. 52, No. 3, June, 1988, p. 158.

Methuen's new 'Teen Collection' gets off to a good start with a thoughtful and exciting novel by a distinguished Canadian writer. Monica Hughes has been best known for her science fiction. Here, although there are esoteric elements, is a story about real people sorting out their problems in the modern world.

Problems there certainly are. One protagonist, Isaac Manyfeathers, is a convict on the run. The other, Leonora Rydz, is a young teenager whose mother has just made what appears to be an injudicious second marriage, presenting her daughter with an unwanted stepfather and two new brothers. Ostensibly to help the young people get to know one another (actually, it would seem, so that mother can do her share of the driving and the men-folk can enjoy uninterrupted fishing and canoeing) the Mathiesons and Lenora have gone on a camping holiday in the Alberta forests. This only confirms Lenora's worst fears about her family. Partly to have a little fun of her own, partly to get back at her stepfather and his selfish elder son, Lenora persuades the younger and more amenable boy to go canoeing with her. The canoe is wrecked and Lenora disappears, feared drowned. Here the paths of Lenora and Isaac meet, and each finds in the other a partial solution to dilemmas. Stepfathers, especially when they are as bossy and capable as Harry, have their uses: they may not even be so bad in other ways. Lenora has learnt a little tolerance; Isaac, back in jail, has found a glimmer of hope for the future.

The absorbing story is drawn in natural colours, not in black and white. There are no baddies. Even Mom is not all fool, and we learn to sympathize with her, if not to love her. The Indian boy's mystical quest for his home is described with great delicacy. His visions may be caused by exhaustion and hunger, they may be real: it is enough that we should understand him and wish him well in his three steps to reality (as the book's motto has it). The writing is excellent. Without the assistance of elaborate descriptive writing, we see this wild country and share in its beauty. Above all it is a story of young people and of the meeting of cultures, and this fundamental theme is conveyed with great conviction. A fine novel, and not just for adolescent girls.

**Roderick McGillis**

SOURCE: A review of *Log Jam,* in *Canadian Literature,* No. 117, Summer, 1988, pp. 151-54.

Monica Hughes's **Log Jam** is a book for adolescents. Here Hughes returns to a contemporary setting to deal with the problems adolescents encounter in growing up—divorce and remarriage of parents, cultural identity, the pull of urban and rural values, and what it means to be free in a world that threatens and squeezes human opportunity—themes and settings she has dealt with in such books as **The Ghost Dance Caper** (1978), **Hunter in the Dark** (1982), and **My Name is Paula Popowich!** (1983). **Log Jam** has both the virtues and the weaknesses of these earlier books, but it also has a more sophisticated structure and a willingness to enter the consciousness of adults as well as adolescents.

Hughes's weakness is a familiar one to reader's of novels for young adults: heavy-handedness. Lenora's stepfather, Harry, appears too insufferably straight, too organized and informative and unsympathetic. His cool explanation as to why lumber companies ought to "exploit" the forests more aggressively and his calculating use of his wife strike us as too unpleasant for us to accept Lenora's change of attitude to him at the end. Hazel, Lenora's mother, is also presented in the extreme: nervous and weak. In theme as in character, Hughes is quick to give the reader more than enough help. The book modulates nicely with images of prison, entrapment, and immovability. Perhaps Hughes thinks her young reader incapable of understanding these images, for at the end she has Lenora say just what the book has been trying to show: *"Maybe all of us are alone most of the time. Each one in his or her own prison."* Emotions can be jammed up, like the log in the river that stopped Lenora's canoe, and until something sets

that log free there will be no connection with others, no passage to understanding of others.

The strengths of **Log Jam** are fine writing, a willingness to show toughness of vision, and a structural complexity that will challenge young readers. The fine writing is especially evident in the sections of the book that deal with Isaac, the Indian boy who has escaped from a prison camp. His feel for the wilderness and his attachment to the old ways and legends of his people allow Hughes to show her ability at poetic writing that captures the spirit of the wild and primitive. At the same time, Hughes does not grow sentimental over this lost boy in the woods. His fierce desire for freedom leaves him gaunt and desperate so that when he meets Lenora his frantic, near crazed, attempt to keep her from signalling her rescuers is believable and frightening. Hughes also manages the bringing of these two together deftly, interweaving chapters devoted to Isaac with chapters devoted to Lenora and her family until the two come together in chapter 9, on the third day of the adventure. For both Isaac and Lenora, their meeting completes a rite of passage that leads to acceptance and understanding.

**Margery Fisher**

SOURCE: A review of *Spirit River,* in *Growing Point,* Vol. 27, No. 2, July, 1988, pp. 4999-5002.

Journeys actual and spiritual make a close web in **Spirit River,** with the accidental conjunction of a Canadian Indian youth and a half Polish Canadian girl providing a strong emotional element. Isaac escapes from a detention centre to which an unfortunate alliance with crooks had brought him, after deciding that his mother's life in the modern world suits him less well than the tribal traditions in which his grandmother had brought him up. While he is trying to find his way back to her in the foothills and forests of the Alberta Rockies, Leonora Rydz is enduring a camping holiday in hostile proximity to her mother's second husband, fussy Harry, and his two teenage sons, disturbed by her father's desertion of her and perplexed by her mother's subservience to a man who seems impervious to anything but fishing and canoeing. In a state of angry confusion she persuades her stepbrother Denis to steal a canoe and join her in an exploratory trip on the river; they capsize in rapids, Denis loses her and returns in terror to camp and the girl is saved by Isaac who, in a hallucinatory state while starving in the search for his 'spirit', takes her for the Daughter of the Sun. The clash of cultures and the instant sympathy between two lonely young people make a strong impact on a story with an impressive craggy, remote setting in which Isaac's mystical experiences are entirely credible and moving.

**Shelia Allen**

SOURCE: A review of *Spirit River,* in *School Librarian,* Vol. 36, No. 3, August, 1988, p. 108.

There are two entirely separate stories in this book, told in alternate chapters until the paths of the two central characters cross. Isaac Manyfeathers, an Indian boy, escapes from a detention centre working party and endeavours to find his way through the vast Canadian woods to his grandmother's cottage. He believes native spirits will help him, and he obeys their imagined 'rules' and goes without eating or drinking for four days. Lenora Rydz is on a camping holiday in the same woods. Her mother is hoping that Lenora will accept her new, well-organised stepfather and two stepbrothers and that they will become one happy family. Lenora finds her younger stepbrother an ally and a good companion. They embark on a secret canoeing trip which ends in disaster. Lenora is swept away and Denis is left to face the family. Isaac finds Lenora and each has to come to terms with the other. At the end of the book both are facing the future optimistically, even though Isaac is in prison. These stories are too disparate to be interwoven happily. The problems and situations of the characters cannot be paralleled to make a satisfying plot.

**Linda Newberry**

SOURCE: A review of *Spirit River,* in *Books for Keeps,* No. 60, January, 1990, p. 10.

Set in the foothills of the Rocky Mountains, **Spirit River** links the stories of Isaac Manyfeathers, a native escapee from a detention centre, and Lenora, a teenage girl on a camping trip with her mother and newly-acquired stepfather and brothers. The friction of the thrown-together family contrasts with Isaac's isolation as he follows his spiritual promptings to join his grandmother. After a canoeing accident, Isaac rescues Lenora but then refuses to part with her, seeing her as a 'Sun Child' and good omen for his quest.

Adventure-story elements combine with strong characterisation and sense of place to make this a moving and engrossing book.

📖 *LITTLE FINGERLING: A JAPANESE FOLK TALE* **(retold by Hughes, 1989)**

**Adele Ashby**

SOURCE: A review of *Little Fingerling,* in *Quill & Quire,* Vol. 55, No. 9, September, 1989, p. 22.

Any new book by Monica Hughes is worth paying attention to. Having established a fine reputation as a writer of speculative, contemporary, and historical fiction, she is now adding folklore to her repertoire.

*Little Fingerling* is a traditional Japanese variant of Tom Thumb, without King Arthur and the unhappy ending. "Once upon a time, in old Japan, there lived a childless couple," it begins. One day their prayers are answered in the form of a son so small he is only as long as his

mother's thumb. Hence, he is called Issun Boshi, or Little Fingerling. He only grows to the length of his father's longest finger, but he is not lacking in a sense of adventure. At 15, he takes leave of his loving parents to make his way in the world, armed with a sword in the form of his mother's sewing needles in a scabbard made of a hollow straw. After several adventures, he joins the house of a nobleman, learns to read and write, and becomes attached to the nobleman's beautiful daughter, Plum Blossom. After saving her from two ferocious demons, he finds a lucky mallet, which, when struck on the ground, grants wishes. Plum Blossom makes use of the mallet, Little Fingerling vanishes, and in his place appears a handsome samurai warrior. Joined by his parents, they live happily ever after.

Hughes's retelling is entirely in keeping with the story—simple and dignified—as are Brenda Clark's full-colour illustrations. Warmth radiates from the faces of the human characters, and Clark's demons are suitably fierce. A successful collaboration.

**Publishers Weekly**

SOURCE: A review of *Little Fingerling,* in *Publishers Weekly,* Vol. 239, No. 36, August 10, 1992, p. 70.

Good things often come in small packages, according to this Japanese folktale. As the answer to his childless parents' prayers, Issun Boshi—"Little Fingerling"—is born. Although by 15 he is only "the height of his father's longest finger," the determined teen leaves his family's farm to seek his fortune in Kyoto. After a brief stint as a comb painter, Issun Boshi is welcomed into the home of a nobleman where he becomes enamoured of the beautiful Plum Blossom. The young woman recognizes a brave warrior trapped in the small body and the couple eventually becomes a perfect fit when they defeat two monsters and obtain a wish-granting mallet. With a nod to the Oriental flair for economy Hughes's phrasing and sentence structure create an air of formality from simple vocabulary. The plot's grand scope, however, detracts from the drama and prevents the reader from becoming more emotionally involved. Clark's pencil and watercolor illustrations are reminiscent of Japanese woodcuts, though her human figures are more animated. The white-capped river waves, thatched roof huts and richly hued kimonos all help to define an Eastern-flavored slice of time and place.

**Lauralyn Persson**

SOURCE: A review of *Little Fingerling,* in *School Library Journal,* Vol. 39, No. 4, April, 1993, p. 111.

This familiar Japanese folktale, a cross between "Tom Thumb" and "David and Goliath," is given elegant treatment in this attractive picture book. Hughes's telling is leisurely and formal, with a ceremonial tone that suits the material. She doesn't spare gruesome details, either;

the battle between Issun Boshi and the giants is quite graphic, in a way that may make even second-grade boys say, "Oh, gross!" In the end, romance prevails. Clark's watercolors are entirely appropriate for the text. The pictures, each of which is bordered with a delicate line and a touch of yellow, are simply and effectively composed. They are realistically done, with soft, true colors; expressive characters; and imaginative use or perspective to show the vulnerability of the tiny hero. Like the text, the pictures do well with both the beautiful (the kindly parents, the lovely Plum Blossom) and the gruesome (the satisfyingly horrible giants). *Little Fingerling* is for a slightly older audience than Morimoto's *The Inch Boy.* Both books are lovely, and make a good contrast to one another.

## THE PROMISE (1989; U.S. edition, 1992)

### Frieda Wishinsky

SOURCE: A review of *The Promise,* in *Quill & Quire,* Vol. 56, No. 1, January, 1990, p. 16.

Sequels do not often achieve the power, fluency, and characterizations of the original. *The Promise,* Monica Hughes's sequel to *Sandwriter,* is an exception. An engrossing tale of love and commitment, it stands fully on its own.

Set in the mythical desert kingdom of Rokam, *The Promise* tells the story of Rania, princess of Malan, who, in fulfillment of a promise, is sent by her parents to live with Sandwriter, an aging priestess with mysterious powers. For four years Rania lives like a hermit, her days filled with observation and learning but few comforts. Eventually the isolation and harsh existence become too much to bear and Sandwriter wisely allows Rania to go into the world. Obtaining work in a bustling seaside inn, Rania is reunited with Atbin, the young man who had escorted her to Sandwriter years ago, and they fall in love. Now Rania knows she must make a choice. Will she live the life of an ordinary woman or return to Sandwriter and become her successor?

Hughes's use of vivid imagery paints an illuminating picture of Rania's world. The stark beauty of the desert is a constant and haunting backdrop to the unfolding events. But more than merely drawing us into an exotic environment, Hughes gives us a sensitive portrait of a young girl who must make an extraordinary choice—one that could affect not only her life but the lives of others.

### Fran Newman

SOURCE: A review of *The Promise,* in *CM: Canadian Materials for Schools and Libraries,* Vol. 18, No. 3, May, 1990, p. 128.

Monica Hughes is a master writer and *The Promise* shows this. The planet on which *The Promise* takes place has two continents named Komilant and Kamalant and there is a great desert and an oasis called Ahman, where beasts similar to camels but seemingly more reptilian called kroklyns are used for transportation. Clothing, food and houses are of the ancient Middle East.

Atbin, blond, blue-eyed, sixteen, son of the elder of the oasis village of Roshan, is given the task of travelling to Malan, the capital of the two continents, with a gift for the Princess Rania on the occasion of her tenth birthday. Sandwriter, ancient priestess who holds the whole planet in her hands, has honoured Atbin with this task.

"Sleeping Beauty" came to mind at the scene of the birthday party as Queen Antia shows her distress before and during the presentation of Atbin's gift—the summons from Sandwriter. Princess Rania is to leave the safety and loving security of her home and travel to live with Sandwriter, where she is to be trained to become her successor.

Like any young girl wrenched from her environment, Rania experiences shock, disbelief, anger and grief. But once the transition to the Great Dune of Roshan and Sandwriter has been made, once the severity and loneliness of this new life have been accepted, Rania draws upon the strength of being a princess.

Alone with Sandwriter, Rania finds her former life becoming dull in memory until, years later, Atbin, bringing food for the two, leaves Rania a doll he has made. This precipitates a crisis in the girl. Torn between her "duty" and her femaleness (a strong attraction to Atbin), Rania is sent away by the enigmatic Sandwriter to sort out her feelings. During her stay in a nearby village, Rania experiences her gifts and makes the difficult decision.

Rania is a very believable character. Sandwriter is wonderfully old, wise and powerful. Female readers will have much to ponder on the direction of Rania's life and of their own.

### Li Stark

SOURCE: A review of *The Promise,* in *School Library Journal,* Vol. 38, No. 6, June, 1992, pp. 115-16.

Twelve years before this story opens, in *Sandwriter,* Princess Antia of Kamilant and Jodril, son of the chieftan of the desert kingdom of Roshan, pledged their first child as apprentice to Sandwriter, an old woman who is revered as the mystical spirit of the kingdom. As *The Promise* opens, it is Princess Rania's tenth birthday, and time for the pledge to be fulfilled. Atbin, a young man from a desert village, is sent to escort her. At each step of their journey, items are discarded, until she arrives at Sandwriter's desert dwelling with all vestiges of her former life stripped away. For four years, living austerely, she learns the lessons of the desert, gradually forgetting her family and friends. One day she sees

Atbin leaving their daily food, and her interest in the outside world is rekindled. Realizing she has demanded too much too soon, Sandwriter sends Rania to spend a year in the town of Monar, at the end of which she may choose an ordinary life or to return to the desert. As the year progresses, she misses and values her desert existence more and more, and, when the time for choosing comes, she returns to it and Sandwriter. Not as fast placed or as obvious in its message as some of Hughes's other works, *The Promise* nevertheless has much to offer thoughtful readers.

### Kirkus Reviews

SOURCE: A review of *The Promise,* in *Kirkus Reviews,* Vol. LX, No. 12, June 15, 1992, p. 778.

Honoring her parents' promise, ten-year-old Princess Rania is taken from her lush palace and thrust into the arid desert home of Sandwriter, the powerful shaman whose magic is essential to survival in their world. When she's 14—wiser, stronger, but still ambivalent about dedicating her life to magic—Sandwriter sends her to choose her future, a choice made more difficult by the love of Atbin, the desert youth who took her to Sandwriter four years ago. Conscience wins: Rania decides that her responsibility to her people outweighs her personal happiness.

The jacket shows Atbin and Rania perched far forward on a two-legged desert beast that, if the laws of gravity hold, is about to go snout-down in the sand; but this is fantasy, so the beast lumbers on. It's not a bad metaphor for the book: lots of suspension of disbelief required. That said, young readers will find some convincing details, while tales of selflessness still have their place. There may even be a subtext about the harsh price society exacts from women who choose wider responsibilities than love and family.

### Deborah Abbott

SOURCE: A review of *The Promise,* in *Booklist,* Vol. 89, No. 4, October 15, 1992, pp. 417-18.

In this sequel to **Sandwriter,** a fairy-tale-like promise sets the course for an engrossing story. At the marriage of Jodril and Antia, which joined two countries, the newlyweds had promised that their first child would be given to Sandwriter, a mysterious goddess-ruler of the continent of Roshan. On their daughter Rania's tenth birthday, much to the distress of Queen Antia, who had not understood the covenant, Sandwriter calls the girl to begin her apprenticeship in an ethereal world far away from all human contact. After instructing Rania for four years, Sandwriter lets her protegee return to a human community for one year to allow the young girl a last chance to discover if becoming the next Sandwriter is the right future for her. Strange beasts, a barren land, an arid climate, and a powerful female ruler enrich a

fast-paced story that deftly explores an unusual world, perfectly meshing the human with the otherworldly condition. Part romance and part coming-of-age, Hughes's novel, which stands alone or as a sequel, will have wide appeal, although readers of fantasy fiction will probably be the most intrigued.

### INVITATION TO THE GAME (1990; U.S. edition, 1991)

### Margery Fisher

SOURCE: A review of *Invitation to the Game,* in *Growing Point,* Vol. 30, No. 2, July, 1991, pp. 5543-48.

A move to a fictional future world means an increased responsibility for the background of adventure; a balance must be struck between invented, unfamiliar details of place and even of people and a certain continuity with the reader's own world. *Invitation to the Game* takes us to 2154, to a robot economy where work has ceased to exist for the citizens. However, the work ethic survives, in strange forms. Although people are boxed in designated areas to prevent conspiracy, groups of subversives have set up house in a disused warehouse and are taking their own individual ways to occupy their energies while evading detection by the helicopters of the secret police. One particular group of young people apply to enter the Game, a treasure hunt activity invented by the government in which simulated adventure promoted by drugs affects Karen (a geologist), Paul (an historian), Rich (son of a psychiatrist) and other associates in various ways. Survival in marsh and forest with adverse weather, scant food and the need to reinvent essential items like salt, fire, paper and shelter, end in a precarious but thriving new world. The scheme of the complex narrative is positive and clear, the incidents in the story exciting and varied, the adventure clichés (lurking animals, dark woods, desert torment) create a believable future in which work is not a burden but a prize. The reference to our own time will not be missed by attentive readers of the latest piece of speculative fiction by an author who understands how to make a metaphor from fantasy.

### Kirkus Reviews

SOURCE: A review of *Invitation to the Game,* in *Kirkus Reviews,* Vol. LIX, No. 14, July 15, 1991, pp. 931-32.

The choice for high-school graduates in 2154: to live on the dole or become colonists. Lisse and her friends are bright, caring young people, but there are no jobs. Thrown together by a computer, they forge a fortress from an abandoned warehouse and learn to live with one another, avoiding the streets' drugs and hedonism. Suddenly, there comes an invitation to the Game: shared computer-induced experiences in a wild, virgin wilderness. Always, when injury threatens, the computer pulls them back—until the last time, when they discover that they have actually emigrated to another part of the galaxy. Using their individual and group skills, they start to conquer the new planet, ultimately meeting and inter-marrying with other groups of colonists.

Hughes, a facile, experienced writer, knows how to keep a story moving. She conveys a real sense of social threat; the reader cares about the group's small victories over the mean streets. Unfortunately, she telegraphs her punch-es: the new planet may astonish the characters, but it won't surprise the reader. The details of environment and skills to cope with it are adroitly done; but the hard technology—e.g., computer-induced reality and painless, undetected transport across light-years—are less convinc-ing, while the tidy conclusion has a perfunctory feel. A mixed effort, but entertaining.

### *The Junior Bookshelf*

SOURCE: A review of *Invitation to the Game,* in *The Junior Bookshelf,* Vol. 55, No. 4, August, 1991, p. 186.

This is Monica Hughes's umpteenth novel and continues her excursions into the fantasy worlds of science fiction for senior readers. We are in the future—the 22nd cen-tury A.D.—and meet Lisse and her friends. They com-plete their schooling as the book opens (the domestic robots strip the beds in the dormitory) and a bleak future appears to stretch ahead. Everything is devoted to 'lei-sure years' and it seems the youngsters have little to live for. However, they arrive at their DA (designated area) and endeavour to find out about The Game. Eventually they receive an invitation, and we are soon into a story detailing various travels and adventures.

The book is a compulsive read. There is pace, energy, and surprise. A considerable reading experience for teen-agers. The setting in which the youngsters find them-selves may not be an attractive landscape or world, but there is a sense of exploration and curiosity which gives the book an optimistic balance. Well written, taut, clev-er, inventive . . . and above all highly readable.

### Li Stark

SOURCE: A review of *Invitation to the Game,* in *School Library Journal,* Vol. 37, No. 9, September, 1991, p. 281.

It is the year 2154. Unemployment is rife, many work-ers having been replaced by robots, and teenagers, as they graduate from school, are either assigned jobs or an unemployed status. Lisse and seven of her classmates are relegated to a DA (Designated Area) for unemploy-ment together. As they begin to explore the area, they hear about something called The Game, and eventually receive an invitation to participate. By computer simu-lation, they experience life in an unfamiliar, wild set-ting. After several sessions, the game intensifies. Sev-eral days into a particularly difficult situation, they re-alize it is no longer a game, but reality, and when,

gazing at the night sky, they see no familiar constella-tions, they know they are no longer on Earth. The future Hughes creates is a logical extension of the disasters of the present day. The characters are likable individuals, each with traits or skills that complement the others. As they grow in ability to work cooperatively, readers will easily accept their selection to populate a new planet. Life there is primitive, but they succeed in making not only useful, but also beautiful necessities of daily life; there are many satisfactions for these latter-day Robin-son Crusoes. This is both a first-rate adventure/survival story and a cautionary tale.

### Sally Estes

SOURCE: A review of *Invitation to the Game,* in *Booklist,* Vol. 88, No. 2, September 15, 1991, p. 141.

It's April 2154. Graduating high school in her highly robotic society, 16-year-old Lisse and seven of her friends find themselves unemployed and assigned to live on welfare in a DA (designated area of the city) with noth-ing to do, despised or ignored by the drab workers, and monitored by the thought police. Finding a vacant ware-house and scrounging workers' castoffs to furnish it, the group settles down to endure a boring life, unable to leave their DA or to get work. Then they receive formal invitations from the government to participate in the Game, which is rumored to be like a treasure hunt in a special place where clues help the searchers move on to another level. On their appointed day, they report to the Game Master and soon find themselves in a vast, empty desert—or are they really experiencing a typical hypnot-ic scenario? During intermittent visits (by invitation only) to the desert, they hone their survival and cooperative skills, always being immediately recalled to their couch-es in the government building when one of them is hurt or in danger—until that final journey when they are not brought back. While the plot flags at times, and charac-terizations, for the most part, lack dimension, Hughes's vivid picture of a society that employs few human work-ers because robots take care of all needs gives one pause as does the society's solution to the overpopulation of nonworkers. Thought- and discussion-provoking fare.

### Roger Sutton

SOURCE: A review of *Invitation to the Game,* in *Bul-letin of the Center for Children's Books,* Vol. 45, No. 2, October, 1991, p. 40.

It's overpopulated, robotized 2154, and Lisse and her friends find themselves in a scenario familiar to most of their fellow school graduates: permanent, subsidized unemployment, and restriction to one small, scary area of a city. But while attempting to build a makeshift life in an old loft apartment, the group hears enticing rumors about "The Game," and soon an invitation arrives, of-fering a chance to join in. While seated in cozy chairs in a secret government building, Lisse and the six others find themselves transported to a deserted landscape for a while, only returning when Lisse has an accident while the group is exploring. Intrigued, the friends go back several times more, arguing whether or not the landscape is real or some kind of electronic or mental manipulation. Both the bleakness of the realistic setting and the wilderness of The Game are convincing, as are the arguments and cooperation among the friends. This is a natural for both fantasy gamers and fans of survival stories, and the eventual revelation of the nature of The Game is surprising but well-prepared.

**Tony Manna**

SOURCE: A review of *Invitation to the Game,* in *Voice of Youth Advocates,* Vol. 14, No. 5, December, 1991, p. 323.

While Hughes anticipates the formation of a more humane world order at the conclusion of this unsettling tale, she also provides a brief glimpse of the social and economic conditions of our own time in history, which could possibly allow an unsavory social climate and ruined environment to develop in the 21st century, the era in which she has set her story. The tale she tells is both a bitter indictment of careless technological progress, unbridled governmental control, human aggression, and an enticing prophesy about human resilience and courage. At the center of the tale is a small group of disaffected and talented young people, all of them recent graduates of a sterile and regimented government school, who, having been denied a career by the authorities at large, must live out their days within the ranks of the Unemployeds, a dread caste of pariahs that is virtually quarantined in squalid urban ghettos where only the most savvy can survive with even a semblance of peace and comfort. Once they settle into the monotony and tension of their predictably strident environment, these youngsters happen upon a glint of hope in the form of a mysterious life-rate game whereby they are transported to some unidentifiable pastoral place. At first, these occasional treks merely provide them with a pleasant respite from the grim realities of everyday life, but when they are carried to the farthest reaches of this universe, the challenges they must face grow more rigorous until they discover that all the preceding journeys constituted an initiation rite that has prepared them for their destiny: to build a new and peaceful society in a far distant galaxy. In the final, hopeful moments of the novel, Hughes shows these youngsters at work, determined to develop a more equitable and sane world with others their own age, who-have been similarly transported.

What prevents this intriguing tale from reaching its full power is Hughes's penchant for hastily drawing a scene and providing only the barest outline for potentially appealing characters. She seems so set on exploring the themes behind the action that she rushes the plot forward without giving adequate attention to the pressures of the moment and her young characters' responses to the enigmas they encounter over time and space. It's as though we are working through the first draft of what could be a full and rich and a truly moving story about the problems that must be solved if we expect there to be a livable world in the future—on the planet we now inhabit.

## THE CRYSTAL DROP (1992; U.S. edition, 1993)

**Celia Barker Lottridge**

SOURCE: A review of *The Crystal Drop,* in *Quill & Quire,* Vol. 58, No. 3, March, 1992, pp. 66-7.

Megan, 14, and Ian, 10, are prairie farm children, living not far from the foothills of the Rockies. The year is 2011; there is a severe drought, and water is nearly gone. Most people have left the prairies; social structures and technology have collapsed. There is no mail, no telephones, no electricity, no towns, no schools. The children's father is long gone, and when their mother dies, the two have little choice but to set out across the burning land toward the mountains in the hope of finding their uncle.

Most of this engrossing novel—told in evocative language which makes the intense heat, the thirst, and the fear felt by Meg and Ian very real to the reader—is taken up with the journey. The children must find enough food and water to survive, and also deal with an odd assortment of people. The most puzzling encounter is with four teenaged Peigan Indian boys who live in the remnants of the Head-Smashed-In Buffalo Jump World Heritage Site. The boys give Megan an abrupt history lesson in how the white settlers ruined the land. They also provide food and shelter, but the food turns out to be Ian's beloved dog made into fried meat and gravy. Other encounters are less ambiguous. There are survivalists with guard dogs and guns, and a kindly and religious old couple who give help when it is needed most.

This is compelling reading. Megan's determination to be "hard" and responsible is convincing, as is Ian's ability to take action when he must. However, the framework around the central story is very unclear. What is happening in the rest of Canada and the world while the prairies become an ungoverned wasteland? Even the question Ian asks early in the story—how come his mom and dad didn't leave when everyone else did—is never answered. The ending, too, is sketchy. Megan and Ian find their uncle, who is a member of a briefly described "Gaia" community dedicated to healing the earth through responsible agricultural practices. The children find a home, but the reader is left with an overpowering image of desolation in which small bits of hope disappear like scattered raindrops in a parched land.

**Chris Sherman**

SOURCE: A review of *The Crystal Drop,* in *Booklist,* Vol. 89, No. 14, March 15, 1993, pp. 1313-14.

Megan doesn't believe there are any options left. Deserted by her father seven months before, and with her mother and the baby now dead, she is responsible for her younger brother, Ian. Leaving the farm couldn't be any worse than dying slowly as the well dries up and the food supply runs out. The year is 2011, the drought seems to have gone on forever, and the only chance for survival is to reach an uncle whom Megan believes has established a commune in the Canadian Rockies, nearly 50 miles away. With only the faintest hope of finding him, Megan and Ian set out across the barren plains. Readers won't be able to put Hughes's survival adventure down. The heat and devastated landscape, the survivalists determined to protect their water at all costs, and Megan and Ian's strained relationship are so realistically and believably portrayed that readers may forget that this is actually science fiction.

**Margaret A. Chang**

SOURCE: A review of *The Crystal Drop,* in *School Library Journal,* Vol. 39, No. 6, June, 1993, pp. 106-07.

By the year 2011, global warming and an enlarged hole in the ozone have turned southern Alberta, once a fertile plain, into a burning desert. Adolescent Megan has grown up watching her neighbors leave and her family's water supply dwindle. Abandoned by her father, she harbors few illusions about human or natural generosity. After her mother dies in childbirth, she and her 10-year-old brother, Ian, leave their home and walk west, toward Lundbreck Falls in the foothills of the Canadian Rockies. There, in the last years of the 20th century, her Uncle Greg helped found a community called Gaia. Drawn by her vision of tumbling water, Megan coaxes and bullies Ian across the ravaged landscape. Every human they meet is a competitor for the scarce resources, from the bitter descendants of the Blackfoot people to survivalists who guard their water with bullets. Readers share Megan's growing horror as she begins to comprehend the enormity of the ecological disaster that is her legacy, and admire her grit as she struggles on. While the trumpet of doom sounds a bit too shrill, and the story ends abruptly, the flaws of this compelling survival story are outweighed by colorful writing, believable characters, and a palpable landscape.

*Kirkus Reviews*

SOURCE: A review of *The Crystal Drop,* in *Kirkus Reviews,* Vol. LXI, No. 11, June 1, 1993, p. 722.

When their mother dies in childbirth, teenaged Megan and her younger brother Ian flee their arid farm—ecological catastrophe has made Canada's Alberta a desert—and, lured by the promise of abundant water, head for the Rockies, braving an array of natural hazards and encountering only a few people (some kind, some not). Setting her story less than 20 years in the

future, Hughes creates a barren, sun-blasted landscape marked by old barbed wire fences and decrepit farmhouses, tumbleweed and hordes of grasshoppers. Unlike Ian, Megan remembers cars, school, and electricity; now, there's neither government nor even rudimentary communication with the outside world. Megan and Ian are strong, believable characters who come through many dangers and reach a haven at the end, but the author's bleak vision of the near future is more vivid than their adventures.

## A HANDFUL OF SEEDS (1993)

**Sarah Ellis**

SOURCE: A review of *A Handful of Seeds,* in *Quill & Quire,* Vol. 59, No. 4, April, 1993, p. 35.

Just how you talk to young children about the poverty and neglect of so many of their contemporaries around the globe is a delicate issue, creating a tension between our desire to make children aware, and our desire to protect them. These conflicting impulses achieve a harmonious balance in *A Handful of Seeds.* Author Monica Hughes and Nicaraguan-born illustrator Luis Garay tell the story of young Concepcion, who is forced to move from a farm to the *barrio* when her grandmother dies. In the city Concepcion joins forces with other street children and teaches them to grow vegetables as an alternative to theft. With its serious message, its endorsement by UNICEF, and its earnest introduction by Sharon, Lois and Bram, such a book could be plodding and dull. It is not. Hughes writes with a clear, pared-down style that gives this story of social realism a fable-like feel. And Garay, too, opts for a very focused, simple approach. His figures are solid—sculptured, monumental, and static. His colours are sombre. He gives the garbage-strewn *barrio* a kind of loveliness which serves not to negate its horrors, but to let us in, to hear and see its story. A young audience more used to sunnier, or more familiar, portrayals of the world in their books may need some adult explanation. But it is worth the effort. "Always save enough seeds for another planting and to share with other children." No, it is not a solution to the complex problems of poverty and development. But it is not a bad place to start, for any age.

**Elizabeth Anthony**

SOURCE: A review of *A Handful of Seeds,* in *Books in Canada,* Vol. XXII, No. 6, September, 1993, pp. 57-8.

The words and images of Monica Hughes's *A Handful of Seeds,* with paintings by Luis Garay, interrelate with a more sober integrity. This is the volume endorsed by Sharon, Lois, and Bram as Friends of Unicef; a percentage of the book's profits will benefit that organization, in keeping with the story's theme of endurance, cooperation, and hard work as the keys to survival in a Central American barrio. Orphaned when her grandmother dies,

Concepcion must head for the city with only a handful of seeds to sustain her. These seeds require not only sun and rain but human commitment in order to become food, and Concepcion secures these vows of cooperation with minimal difficulty from the several gangs of her barrio. Laudable. It is with sadness that I report, however, that my daughter was not convinced, nor was I. While this book is ostensibly addressed to children of all ages, its naïve idealism best suits the very young, who are novices to, not veterans of, the playground: those whose overtures of generosity are minimally bruised by the realities of human nature. While Hughes's moral aim is commendable and high, this question bears some thought: do we serve our children well with tales less complex than they themselves are?

**Patricia L. M. Butler**

SOURCE: A review of *A Handful of Seeds,* in *CM: A Reviewing Journal of Canadian Materials for Young People,* Vol. 21, No. 5, October, 1993, p. 187.

Concepcion is one of the thirty million children around the world who live in the streets. She is forced to make her home in the barrio of a Central American city when her grandmother dies and the landlord must rent the land to a family who can afford more rent. Concepcion takes with her to the city the only legacy possible from her grandmother—the resolve to survive, a handful of bean, corn and chili seeds, and the knowledge that in order to survive one must always save enough to plant and share.

The life of barrio children is a shock to her after her peaceful life with Grandmother, but she quickly sets about planting and tending her garden. Through her determination, the plants survive, bringing both food and hope to the children who have learned to co-operate through her example.

Barrio life is, thankfully, not first-hand knowledge for most of our children, and this poignant introduction to the plight of others carries just the right tone to make its point without being overbearing or frightening. This is Garay's first children's book and he uses the experience of his native Nicaragua to depict the realities of the children who must live in this way. Hughes, an experienced story-teller, gently leads the reader through the story, imparting a sense of hope to the younger reader newly faced with this ugly side of the world. The message, its illustration and overall presentation make this book a highly recommended addition to the collection.

**Publishers Weekly**

SOURCE: a review of *A Handful of Seeds,* in *Publishers Weekly,* Vol. 243, No. 9, February 26, 1996, p. 105.

When her grandmother dies, all Concepcion possesses is a bag of beans, corn and chilies, and her grandmother's advice: "Save enough seed for the next planting . . .

then you will always have something to eat." With nowhere else to turn, Concepcion joins a band of orphans who live next to the dump and steal food for survival. But Concepcion plants a garden and eventually teaches the barrio children to do the same. Without sensationalizing, this tale presents a gritty picture of Latin American children living in poverty, idealizing only their instant solidarity and not their surroundings. First-time illustrator Garay's intriguing combination of paint and cross-hatching is theatrical, posed and yet honest, akin in its tone and scope to the work of Diego Rivera. In both these masterly illustrations and in Hughes's text, the children are dignified and even heroic in their self-reliance. A bittersweet, well-crafted story, it gently opens eyes to the very different lives children lead.

**Roger Sutton**

SOURCE: A review of *A Handful of Seeds,* in *Bulletin of the Center for Children's Books,* Vol. 49, No. 10, June, 1996, p. 339.

When her grandmother dies and Concepcion is forced to leave her village to try and survive in an unnamed city, she recalls the wise woman's adage, "Remember to save enough seed for the next planting. . . . Then you will always have something to eat." When she reaches a miserable barrio, Concepcion is shocked at the other children's suggestion that she steal food; instead she plants corn and beans and chilies, only to see her garden destroyed when police come and chase and beat her new friends. With the help of these friends and her cache of seeds, she plants again, and Concepcion's vision of self-sufficiency spreads through the shantytown. This is a pretty fable, but begs too many questions of reality—most notably, what did Concepcion eat while waiting for her crops to grow?—to be convincing. Like the text, the textured illustrations are a bit too elegantly stylized, with tidy fine lines making even the garbage picturesque. This is pitched in a lower key than such ostentatious lesson-stories as Mem Fox's *Feathers and Fools,* but it lacks the hardiness that would allow it truly to flower.

## THE GOLDEN AQUARIANS (1995)

**Barbara Greenwood**

SOURCE: A review of *The Golden Aquarians,* in *Quill & Quire,* Vol. 60, No. 3, March, 1994, p. 82.

Set a century in the future, on a distant planet colonized by scientists who are "reforming" its topography to produce oil for Earth, ***The Golden Aquarians*** tackles the ethics of ecological tampering. The problem is dramatized in the confrontation between sensitive, liberal-thinking Walt Elliot and his obsessive and ruthless father, Angus, boss of the project. Colonel Elliot has summoned his 13-year-old son from Earth convinced that Walt will learn to be a man in the harsh conditions of Aqua. The toughening-up begins with the gauntler of bullies Walt has to run each day after school. To escape briefly from his grim new life, Walt turns to exploring—and discovers intelligent life, in the form of telepathic amphibians, in Aqua's dank and gloomy marshes. It is against the laws of the galaxy's ruling Federation to restructure a planet that supports intelligent life. How is Walt going to tell his father, who boasts of never giving up on a job, that he must abandon Aqua? Worse still, how can he convince the Colonel that, according to the Aquarians, in six days the Earth colony will be wiped out by a tidal wave? Helped by his one friend, Solveig, Walt first manages to convince the workers. Then he has to confront his father.

While Hughes presents these ethical problems clearly and simply, her characters never quite come to life. The Colonel's transformation at the end of the book has nothing to do with a change of heart or mind but is instead the result of amnesia. Given all that has gone before—the Colonel seemed almost pleased when his son was beaten up at school; when Walt confronts him with the truth about Aqua, he slaps him across the face then seals him into a shed to die of starvation—it seems incredible that Walt would forgive him. Although the novel poses a valid problem, it falls short of an emotionally satisfying resolution.

**Douglas H. Parker**

SOURCE: A review of *The Golden Aquarians,* in *Canadian Children's Literature,* Vol. 20, No. 1, Spring, 1994, pp. 68-9.

Monica Hughes has created another monster in her most recent futuristic work, and, as is her wont, this creature is all the more frightening because he is human. Colonel Angus Elliott, a realistic amalgam of George Patton, Kurtz and Dr. Strangelove, is the *non pareil* of Terraformers, a "planet-maker" who transforms planets into "habitable" environments and in the process destroys whatever life forms exist thereon.

The Colonel hasn't been home for years, home being Lethbridge, Alberta, where his teenage son, Walter, lives with the Colonel's caring sister, Gloria. One day Walter gets the call from his father, whom he hasn't seen for years, and is transported to the planet Aqua to join him in order that he might be made into a man. In short, the Colonel wants to remake his poetry-loving, piano-playing sissy son in the same way that he remakes planets. Happily, appearances to the contrary, Walter is made of stronger stuff than his father thinks. Despite being physically beaten by the Colonel (and by his school-mates), his inherent kindness, good sense, and concern for life wins out in the end. Along with his female companion Solveig, whose mother is the sympathetic and caring doctor on Aqua, Walter, in the face of overwhelming opposition, saves the planet Aqua from the physical ravages his father inflicts on it, and, in the process, saves the lives of those working to transform it. In a somewhat contrived fashion, I feel, father and son are

reunited at the end and spend happier days together in Lethbridge, reunited with Gloria.

Initially, Walter knows nothing about his father—not even his first name—until he reads about his exploits in the newspaper; indeed, his knowledge of what he looks like comes only from the photograph that his aunt keeps of her brother on the top of the piano. Neatly and with masterful irony, Hughes allows Walter to see his father as a kind of magnificent creator: "He used to imagine him, a bit like God, rolling up pieces of clay into worlds and spinning them out into the galaxy." Naïvely, Walter calls his father "godlike," compares him to "Superman" and "King Arthur," and imagines "his big hands [moving] together, almost as if he were moulding a lump of clay." What Walter initially fails to realize is that his father is working to mould him in the same way as the planets he claims to challenge and in the same frighteningly destructive manner. The Colonel is a "remaker" to be sure but he does it by "pulverizing" and "gouging." Hughes lets us know that he is as much a force of nature as the various lands he re-shapes, but she also skillfully informs us that he is an unenlightened brute lacking the finer qualities of even the lowest life forms he sets about to destroy. Indeed, one of the disturbing elements in this story is that readers never get to revise their negative opinion of Walter's father, even though Hughes—who never leaves any threads dangling—intimates that the Colonel's drive to conquer is born of his sorrow for the loss of his wife.

The Colonel and his son are harmoniously reunited at the end of the novel to be sure, but not because the Colonel has learned the error of his ways and repented. Rather, the Colonel suffers amnesia and returns to earth having forgotten about his past. Those looking for a stock ending involving a repentant villain will perhaps be disappointed with the conclusion of *The Golden Aquarians.* But those who know Hughes's other work will understand that she never allows her readers the facile satisfaction of witnessing a 180 degree turn in her characters' behaviour just to bring things to a "happier ever after" conclusion. At the end of this novel, one is left with the ominous feeling that below the blocking level of amnesia the same frightening person lurks. The Colonel has not changed, he has simply forgotten. Throughout the course of the novel, Walter has admired, feared, hated, and, finally, come to accept his "transformed" father. The reader, both less initially naïve than Walter and, finally, less forgiving than him, is left feeling profoundly uncomfortable as *The Golden Aquarians* draws to a close, a feeling that dedicated readers of Hughes's novels will recognize as one of the hallmarks of her craft.

***Kirkus Reviews***

SOURCE: A review of *The Golden Aquarians,* in *Kirkus Reviews,* Vol. LXIII, No. 10, May 15, 1995, p. 712.

The spiritual metamorphosis of a boy into a man is

juxtaposed with the transformation of a pacific planet in this intergalactic thriller.

Raised on Earth by a doting aunt, Walt is completely unprepared to join his father, famed terraformer Colonel Angus Elliott, on the planet Aqua. Walt's hero-worshipping fantasies fade beneath the barrage of beatings from classmates and his sadistic father's lack of interest. Walt's accidental fall into a hidden cave leads to a meeting with Aqua's telepathic amphibious life forms, nicknamed "Greenies." When Walt learns that tidal waves are about to sweep over the entire planet, he and his pal Solveig must convince the colony to evacuate.

Looming disaster pushes the plot forward at a compelling pace, but Hughes drains excitement from such pivotal moments as Walt's departure from Earth and the initial meeting with the Greenies, both presented in a straightforward, anticlimactic manner. Some scientific methods used by the terraformers seem a bit questionable, yet readers can put their faith in the future of the men's movement. Although Angus is a one-dimensional tin soldier, the character of Walt is a realistic, sensitive portrait. A case of "hysterical amnesia" catapults the colonel from being all-bad to all-good, but fans will welcome Walt's forgiveness as genuine.

### Heather MacCammond-Watts

SOURCE: A review of *The Golden Aquarians,* in *Bulletin of the Center for Children's Books,* Vol. 49, No. 2, October, 1995, p. 57.

The planet Aqua is the "biggest, most beautiful 'aggie' in the galaxy." Its blue-green surface is mostly water, and Colonel Angus Elliot has proudly taken charge of terraforming it into an industrial site. Thirteen-year-old Walt Elliott joins his father on his godlike mission to transform a hostile world into an exploitable resource. Walt and the Colonel are painfully estranged after years of living apart, and when Walt discovers that intelligent, telepathic, amphibianlike creatures inhabit Aqua, he comes to blows with his father. The tension keeps the pages turning; Walt's beleaguered attempts to connect with his father are rebuffed by the Colonel's harsh, grief-bitten attitude (Walt's mother died on a non-terraformed planet), and Walt gets beaten up after school everyday because he's the Colonel's son. Walt and his friend Solveig are able to communicate with the Aquarians who are unconvincingly calm about the destruction of their home; they even warn the humans about an upcoming planetary disaster. Monica Hughes, author of *Invitation to the Game,* uses her considerable skill in creating believable science fiction to fashion this dripping, distracting atmosphere of exploration, funky aliens, and family antagonism. The ending is too good to be true (conveniently resolved with the Colonel's amnesia), but it's like a good Hollywood movie, and kids immersed in Aqua will be having too much fun to notice.

### CASTLE TOURMANDYNE (1995)

### Mary Beaty

SOURCE: A review of *Castle Tourmandyne,* in *Quill & Quire,* Vol. 61, No. 7, July, 1995, p. 61.

Poor Marg is having a bad summer. Her sophisticated Toronto cousin, Peggy, has been shipped to Edmonton while her Rosedale parents are on an antique-buying jaunt in Thailand. Peggy's condescending behaviour conceals a heart tormented by the failure of her family to provide the king of support and closeness she craves. Nonetheless, she predictably impresses the adults while making her cousin's life miserable. Enter the plot device. Grandma Pargeter sends Marg an antique paper doll house, with a warning to "make it with love." As love is in short supply, the omens and the thunderclouds gather. Despite the local museum curator's admonition that the creator of the doll house met a nasty end, Peggy compulsively assembles it—and of course finds herself trapped inside, pursued by demonic paper dolls. Through the power of love, the two cousins finally enter the house together and defeat the evil paper doll schoolmaster (with the red ring a-round his neck and the glowing eyes and the riding whip). Both girls decide their families are pretty nice, after all.

Monica Hughes's 28th book is a simple ghost story for grade 4-5 students. Although the characters are ages 12 and 14, this story is better suited for 9- and 10-year-olds. It wasn't possible to assess the layout or the all-important cover art from the unbound review galleys, but the writing style is definitely pre-adolescent, fitting in nicely with Nancy Drew and easy R. L. Stine. Like such competitors, this is also a formula book, although it is written with real skill. The plot is so familiar we could finish it ourselves after the first few chapters. The dénouement is nicely scary with just the right sprinkle of self-realization, and nothing is over-explained or analyzed. We never find out why the bad guy hung himself, why he's back hunting people, why Peggy's parents don't have time for her, or any other deeper characterization. But Hughes is such an experienced writer that we don't mind the lack of continuity or exposition. Her assured narrative powers sweep us past the sad emotional moments and into the delicious chills of the scary bits. The prairie setting, the anachronistic slang ("swanky," "posh"), and the childhood references from an older time (pretty Peggy has "gorgeous dresses" on padded hangers rather than expensive grunge) all seem oddly old-fashioned, as if this were a book of the 1960s. As such, in these retrograde times, it should have a happy and comfortable readership—the cover will determine the market.

### Dave Jenkinson

SOURCE: A review of *Castle Tourmandyne,* in *Canadian Book Review Annual,* 1995, pp. 503-04.

On her 12th birthday, Marg Pargeter receives an antique

cardboard house that is accompanied by a handwritten warning: "Be careful to make this house with love." The toy, however, is assembled in an atmosphere of anger, for an unwilling Marg is sharing her bedroom over the summer holidays with her pushy cousin, Peggy, who has been sent to Edmonton by her globetrotting parents. Feeling deserted and unloved, Peggy is jealous of Marg's supportive home life. Marg in turn feels threatened by her older cousin's looks and talents. As Peggy selfishly monopolizes the house's construction, Marg angrily cuts out the building's paper inhabitants, names them, and creates a story about their relationships; the child figure is an orphan named Celine who resembles Peggy and is mistreated by her guardians, the evil, greedy Lady Tourmandyne and her cowardly husband, Sir Basil. The torment Celine undergoes is reflected in Peggy's deteriorating emotional state. In the end, Marg and Peggy join forces to undo the damage caused by their former animosity. Middle-school girls, in particular, will enjoy this tightly written tale.

**Alison Sutherland**

SOURCE: A review of *Castle Tourmandyne,* in *Books in Canada,* Vol. 25, No. 4, May, 1996, pp. 19-20.

Monica Hughes, as omnipresent as Jean Little, writes science fiction and fantasy. Although I enjoy this genre more than Little's, Hughes is arguably not as good a writer, and certainly not as widely read by children. I keep urging her books on the young, but haven't found a sure-fire way of getting them read. Personally I'm a sucker for a good plot, and Hughes has come up with some dandies, but as a discerning fourteen-year-old rural male said to me, "She's in too much of a hurry with it." We assume that young readers are mainly captivated by action, but this is not necessarily so. An eleven-year-old urban female loved Little's *Look Through my Window,* explaining, "I enjoyed the personalities and the situation." But she was disappointed by its sequel, *Kate:* "She was just telling a story, that's all." Hughes's **Castle Tourmandyne** concerns two girls of roughly the same ages . . . and there is another over-sophisticated little madam—whose mind we do enter. She seems to have a headache throughout most of the book, and you don't get that marvellous sense of smug self-righteous superiority that comes with being tidy and well-dressed. The two girls build an antique paper doll's house, and their animosity sets free an evil power associated with its first owner. It's a page-turner, though; I missed my subway stop reading it on the way to work.

## WHERE HAVE YOU BEEN, BILLY BOY? (1995)

**Kenneth Oppel**

SOURCE: A review of *Where Have You Been, Billy Boy?,* in *Quill & Quire,* Vol. 61, No. 11, November, 1995, pp. 44-5.

Keeping secrets from Mom and Dad is an age-old convention of children's literature, and in Monica Hughes's latest novel, there's a biggie. Thirteen-year-old Susan discovers a young street urchin named Billy, who has travelled through time on a magic carousel.

*Where Have You Been, Billy Boy?* actually begins in the past, in 1908, with Billy taking refuge from the police in the carnival grounds. Befriended by the old groundskeeper, Johannes, given a new set of clothes and a cozy place to sleep, Billy thinks he might finally be able to stop running. But he is unable to control his curiosity when he sees Johannes riding his beloved carousel in the middle of the night, faster and faster so that it seems to shimmer out of sight momentarily. When Billy decides to try for himself, he ends up in 1993, in a Kansas barn; the carousel's there, too, though now horribly decrepit. It's here he meets Susan, and together, the two have to figure out how to get Billy back to the past.

Hughes has a fine eye for detail, and her writing is graceful and vivid. Her early depiction of Billy and his growing affection for Johannes is subtle and convincing. But when the story shifts to modern day Kansas, so does the point of view, and we increasingly lose track of Billy as Susan takes over the story. Susan is an able and likable character, but not as interesting or original as Billy.

Exciting complications abound as the kids try to get the carousel up and running, but the story gets a bit too bogged down in procedural as Susan's bossy brother and friend all join in the effort. Hughes's premise is so rich, it's inevitable there are missed opportunities here. The magical nature of the carousel is largely ignored—we never do find out why or how. Nor do we get enough of Billy's reaction to his new world. As well, there isn't as much connection between present and past, thematically or logistically, as one might expect from a time-travel story.

As for keeping all this secret from Mom and Dad, the cover-up Susan devises to explain Billy's presence (for a whole month) is so precarious, it rather stretches credulity when neither parent figures things out. Nonetheless, this is an entertaining, if somewhat easy story, filled with fine writing and intriguing ideas.

**Gerald Rubio**

SOURCE: A review of *Where Have You Been, Billy Boy?,* in *Canadian Children's Literature,* Vol. 22, No. 2, Summer, 1996, pp. 92-3.

In her latest novel Monica Hughes (to paraphrase *Star Trek*) "boldly goes where [she] has not gone before," and in so doing has produced a novel that will win her new fans as well as praise from educators. Instead of using the techniques of science-fiction to construct a possible future as in so many of her best-known novels, she here compares past and present through a plot which depends upon fantasy. Her characters, however, are as realistic, problem-prone, daring and as easy to identify with as in her best previous works.

As the title suggests, eleven-year-old Billy is both the youngest and least socialized of her major characters: as we meet him in 1908, he is a parentless, shoeless street urchin who steals food, sleeps outdoors wherever he can find a hiding place, and is planning to steal the savings of a sick old man as soon as he gets the chance. (His situation echoes that in Hughes's earliest novel, *Gold-Fever Trail*. Billy's father was away prospecting for gold in the Klondike when his mother died; in both works, the children prefer striking out on their own to orphanages.)

Hughes transports Billy 85 years into the future (our present) via a ride on a high-speed carousel. Billy had seen old Johannes, the carousel operator, speed it up until both it and he simply disappeared, but then reappeared in the morning. Billy, of course, awaits his chance to do the same; Billy faints during the ride, and awakes to find himself (in an allusion to *The Wizard of Oz?*) on a farm overlooking "the corn country of Kansas." It is only here that Hughes introduces her more typical characters—fourteen-year-old Susan, her schoolmate George, her sixteen-year-old brother Jim—who are daring, cooperative and inventive enough to find the way to send Billy back to his own time.

Of particular interest to educators is Hughes's semi-comic but realistic descriptions of the mutual cultural shocks all the youngsters experience: Billy's '90s friends (and their families) are horrified as he (following practices of his day) "spits" on the floor, blows his nose into an embroidered dinner napkin, and the like; he is mystified by television, freezers, aeroplanes, and such. The moderns, of course, cannot understand why Billy is frantic to return to his own time where nothing awaits him but homeless misery, but he has come to realize that his love and concern for the sick Johannes he left behind is more important than our brave new world. His friends use '90s technology to return him to his own time (by rebuilding the carousel with a powerful new high speed engine). The novel ends with Billy's descendants visiting the teenagers who sent him back to his own time and who are responsible for restoring the carousel to its original condition.

## 📖 THE SEVEN MAGPIES (1996)

### Dave Jenkinson

SOURCE: A review of *The Seven Magpies,* in *Canadian Book Review Annual,* 1996, p. 480.

In the early days of World War II, Maureen Frazer, 14, is sent to a boarding school in the Scottish highlands. Largely ignored by her seven roommates, Maureen learns that they belong to a club, the Secret Society of Magpies. In order for someone to join the Magpies, Kathleen, the prefect who controls the club, must leave a "sacrifice" at full moon before a Celtic standing stone. The disappearance of the sacrifice fuels the girls' imaginations, so that when Maureen spots a furtive stranger in a nearby valley, in the minds of the Magpies he becomes a German spy.

This evocative novel offers rich historical detail. Middle-school girls will empathize with the sense of isolation associated with observing an in-group from the outside.

### Maureen Garvie

SOURCE: A review of *The Seven Magpies,* in *Quill & Quire,* Vol. 63, No. 1, January, 1997, p. 39.

Monica Hughes's 30 books for young people are remarkably varied, from her celebrated Isis sci-fi series to historical fiction to realism. What they share is engaging, forthright characters with a keen awareness of the world. Hughes's latest, *The Seven Magpies,* employs that genre still so dear to the hearts of young female readers, the school story, and adds history and Hughes's trademark streak of fantasy. Notably absent is Canadian content: the setting is Scotland, the characters Scottish. The Celtic magic goes back to the dawn of time, while the story starts in the early days of the Second World War—an era that must itself seem like ancient history to young readers. It's a period Hughes has explored before, for example, in *Blaine's Way,* and she is thoroughly at ease in it.

War has suspended ordinary life for "the duration," sending 14-year-old Maureen Frazer's father to the front, and Maureen herself to a remote boarding school in a castle at the edge of the highlands. She arrives to find the rest of the Lower Fifth class have already bonded, Enid-Blyton fashion, around their Secret Seven society, leaving Maureen odd one out. She misses her beloved father and resents her mother who, after packing her off in the name of safety, is (in Maureen's opinion) having far too good a time in the women's naval service.

Hughes writes wonderfully about lochs and burns and cattle "with hides like hearthrugs and great horns curving like bicycle handles." There's suspense and palm-dampening danger, late-night sacrifices at the foot of a Standing Stone, and a mysterious man—a deserter or maybe a German spy?—lurking in the heather. The cast has fine bit parts, and Maureen is a well-developed character who finds adults interesting, doesn't hold grudges, and appreciates the civilized comfort of a hot cup of tea. From the familiar base of schoolgirl bitchiness and boarding-school food, Hughes widens the focus to larger—international—dramas and issues of truthfulness and conscience in a world badly in need of good magic. *The Seven Magpies* should export well while delighting domestic readers.

## Frieda Wishinsky

SOURCE: "Strength from Solitude," in *Books in Canada,* Vol. 26, No. 2, March, 1997, p. 36.

The stories of the prolific young adult writer Monica Hughes seem to flow from her pen. But each of her carefully crafted tales simmers in her mind for a long time before she puts it down on paper.

"I keep an idea in my head and let it grow there," she says.

And as the idea grows, she develops a plot, builds characters, envisions places, and nurtures the theme that ties it all together.

What are those themes? What are the concerns and issues that link her stories?

Her stories often focus on environmental problems. She has a deep concern for the damage humans inflict on the planet. She also has a profound understanding of the loneliness young people experience as they strive to find a place for themselves in a difficult, complex world.

"The most intense agony of a child is loneliness," she says. Yet despite the loneliness, her characters learn how to draw on their strengths to cope with their feelings and predicaments. Many of them display ingenuity, curiosity, and an independent spirit.

Hughes intimately understands the intense loneliness of childhood and the search for a place in the world. Born in Liverpool, England, she grew up in Egypt and Great Britain. Her father was a mathematician and somewhat of a hermit. Her mother was quiet and unobtrusive.

She and her only sister were given freedom to think, to dream, to discover their interests. "You had your own time," says Hughes. "There wasn't much external entertainment. You played your own imaginative games." . . .

*The Seven Magpies,* though not truly a science fiction tale, does have deep elements of magic and the unknown. It also explores other themes that resonate in many of Hughes's stories: a lonely heroine, a strange setting, and mysterious events. And it is set during World War II, a time she vividly recalls.

In this story, Hughes describes the hauntingly beautiful Scottish Highlands. She conveys the sense of looming fear that pervaded the troubled and trying war years. The tension of the war's horrors, even for those who lived in remote parts like the Highlands, hangs like a curtain over the story and the heroine, Maureen Fraser.

Maureen has been forced by her parents to attend the Logan Academy for Young Ladies. Her father is off fighting in the war and her mother is busy with the WRNS [Women's Royal Naval Service] in London. Her parents are confident that in Scotland, Maureen will be shielded from the dangers of the war. But even in the Highlands, there is no escape from it or from the complexities of life.

Maureen soon contends with the girls at her new school. She's left out of their tight clique, strange whisperings, and rules. She's affected also by the stark Highland landscape, which both fascinates and frightens her. It too seems to hold secrets, mysteries, even magic.

Suddenly the war intrudes on the eerie quiet of the ancient Highland hills. And as it does, it draws Maureen into dangerous situations and questions of loyalty and betrayal. In the process, she has to draw upon her reserves of intelligence, intuition, and courage.

*The Seven Magpies* touches on a place and a past Hughes knows well. Yet she is just as comfortable and adept at setting her tales in the future, in places that exist only in her imagination.

"The basic issues are the same," she says. Matters such as the desire to belong, the hurt in being left out, and the need for empowerment and control are perennial conditions of childhood.

But futuristic settings have given Hughes a special kind of freedom. They've allowed her to explore the possible consequences of present actions—such as society's wanton destruction of the earth's natural resources and the deterioration of the elements that make life possible and pleasant on earth.

And from those concerns, Hughes has fashioned a steady flow of stories. How does she create so many plots in so short a time? Perhaps it's because she is also always open to new story ideas.

The plot for an upcoming book, for example, took shape after a conversation with a teacher on a plane. The teacher was returning to her teaching job abroad after a six-month sabbatical. "She could almost not bear to go back," says Hughes. "They read no fiction at all in her country. They play no imaginative games. She told me how hard it was to teach only facts."

That conversation saddened and intrigued Hughes. And soon a story was born. And although the final manuscript was not set in the teacher's country, but in a mythical island Hughes created, the theme inspired by that conversation set the stage.

It's a creative process that's as magical as any plot. And Hughes knows that and enjoys every aspect of it. "It's wonderful fun," she says with a twinkle of delight.

## Ronald Jobe

SOURCE: A review of *The Seven Magpies,* in *Journal of Adolescent & Adult Literacy*, Vol. 40, No. 8, May, 1997, p. 676.

"But I won't be here, . . . she promised herself fiercely. By spring the war will be over. Everyone says so."

A sense of abandonment sweeps over 14-year-old Maureen as she arrives at the Logan Academy for Young Ladies, recently evacuated to the west side of Scotland to avoid any German raids during the war. She is upset at her parents for forcing her to leave home for her own safety and because she will stand out "like a lump of coal" by starting late.

Maureen's isolation heightens when she is placed in the lower fifth form, a closely knit group of seven girls. She gets over her loneliness by reading about the region and exploring it. The discovery of an ancient headstone strangely fills her with courage. She learns more of the area, as well as the meaning of the seven magpies on the sampler in her home, from the wife of the gatekeeper.

Accepted at last, Maureen is invited to join the girls in their secret seven magpies society. As an act of courage she must take an offering at night to the strangely carved four-sided pillar overlooking the coast. The next day the offering is gone, the girls don't believe it, but Maureen remembers a man hiding in the bracken. Could he be a spy?

"One for sorrow, two for joy, three for a girl, four for a boy, five for silver, six for gold, seven for a secret that can ne'er be told." The author cleverly makes use of the old magpie rhyme to structure the events in the story. Readers will anticipate the possibilities by referring to the pattern. Hughes develops a strong sense of the Scottish landscape through Maureen's eyes. Tension is created in the story when the girls' active imaginations focus on the possibility of German spies being in the area.

Then comes the revelation that the young man who was hiding is actually a deserter from the British army. The agony he and his parents go through is warmly and sensitively disclosed. Teen readers could compare this novel with Mary Downing Hahn's *Stepping on the Cracks* for the images of deserters from modern armies. What makes them break? Who is hurt by their actions? What is the response of the people around them?

### 📖 *THE FACES OF FEAR* (1997)

#### Anne Louise Mahoney

SOURCE: A review of *The Faces of Fear*, in *Quill & Quire*, Vol. 63, No. 10, October, 1997, p. 36.

After a car accident leaves 15-year-old Joan Sandow without the use of her legs, Joan's world looks pretty bleak. So when she and her Internet buddy, Steve (alias Whizkid), get a chance to test a new virtual reality computer game, Joan is thrilled. What they don't know is that Jason, the game's designer, has filled it with situations aimed at triggering their deepest, darkest fears.

As they move through the four parts of the game, which involves finding four artifacts and saving the world from an asteroid, Jason's malevolent plan backfires. Instead of succumbing to their fears, the two teens overcome them in the virtual world and bring their newfound confidence and sense of triumph back to their real lives.

This fascinating tale by master storyteller Monica Hughes is a nicely balanced story within a story. The virtual reality adventure is more compelling reading due to the challenges that Joan and Steve take on (finding their way out of a complex maze, climbing a mountain). Although they know it is "just a game," they push themselves to the limit physically and mentally. But the story of their real lives is interesting, too. Because we see them between episodes, we can see subtle changes that the game is working on them. Joan becomes more motivated and positive; Steve starts listening to his heart. Both characters are believable as teens struggling with various aspects of growing up.

Although Jason, the only other significant character in the story, remains in the background, his presence is felt throughout the game. He seems underdeveloped—all we know about him is that he rarely bathes, which is what Joan insulted him about before the story begins. That a spontaneous comment about personal hygiene should provoke such a vengeful response, even when the comment comes from the boss's daughter, is a bit of a stretch. So is Jason's unexpected remorse at the end of the story: all of a sudden, he realizes his revenge has gone too far and decides to resign from his job. Apart from this minor weakness, this is a gripping story of triumph over the fears that keep people from being free to be themselves.

#### Dave Jenkinson

SOURCE: A review of *The Faces of Fear*, in *Canadian Book Review Annual*, 1997, pp. 511-12.

A car accident, which killed her mother, has left Joan Sandow, 15, a paraplegic. Her guilt-ridden, wealthy, and indulgent father allows his "Princess," once a star athlete but now wheelchair-bound, to disassociate herself completely from her friends and receive homeschooling. Joan's outside contacts are limited to the Internet, where, as Joanna, she masks her physical condition. Joanna's response to an invitation from Whizkid to play chess online initiates a series of events that ultimately takes her life in a positive direction.

The key to the change is Joan's and Whizkid's participation in a sophisticated interactive virtual reality computer adventure game that allows them to feel as if they were warriors who were actually "in" the game. Developed by Jason Bedard, a precocious program designer, the four-part game has a malevolent side: a vengeful Jason, rejected by Joan during her able-bodied days, has incorporated her fears into the game and later adds those of Steve Andersen, a.k.a. Whizkid.

Teens who play computer simulation games will be attracted to Hughes's novel plot device.

## Katherine Matthews

SOURCE: A review of *The Faces of Fear,* in *Books in Canada,* Vol. 27, No. 5, June, 1998, p. 34.

In **The Faces of Fear,** Joan Sandow uses her computer to escape the confinements of her wheelchair. Using the alias "Joanna", she connects with Whizkid (aka Steve Andersen) in a computer chat room.

Both these teens are dealing with pressures: Joan, to adjust to life as a paraplegic; Steve, to succeed at school or baseball. The common need for self-determination unknowingly unites them. They join forces to test a new virtual reality game from Joan's father's company, but unbeknownst to either of them, the game contains traps set out by its designer, Jason Bedard, a hot-shot computer geek who holds a grudge against Joan. Whizkid and Joanna learn that they must draw on the strengths of Steve and Joan in order to successfully survive the game.

Monica Hughes is no stranger to alternate worlds, although typically she sets these worlds on other planets or in other times. It is no surprise, then, to find her exploring the world of virtual reality, and it is when Whizkid and Joanna enter the game that Hughes is at her most successful. The game is intriguing and fast-paced, with enough thrills and challenge to keep both players, as well as the reader, engaged.

Characterization and character development, however, are weak. Joan tends to be a bit of a one-note; the reader may feel some sympathy for Joan and her challenges, but she rarely engages us emotionally. Jason is overdrawn, and the ending, in which he has a sudden change of heart, is far too pat to be believable.

Despite this, Hughes is a skilled enough writer to keep us interested. In **The Faces of Fear,** as the two protagonists learn about themselves through the game, so does the reader learn the importance of facing fear and remaining true to oneself.

## 📖   *JAN'S BIG BANG* (1997)

## Lisa Arsenault

SOURCE: A review of *Jan's Big Bang,* in *Canadian Book Review Annual,* 1997, p. 512.

Even though they are only in Grade 3, Jan and her friend Sarah decide to participate in the school science fair. The projects they attempt—an erupting volcano, an ant farm, and a worm composter—all turn out to be unworkable for various reasons. Running out of time and beginning to despair, they finally manage to develop a viable experiment out of the failed attempts.

This enjoyable novel's central themes—protecting the environment and the importance of perseverance—are well developed. The book is also quite humorous. A Very Distinguished and Important Visitor to the science fair insists on testing the "explosive" aspect of the girls' project, thereby causing the "big bang" of the title. The fact that the two budding scientists are girls is another plus, given that the disciplines of math and science are sometimes still considered to be male preserves.

## 📖   *THE STORY BOX* (1998)

## Gwyneth Evans

SOURCE: A review of *The Story Box,* in *Quill & Quire,* Vol. 64, No. 12, December, 1998, p. 38.

A place where stories are forbidden, where all of life is dedicated to practical tasks, and where children are punished for speaking of their dreams—such is the world created by Monica Hughes in **The Story Box.** The islanders of Ariban work at their traditional crafts of fishing and weaving in a pre-industrial society marked by their dread of contact with foreigners, and their strange refusal to permit any mention of dreams, stories, or other products of the imagination. Into this stern world comes a shipwrecked stranger, the beautiful Jennifer, who clutches a chest of books and tells the horrified islanders that she is a storyteller. She is discovered, half-drowned, by young Colin, and his decision to save her rather than let the sea take her away is only the first in a series of increasingly agonized choices he must make. Family loyalties and love of his home conflict with a growing interest in the larger world and curiosity and admiration for the wise, resourceful Jennifer. Can Jennifer's stories help him to understand himself and choose the right path?

A masterly storyteller herself, Hughes grabs the reader's attention from the opening lines of the novel and holds it until its dramatic open-ended conclusion. The conflict between a virtuous puritanical community and the artistic and imaginative expression that it considers threatening is a recurring theme in literature, from Swift's horses in *Gulliver's Travels* who cannot conceive of speaking "the thing which is not," to the isolated fishing community that tries to stifle musical creativity in Anne McCaffrey's *Dragonsong.* Hughes's focus on brave but troubled Colin, rather than the almost too self-assured Jennifer makes the conflict real and understandable. Ultimately, **The Story Box** is a celebration of the liberating power of fiction.

**Additional coverage of Hughes's life and career is contained in the following sources published by The Gale Group:** *Authors and Artists for Young Adults,* **Vol. 19;** *Junior DISCovering Authors; Major Authors and Illustrators for Children and Young Adults; Something about the Author Autobiography Series,* **Vol. 11; and** *Something about the Author,* **Vols. 15, 70.**

# Satoshi Kitamura

## 1956-

Japanese illustrator and author of picture books.

Major works include *Angry Arthur* (written by Hiawyn Oram, 1982), *What's Inside* (1985), *When Sheep Cannot Sleep* (1986), *UFO Diary* (1989), *Sheep in Wolves' Clothing* (1995).

## INTRODUCTION

Praised for his colorful, angular style as well as his whimsical humor, Kitamura uses simple lines to express a wide range of feelings and events in his picture book illustrations for preschool and elementary grades. With strong technical abilities and a gift for visual comedy, Kitamura adds an unconventional touch to many traditional children's book formats, including alphabet and counting books. His pictures often reflect Japanese scroll stories: as the action moves from one spread to another, the central character appears in various locations at once, moving through the narrative in a nonlinear fashion. Several critics have expressed their enthusiasm at finding Kitamura's work on their desk. His alphabet books, such as *What's Inside* and *From Acorn to Zoo* (1991), are filled with throwaway details, all of them sweetly funny and many too subtle for a small child. He told *Something about the Author* (*SATA*), "I am interested in different angles of looking at things. I find great potential in picture books where visual and verbal fuse to experience, and I also experiment with these angles." As stylized as Kitamura's works are, they are recognized for their rich palette of earth and sky tones and for, as David Weisner noted, their "warmth and wit." Weisner added, "The simplicity of Mr. Kitamura's art is deceptive. A superb draftsman and colorist, he uses pen and brush to create remarkably lush and textured illustrations." A master of linear simplicity and an imaginative narrator, Kitamura takes advantage of the power of a single stroke, using it to depict universal expressions, which are necessary, he feels, to communicate with young readers, whether he is illustrating his own books or the works of others.

Jane Doonan was full of praise, commenting, "Kitamura offers an interpretation of life as we experience it emotionally; his paintings strike a chord of recognition." John Mole, writing in *The Times Educational Supplement,* echoed Doonan's regard: "Satoshi Kitamura's pictures are rich in character and full of incidental detail, but what really stands out is his wonderful way with faces. Huge, round white eyes with perfectly placed dots combine with the single line of a mouth to express a whole range of emotions—surprise, anxiety, cunning, triumph. This is the cartoonist's art, and Kitamura's originality lies in the imaginative use he makes of it.

Deceptively simple, it is at the service of a remarkable sense of design and real gift for narrative."

## Biographical Information

Kitamura was born in 1956 in Tokyo, Japan, where he was raised by his parents, Testuo and Fusae Kitamura. In 1983, after the publication of *Angry Arthur*, he moved to London, which has become his permanent home. The critical success of *Angry Arthur,* both in England and in America, caught the attention of publishers, and Kitamura was soon busy with numerous projects. Married to an interior designer, Yoko Sugisaki, in 1987, the couple live in a London flat.

## Major Works

*Angry Arthur* is a visual analogy of a child's explosive anger. Arthur is not allowed to stay up to watch a Western on television, and his anger summons thunder and lightening, then a typhoon that blows the house apart, then an explosion that destroys the town. Eventually, the earth cracks like an egg and the universe disappears, leaving Arthur sitting on "a piece of Mars" in outer space, trying to remember what made him so angry. Kitamura's furious child is surrounded by violent colors and shapes as the world around him succumbs to his wrath. Critics appreciated Kitamura's evocative display of an out-of-control young child's frustrated rage, noting the humor and sheer extravagance of the entire presentation.

*What's Inside* is an alphabet book that resembles a long scroll moving from page to page. The first page shows boxes of fruit and two closed boxes marked "a" and "b." The next page shows those boxes to the left edge of the picture, but opened to reveal apples and bananas, with the words written on the box lids. On the opposite page is a closed garbage can with the letters "c" and "d"; as the page is turned, readers see a cat and a dog coming out of the can with hidden items beginning with the letters "e" and "f." The pictures move along a vista, and each object sometimes moves through several spreads; for example, on the next page, the dog has chased the cat up a lamppost. Although some reviewers found the book too sophisticated for a first alphabet, others considered it completely charming, praising its illustrator for both his ingenuity and humor.

An unusual counting book, *When Sheep Cannot Sleep* does not contain numbers, yet, offers a growing number of things to count from beginning to end. In the story, Woolly, a goofy looking sheep with a single-lined, but very expressive mouth, wanders around during the night because he is unable to sleep. He chases one butterfly, watches two sleeping lady bugs, and so on, and ends up in bed snoring 22 zzzzzs. Reviewers appreciated Kitamura's whimsy and noted the lovable Woolly's vast appeal for both children and adults.

Praised for being consummately artistic while retaining the simplicity appropriate to its audience, *UFO Diary* is the travelogue of a lost alien who lands on earth but who the audience never sees. According to the diary, the alien is greeted by a young child, and the two play together although they cannot understand each other's language. They also take a flying saucer ride around the earth before the alien leaves for home. The book contains little text while Kitamura's humorous and refreshing illustrations advance the narrative.

Kitamura's sheep return in *Sheep in Wolves' Clothing*, this time as Hubert, Georgina, and Gogol. The sheep are spending the day at the beach when four wolves convince them that the saltwater will spoil their wooly coats. The wolves offer to watch the coats, but of course, they take off with the goods. The sheep consult Georgina's cousin, detective Elliott Baa, to help them find their clothes. They careen about town in their underwear, and eventually discover the wolves' knitwear factory, where they acquire colorful sweaters for themselves. Told in few words with full-page spreads of hilarious activity, *Sheep in Wolves' Clothing* was greeted joyously by reviewers, who found the illustrations

kid-pleasing, maniacal, and highly amusing; some even thought the words were extraneous.

## Awards

*Angry Arthur* received the Mother Goose Award from the Books for Children Book Club. In 1985, *What's Inside* was selected a *New York Times* Notable Book. *When Sheep Cannot Sleep* won the Children's Science Book Award in Great Britain and the Children's Science Book Award from the New York Academy of Sciences, both in 1987.

---

# GENERAL COMMENTARY

## Karla Kuskin

SOURCE: A review of *What's Inside?*, in *The New York Times Book Review,* June 16, 1985, p. 30.

Arthur, a furious black-haired, white-faced child, was the protagonist of Hiawyn Oram and Satoshi Kitamura's first book, **Angry Arthur.** When his mother told him to turn off the television, Arthur turned on a tantrum so world-shaking that it destroyed the planet and made the universe tremble. This was Max minus the Wild Things; a neat variation on a contemporary picture-book theme.

The protagonist of **In the Attic** looks just like Arthur. But this child is not angry, he is a dreamer. "I had a million toys" he begins, "but I was bored." So he climbs the accommodating ladder on his toy fire engine into an attic that soon fills with his daydreams. The first of these features a family of hyperactive mice up to all kinds of mischief. They are followed by an interlude in a tropical garden growing out of the attic floor, a short visit with an industrious spider and lasting friendship with a tiger. At the end of the day, recounting these adventures, the child tells his mother where he has been. When she replies, "But we don't have an attic," he calmly concludes, "She hasn't found the ladder."

Like that small but expandable ladder, this slim story is a springboard into imaginary realms. Mr. Kitamura takes full advantage of it. To illustrate the child's rather adult phrase "I opened windows to other worlds," the artist, who has a fine feeling for rearranging space, juxtaposes close views and far horizons as deftly as the eye of a camera. Under a night sky the attic floor hovers over the Earth, while here and there free-standing windows reflect diverse scenes. It is an attractive, surreal setting. A strange land for a child, but probably an interesting one.

An equally well-designed double-page-layout farther on is less successful at communicating mood. It animates the line "My friend and I found a game that could go on forever." Instead of a recognizable game, Mr. Kitamura has created what looks like a midair collision between paintings by Paul Klee and Joan Miró over an elliptical chessboard. In a rain of squiggles and exploding stars, the child descends his ladder, a planet in hand. He is smiling. The tiger waits below looking baffled. Perhaps, like the very young children for whom this book is meant, the child is not a symbolic thinker quite yet. What has happened here occurs in sophisticated picture books when an illustrator, caught in his own designing, forgets who his audience is. In this case the moment passes as the page is turned and the child returns to a kitchen full of the familiar, including mother. Using quick, angular pen strokes, Mr. Kitamura delineates the commonplace with style. And he delights in tiny details—miniature boxes, a carrot dropped near the garbage—that will reward searching young eyes.

Pursuing his talent for detail, Mr. Kitamura lays out busy pages in his alphabet book, *What's Inside?* The format is a graphic game of hide-and-seek. The rules are loose. A closed container, a garbage can for instance, is marked with the initials of its contents ("c d" in this case). When the page is turned, the can disgorges a frantic "cat and dog." An enormous suitcase marked "g h" and shaped like a guitar *and* a hippopotamus holds, by golly, a guitar-playing hippopotamus. And a coffin marked "u v" releases a vampire bat clutching an umbrella. An elephant accompanied by a fire engine simply materializes on a street marked "e f," and the woodpecker plus xylophone are found behind a tree marked "W X." These last two letters are the only capitals in the book. Here and there the alphabet gets upstaged by the bold drawings and lush washes.

On the back cover is an illustration unrelated to what is inside: a crowded desk under a window faces a detailed outdoor scene. Each drawn object has been cleverly paired with its initial. A "b" lies like a bookmark in a book; an "e" sticks out of a envelope; outside, a kangaroo dozes with a "k" in its pouch. This amusing, logical way of linking letters to objects has room for expansion. Every illustrator worth his ink has an alphabet book in him. Mr. Kitamura may have two.

### Jane Doonan

SOURCE: "Satoshi Kitamura: Aesthetic Dimensions," in *Children's Literature,* Vol. 19, 1991, pp. 107-37.

Satoshi Kitamura, a Japanese artist now living in London, won the 1982 Mother Goose Award, given annually to the most exciting newcomer to British children's book illustration. His subsequent picture books have fulfilled this promise. They show a striking originality of vision, a criterion Maurice Sendak considers paramount for the judgment of picture books. Sendak suggests that we should look for "someone who says something, even something very commonplace, in a totally original and fresh way. We shouldn't look for pyrotechnics but a person who thinks freshly." Kitamura's work

is notable as well for the artist's material skills and for his distinctive relationship to the pictorial tradition of Japan. Consideration of all three aspects—vision, material skills, and tradition—is a way of traveling toward a sympathetic understanding of Kitamura's accomplishment.

Kitamura's first three picture books—the prize-winning *Angry Arthur, Ned and the Joybaloo,* and *In the Attic*—were produced in collaboration with Hiawyn Oram, who wrote the texts. Each is an extended metaphor for one of three very different states of being. *Angry Arthur* exemplifies, the destructive rage of a thwarted small boy who does not want to go to bed, *Ned and the Joybaloo* gives form to the human frailty of wishing to control and perpetuate happiness, and *In the Attic* celebrates the imagination as a source of nameless and profound satisfactions. Each story sends its central character traveling out to the farthest reaches of the physical universe, deep into the psyche, and away to the wildest stretches of childhood's imaginings. The barriers between inner and outer lives are removed.

These collaborative works were followed by educational picture books for which Kitamura was wholly responsible: *What's Inside? The Alphabet Book* and *When Sheep Cannot Sleep: The Counting Book.* The former, virtually textless, involves the beholder in a guessing game and in opportunities for do-it-yourself story making; the latter has a memorable hero, Woolly the Sheep, with all the appeal of a Snoopy, whose adventures are well worth watching whether or not one counts as the pages turn. Both books go far beyond increasing literacy and numeracy; each has an inventive approach to a traditional form. Other picture books have followed which are charged with honest humor.

The values Kitamura promotes are aspects of an independent and creative nature: curiosity, resourcefulness, self-sufficiency, and the need for self-expression. One suspects that if he had his way, artists' materials and the means of making and listening to music would be every child's right. Arthur has a gramophone and piano; Ned, when not occupied with the Joybaloo, practices his recorder and relaxes to the sounds of Erik Satie and Charlie Parker. The child who explores the attic owns an accordion and a trumpet, and mathematician Woolly tunes in to the radio. H for Hippo playing his G for guitar has enough musical instruments in his soundproofed studio to service a symphony orchestra, a jazz band, jungle drummers, gypsy fiddlers, pipers Aegean and Scottish, harpers Jewish and Welsh. Sharpened pens, paints, sketchblocks and easels also are at hand. The omnipresence of musical and artistic instruments reveals Kitamura's focus upon the inner life, as well as providing intertextual reference to the artist's own creativity, and indicates a source for the self-reliance and independence of his characters.

With the exception of the alphabet book, each story features a single character accompanied, if at all, only by an animal, though friendly relatives are never far away. These independent youngsters are able to resolve most of the difficulties they encounter from strengths within themselves. Kitamura's task is to find graphic equivalences for both their outer and their inner worlds that are sufficiently seamless and convincing to provide his reader with opportunities for identification. He brings out the abstract qualities of both worlds. Through particular emphases in depictive style he captures on the page the effects of physical objects as we experience them; the imaginary inner life, "past everyday night and everynight dreams" (a quotation from *Ned* which applies to most of the picture books) often is visualized through innovative organization of the spatial and temporal framework of his compositions and by an evocative use of color.

Kitamura uses simple materials, pen and watercolor, to construct compositions of extraordinary subtlety. In this as in other characteristics of his style, his indebtedness to the pictorial traditions of Japan and such artists as Utamaro, Hiroshige, and Hokusai is evident. When faced with a graphic problem, his instinctive response is to find a compositional solution which has its origins in the Japanese print or scroll. Such solutions in conjunction with Western imagery give his style a strong individual identity.

The quality of Kitamura's line is one of the distinctive aspects of his artwork, though it can hardly be separated from other such vital elements as his use of color. There is no underdrawing, so the line goes down once and for all, with no margin for error, no chance to reconsider. The line is fine, unbroken, and exhibits a slight tremor which charges the drawing with energy. It is as if the concentration required to limn the line is still present in the record of the movement of the artist's hand.

To define objects Kitamura uses a closed contour line precisely filled with color. A closed contour contains an object and separates it from its surroundings. This mode of drawing separate attention to an object suits Kitamura's purpose well, since many of his images have symbolic or narrative value and thus reward close looking, and since he often is concerned to promote a surreal effect by juxtaposing unlikely objects to suggest his characters' inner lives.

If he used the continuous line and local color alone, Kitamura would have no way of softening the passage from the shape of one object to another, no way of suggesting the relativity of existence or the connections between objects. To some extent he resolves this problem by plain water or water paint washes. In places, the precise definition of the line is modulated by a wash which causes a slight bleeding (either blue-black or sepia, according to the type of ink chosen for a particular set of illustrations). These passages, with their cunning shifts and drifts of color and tone, have a unifying effect on the composition as a whole. Often they refer to background motifs or textures—bricks, tiles, foliage—against which the objects with closed contours are thrown into sharp contrast. The tension between the tightly

controlled line and the escaping watery staining gives the picture much of its sense of movement and vitality.

Kitamura is always a sophisticated colorist; he uses white areas skillfully in conjunction with subtle combinations of hues like cinnabar and ocher opposed by intense inky violet. Pale milky tints and chalky grays are contrasted in hue and tone with full grape red, with hyacinth and Prussian blues. Color modifies the directness of his forms as well as having a vital expressive function.

The emotional use of color is in accord with the artist's style of drawing. Kitamura draws intuitively rather than from life, a quality foremost in Japanese and Chinese art, as Frederick Gore suggests [in *Painting: Some Basic Principles*]. The shapes of Kitamura's forms are sculptural, simplified, and tend toward the angular, with scant concern for anatomy or the rules of projective realism. He is after the essence of things rather than their (mere) appearance. Kitamura emphasizes the clumpfootedness of a child wearing training shoes, the snaking hazards of electrical cords, the comforting possibility of delving deeply into a stew pot, the cheery stir-it-all-about directness of the frying pan. He often gives two viewpoints on individual objects; we may look at something—say a jar—at eye level, the better to read its label and observe how solidly it sits upon a surface, but in addition we may look down on it from above, the better to enjoy its contents. The effect of the second viewpoint is to tilt the upper surface toward us and to make the total form more accessible. This is how we "know" a jar, as we handle it and glance at it from different angles.

Kitamura's use of perspective is eclectic. He readily juggles between the Western Renaissance convention, which dictates that parallel lines should converge in the distance, and a system of perspective widely used in China and Japan which may be related to the concept of the "traveling eye." The beholder is assumed to be scanning the painting in different directions rather than maintaining one fixed viewpoint and is not looking at a scene so much as wandering about in it. Kitamura also favors inverted perspective—diverging rather than converging parallels—on furniture like sturdy wooden beds, tables, and chairs; inverted perspective maintains symmetry as a whole and exposes both sides of an object to the spectator. As well as offering much more access to and information about an object, inverted perspective gives it an air of stability. This quality acts as a comforting counterbalance to the unsettling, sometimes intemperate, and often mysterious happenings in the stories themselves.

Through such stylization Kitamura offers an interpretation of life as we experience it emotionally; his paintings strike a chord of recognition. Nothing could be more down-to-cement than his depiction of a busy and cluttered urban domestic environment with many things to mind and tasks to do. Toys must be tidied away, musical instruments have to be practiced, house plants wilt for want of water, dishes wait to be dried, dust bins overflow. Every viewer, whether child or adult, recognizes this world firsthand and easily identifies with it. Taken together, the unbroken tremulous contour, the simplified shapes, and the multiple viewpoints cause objects to impinge upon the consciousness of the picture-book beholder, just as the maintenance and manipulation of objects impinge in reality. Thus Kitamura draws us into the lives of his protagonists. . . .

*Angry Arthur* is the portrait of a rage. Arthur wants to stay up to watch a Western on the television but is told that it is time for him to go to bed. "'I'll get angry,' said Arthur. 'Get angry,' said his mother." And he does. Arthur goes on to indulge in the terrible and secret urge of the impotent child to annihilate everyone and everything which oppose him. Hiawyn Oram's text is flat, unadorned matter of fact, with the interjection, "'That's enough,' But it wasn't" repeated at spaced intervals, as each member of the family in turn attempts to pacify the child. His response is to notch up the force of his tantrum which becomes a storm cloud, a hurricane, a typhoon, an earth tremor, a universe quake in which all perish except the protagonist and his pet. Two elements make a major contribution to the mood of intensive emotional energy of this picture book. One is the color, which includes the open face of white, and the other is the sparseness and intricacy of the forms and the quality of space surrounding them, which sets up waves of visual rhythms.

On the very first opening, Kitamura uses color and white to carry a carefully constructed emotional charge. To the left, Arthur is placed on a white unworked page, watching a Western on the television in a relaxed pose, while the kettle puffs cheerfully on the stove and the cat snoozes contentedly. The strong vertical emphasis of the stove pipe and the flattened perspective of the television set give stability to this scene of the child absorbed in what is, at present, a secondhand experience of conflict. Arthur is viewed from above, on a reduced scale, as if to emphasize the physical insignificance of the small being from whom the mighty drama is soon to spring. The pure white space surrounding him signifies his total concentration. Nothing but the film exists for Arthur, and little else but Arthur exists for the beholder. The composition is a pleasing adaptation of a visual technique used for representing interior scenes in Japan since the mid-seventeenth century. Its essence—simple but forcible and flexible—is the omission of any background except for a few indicators left as clues.

Opposing this comfortable scene is a full plate in somber grayish hues of ocher, violet, and Vandyke brown. Still small in scale and viewed from above, Arthur is now placed against a painted background which represents a darkened room. The outside world intrudes. A block of light falls across the planked floor by way of the open door. Arthur's mother is on the threshold. Her figure throws a huge diagonal shadow across the floor and across the picture plane. We see only her feet, but her presence is unavoidable. Arthur's form and those of his cat, the television set, and his toys are all aligned with the direction in which the floorboards run. These present

a series of rising diagonals (thus mirroring the child's rage) across which the mother's shadow is cast. Arthur and his mother are visually, verbally, and metaphorically on a collision course.

Kitamura fractures the picture plane on the next opening as Arthur's rage is unleashed. From the evening sky outside the window it strikes, Jove-like, ricocheting off the walls, smashing the furniture, and concentrating in an explosive flash at the lower edge of the picture plane. The surface of the flash acts as a label for the brief text, making a perfect example of the integration of typographical word and plastic image. Furniture and household objects are flung across space. The hues which so ominously echoed Arthur's mood in the previous painting have now lightened in tone as this therapeutic rage rises and erupts.

Over the next four page openings the proportion of details in each painting crescendos to a climax as Arthur systematically destroys his room, his garden, his house, his street, his town, and his country. Terraces tilt, horizons heave, trivia and treasures tumble.

As Arthur goes on to attack the surface of the earth as if he were a giant cracking eggs, so the details fall away. Galactic acrobatics soothe the child. He and his pet—depicted in small scale—twist and turn, rise and descend in a starry continuum. Material means match the emotional tenor: the fluid brushstrokes stain the paper with floating, weightless, incandescent color. As the last pages turn, aerial tissues of luminous gold and violet give way to dusky blue, then return, and finally fade away altogether. Arthur's bed on its fragment of Mars drifts above a generous area of unworked white open space, symbolizing a return to normality, blessed sleep. The storm has blown itself out. A musical analogy suggests itself. This final sequence is like a coda which returns us through a series of cadences to a tranquil conclusion. The ebb and flow of images, the balance of saturated and unsaturated hues and of light and dark tones form a visual counterpart to a musical rhythm which is at one with the impulse of the text.

Any work of art creates its own universe, which is a whole, built upon a space-time framework. Kitamura's aesthetic arrangement of this framework is one of the most innovative features of his next collaboration, *Ned and the Joybaloo.* Space (what's inside and what's outside) and time (how the speed of its passage varies according to circumstance) are central to the story and its themes. Ned quests for happiness and finds it in the form of a big and beautiful creature, resembling a seaside inflatable toy. A cross between a dog and a seal, the Joybaloo has "a funny leathery nose and its breath full of paper roses." Every Friday the Joybaloo takes Ned to its playgrounds, where they squeeze "the last drop of mischief" out of the night. But this is not enough for Ned. He wants every night to be a Joybaloo night. Through his insatiable greed and selfishness he exhausts the Joybaloo. And after that he has no choice but to set about making his own happiness, which is not so difficult after all, given his creative nature. The picture book concludes with Ned dreaming happily of the Joybaloo, knowing that one day it will return, in its own good time. Happiness cannot be commanded.

Here is the classic tale of the rise and fall and coming to wisdom of the hero, shaped for a child. It shows that happiness, especially when entirely dependent upon outside factors, is elusive and ephemeral; we may enjoy moments of unlooked-for happiness, but may equally well take pleasure in more modest forms which we create for ourselves. As befits the nature of childhood, Joybaloo-happiness is linked to extreme physical gratification: dancing, bouncing, laughing, flying, playing sensuously in mud and water, and "running wild." On the other hand, there is contentment to be gained from music, toys, and delighting others, as when Ned picks some flowers for his mother. Summarized as baldly as this; *Ned and the Joybaloo* sounds fiercely didactic. The good humor which pervades the visual narrative ensures that the total experience offered by the picture book is thoroughly enjoyable, as well as morally sound.

In six of twelve page openings in this book, Kitamura uses what Joseph Schwarcz [in *Ways of the Illustrator*] calls a "continuous narrative" technique which emphasizes the space and time spans of the story. In each of these illustrations, either Ned alone or Ned and the Joybaloo appears several times at different places, while the background remains broadly the same. A similar device is common both to Western late medieval narrative painting and to the scroll of the Far East, whereby a progression through time is suggested by a repetition of the figure of the protagonist. Such compositions not only incorporate in their structure a strong sense of time; they also ask for time from the beholder.

The continuous narrative needs to be read in a certain order—that is, the one which indicates progress in space and time of the recurring figure(s). Therefore the beholder is obliged to spend a period of dynamic contemplation—a time in which to do visual thinking and attend to inner speech—in order to make meaning. Both the story's participants and the beholder are taking up more time than is perhaps generally the case in a single picture in a children's picture book. Studying the illustrations, one cannot help but be impressed by the different ways Kitamura structures his continuous narrative composition, thus demonstrating that the same technique can serve a variety of effects. Each composition presents a fresh challenge for a young viewer, who, like Ned, must consciously spend time and effort in his search for pleasure. The search becomes the pleasure, through effort.

The continuous narrative is introduced first to show the search for the Joybaloo, a protracted and daunting task. A rising diagonal, from lower left to approximately top right, divides the two-page spread into halves. The resulting smaller upper inverted triangle, which carries the text upon the open face of white, provides a restful contrast to the lower, larger, near-triangular shape, which is colored, dark in tone, and seething with images. A

stretch of brown background reads as carpet or garden, depending on whether Ned's activity suggests that he is indoors or outside. To the right is a section of a house facade, complete with an open back door we can see through.

Disposed over the picture plane of this lower shape, nine little Neds look in, under, through, and behind the likely and unlikely places for finding a Joybaloo: in the cellar, vase, flower pot, boot, vacuum cleaner bag, washing machine, dog kennel, under the couch, and (very sensibly, Ned has donned a rubber apron for this) in the dustbin. In the upper right of the picture plane we see a tenth Ned, backview in pajamas—see how time has flown—peering into the dark depths of the airing cupboard. A huge pair of eyes stares back. The triangular wedge of color and activity created by the rising diagonal is a fitting visual metaphor in itself for Ned's uphill struggle, finally to be crowned by success. His changes of costume, the scattered tools he has used for dismantling and smashing objects, the opened doors and disturbed drawers signify the long passage of time in which Ned has been engaged upon his search. Every element in the busy composition contributes to exemplifying the keyed-up intensity of Ned's feelings, his determination and single-mindedness. And while Ned has been looking for the Joybaloo, the viewer has been looking equally hard, making a logical sequence out of a chaos of instances.

Kitamura's inventiveness allows him another arrangement when, in a collection of little separate episodes, he depicts Ned, hell-bent on making everyone's life as miserable as his own, as he waits from one Joybaloo night to the next. Ned is remarkably busy.

This time the composition is based on a fan-shaped arrangement of forms with oblique or vertical emphases that suggest spokes. Just as a fan opens by separate movements of the spokes, so, by association, here they evoke the temporal breaks Ned experiences in the course of the week. Once again, there is no distinction made between the inside and outside of the house. Roof and walls have been taken away. In both the illustrations discussed, Kitamura has adapted and extended the convention known as "taking off the roof," as seen in early Japanese prints, which allows the beholder to dive in and out of doors and follow the action from one room to the other. It makes a particularly effective way of letting the picture-book viewer into Ned's life. Very different in feeling and appearance, the painting of the playground of the Joybaloo is structured in four curving horizontal bands, which suggest that we are looking at a section of something like a huge roundel composed of ceaseless pleasurable physical experiences. The figures of Ned and the Joybaloo are seen four times, in four different locations, experiencing four different sensations; the transitions from one to the other are seamless, as in dreams. Overleaf Kitamura temporarily abandons continuous narrative, and, in a typically Japanese way of making space, he gives his reader a ride on the Joybaloo.

This memorable composition depicts Ned in his aviator's goggles hanging onto the Joybaloo's ears as they dive diagonally across the picture plane, exemplifying an excess of daring, buoyancy, exhilaration. The saturated violet night sky concedes to the approaching dawn with its open face of white (white also being used for the pure-joy-Joybaloo). Multiple viewpoints of the landscape are from above. Kitamura creates the impression of circling and soaring by curling the horizon, metaphorically transferring loops from the motion of flight to the Joybaloo landscape. It is as if there is no beginning or end to the picture, as in a Japanese hand scroll which can be unrolled either way, and what is space spreads out in all directions. The beholder might well start by looking at the illustration with the book held upside down and gradually turn it, enacting the flight, sharing the view with Ned.

The illustrations for *In the Attic* display a more cerebral and reflective mood. A small boy, the narrator, sits bored in a sea of toys, the forms of which incidentally contain apt visual allusions to works by Tatlin and Brancusi, artists who extended the boundaries of sculpture. Climbing up the ladder of his toy fire engine and going into the attic is a metaphoric trip extending the boundary of the narrator's mind.

Kitamura depicts the young narrator's changes of thoughts in successive openings by changes of settings and of pictorial style. The text is virtually superfluous until the penultimate illustration, when the child goes to tell his mother about where he's been. "'But we don't have an attic,' she said." He smiles.

As each page turns we watch his thoughts traveling far and wide. His building blocks become immense cavernous architectural edifices which hint at the structures of Piranesi. Then toy mice take on life and organize heroic games with everyday objects, such as a toothbrush and a corkscrew. Further on, the child rests and reflects in the middle of a colony of Klee-like insects, which hum and buzz with the music of whirring wings. Next he meets a spider and joins it in making a web, the pair of them thus matching the extraordinary engineering feat of the pyramids pictured below them. The connection between web and mausoleum is waiting to be made in terms of the materials, construction methods, aims, survival span, and symbolism, according to the "reading" skills and experience of the beholder. Later the boy opens surreal windows in space and traveling on, meets and makes a friend—a tiger—with whom he can share his wonders. And, best of all, the two of them find a "game that could go on for ever because it kept changing."

*In the Attic* has one quality I would like to single out above others. Some of the illustrations do not offer much scope for making a literal story from what they denote, though they display qualities which encourage active contemplation and response of a nonverbal kind. Too often children see pictures as just more words in a different form, not a different symbol system with its own

language. As John Dewey points out, reading pictures is thinking directly in terms of colors, tones, images, and their disposition on the picture plane and in imagined space. Pictures have values and meanings which cannot be expressed in words without loss in translation, and this applies to pictures in picture books as well as those on walls.

The needs of our daily life have given superior practical importance to speech, and picture books are used for language development, teaching children how to point and say, read, and generally generate talk. As parents and teachers we foster the impression that pictures are for talking about. But pictorial art is specifically made for looking at; a feature of seeing and looking is silence, though it may be accompanied by what Dewey calls "inner speech." Galleries are full of people reading the attribution labels and exhibition catalogs, listening to lecturers, talking about what paintings denote, and sparing little time for reading the painting itself. Nonrepresentational art gets the shortest shrift; since it appears to be about nothing, what is there to say? It is as if we are at a loss to know how to approach visual art without the written or spoken word in attendance.

Among the many reasons why we should have become so dependent upon words, one could well be the outcome of our earliest experiences with pictures—the picture book. In a paper exploring the apparent compulsion, as well as the difficulties and dangers, of translating visual experiences into language, Ciaran Benson examines the role images play in teaching literacy, the narrative traditions of picture-book illustration, and the research on aesthetic responses of young children to the visual arts. He argues that if children grow up thinking visual art is only to be talked about, as well they might, then the effect of such a theory on their relation with the visual arts will be positively procrustean.

*In the Attic* is the perfect book for exploring what properties the pictures display as well as denote, because the text has minimal narrative thrust, and the layout is organized in a series of self-contained, separate plates; measured rhythms encourage a reflective stance. For example, Kitamura's illustration of the "game that could go on for ever" cannot adequately be translated into words. The game is depicted in Kandinsky-like free form and geometric symbols because it is too wonderful for words. Children might be encouraged to contemplate such a picture, or the one in the insect colony, confident that to feel something and say nothing is still a valid response.

As well as an illuminator of the texts of others, Kitamura is a picture-book maker. His alphabet and counting books bring to his youngest audiences delightful instruction and instructive delight. *What's Inside? The Alphabet Book* poses just that very question: we look inside assorted containers including a carton, dustbin, crate, cases, tubes, and even a spine-chilling coffin lying in the snow. The most innovative technically of the books for which he has had sole responsibility, the layout and dynamics are complex, though regular in pattern, and exert a strong influence on the rhythms of reading the pictures. On each page opening, a puzzle is posed on the right half of the picture, cued by a pair of initials on or by a container; the solution appears overleaf on the left, where the hidden objects are revealed and labeled by words. In addition to the strong linear thrust from one page opening to the next, generated by the curiosity to discover "what's inside," the focus of the picture also alternates rhythmically between large-scale close-ups and small-scale wide-angled views, as selected details on one page become the main subject matter on the next. Furthermore, the spectator's viewpoint shifts between inside and outside localities. This picture book, like others by Kitamura, exhibits a strong kinship to musical form. Here he extemporizes with the letters of the alphabet as in jazz, where the rhythmic framework allows for tremendous energy and freedom. . . .

One of the strengths of this picture book lies in the different ways it can be used, for it is capable of sustaining many pictorial re-readings long after the puzzles have been solved and the alphabet sequence mastered, by virtue of the detail in the compositions. . . . In the artist's perspective, detail makes a distinctive contribution to the whole while, in the spectator's perspective, it elicits and rewards focused perception. Traditionally, detail has been the locus both of personal imprint and of heightened pleasure; however, too often in picture-book illustration it fails to meet either condition. Not so in Kitamura's case. The detailed compositions in *What's Inside?* invite the viewer to read visually all over the picture plane, to search, observe, discover, test, ponder upon, make connections, and construct subplots from this idiosyncratic assembly of characters, objects, and settings.

In *What's Inside?* we see musical and writing instruments, ladders, black bats, striped clothing, empty streets, the friendly tiger—all recurring motifs in Kitamura's work, linking them to a larger whole. Observant young viewers, spying a detail in one picture, may well greet its relocation in another picture or picture book with a sense of delighted recognition. Particularly intriguing are glimpses of characters like two small boys and a tiger, who have made the journey from other works to *What's Inside?* and appear to be waiting to be given new roles in stories from the viewer's imagination. These compositions have the same kind of flexibility and story-making potential as the game which the little attic explorer found that "can go on for ever, because it keeps changing."

And so to bed. *When Sheep Cannot Sleep,* or small children either, what better than to start counting? The nature of a counting book generally works against coherence and flow, normally essential elements of the picture-book experience; not so with Kitamura's, which eschews stereotype. One rare feature is the absence of explicit instruction. The verbal text, apart from one instance, is free from any mention of number, though there are clues by name or sound as to what might be

counted. Nor are there any depicted numerals; it is as if the pictures just happen to display increasing numbers of interesting objects within them.

The story addresses itself to the child with unforced humor. Woolly the Sheep goes on his insomniac rambles under dramatic night skies. He observes first a butterfly and then a pair of ladybirds, plays hide-and-seek in long grass with fireflies, and so on until, finally exhausted by his adventures, he falls asleep counting his relatives. The layout is simple. Nothing distracts from the orderly sequence of three-quarter plates, beneath each of which is set a brief portion of text. There is an airiness about the generous proportion of open face of white which frames the narratives, providing an area of contrast to the richly colored plates. The compositions are masterly, with flawless clarity of communication.

Woolly is an endearing creature with a sagacious look, a thoroughly credible being. Anthropomorphized by expression and pose, he is to be seen more often on two legs than on four. Though he looks very funny he is never a figure of fun; Kitamura no more trivializes Woolly than John Tenniel trivializes the White Rabbit, nor is there a trace of sentimentality.

One touching portrait shows Woolly alone in an unoccupied house and engaged in what everyone does—telling stories to himself about himself in order to make sense of what is happening. Being a Kitamura hero, Woolly does this storytelling by drawing. Serene hues of light rose and light ocher dominate a composition which exemplifies Woolly's happy, childlike absorption, and the results of his labors are to be seen overleaf. Woolly has painted fifteen pictures, one for each of his night's encounters, which he now hangs upon the wall and stands back to admire. Kitamura is playing a game with continuous narrative technique of a very special kind, in which everything counts for Woolly as well as for his beholder. The latter has the chance to tally the score and also benefit from a pictorial summary of the story so far; Woolly's memory of time past gives him a sense of identity in time present—a comforting feeling for an isolated being to have in an unfamiliar setting, and a sophisticated comment on the nature of the text itself.

In common with all the other books, there are little running jokes, meaningful details, faultlessly placed and spaced elements; but the most outstanding feature is Kitamura's use of color and tone. I have been suggesting throughout that the distinctiveness of Kitamura's picture books can best be understood by situating them within his own culture; particularly in Woolly's tale, the artist's preference for rich and often somber color characteristic of Japanese traditions finds its expression in his painting. . . .

In Kitamura's picture books color offers sensuous delight, reflects the tone of the text, and heightens the drama. Just by looking at the portraits of Woolly at work and of Woolly tucked up in bed under his feather-white coverlet, in his room with its walls in many tints of gray, its terra-cotta curtains, deep vine red carpet, and beech brown bed, a child is exposed to the possibility of appreciating differences in hue and tone, contrasts and similarities in relationships. Color, the child discovers, tells its own kind of tale.

In less than a decade Kitamura has made, and continues to make, a distinctive contribution to the art of the children's picture book. The fresh way of saying "even something very commonplace" is evident in all he does.

**Mary Gribbin**

SOURCE: "The Inside Story," in *The Times Educational Supplement,* No. 4089, November 11, 1994, p. 18.

This new series for key stages 1 and 2 is inspired by the exhibitions at Eureka!, the hands on museum in Halifax. *Me and My Body* features a robot called Scoot who wants to find out everything it can about the children reading the book. Scoot isn't just interested in what the readers look like, but also their likes and dislikes, why and how they grow, their emotions, needs and feelings.

The illustrations by Satoshi Kitamura are the most striking feature of the book. They are lively and charming but there just aren't enough of them. Most of the illustration is photographic—clear and straightforward but nothing new. Having the book totally illustrated by Satoshi Kitamura would have lifted it way out of the ordinary. The text is also clear and straightforward.

It doesn't patronise and this book would be useful to any class learning more about themselves and how they work both mentally and physically.

*Inside My House* is aimed at the same readership. Where *Me and My Body* has Scoot, *Inside My House* has Tweet the Bird who hops through the book looking at what goes on and passing pious comments: "You all need a few rules to help things run smoothly," twitters the merry bird.

Tweet is undoubtedly a very sensible bird, but he could do with lightening up now and again.

*Inside My House* concentrates on what goes on inside homes and why caring for homes and the people living in them is important. But it cries out even louder than its companion for more Kitamura drawings, because sometimes the photographs are downright incomprehensible. Page 13 has a series of three smallish photographs of a working exhibit at the Eureka Museum.

Each photograph, of Archimedes in his bath, looks staggeringly similar to the others. They disprove the claim that one picture is worth a thousand words. How a six-year-old is supposed to comprehend Archimedes Principle from this I do not know.

Both books are full of ideas for class activities and individual projects. They are clear and jolly and would be fun to have in class. If they had more of the Satoshi Kitamura magic and were a bit cheaper they would be snapped up by children's pocket money shopping as well.

---

# TITLE COMMENTARY

📖 *ANGRY ARTHUR* (written by Hiawyn Oram, 1982)

**Holly Sanhuber**

SOURCE: A review of *Angry Arthur,* in *School Library Journal,* Vol. 29, No. 1, September, 1982, p. 110.

Arthur's anger may frighten children and disturb adults who do not recognize it as anger acted out in the realm of imagination—or is it? That ambiguity is also disturbing—and out of place in a picture book that the jacket copy claims will ". . . appeal to every reader who has ever been disappointed or frustrated . . . [and] will help children put their feelings in proper perspective." This cheery bibliotherapy is at variance with the book in two ways. First, Arthur's anger is out of all proportion to the provocation offered. Second, the violence of the pictures, increasingly crowded and purple, showing Arthur with hatred distorting his small ferocious face, are unlikely to reassure anyone, adult or child. The ending, although a sad commentary on every act of carnage that ever was, is hardly satisfying. Arthur's anger has become cosmic, causing a "universe quake," and "Arthur

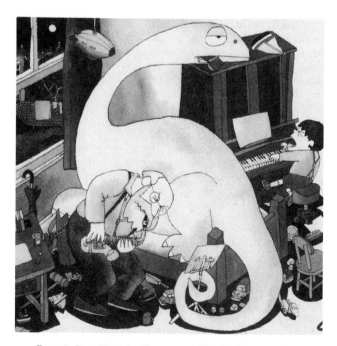

*From* A Boy Wants a Dinosaur, *written by Hiawyn Oram. Illustrated by Satoshi Kitamura.*

sat on a piece of Mars and thought. He thought and thought. 'Why was I so angry?' he thought. He never did remember. Can you?" Teaching picturebook audiences the futility of vain regrets? That's bibliotherapy with a vengeance!

## A. Thatcher

SOURCE: A review of *Angry Arthur,* in *The Junior Bookshelf,* Vol. 46, No. 5, October, 1982, p. 183.

Young Arthur is angry because he is not allowed to watch a Western on Television. His anger explodes into a storm cloud, a hurricane, a typhoon, an earth tremor, and a universe quake. As he sits on his bed floating in space on a chunk of Mars, he cannot even remember what started it all. The short, simple text complements full-page brightly coloured, original and imaginative illustrations. Arthur and his dog, and family are cleverly drawn cartoon figures—grandma sits knitting in her rocking chair in space wearing a helmet! Young readers will enjoy looking at this picture book.

## 📖 NED AND THE JOYBALOO (written by Hiawyn Oram, 1983; U.S. edition, 1988)

### Joan Wood Sheaffer

SOURCE: A review of *Ned and the Joybaloo,* in *School Library Journal,* Vol. 30, No. 10, August, 1984, p. 63.

In this story that is awkwardly written and moralistic, a small boy discovers a Joybaloo, a huge dog-like creature, in his closet. On Friday evenings he and the Joybaloo travel wherever their dreams may take them. While Ned has his creature for companionship, he behaves horribly between the joy-trips. When he insists that the Joybaloo play with him every night, the creature gradually weakens and fades away. The creature's disappearance forces Ned to amuse himself and he learns that it isn't difficult to find constructive entertainment. The full-page illustrations are vibrant and filled with humorous details, but children may be confused by the multiple images of Ned and the Joybaloo in some of the pictures.

### Publishers Weekly

SOURCE: A review of *Ned and the Joybaloo,* in *Publishers Weekly,* Vol. 233, No. 25, June 24, 1988, p. 110.

Ned is impatient for Fridays, the "day of the night" that he and the Joybaloo play together. The Joybaloo, which is the size of a dragon, but most closely resembles a white dog bearing confetti-like spots, is a friend Ned found in the cupboard; it can fly and make Ned laugh for hours on end. But Ned demands the attention of the Joybaloo so often that it loses its joy. And Ned learns to have fun on his own. Perhaps this is Oram's comment

on the logic that rules imaginary friends, the troubles of addictive behavior or simply a glimpse of a boy who learns to look to himself for happiness. Kitamura chooses the latter of these three to interpret Ned's plight; offbeat perspectives show a button-eyed Ned making mischief in a cluttered, chaotic household and soaring through the skies with the Joybaloo.

### John Cech

SOURCE: "Every Kid Needs a Friend," in *The New York Times Book Review,* May 21, 1989, p. 41.

A Joybaloo is "big and beautiful, with a funny leathery nose and its breath full of paper roses." At least Ned's is, the one that he finds unexpectedly in the linen closet while looking for "an important piece of a thing he was making." The discovery of this enormous imaginary friend means that Ned can bounce past "every-day night and every-night dreams" to other places that only an empowered creature like the Joybaloo is able to take him. Clinging to his friend's striped ears, Ned can leave behind the daily routines that bore him to anger and tears and, with them, the mother "who seemed to expect him to wash, dress, have breakfast, and get to school all in the same moment." On Friday nights—Joybaloo nights—Ned can fly.

Fantasy sees what is unseen, brings to light what is in the shadows. It is one of the primary ways we have for adapting psychologically to the new and unfamiliar, the frustrating and the frightening. Children find fantasy a natural and ready means for solving the pressing emotional problems of their lives, turning, as Maurice Sendak's star-child Rosie puts it, "twelve boring hours into a fascinating day." So, too, Ned's ecstatic fantasy helps him to soar out of his doldrums.

But, as anyone who has ever had a good fantasy knows, there is a downward arc after the euphoria. Joybaloos can get overworked and lose their exhilarating energy. Hiawyn Oram does not spare the reader that reality, nor the one that gently insists those supreme fantasies are rare. But they are also sustaining, and the vitality that they release helps Ned to rediscover meaning—and joy—in his everyday world and those who inhabit it with him.

Satoshi Kitamura's spirited watercolors capture the fluid essence of Ned's fantasy. In fact, both Ned—a tousle-haired, expressive little boy—and the Joybaloo—an overstuffed, shape-changing dog-cloud with red, blue and yellow spots and abstract striping—are completely his vision. At times, Mr. Kitamura makes Ned a little too cute, thus sweetening the fantasy unnecessarily. But he is at his best when he lets Ned be himself—grumpy, brooding or unselfconsciously intent upon the purposes of his fantasy, as he is when Mr. Kitamura draws him in goggles and gloves jetting across a swirling, crazy-quilt landscape on the Joybaloo's streamlined back. At moments like these, when the artist quite literally opens up the roof of Ned's house to let the bouncing child and his friend out, Mr. Kitamura is truly and completely at one with the emotional dimensions of Ned's fantasy.

*Ned and the Joybaloo* is the third book in the happy collaboration between Ms. Oram, a British writer, and Mr. Kitamura, an illustrator who was born in Japan and now lives in England. Their two other books have explored similar themes concerning the powerful role that fantasy plays in children's lives. In *Angry Arthur,* taking their inspiration from Maurice Sendak's pioneering *Where the Wild Things Are,* Ms. Oram and Mr. Kitamura sent a little boy (the prototype for Ned) to the outer limits of his temper-tantrum-induced fantasy, turning his rage into "a universe quake" that leaves him floating on "a piece of Mars," wondering what made him so mad in the first place. *In the Attic* lets another little boy (Ned again) discover a new room for his imagination— the attic—in a house that doesn't have one. But, of course, it does.

*Ned and the Joybaloo* reminds one of the line in Ruth Krauss's poem *A Very Special House* that locates imagination so precisely: "Oh it's right in the middle . . . of my head head head."

## 📖 *IN THE ATTIC* (written by Hiawyn Oram, 1984; U.S. edition, 1985)

### *Publishers Weekly*

SOURCE: A review of *In the Attic,* in *Publishers Weekly,* Vol. 227, No. 8, February 22, 1985, p. 158.

Kitamura's debut as the illustrator of Oram's *Angry Arthur* won him England's Mother Goose award. His inventiveness complements the new, rhythmic, enticing story by the author, who shows she's in on a secret known to children all over the world: anything is possible. Firmly etched pictures in striking, contrasting hues reveal the escapades of a toddler who's bored with his roomful of toys. "So I climbed to the attic," he says, on the ladder of a miniature fire truck. The dream adventures entertain the boy for hours; he hates to leave the friends he has made, but it's time for dinner. When he tells his mother where he's been, she says, "But we don't have an attic." Gazing confidently at the reader, the voyager concludes, "I guess she doesn't know . . . she hasn't found the ladder."

## 📖 *WHAT'S INSIDE? THE ALPHABET BOOK* (1985)

### *Kirkus Reviews*

SOURCE: A review of *What's Inside? The Alphabet Book,* in *Kirkus Reviews,* Vol. LIII, No. 10, May 15, 1985, p. J26.

Kitamura's clever alphabet page-turner proceeds some-

thing like a film: one uninterrupted camera pan that meanders from city street to country lake, growing less realistic as it proceeds. The first spread shows scattered pieces and boxes of fruit with the letters "a" and "b" on two closed boxes on the right-hand page. On the second spread, those two boxes, now toward the left edge of the picture, are open to reveal *apples* and *bananas*—pictured inside the boxes and printed on the inner raised lids. Nearby, on the right, a garbage can marked "c" and "d" has come into view, and a further turn brings a scared *cat* (treed on a lamppost) and a fierce *dog* from the can. From there to "z," Kitamura's ramshackle pictures become more cluttered, nutty, and surreal, with a *tiger* in a *snow*-covered graveyard yielding to a flying *vampire* bat with an *umbrella,* and with "m" and "n" on toothpaste tubes unfurling to depict *morning* (sunny blue sky) and star-studded *night.*

Far too tricky for a first alphabet book, but too genuinely ingenious to pass up.

### Denise M. Wilms

SOURCE: A review of *What's Inside? The Alphabet Book,* in *Booklist,* Vol. 82, No. 1, September 1, 1985, p. 64.

Kitamura's adept, whimsical full-color paintings are the basis of an offbeat alphabet book that will intrigue older children who already know their letters but aren't above partaking in some visual fun. Letters are here, but not in the way you would expect; they appear only in lowercase forms of varied size, placed on the page as a signal to the pair of words that will appear next. For example, the first spread features a group of partially opened boxes with fruit spilled about. One box has an *a,* another a *b;* the following page shows them opened with apples and bananas inside. Then, just around the corner is a trash can with *c* and *d* written on its side. On the next page a dog has chased a cat atop a lamppost while a discreet sign carries the words *cat* and *dog.* The scenes often reflect a spirit of fun. An elephant and a fire engine come head to head on the same street; and a hippopotamus strums his guitar in a room filled with a jumble of musical instruments. The imaginative quality of the pictures coupled with the artist's precise way with line and wash make for a fresh, engaging display of letters that will stand up to more than one close look.

### R. Baines

SOURCE: A review of *What's Inside? The Alphabet Book,* in *The Junior Bookshelf,* Vol. 49, No. 5, October, 1985, p. 212.

This gloriously exuberant alphabet book uses lower case letters throughout, introducing two at a time then expanding the same pair on the following page. Thus boxes marked a and b open to reveal that they contain apples and bananas, whilst o and p are developed in a picture of an octopus playing a piano.

Other intriguingly unconventional subjects are selected: e and f juxtapose the vast shapes of an elephant and a fire engine, whilst u and v are illustrated by a cheerful vampire bat sheltering under an umbrella. The pictures also spring surprises: toothpaste squeezed out by a small boy swells into an ocean, and a guitar-playing hippopotamus lives inside a hippopotamus-shaped case.

Every page is filled to the edge with vivid colour and the good quality paper has an attractive gloss. Altogether a very pleasing book.

### WHEN SHEEP CANNOT SLEEP: THE COUNTING BOOK (1986)

#### Ilene Cooper

SOURCE: A review of *When Sheep Cannot Sleep: The Counting Book,* in *Booklist,* Vol. 83, No. 3, October 1, 1986, p. 273.

A clever counting book for older children. One night an insomniac sheep named Woolly is wandering through the meadow. As he walks along he chases (one) butterfly, watches enviously as (two) ladybugs sleep in a tree, and tries to reach (five) apples among the leaves. But after other adventures, including going to an art gallery and admiring (fifteen) paintings, he finally goes home and counts his *zzz*'s. All 22 of them. This book has a number of things going for it. The subtle counting element is unusual because no mention of the numbers appears in the text. Children are given a written hint of what they are to count; sometimes, as in the case of nine grasshoppers, the objects are difficult to spot. For those who need help, a key is appended. The other plus is Kitamura's whimsical full-color artwork. The squared-off sheep has an endearingly goofy look that kids and adults will love. The pictures are offbeat and funny, making this just fine for those who want to put their counting skills to use and enjoy a guessing game along the way.

#### Jane Doonan

SOURCE: "The Pictured World," in *The Times Literary Supplement,* No. 4365, November 28, 1986, p. 1345.

Most counting books overtly declare their laudable aim in the text and pictures, whereas Satoshi Kitamura's **When Sheep Cannot Sleep** is a perfect picture book free from stereotype images, brimming with unforced humour, which appears just to happen to have some beguiling things worth counting, as the pages turn. Woolly the sheep, an expressive animal with some of the appeal of a Snoopy, goes on his insomniac rambles under dramatic night skies. He chases a butterfly, envies a pair of sleeping ladybirds, is amused by a trio of bats. Grass-

hoppers sing to him, flying saucers zip overhead. Taking refuge from a storm in an empty house Woolly finally falls asleep totting up his extensive family, while the reader is left to tally the snores. Kitamura's style counts for still more. Economical compositions in masterly pen and watercolour show every element unerringly spaced and placed. Use of colour is sophisticated with subtle combinations like cinnabar, ochre and intense inky-violet. Shapes are pure and sculptural, bestowing reassuring solidity on the pictured world.

#### Donald Fry

SOURCE: A review of *When Sheep Cannot Sleep: The Counting Book,* in *The School Librarian,* Vol. 34, No. 4, December, 1986, p. 337.

There have been many counting books, but none so witty and enjoyable as this one. Woolly, a sheep with lunatic eyes and a wonderfully comic range of facial expressions, cannot sleep and goes for a walk. Each page keeps track of his journey, a journey that steadily takes on the crazed appearance of a dream, until he ends up in bed. Woolly does no counting until the end, and most readers probably won't realise that there is counting to be done. It is a pity that the book announces itself as a counting book on the front cover instead of letting readers discover this for themselves. Even when you find out, you still have to work out what it is that is there to be counted, and such is the author's humour that this never becomes boring. Even the endpapers are part of the fun. Readers will learn about counting, but this is a literary and visual experience of comedy too.

#### Lorraine Douglas

SOURCE: A review of *When Sheep Cannot Sleep: The Counting Book,* in *School Library Journal,* Vol. 33, No. 4, December, 1986, pp. 90-1.

Woolly, 1 sheep, has insomnia, and so he goes to the meadow where he finds 2 ladybugs, 3 owls, 4 bats, etc.—all the way up to 22 "z's" when he finally nods off in an unoccupied house that he has discovered. The droll watercolor illustrations contain the items to be counted, but they are not enumerated in the text, and so it is a game to find and count them. An index at the end of the book lists the numbers and the items. . . . Like Kitamura's **What's Inside? The Alphabet Book,** this presents an engaging and fresh approach that young readers will enjoy on their own.

#### Margery Fisher

SOURCE: A review of *When Sheep Cannot Sleep: The Counting Book,* in *Growing Point,* Vol. 25, No. 5, January, 1987, p. 4745.

A square-shaped sheep with the face of a demented granny

wearing a nightcap wanders sleeplessly, noticing objects in varying numbers. This is an unusual counting-book because no figures are given on the pages and the child must count, each time, squirrels, plates, apples, stars, flying saucers and so on, until the sheep finally falls asleep in a convenient house along its route. Comically exaggerated shapes in bold paint give an air of exhilaration and surprise to a most attractive book for the youngest to pore over.

## Liz Waterland

SOURCE: A review of *When Sheep Cannot Sleep: The Counting Book,* in *Books for Keeps,* No. 52, September, 1988, pp. 8-9.

Despite its subtitle, this is a very unobtrusive counting book; it's perfectly possible to read the whole thing without counting anything at all if you don't want to. This is because it also has a story, about an insomniac sheep, which doesn't mention numbers and which therefore extends the book's appeal beyond the stage at which counting to 20 is an interesting activity.

The pictures are entertaining (the sheep's expressions are wide-ranging and shown entirely by the one line that delineates his mouth . . . very economical) and the story has that unexplained arbitrariness which children's writing and dreams can have. It was popular with the children, despite the rather unsatisfactory ending . . . what is going to happen when the owners of the house come home and find a strange sheep in bed? Shades of Goldilocks.

## LILY TAKES A WALK (1987)

### Publishers Weekly

SOURCE: A review of *Lily Takes a Walk,* in *Publishers Weekly,* Vol. 232, No. 11, September 11, 1987, p. 92.

In Hiawyn Oram's **Angry Arthur,** Kitamura illustrated the violent, intense rages a child sometimes feels. Here, he addresses the subject of childhood fears. When Lily and her dog Nicky go out walking, Lily loves to look at the world around her. For Nicky, however, the walk is a hair-raising experience: a face grins evilly from a tree; monsters rise from a trash can; streetlights become staring eyes. Kitamura simultaneously and humorously depicts Lily's and Nicky's divergent perceptions of the same walk; he is adept at tinging reality with the surreal elements that give rise to Nicky's fears. A gatefold last page reveals a heart-stopping finale for Nicky (and a hilarious coda for readers). Children will enjoy identifying with the imperturbable Lily ("Aren't they clever?" she says when faced with very real, swooping bats) and feeling superior to Nicky, who in fact experiences many of the fears they themselves are prone to. Nicky's nervous antics and his overactive imagination give this stroll a delicious scariness; inventive details on each page make this a walk well worth taking.

## Kay E. Vandergrift

SOURCE: A review of *Lily Takes a Walk,* in *School Library Journal,* Vol. 34, No. 3, November, 1987, pp. 93-4.

The straightforward text tells of Lily and her dog Nicky's stroll through town, while the illustrations show Nicky fending off real and imagined monsters on every page (a snake, a mailbox with teeth, a dinosaur). At the end, Nicky is safe in his basket when, on a final fold-out page, he is frightened by a family of mice. The simple childlike drawings of Lily and Nicky and the details of the city setting have a charm that should appeal to children, but the book does not work successfully as a whole. Some of the "monsters" that the dog sees are so subtly portrayed that they may be missed until Nicky reviews them in image balloons near the end of the story. The playful visual activity of looking for monsters in everyday items is abandoned for very obvious fantasy near the end. This book is a clever idea with an appropriately humorous ending, . . .

### Kirkus Reviews

SOURCE: A review of *Lily Takes a Walk,* in *Kirkus Reviews,* Vol. VI, No. 21, November 1, 1987, pp. 1575-76.

When Lily takes a walk, she sees only the evening star and the ducks on the canal; but her dog Nicky sees sea serpents and vampires lurking in the shadows.

Kitamura, who won the 1983 Mother Goose Award for his illustrations to Hiawyn Oram's *Angry Arthur,* has a wonderfully quirky style that combines a Japanese sensibility with a Western-style sense of humor. As Lily walks through the streets of her town, insensible to the offbeat and threatening monsters, poor Nicky stares aghast. At dinner, Lily cheerfully tells her parents about her day, while cartoon balloons picture what Nicky would say if only he could talk.

This understated, subtle, and delightful story offers no moral, but children will enjoy its double world of fantasy and reality.

## Margaret Meek

SOURCE: A review of *Lily Takes a Walk,* in *The School Librarian,* Vol. 36, No. 1, February, 1988, p. 16.

Accompanied by her dog, Nicky, Lily enjoys evening walks. It's Nicky who sees the spooks as, in well-authenticated fantasies, bushes, dustbins, trees, letterboxes become haunting monsters. Lily isn't in the least afraid. Kitamura has a special drawing skill, a strong-edged clarity, for both realism and fantasy. The trick is to redraw the scene with the everyday objects looking like horrors. The details are clear, the colours strong, so that each object and the possibility of its transformation are seen together. First rate.

## 📖 *CAPTAIN TOBY* (1987; U.S. edition, 1988)

### *Publishers Weekly*

SOURCE: A review of *Captain Toby,* in *Publishers Weekly,* Vol. 234, No. 14, September 30, 1988, p. 65.

One stormy night a boy named Toby embarks on a terrific journey. One minute he is lying in bed, as the howling of the winds and rattling of the windows begin a horrible crescendo; before Toby knows what has happened, his house has rolled and pitched out to sea. Aided by his pet cat, Toby bravely charts a course. An enormous octopus swims menacingly near, but luckily, reinforcements arrive—Captain Grandpa and Chief Gunner Grandma, in their own house-submarine. Grandma shoots balls of yarn at the surprised octopus ("She never missed a shot"). Later, in calmer seas, the octopus is found knitting busily. By the creator of **When Sheep Can't Sleep** and **Lily Takes a Walk,** Kitamura's nautical romp is a combination of sweet charm and raucous revelry. Both violent storms at sea and the halcyon morning after are conveyed with equal intensity. The artistry displayed in the jewel-colored illustrations is considerable: prismatic blues of the ocean and the varying greys and blacks of stormy skies (occasionally streaked with brilliant bolts of lightning) make the book a satisfying visual treat.

### Patricia Pearl

SOURCE: A review of *Captain Toby,* in *School Library Journal,* Vol. 35, No. 7, March, 1989, p. 164.

While a thunderstorm howls outside, Toby has a fabulous dream in which his house becomes a ship tossing on the ocean, he is the captain, and his cat the mate. A tremendous octopus shoots two huge tentacles through the bedroom windows when a smaller, submarine-house manned by Toby's grandparents surfaces and fires a barrage of yarn balls at the monster, subduing it. After the house-ships dock safely in the harbor, Toby sets out again in a bathtub-dinghy to fish for breakfast and passes the octopus, now peacefully knitting. A clever premise is carefully realized in the illustrations but not so carefully in the text. Although the writing is simple, brisk, and suspenseful most of the way, the ending is lame, without a satisfying conclusion. The deep-toned, vibrant watercolors carry the action forward with humor and excitement. Toby and his cat are simplified, almost cartoon-like figures, but they are lively, expressive, and funny. The violence of the storm and its sizzling lightning tapers off effectively to a calm cobalt sea, with blocky houses squatting comfortably on its shore. With its tame monster, boy hero, and amusing plot, the book will show and tell nicely to young children.

### Margery Fisher

SOURCE: "Picture-Book Adventures," in *Growing Point,* Vol. 28, No. 5, January, 1990, pp. 5269-72.

A child with jagged hair, a bumpy face with huge bulbous eyes—Kitamura is an artist with a conception of the imaginative young that carries over from one book to another; moods may vary but the child's alert, resourceful attitude to surprising events remains consistent, amusing and most flattering to the young. When his home takes off in a storm 'like a ship in the middle of the ocean', Toby is ready with ship's chart and binoculars and with the help of the crew (an equally idiosyncratic and alert cat) and grandparents turning up efficiently at the critical moment (in *their* house, now a submarine) a terrifying octopus is warded off and is last seen offshore 'knitting very peacefully' as the energetic small boy sets out in a boat to catch something for breakfast. The deadpan text confirms the impressions of a splendidly dreadnought child which is carried on in scenes at sea and in a seaside town; improbability is beautifully contained within supremely neat paint and line in a book that moves like a film from one frame to another, subtly domesticating humour and creating a complete and believable fantasy.

## 📖 *UFO DIARY* (1989; U.S. edition, 1990)

### Liz Brooks

SOURCE: "Picturing Pets," in *The Times Literary Supplement,* No. 4501, July 7-13, 1989, p. 757.

One definite advantage of the internationalization of the children's picture book is that it has opened the way for the translation of high quality Japanese work. Satoshi Kitamura was awarded the Mother Goose prize for newcomers for his illustrations to **Angry Arthur** in 1983. His new book **UFO Diary** is the most consummately artistic of the books under review, while retaining the simplicity appropriate to its audience. Kitamura has interpreted the commonplace of the "Martian observer" literally, presenting a close encounter from the unseen alien's point of view. His spaceship first appears as a miniature golden Samurai helmet, floating around in a vast starry ether, with the spacious naturalism of the artwork paralleled in a cool deadpan narrative. "On Monday," it relates, "I took a wrong turn in the Milky Way." The distant earth is portrayed with photo-precision, while the scenes on land echo the astral experience of boundless expanse.

### Susan Perren

SOURCE: A review of *UFO Diary,* in *Quill & Quire,* Vol. 55, No. 10, October, 1989, pp. 17-18.

Satoshi Kitamura's **UFO Diary** is a charming tale about interplanetary travel for small and not-so-small children, told from the point of view of the pilot of an unidenti-fied flying object from outer space.

"On Monday, I took a wrong turn in the Milky Way." Thus begins the account of the UFO's voyage to a new world. A strange blue planet, "bright as a glass ball," comes into view. As the UFO gets closer to this ball the shifting patterns become differentiated into islands, mountains, seas, ice floes, and deserts, until finally a creature can be observed, one that stares in goggle-eyed amazement as the UFO lands. This earthling speaks but cannot be understood; however, when the UFO pilot smiles the earthling smiles back.

The two play for hours until it is dark and time for UFO and pilot to head back to the friendly lights of their own planet. Before parting, though, the two new friends take a spin around the earth in the UFO, whirling until the earthling is quite giddy.

Kitamura uses very little text; the illustrations—the yel-low cone-shaped UFO in the inky blue-black sky, bisect-ed by the Milky Way, the gentle verdant landscapes of Earth, and the sweet, strange earthling—say it all, and, in doing so, convey the humour, the mystery, and the sense of possibility that is at the heart of this book.

**Sue Smedley**

SOURCE: A review of *UFO Diary,* in *The School Li-brarian,* Vol. 37, No. 4, November, 1989, p. 145.

A special book with appeal across a wide age range. It tells the story of a visitor from outer space arriving on earth by mistake, as a result of a wrong turn in the Milky Way. The visitor is the 'I' of the story, creating a fascinating position for the reader, as the visitor is not described in text or illustration (plenty of work for the reader to do here). When the spaceship lands on earth the visitor meets a young boy and the rest of the story describes sensitively how they become friends and play together until the visitor departs. The boy gives the visitor a present when he leaves and we see him waving, a small figure standing on a rooftop amidst hundreds of other rooftops against a night sky, creating an atmo-sphere of enchantment and wonder. Other illustrations in the book are equally effective and intriguing, for exam-ple the perspective when the spaceship comes in to land and when a ladder is lowered for the visitor to descend. A sophisticated book acknowledging that children deserve quality texts and illustrations. Strongly recommended.

**Nancy Vasilakis**

SOURCE: A review of *UFO Diary,* in *The Horn Book Magazine,* Vol. LXVI, No. 2, March-April, 1990, pp. 190-91.

Kitamura's inventive mind and his artist's eye work together harmoniously in this unusual picture book that presents an alien's fresh view of a lush, inviting planet Earth. Written in the first person, the text thrusts the reader into the unconventional perspective of an alien creature as its spaceship is about to land. We are greet-ed silently by a boy and assorted beasts and reptiles who stare wide-eyed out of the pages at the reader—or alien—in transfixed bemusement. Deep, velvety colors and vast panoramas commingle to create a sense of awe at the planet's rich and varied topography. The boy is taken on a quick journey in the yellow, hat-shaped spacecraft before being dropped off at twilight on the roof of his house, where he is surrounded by the twinkling lights of the city and the stars above. He offers the alien a present in return—a dandelion. A beautiful, quiet, respectful reminder of who we are and whence we come.

### SPEAKING FOR OURSELVES (written by Hiawyn Oram, 1990)

**Angela Redfern**

SOURCE: A review of *Speaking for Ourselves,* in *The School Librarian,* Vol. 38, No. 4, November, 1990, p. 156.

*Speaking for Ourselves,* a child's-eye view of the world, invites you right in with its Rogues' Gallery cover. Hiawyn Oram has complete control over her material and her appealing trio of mischief-makers keep us enter-tained from start to finish with their humorous reflec-tions on life's everyday events. A clutch of rhyming four-liners will be chanted in the playground in next to no time. The partnership with Satoshi Kitamura has paid off once more—he matches her text exquisitely. The author is obviously tuned to young children's wavelength but adults—who, of course, come in for criticism—will delight in this collection too. Lots of shared pleasure guaranteed.

**S. M. Ashburner**

SOURCE: A review of *Speaking for Ourselves,* in *The Junior Bookshelf,* Vol. 55, No. 1, February, 1991, p. 26.

The poems in this collection are ostensibly spoken by three children, aged 6, 4 and 1½. They deal with every-day incidents: quarrels, meetings, activities and familiar people.

The writer has been reasonably successful in her en-deavour to see life 'through the eyes of a child.' There is a pleasing lack of condescension, and the style is colloquial without having too much trendy slang. There is humour but also pathos.

The cover describes the poems as 'Read Aloud Poetry', and they would certainly work well read aloud by an adult to a group of children. They could also be enjoyed silently by an individual child. The illustrations would be especially appreciated in the latter instance; these are black and white caricatures full of life and detail.

*From* Goldfish Hide-and-Seek, *written and illustrated by Satoshi Kitamura.*

*Speaking for Ourselves* would be a welcome addition to a larger library collection; however, it is not sufficiently outstanding to merit inclusion in a restricted classroom or library collection.

## A BOY WANTS A DINOSAUR (written by Hiawyn Oram, 1990; U.S. edition, 1991)

### Val Booler

SOURCE: A review of *A Boy Wants a Dinosaur,* in *The School Librarian,* Vol. 39, No. 1, February, 1991, p. 20.

The team of Oram and Kitamura are a familiar sight—the offbeat stories and the complementary quirky illustrations have come together in some notable books. Of course a boy wants a dinosaur, and many girls do too, so what more natural than that Alex's grandfather should take him to a Dinostore to choose one for himself. Alex's eyes and mouth grow wide at the prehistoric monsters, but which one to choose? The Massospondylus catches his eye and they take her home, but keeping a hugely hungry and lonely dinosaur as a pet is no easy matter. . . . To reveal the ending would spoil the fun; as we expect from this team, the story can work on several different levels and can be enjoyed more than once, even when the denouement is known. There is a lot to notice in the seemingly simple pictures and I especially enjoyed the long-suffering and saxophone-playing grandfather. The book provides more to think about than just the problem of choosing a suitable pet; it is very enjoyable and warmly recommended.

### Stephanie Zvirin

SOURCE: A review of *A Boy Wants a Dinosaur,* in *Booklist,* Vol. 87, No. 16, April 15, 1991, p. 1651.

Some boys want a dog for a pet. Not Alex, though. He wants a dinosaur. So his devoted grandpa takes him to the "Dino-Store," a fascinating glass building shaped like a prehistoric beast. There, the two view the grazing stock, finally settling on a playful massopondylus to bring home. To the great dismay of Alex's parents, dinosaur Fred makes a mess of the bath, destroys Alex's room, takes a bite out of the neighbor's cat (onlooker Grandpa treats the wound), and leads Alex and Grandpa on a chase through a swamp to find friends. Then, just when things are really getting out of hand, Alex wakes up. There's nothing coy about illustrator Kitamura's goggle-eyed Alex or Fred; their simple outlines have distinctive child appeal and are particularly striking set against the richly colored backgrounds filled with crosshatched shadings and clever details. A lively, inviting twist on a familiar scenario, this fits in nicely with children's on-going fascination with dinosaurs.

### Francine Prose

SOURCE: "A Boy and His Lizard," in *The New York Times Book Review,* May 19, 1991, p. 23.

*A Boy Wants a Dinosaur,* written by Hiawyn Oram and illustrated by Satoshi Kitamura, [takes] on the essential differences between wilderness and civilization, between Nature and Your Room, between natural world and man-made object—a seemingly obvious distinction about which children may need reminding, as do, apparently, adults with trouble telling desert from Nintendo. . . .

Little Alex does indeed want a dinosaur, and Alex's grandfather—a faintly raffish and endearing saxophone-playing old hipster—takes on the surprisingly simple task of satisfying his grandson's desire. Fans of Satoshi Kitamura's previous books—among them **When Sheep Cannot Sleep** and **Angry Arthur,** which were also written by Hiawyn Oram—will recognize the wittily detailed, wildly animated London cityscape, and perhaps even Fred the dinosaur, a benign version of the monsters lurking everywhere (though noticed only by Lily's dog) in Mr. Kitamura's *Lily Takes a Walk.*

Buying a pet at the Dino-Store is a simple transaction, but dinosaur care and maintenance prove to be a tall order. Fred, a female whose apt real name is The One Who Eats Everything, is an affectionate but high-maintenance family addition. . . . Fred has demanding dietary requirements ("two bags of fossils soaked in all the milk in the fridge, one drum of dried club-moss tree, three sacks of pine needles, the washing, the neighbor's zucchini, and a bite out of the next-door-but-one's cat") and her own design and comfort ideas: interior redecoration through chewing. Fred's stressful efforts to adjust to her new environment, and to lonely exile in the Pets' Corner of Alex's restrictive classroom, soon take a heavy emotional toll on the sensitive dinosaur. When a sympathetic veterinarian advises a restorative walk in the country, Alex and his grandfather discover that a "crusty old swamp" offers Fred the joys of home for which she has been pining.

Here, too, the drearily literal-minded may feel compelled to point out that extinct species are not a shopping item for sale at the local Dino-Store–a caveat that even small children will no doubt reward with superior, knowing smirks. They know dinosaurs are extinct, just as they know their room is different from the forest. And the more fully they understand this—the more engagingly it's suggested in the most inventive and least literal-minded books—the better the chance that all of us won't go the way of Dinosaur Fred.

## 📖 *A CREEPY CRAWLY SONG BOOK* (written by Hiawyn Oram, music by Carl Davis, 1990; U.S. edition, 1993)

### Jane Marino

SOURCE: A review of *A Creepy Crawly Song Book,* in *School Library Journal,* Vol. 40, No. 1, January, 1994, pp. 108-09.

Yes, indeed, a song book about bugs. An itchy-scratchy, flying, crawling collection of 17 selections presented with style and humor. And no stone is left unturned, from "A Hundred Feet Ahead: The Dance of the Centipede" with its gavotte tempo and "Slow, Slow Snail," a slow march through the leaves that decorate the pages. There's a quick little ditty about lice with thin strands of hair decorating the pages' edges, and industrial-strength ants who dot the edge of the pages as "The March of the Worker Ants," drones slowly on. From "The Flea Circus," "The Black Widow's Waltz," "The Lament of the House Fly," and "The Ladybug's Lullaby," the rhythms, creative arrangements, well-chosen lyrics, and colorful watercolor and black-ink drawings all work together to deliver songs that are for the most part easy to sing and

contain great possibilities for creativity and dramatics. A good choice, especially for collections with large music sections.

### Nancy Vasilakis

SOURCE: A review of *A Creepy Crawly Song Book,* in *The Horn Book Magazine,* Vol. LXX, No. 1, January-February, 1994, p. 83.

Seventeen fresh, original melodies accompanied by droll lyrics and exuberant drawings that fill the pages with color and crawling insects mark this irrepressible song book. A black widow spider laments the shortage of available mates, forgetting she "ate every one"; a praying mantis confesses to worldly appetites; in a tender, lilting melody a can full of gullible worms disappear one by one onto the fisherman's hook. The refrain in "Busy Bee" with its last two lines, "Busy in the beehive and busy in the trees, / Busy feeding future busy, busy, busy bees," is hypnotically irresistible. The rhythms range from marches to waltzes and polkas. There is even a round for three voices about a green and slimy slug. Kitamura's artwork, from its decorative endpapers to the drawings of insects and lush greenery that crawl up and down the pages, adds its own happy chaos to the mix. A must for music classes, family sing-alongs, and general all-purpose revelry.

## 📖 *FROM ACORN TO ZOO* (1991; U.S. edition as *From Acorn to Zoo and Everything in Between in Alphabetical Order,* 1992)

### Nancy Vasilakis

SOURCE: A review of *From Acorn to Zoo and Everything in Between in Alphabetical Order,* in *The Horn Book Magazine,* Vol. LXVIII, No. 3, May-June, 1992, p. 330.

Combining Anno's artistry with Waldo's appeal, Kitamura has created an alphabet book that is ingenious, fun, and accessible. Marked by highly charged, deep-toned colors and sharp, unexpected diagonals, each page is an exciting visual experience. The artist juxtaposes an incongruous assortment of objects beginning with the same letter, all of the items being neatly and clearly labeled. Thus, a hippopotamus plays the harmonica in a hammock while a harp leans against a tree and a hanger swings from one of its branches; a kangaroo in a knotted apron fries an egg in the kitchen for a king and a koala; a masked monkey poring over a map is overseen by a mammoth and a moth peering in through the window. Beneath the scene portrayed on the top two-thirds of the page appears a question, accompanied by a pictorial clue, that can be answered only by careful scrutiny of the illustration above. While children will enjoy the guessing game, adults will see this clever book as a creative and painless way to develop a beginning reader's vocabulary. The few British terms that occasionally appear—*nappy* for *diaper* and *aubergine* for *eggplant,* for example—shouldn't detract from the wholesale fun of the book. Alphabet books are plentiful, but this one should be at the top of everyone's list of essential purchases.

## Deborah Abbott

SOURCE: A review of *From Acorn to Zoo and Everything in Between in Alphabetical Order,* in *Booklist,* Vol. 88, No. 21, July, 1992, p. 1943.

In his second alphabet book, Kitamura again uses a zany art style to illustrate many words that begin with the same letter, but not necessarily with the same sound (knife, knapsack, ketchup, king). One letter is presented per page, except for x, y, and z, which are combined on a single page. The upper two-thirds of each page consists of a landscape speckled with objects. Although the incongruous juxtaposition of neatly labeled items adds humor (for example, the "I" page shows an iguana on ice next to a small child eating ice cream and holding an iris, with an iron between the two), it may also engender confusion in very young children, who may not appreciate the subtlety because of their limited experience. The bottom third of each page contains a picture riddle and a question featuring several of the objects from above. The slightly stiff people and animals (many with deadpan expressions), often colored in dark or muted hues, add to the overall appeal of the artwork. Much is alluring about this offbeat alphabet, and the soft British accent in some of the terms (hedgehog, nappy, queue) slides by easily.

## Mary Lou Budd

SOURCE: A review of *From Acorn to Zoo and Everything in Between in Alphabetical Order,* in *School Library Journal,* Vol. 38, No. 7, July, 1992, p. 60.

With three exceptions (X, Y, and Z all together), each page in this book is devoted to one letter of the alphabet. Wide spaces frame the illustrations that depict articles, animals, or plants that begin with the featured letter. A question is posed next to a small picture at the bottom of each page; the answer is found by comparing aspects of that scene with the main picture above. These questions are subtle and require some deductive reasoning and close scrutiny. Many of the words, e.g., eider, ukulele, ocarina, will be unfamiliar to children, providing an exercise in vocabulary expansion. The detailed pen-and-ink drawings, done in flat perspectives, are accompanied by labels with tiny print, giving a somewhat cluttered appearance. The labeled items are shown in light colors with placement on dark backgrounds of blues, greens, and browns. Unfortunately, whimsicality is lost because of the rather austere expressions borne by both animals and people.

## I. Anne Rowe

SOURCE: A review of *From Acorn to Zoo and Everything in Between in Alphabetical Order,* in *The School Librarian,* Vol. 40, No. 3, August, 1992, p. 97.

I reached for this book with a strong sense of anticipated pleasure. A familiar beastie on the cover directly engages readers as it prowls a stylised landscape set against a sky of Satoshi blue. The delight continues through the alphabetical endpapers, the title page which is reminiscent of American patchwork 'friendship quilts', to the main text which explores all alphabetical possibilities. The sense of the artist is palpable in the cultural heritage of Japan that shapes his vision.

Each page is divided into a rectangle perfectly balanced in its size, placement on the page, and relationship to the surrounding white space. Each frame is flooded with colour from the particular palette we have come to recognise from Satoshi's other work; each reveals detailed worlds filled with objects neatly captioned with small white cards. It is like wandering back into certain infant classrooms of the 60s! The pictures are full of life and sound, as well as the humour that we have come to expect in Satoshi's work. Beneath each rectangle is a story. Satoshi selects from his alphabetical images and combines some into delicious little anecdotes. The choice of language will carry this book way beyond the traditional audience of alphabet books. My anticipation was delightfully realised.

## SHEEP IN WOLVES' CLOTHING (1995; U.S. edition, 1996)

## Wendy Cooling

SOURCE: A review of *Sheep in Wolves' Clothing,* in *Books for Keeps,* No. 93, July, 1995, pp. 24-5, 28.

In Satoshi Kitamura's **Sheep in Wolves' Clothing** wolves, as so often in children's literature, are the baddies. It's always a pleasure to open a new book by this illustrator whose distinctive style is full of humour and originality. Three sheep decide to go for a swim and foolishly leave their coats in the care of four wolves—the expected happens, both wolves and coats have gone by the time the sheep leave the water. They call on a detective friend, Elliott Baa, for help and come upon a gang of cats playing rugby with a slowly unwinding ball of wool. Following the wool into the building of Wolfgang and Bros, Quality Knitwear, they defeat the wolves in a wonderfully visual battle. The illustrations are superb and changes in mood are established by using the pages in different ways as well as with the use of colour. By breaking up the page the battle comes alive and full of action—these extraordinary scenes contrast well with the last double-page which shows the sheep back home, grazing peacefully.

## Publishers Weekly

SOURCE: A review of *Sheep in Wolves' Clothing,* in *Publishers Weekly,* Vol. 243, No. 19, May 6, 1996, p. 80.

In this kid-pleasingly convoluted effort, three unwary sheep are fleeced of their outerwear by four wily wolves (or, perhaps, "woolyes"), the mafioso-like manufacturers of Wolfgang & Bros. apparel. The sheep enlist the help of a detective cousin to win back their wool, and further adventures ensue. Kitamura's elaborately spun plot has more twists and turns than a ball of yarn. Panel insets and cartoons with dialogue balloons mix manically with half-, full- and double-page spreads. Every blade of grass and cobblestone gets careful attention in Kitamura's precise, rectangular renderings, painted in slightly muted, subtly mottled watercolors. The effect is of controlled chaos—high comedy that stops just short of baa-laboring its own jokes.

## David Wiesner

SOURCE: "A Job for Elliott Baa, Private Eye," in *The New York Times Book Review,* May 19, 1996. p. 27.

It is a funny, action-packed adventure about three sheep who want nothing more than one last swim in the ocean before winter. At the beach, Hubert, Georgina, and Gogol meet a group of wolves playing golf. With its clubs, striped ties, sunglasses, and drinks in hand, this wolf pack would feel right at home with Frank Sinatra's Rat Pack out on the course.

The slick wolves announce their fears about the ill effects of saltwater on that beautiful wool, and generously offer to watch over the fluffy white coats while the sheep swim. Needless to say, when Hubert, Georgina, and Gogol return, neither the coats nor the wolves are anywhere to be seen. Cold and wet, the three sheep, in their underwear, boots, and gloves, set off to track down their wool. What follows is a rambling mystery, replete with a nighttime trek through the city, kitties who play rugby, a jazz-filled wolf hideout and, of course, Elliott Baa, sheep detective.

Satoshi Kitamura, who lives and works in London, has produced some of the most delightful picture books of the last dozen years. Whether he's illustrating his own stories or those written by his frequent collaborator, Hiawyn Oram, his distinctive books—*Angry Arthur, A Creepy Crawly Song Book* and *A Boy Wants a Dinosaur*—are suffused with both warmth and wit. Just remembering the titles brings back a smile.

There is a recurring cast of winsome and amusing characters in Mr. Kitamura's work. The children, sheep, dogs, dinosaurs and alien visitors who appear again and again are rendered in utterly simple geometric forms. They are angular, their mouths are mostly just straight lines, their eyes are circles with dots in them. His sheep, for example, have amorphous bodies—white blobs with stick legs. Yet with the subtlest of alteration in the line of the mouth or repositioning of the eye dots, Hubert, Georgina, and Gogol are alternately joyful, freezing, terrified or—and this is Mr. Kitamura's specialty—completely bewildered.

In books like **When Sheep Cannot Sleep, Lily Takes a Walk** and **UFO Diary,** a sheep, a dog and an alien, respectively, react to strange and often surreal surroundings with a mixture of anxiety, wonder and benign pleasure. The simplicity of Mr. Kitamura's art is deceptive. A superb draftsman and colorist, he uses pen and brush to create remarkably lush and textured illustrations. The riot of crosshatching and scribbles that defines his foliage, shrubbery and landscape is unique.

There's a wonderful example of Mr. Kitamura's artistic ingenuity in **Sheep in Wolves' Clothing.** Hubert and Georgina are in Gogol's car, driving fast down a country lane. Mr. Kitamura avoids the typical ways of conveying speed, like motion lines streaming out behind the car or clouds of dust being kicked up. Instead, he shifts the lines within the tree shapes and in the fields from vertical slashes and curves to more horizontal strokes, and, just like that, the three sheep appear to be zooming down the road. Very simple. Very effective.

Mr. Kitamura's palette is rich and sumptuous. He uses a wide range of grays and earth tones side by side with deeply vivid blues and greens. His night scenes are particularly striking. The intensity of color in these skies makes them suggest not just another time of day but another world altogether.

Set amid all this texture and color are Hubert, Georgina, Gogol and Elliott—little round shapes that by their mere simplicity become the focus of each page. Always an inventive book designer, Mr. Kitamura tests the limits in **Sheep in Wolves' Clothing.** Using double-page spreads, full-page pictures with small panel inserts and pages with two and three scenes in them, he packs in more visual storytelling than in his previous books.

As the story grows wilder and woollier, and the number of characters begins to pile up, the density of images keeps up with the increasing narrative chaos. The design reaches its peak at the climactic moment of the adventure, as four sheep, four cats and four wolves engage in a yarn-throwing, room-wrecking free-for-all in the wolf hideout, a gloomy house in a dank, dark city. As Elliott throws a basket of yarn into the air and yells, "At 'em, cats!" the page breaks up into 30 small panels, each isolating a small moment in the mayhem.

Turning the page, we then find a double-page spread of total chaos as yarn, cats, furniture, wolves and everything else that isn't nailed down is sent flying across the room. Standing in the corner all the while like the calm eye in this hurricane, with his sunglasses on and hat in place, is Elliott Baa, pouring a cup of coffee.

With so many pictures, the text to **Sheep in Wolves' Clothing** unfortunately gets cramped on a few pages. Given that some of the prose merely states what is obvious in the illustrations, one solution would have been less text. Art as expressive as Satoshi Kitamura's doesn't need extra help.

## Margaret A. Bush

SOURCE: A review of *Sheep in Wolves' Clothing,* in *The Horn Book Magazine,* Vol. LXXII, No. 4, July-August, 1996, p. 450.

In Satoshi Kitamura's silly takeoff on the old maxim, the comic scenario begins as three endearingly goofy sheep, Georgina, Hubert, and Gogol, set off in Gogol's convertible for a day at the beach. There, four wolves playing miniature golf on the sand offer some advice: "'I don't want to be rude,' said one of them, 'but think of your beautiful coats! The salt water will ruin them.'" The trusting sheep slip out of their sheepskins (the boys cheerfully emerging in striped boxer shorts, Georgina in a white slip) and go for a swim; when they return, their skins—and the wolves—are gone. Sounds like a case for Georgina's cousin, Elliott Baa, Private Detective, who eventually tracks the sheepskins to a seedy building where the wolves are operating—what else?—a knitwear factory. Total chaos erupts as a gang of rugby-playing cats in Elliott's employ make a fine mess of the operation. Full-page scenes filled with congenial clutter are interspersed with assorted vignettes of the jauntily cartooned characters. Younger children will delight in the climactic brouhaha and will also find this a satisfying mystery story. Older children will enjoy the detective story spoof and the new twist on the old sheep/wolves theme. The deft cartoonery is sure to tickle a wide audience.

## Luann Toth

SOURCE: A review of *Sheep in Wolves' Clothing,* in *School Library Journal,* Vol. 42, No. 8, August, 1996, p. 124.

Georgina, Hubert, and Gogol go to great lengths to get to the beach for one last carefree day of summer sun, surf, and fun. Once there, these innocent lambs get fleeced (defleeced?) by some cagey characters (miniature-golf playing wolves) who smooth talk them out of their fur coats. Cold, exhausted, and feeling rather sheepish, the trio follow the trail of the culprits and wend their way to town. With the help of Georgina's cousin, Elliot Baa, Private Detective, and some rugby-playing cats, the mystery of the missing fleece is unraveled and the wolves are caught redhanded. All is tied up neatly at the end with the sheep returning to their meadow, slightly wiser and none the worse for wear. Kitamura's deadpan delivery and cinematic cartoons work together

swimmingly. The bold-print text with occasional dialogue balloons is easy to read and has a fine sense of comic timing. Bright kinetic illustrations are filled with sly jokes and clever details. The enormously expressive characters are endearing (even the big, bad Wolfgang & Bros.) and absurdly funny. Kids will love to watch and listen as this rollicking yarn unwinds.

### FLY WITH THE BIRDS: AN OXFORD WORD AND RHYME BOOK (written by Richard Edwards, 1995; U.S. edition as *Fly with the Birds: A Word and Rhyme Book,* 1996)

## Sally R. Dow

SOURCE: A review of *Fly with the Birds: A Word and Rhyme Book,* in *School Library Journal,* Vol. 42, No. 3, March, 1996, p. 173.

In playful rhymes, a child narrates her day, from waking up and selecting an outfit to wear, through myriad activities, and finally to bedtime and dreamland. The narrative is imbued with a strong sense of adventure, lifting everyday happenings from the mundane to the fanciful. "Stuck in the traffic, we creep and we crawl,/ Buses and cars hardly moving at all,/ So closing my eyes/ I say two magic words . . . Hey, presto! A bus that can fly with the birds." Bright, childlike illustrations with fold-out flaps that label items depicted in the art and reveal surprises enhance the fun and capture the imagination.

## Publishers Weekly

SOURCE: A review of *Fly with the Birds: A Word and Rhyme Book,* in *Publishers Weekly,* Vol. 243, No. 13, March 25, 1996, p. 82.

[Richard] Edwards and Kitamura follow a child through an ordinary day in this well-organized, imaginatively designed vocabulary-builder. Each spread includes a triptych of the blond narrator's daily activities, a poem and a gatefold flap that lifts to reveal the poem's final line. On the flap appears a group of words and pictures that can be matched to the illustrations. When the child imagines escaping a traffic jam, for instance ("Stuck in the traffic, we creep and we crawl, / Buses and cars hardly moving at all, / So closing my eyes, I say two magic words . . . / Hey, presto! A bus that can fly with the birds!"), the vocabulary list sends readers on a search for a bicycle, van and trailer; the first picture shows passengers sitting miserably on a stalled bus, but the concealed picture is of a bus hoisted into the air by a flock of birds. Edwards's 11 rhymes about pets, shopping and the weather prove serviceable at best. However, Kitamura's angular illustrations, drawn with a steady pen and filled with compatible solid colors, nicely serve the word-game setup. Despite the complex arrangement of images, text and gatefolds, the overall effect is invitingly clean.

## 📖 *CAT IS SLEEPY; DOG IS THIRSTY; DUCK IS DIRTY; SQUIRREL IS HUNGRY* (1996)

### Kirkus Reviews

SOURCE: A review of *Duck Is Dirty,* in *Kirkus Reviews,* Vol. LXIV, No. 12, June 15, 1996, p. 906.

[*Duck Is Dirty*] recounts the modest tribulations of Duck during a potentially pleasant stroll. It starts raining, he gets his feet muddy, is buffeted by winds, papered by leaves, and takes a header into the muck. A dip in the pond and Duck is good as new. Kitamura coaxes an appealing story from this 19-word trifle; one, moreover, that will ring familiar with the intended audience. The misleadingly simple artwork is graphically sophisticated, with Duck coming across as a winsome geek. Companion volumes are *Squirrel Is Hungry, Cat Is Sleepy,* and *Dog Is Thirsty.*

### Publishers Weekly

SOURCE: "Animal Pragmatism," in *Publishers Weekly,* Vol. 243, No. 26, June 24, 1996, p. 62.

Each of the four furred or feathered heroes in Satoshi Kitamura's quartet of board books solves a problem after exploring several options. In *Dog Is Thirsty,* a parched pup finds a bone-dry garden hose, a too high water fountain and a fenced-off river before a precipitous change in the weather saves the day; in *Cat Is Sleepy,* a baggy-eyed feline finds the perfect lap-sized spot to take a nap after trying out several uncomfortable alternatives (a saucepan, a sink, a piano). Aimed at the nursery crowd, Kitamura's trademark angular lines are slightly heavier here, while the details and objects that usually crowd his tableaux are sparser and larger in size. Other titles include *Squirrel Is Hungry* and *Duck Is Dirty.*

### Ann Cook

SOURCE: A review of *Cat Is Sleepy,* in *School Library Journal,* Vol. 42, No. 8, August, 1996, p. 124.

A winning quartet of board books. In a style reminiscent of Dav Pilkey's work, Kitamura has created four animal characters, each faced with a decision: where to sleep, what to drink, how to bathe, and what to eat. Resolving these dilemmas requires hilarious experimentation (the cat curling up in the saucepan is a hoot) and myriad facial expressions, from bewilderment to frustration to satisfaction. The straightforward texts are a perfect fit for the illustrations. Youngsters will connect immediately with the simple plot lines and familiar sit-

uations. No cutesy, patronizing stuff here—these genuinely funny books assume that toddlers have a sense of humor.

## 📖 *GOLDFISH HIDE-AND-SEEK* (1997)

### Publishers Weekly

SOURCE: A review of *Goldfish Hide-and-Seek* in *Publishers Weekly,* Vol. 244, No. 23, June 9, 1997, p. 44.

Kitamura serves up an attenuated tale only partially redeemed by his dynamic illustrations. The narrator, a goldfish, searches every inch of his apparently vast watery home for a playmate named Heidi, consulting fellow fish, frogs and octopus. He next tries land, but leaps into the clutches of a hungry cat. An inadvertent dance between cat and fish ensues before the fish is accidentally vaulted back to his home, which the art now reveals as a fishbowl. Although the story lacks cohesion and the writing is stilted in places, Kitamura's humor comes through in the cartoon illustrations, which are at once luminous and daffy. Using subtle gradations of his rich palette, his colors seem to shimmer and bloom on the page—an especially pleasing effect for a book largely set underwater. At the same time, Kitamura has a keen, almost cinematic sense of the visually comic. To suggest the growing frenzy of the story, he moves from neatly framed scenes set in the middle of the page to sprawling, distorted compositions that cover the entire spread (one such scene shows the protagonist looking in 15 different locations at once). Yet young children may be confused by the number of fish that look so similar, and may wonder why the initial cast of characters goes missing in the last view of the fishbowl. Even the many sight gags can't compensate for the shortcomings here.

### Kirkus Reviews

SOURCE: A review of *Goldfish Hide-and-Seek,* in *Kirkus Reviews,* Vol. LXV, No. 12, June 15, 1997, p. 951.

Where is Heidi hiding? This single question forms the premise for a goldfish game of hide-and-seek. The seeker is an unnamed friend and fellow goldfish who asks the question of Miss Frog, Mr. Octopus, Doctor Angler, and others who inhabit the fishbowl universe. But Heidi is not to be found in this watery world. When the fish jumps out to have a look around, it finds that danger lurks outside the fishbowl in the form of Mr. Cat. As a distraction, the fish does a little dance and gets away, splashing into Heidi's path in a now uncluttered two-fish bowl, earlier shown profuse with underwater flora and fish, not to mention household items. The ending shortchanges its audience: Heidi appears out of nowhere, without an explanation for her previous whereabouts, nor visual clues for those preschool sleuths who may have wanted to join the search. It's a storyline that lacks the splash readers expect from Kitamura.

## Karen James

SOURCE: A review of *Goldfish Hide-and-Seek*, in *School Library Journal*, Vol. 43, No. 10, October, 1997, p. 100.

Two big-eyed cartoon fish decide to play hide-and-seek. Heidi hides, the other almost identical but unnamed fish searches for her behind a rock and in some seaweed. Two turtles playing checkers claim they haven't seen Heidi, and an artistic octopus only has eyes for his own canvas. On a cluttered two-page spread filled with multiple images, the seeking fish looks for its friend in everything from a desk drawer to a piano. The fish then jumps out of the bowl to look further, encounters a cat, and encourages him to dance with it. While spinning and twirling, the fish flies through the air and lands back in the bowl where Heidi is waiting. While a simple text can be admirable in a picture book, this one just seems abrupt and the whole story sinks. The fun of reading about hide-and-seek is the chance to participate vicariously in the game. Here, neither the pictures nor the brief text encourage this participation.

## Lynne Taylor

SOURCE: A review of *Goldfish Hide-and-Seek,* in *School Librarian,* Vol. 45, No. 4, November, 1997, p. 187.

Original, playful, absurd, superlative, inspired: this is another winner from Satoshi Kitamura. Goldfish is playing hide and seek with his companion Heidi, who disappears while he counts to ten. He looks everywhere for her in the goldfish bowl and as he searches his world gets progressively more bizarre, full of wonderful fishy characters none of whom can help. Eventually Goldfish jumps out of the bowl where he encounters a hungry cat. He persuades the cat to dance (of all things!), and ends up falling back in the goldfish bowl with Heidi.

As usual, Satoshi's distinctive use of colour and visual detail is superb, and each page is full of his unique deadpan humour. Children enjoy the book just as much as grown-ups. You'll be asked to read it over and over, and—the mark of an excellent picture book—you won't mind. It's a great book for encouraging young children to join in, with the counting, the repetition in the easy-to-remember text, and the lively sense of movement. A surreal marine world in a 'Tardis' goldfish bowl, corny jokes galore, a goldfish that can dance in a living room; this is wonderful stuff.

---

Additional coverage of Kitamura's life and career is contained in the following sources published by The Gale Group: *Contemporary Authors*, Vol. 165 and *Something about the Author*, Vols. 62, 98.

---

# Caroline Macdonald

## 1948-1997

New Zealander author of fiction and picture books.

Major works include *Elephant Rock* (1984), *Visitors* (1984), *The Lake at the End of the World* (1988; U.S. edition, 1989), *Speaking to Miranda* (1991; U.S. edition, 1992), *Hostilities: Nine Bizarre Stories* (1991; U.S. edition, 1994).

## INTRODUCTION

An author born in New Zealand who spent much of her life in Australia, Macdonald is respected as a writer who created unusual, dramatic, and thought-provoking books for children and young adults. She is also commended for exploring human relationships, especially between parents and children, and the search for identity with accuracy and sensitivity. Often structured as genre fiction such as the horror story and the science fiction novel, her works are thought to transcend their genres by virtue of their author's imagination and literary craftsmanship. Macdonald set her books in her native New Zealand or in her adopted homeland of Australia, landscapes noted for being vividly described by the author. She placed her books in both contemporary and future times and used the time-slip technique, by which characters are magically transported back into time, as a vehicle for them to find out the truth about themselves and their family histories. Thematically, Macdonald characteristically demonstrated how her protagonists, boys and girls who are isolated either physically or emotionally, learn to accept themselves and others through confrontations with the supernatural and the fantastic. The young people encounter aliens, ghosts, doppelgangers, imaginary friends, and children from the past or from unfamiliar cultures. Through their experiences, Macdonald's main characters have their notions of reality changed and make decisions that reveal their growth.

Macdonald often wrote about communication—and the lack of it—between parents and children; in addition, she addressed such issues as cooperation, power, the meaning of family, and responsibility toward the environment. Furthermore, she created utopian societies in her futuristic stories that turn into dystopias through mistreatment of people and misuse of natural resources. As a prose stylist, Macdonald favored spare but precise writing; she also used different literary techniques, such as alternating first-person narratives and those told by an adult character who introduces himself as a teenager. Although she was criticized for both strained plots and gaps in information, Macdonald is generally considered a writer of range and depth who created insightful, challenging, and enjoyable books.

## Biographical Information

Born in the small town of Taranaki, New Zealand, Macdonald was the youngest of four children. Since her older siblings left home when she was still very young, she spent a great deal of her childhood reading. She wrote her first books while working as an editor of teaching materials at Deakin University in Geelong, Australia; she became a freelance writer in 1989. Her first book, *Elephant Rock,* features Ann, a twelve-year-old girl whose mother is dying of cancer. After a time-slip device allows Ann to relive her mother's youth, she begins to accept her loss. In an interview with Alf Mappin, Macdonald said, "I knew that the mother was going to die at the end, but I didn't know quite how it was going to resolve itself; if it was going to be satisfactory. In the end I was really elated by the way that it worked. It was like working out a puzzle: is this going to work or not? That was what was exciting. I guess if I had seen it a long way ahead, I would not have been so keen on finishing it."

Macdonald wrote several of her books in first person. She stated to Mappin, "I'm never going to write a first person novel again in my whole life! I wrote two in a row and I suddenly thought 'first person present tense' and decided, 'this is enough.'" One of these first-person novels, *Speaking to Miranda,* describes how eighteen-year-old Ruby, raised in Australia, finds out the truth about her deceased mother's mysterious life when she decides to go to New Zealand. Miranda, Ruby's imaginary friend from childhood who is now a voice in her head, provides a connection to the past for both mother and daughter. In speaking to Mappin about this novel, which took her two years to write, Macdonald stated, "I definitely spend time planning and choosing the sort of narration which is appropriate for the story I am telling. Before I start I spend a long time thinking about the journey. . . . I had been thinking and planning [*Speaking to Miranda*] for at least eighteen months. . . . " She added, "Prior to writing I know I'm going to begin at A and I know what Z is going to be like. *Miranda* gave me a lot of trouble with MNOP. In fact, I really left it for almost a year in the middle. It is exactly the part where I think Ruby is saying, 'I don't know what I'm going to do next. Shall I go to New Zealand? I'm not a detective. How am I going to do this?' I was going through a similar undecided state myself at the time." In her volume of short stories for children, *Hostilities: Nine Bizarre Stories,* Macdonald explores the theme of hostility toward young people by describing how her protagonists encounter hostile supernatural forces. In speaking to Mappin about *Hostilities,* she said, "I was trying out my preoccupations, all my ideas on different kinds of writing I like to do, like science fiction, relationships, the tyrannies or alliances within families. . . . [T]he thing that the stories have got in common is the idea of hostility. Children go through lots of hostility growing up, whether it's huge hostility or very minor, real or imagined. I think that adults are in some ways hostile to children, whether they get the message or not. So all the stories have some element of testing of the water by the child character."

All of Macdonald's works were written while she was away from New Zealand. She told Mappin, "I am not sure why I keep moving around. . . . I have a real emotional tie to New Zealand. It's a bit like your family; you grow up and you leave and go and live among friends, but there's still this emotional tie to the family. I feel a bit like that about New Zealand, but I operate much better if I am detached from it. It has something to do with being an expatriate. . . . Everything I've ever written I've written in Australia." Macdonald once wrote in *Twentieth-Century Children's Writers,* "Future fiction, science fiction, the supernatural and the mystical are the thematic areas I'm interested in. I like to suggest there's a strange edge to be found in a mundane world. I enjoy forming characters who are for some reason removed from the usual processes of conditioning." In discussing her writing, she told Mappin, "It's a job with an enormous amount of job satisfaction. It is never boring. I like the people that are involved. . . . And I like books so much. I love novels and I admire people who do them successfully. It's a great incentive for me to strive to do the same." Suffering from cancer, Macdonald died July 24, 1997, in Australia.

## Major Works

*Elephant Rock* is considered a daring and unsentimental exploration of a child's reaction to the death of a parent. Writing in *Twentieth-Century Children's Writers,* Betty Gilderdale stated, "Kaye Webb once quoted a child who said of another novel, 'I felt older after reading this.' The same statement could apply to *Elephant Rock;* the reader will grow through experiencing it." Macdonald's next book, *Visitors,* is a science fiction novel for middle graders. The "Visitors" are aliens from outer space who have been trapped on Earth for hundreds of years because no one can understand them. After they select Terry, a boy who is a television addict and is ignored by his parents, to help them get back home, Terry picks up pictures of the Visitors on video; he also pockets a fossil fragment with a significant pattern. Terry is helped to connect with the Visitors by Maryanne, a disabled classmate who communicates best through a word processor. By joining together to work out various aspects of wavelengths and light refractions, the children free the Visitors and become friends. As a result of their experience, Maryanne is revealed to be intelligent and capable and Terry begins to be noticed by his parents. Betty Gilderdale said of *Visitors,* "In addition to investing fantasy with a compelling life of its own, Macdonald demonstrates considerable scientific acumen. . . . "

*The Lake at the End of the World* is one of Macdonald's most well-received works. In this young adult novel set in 2025, the author created a post-apocalyptic world in which pollution has killed most living things. The only surviving area is a New Zealand lake, near which live two communities, a highly structured group that lives in underground caves, and the Redfern family, teenage Diana and her parents, who farm above ground. The novel describes how Diana meets Hector, a teenage boy from the underground world, and how they learn to cooperate in order to save their world. Telling their stories in alternating narratives, Hector and Diana discover that the leader of the underground community, the Counselor, is a maniac who plans to destroy the lake. At the end of the novel, which has been compared to *Robinson Crusoe* and *Swiss Family Robinson,* Hector and the Redferns are joined by scientists, artists, musicians, cooks, and other members of the underground community, a conclusion considered hopeful for the continuation of humankind and the regeneration of the earth. Roger Sutton commented that on the whole, "this is a fresh conception, with more subtly crafted characterization than most post-doomsday fiction," while George Hunt called *The Lake at the End of the World* "an enthralling adventure story, embellished with eerie folklore and loaded with topical issues."

In the author's next book, *Speaking to Miranda,* eighteen-year-old Ruby learns on her trip to New Zealand that her mother Emma, who drowned when she was a baby, had been married to a Maori husband and was actually named Magda. Ruby also discovers that she was originally named Miranda and that she had a sister named Ruby, who died as a baby. At the end of the novel, Ruby decides to call herself Miranda. Marcus Crouch observed, "The search for identity has been a common theme in many novels for young adults recently. I have rarely been more moved than by this very remarkable story by a New Zealand writer. . . . Where Caroline Macdonald excels is in management of narrative. . . . [H]ere is a writer firmly in control of her material, her characters and her tone. Many young readers troubled by the problems of their growing maturity will find this both a great story and a guiding light." Carolyn Phelan added that this "well-written novel, with its memorable characters, will stay with readers for a long time."

In *Hostilities: Nine Bizarre Stories,* Macdonald presents young readers with eerie tales that draw parallels between the supernatural and adolescent angst. Ranging from mildly spooky to truly unsettling, the stories include elements such as soul-switching, seances, and ghostly promptings from beyond the grave. The young protagonists move from city to country and encounter unearthly forces that test both their emotions and their conceptions of reality. Chris Sherman noted that *Hostilities* contains the kind of stories "you don't want to read when you're in the house alone and it's time for bed; the kind you continue to think about hours later." In addition to these works, Macdonald has also written stories about a boy who is nearly lost at sea, a girl who inadvertently becomes involved with a drug-smuggling gang, a boy who creates a fictional character in a school writing assignment that begins to commit real-life dangerous acts, a girl who attempts to save her family from the cruel couple that try to steal their home, and four children who believe that a lady who collects metal in a junkyard is a witch.

## Awards

*Elephant Rock* won the Esther Glen Award from the New Zealand Library Association and the Choysa Bursary Award for Children's Writers from the New Zealand Literary Fund, both in 1984. *Visitors* won the New Zealand Children's Book of the Year Award and the AIM Children's Book Award from Booksellers New Zealand in 1985. *The Lake at the End of the World* received the Victorian Premier's Award, the Diabetes Australia Alan Marshall Prize for Children's Literature Studies, and the Australian Children's Book of the Year Award Honour Book from the Children's Book Council of Australia, all in 1989. It also received the AIM Children's Book Award and the Guardian Award (runner-up) in 1990. *Joseph's Boat* won the Russell Clark Award from the New Zealand Library Association in 1989. *Speaking to Miranda* was shortlisted for the Australian Book of the Year Award and was awarded third prize by the AIM Children's Book Awards committee in 1991.

---

# AUTHOR'S COMMENTARY

## Alf Mappin

SOURCE: "Know the Author: Caroline MacDonald," in *Magpies,* Vol. 6, No. 5, November, 1991, pp. 16-7.

Some authors seem to have such success with their books from their first piece of writing that it almost appears as if they have been created as fully grown authors right from the beginning. Caroline Macdonald's first novel *Elephant Rock* was given two awards: The Choysa Bursary Award for Children's Writers and the Esther Glen Memorial Award. Her next book *Visitors* gained the New Zealand Book of the Year Award. *The Lake at the End of the World* received several awards and shortlistings, including the Victorian Premier's Award and Honour Book for the Australian Children's Book of the Year Awards: Older Readers. *Speaking to Miranda* was shortlisted for the 1991 Older Readers' section of the Book of the Year Awards. Not a bad record for someone whose published writing career began in 1982.

Macdonald is a New Zealander, growing up in the small

town of Taranaki, the youngest of four children. However her older siblings had left home while she was still very young and a great deal of her childhood was spent reading. Interestingly her books have only been written when she has been away from New Zealand. *Elephant Rock* was written while she was in Hobart. She moves frequently. "I am not sure why I keep moving around. I've shifted all my possessions backwards and forwards three times across the Tasman now. I have a real emotional tie to New Zealand. It's a bit like your family; you grow up and you leave and go and live among friends, but there's still this emotional tie to the family. I feel a bit like that about New Zealand, but I operate much better if I am detached from it. It has something to do with being an expatriate, though it may seem odd to talk in this way when New Zealand and Australia are so close, but the same sort of dynamics work. Everything I've ever written I've written in Australia. I went back to New Zealand in 1989 as an experiment and everything I wrote there I threw away.

"I love Australia and I love being here, but I also find it extremely challenging, particularly in the field I work in."

["Writing is] a job with an enormous amount of job satisfaction. It is never boring. I like the people that are involved. It's not like working in some occupations; people who work in the book trade are generally pretty good people to deal with. And I like books so much. I love novels and I admire people who do them successfully. It is a great incentive to me to strive to do the same.

"The monetary rewards are lousy. If you write something that takes off you can make lots of money (like Roald Dahl) but that it something that is very rare. There's a great temptation to churn books out too quickly in order to make sufficient money to live on. I am in a situation at the moment where I have to really get a new manuscript in to the publishers by the end of next week to have it published this year, because I need that continuity of income—and, at the same time, I want to make it as good as possible. . . . I'd need at least three novels every two years [to make a reasonable living] and that's pretty difficult to achieve when you consider that I can manage to fit in every year an average of about three months of writing fresh material, that is new drafts. There are so many other things to do: re-writing, proof-reading, re-reading, chatting to school groups. And also a lot of my time seems to be taken up shifting. I keep moving and have to settle in. I hope I'll be settled in Adelaide for a few years now."

The subject of Caroline's latest book, *Hostilities,* naturally entered the conversation. This is a collection of short stories published by Omnibus Books. "I was trying out all my preoccupations, all my ideas on different kinds of writing I like to do, like science fiction, relationships, the tyrannies or alliances within families. I expect it will have charges of being uneven because all the stories are different, but the thing that the stories have got in common is the idea of hostility. Children go through lots of hostility, face a lot of hostility growing up, whether it's huge hostility or very minor, real or imagined. I think that adults are often in some ways hostile to children, whether they get the message or not. So all the stories have some element of testing of the water by the child character.

"The title story has the child character in fact perpetrating hostility against another child. She has made a tremendous error of judgement about her stepbrother, so she finds that war has been declared between them and she is going to win. As it gets towards the end she feels she is losing her grip. There is one sentence in which she says that his eyes seem to glitter when she thinks she might lose this war.

"I hear comments that people are getting used to publications of collections of short stories for children being very homogenous. A collection of love stories, or ghost stories, for instance. I don't think this collection of mine is going to do that at all. There are a lot of genres within the book; they aren't all supernatural, or all science fiction. There are three that have no hint of the supernatural at all. There's future fiction, speculative fiction, there's family fiction, but not really family stories.

"It's interesting that this comment about homogenous groups of stories is not a criticism which would be levelled against an adult collection, isn't it?

"While my stories loosely comment around the theme of hostility towards children, they are all very different. They are different lengths, have different narrators, and particularly they have different styles of narration.

"One particular style of narration I really love. This is the idea of the unreliable narrator. Robin Klein does it so interestingly in *Came Back to Show You I Could Fly* where the child narrator who is describing the girl says what beautiful clothes she wears. We all know the girl has terrible tawdry stuff from op shops. He says she is not well, poor girl, sometimes in the morning she's not well. We know she's a hopeless addict to drugs.

"I like that idea of the unreliable narrator. It's interesting to talk about it to older school groups. You see the penny suddenly drop as they begin to think, Yes, that's right, you can have a narrator who is actually lying to you whether they mean to or not. It is just an added trick that the writer is using."

The question of the number of books for young people being written in the first person came up: "I'm never going to write a first person novel again in my whole life! I wrote two in a row and I suddenly thought 'first person present tense' and decided 'this is enough.' Both of them seemed to need it, I thought. *The Lake at the End of the World* and *Speaking to Miranda* really required that first person present tense. To be done well, it is a difficult form. You know only what the character knows. But you can do that sort of thing using third person past tense only using a single point of view.

"I think I always use a single point of view. In *The Lake at the End of the World* there were two, but each of them was told as a single view point narration.

"I definitely spend time planning and choosing the sort of narration which is appropriate for the story I am telling. Before I start I spend a long time thinking about the journey. *Speaking to Miranda* took two years to write, and I had been thinking and planning it for at least eighteen months before then. So it's cooking for a long time.

"Prior to writing I know I'm going to begin at A and I know what Z is going to be like. *Miranda* gave me a lot of trouble with MNOP. In fact, I really left it for almost a year in the middle. It is exactly the part where I think Ruby is saying, 'I don't know what to do next. Shall I go to New Zealand? I'm not a detective. How am I going to do this?' I was going through a similar undecided state myself at the time.

"In my very first published novel *Elephant Rock* I knew that the mother was going to die at the end, but I didn't know quite how it was going to resolve itself, if it was going to be satisfactory. In the end I was really elated by the way that it worked. It was like working out a puzzle: is this going to work or not? That was what was exciting. I guess if I had seen it a long way ahead, I would not have been so keen on finishing it."

---

## TITLE COMMENTARY

### *VISITORS* (1984)

**A. R. Williams**

SOURCE: A review of *Visitors,* in *The Junior Bookshelf,* Vol. 49, No. 5, October, 1985, p. 230.

It is not a simple matter to explain Miss Macdonald's fantasy of alien influences seeking to communicate with a brainy New Zealand boy addicted to television who has by sheer chance pocketed a fossil fragment with a peculiar, and, as it turns out, significant pattern. Plot and style may tax the resources of senior-junior and junior-senior readers. It is through the medium of sabotaged television that the Visitors seek to communicate with Terry to make known their need and this they can do only through the medium of a sporadic documentary of the work and despair of a scientist some three hundred years into history. Aside from the technicalities which pervade the story, one feels sorry for Terry whose parents are too busy to do much more than eat meals with him, and it is not an entirely romantic attachment which develops a companionship in mystery with a handicapped girl contemporary who can express herself in decent fashion only with the aid of a word-processor. Family relationships are nevertheless an integral part of the story.

## THE LAKE AT THE END OF THE WORLD (1988; U.S. edition, 1989)

### Publishers Weekly

SOURCE: A review of *The Lake at the End of the World,* in *Publishers Weekly,* Vol. 235, No. 17, April 28, 1989, p. 82.

The end of the world is not a place but a time not too far in the future, a premise that is not as farfetched today as it would have seemed a decade ago. The world is practically dead, because its ecology has collapsed. At Redfern Lake, in Australia, preserved as a wilderness, live Evan Redfern, an ornithologist, his wife Beth and their daughter Diana. One day, Diana stumbles across a young man, Hector, escaped from a community that has lived for decades in a cavern deep below the lake, unbeknownst to Evan and Beth. The community's megalomaniac leader, the Counselor, had virtually kidnapped bright young scientists to found an underground utopia. Hector's narrative alternates with Diana's; at first, because Diana's thoughts are printed in italic, this looks confusing, but the device makes the story more immediate and the characters easier to identify with. When Beth falls ill and needs medicine, Diana and Hector brave the Counselor in his cavern and fall foul of his plot to destroy the lake. But all ends well, and when the Redferns are joined by many from underground, there's hope for humanity's survival and the earth's renewal. A satisfying work of future fiction.

### Roger Sutton

SOURCE: A review of *The Lake at the End of the World,* in *Bulletin of the Center for Children's Books,* Vol. 42, No. 9, May, 1989, pp. 229-30.

Neither Hector, who lives in an underground community much like the one described in Maguire's *I Feel Like the Morning Star* nor Diana, who lives with her family at the edge of a mysterious lake, are prepared for their first sight of each other. Both had thought no one else was left in the world since "it all happened." Not nuclear war, but an inexorable breakdown of the earth's resources—a whimper, not a bang. Gradually learning to trust each other, Hector and Diana become friends when he escapes the caves and comes to live with her family. Survival within the family and as a family is the theme, the "war of love" that is fought among Diana and her parents, and

the exacerbating relief and tension that Hector's presence brings to them. Their Robinson Crusoe-like existence is involvingly particularized; less successful, although suspenseful, is a subplot about the evil machinations of the charismatic leader of the cave community, which is resolved through an insufficiently prepared fantasy element. On the whole, however, this is a fresh conception, with more subtly crafted characterization than most post-doomsday fiction.

### Pam Spencer

SOURCE: A review of *The Lake at the End of the World,* in *School Library Journal,* Vol. 35, No. 9, May, 1989, p. 127.

The 21st century begins with the signing of a worldwide nuclear disarmament treaty thought to be earth's salvation; unfortunately disaster and decimation arise from a combination of nuclear accidents, toxic oil spills, and experimentation with dangerous herbicides, which cause everyone to die. In the year 2025 Diana and her parents, living on a farm beside beautiful, self-preserving Redfern Lake, have had no contact with any other settlements in a year and realize that they are probably the last of all humans. One day Diana stumbles across Hector, a boy who has been part of a secret society living underground since 1968, who just happens to have followed his dog out of the underground maze of tunnels. The lives of Diana, Hector, and Redfern Lake follow an intertwining course from that initial meeting. The Eden-like setting of Redfern Lake, an oasis in a devastated world, offers a plausible rationale for Diana's family to still be alive. Reading of their survival techniques is akin to reading a modern version of *Swiss Family Robinson;* although rescue is not possible, the discovery of this secret society, a handpicked assortment of scientists, artists, musicians, cooks, etc., grants Diana's family hope for companionship in their isolated world. The characters, dialogue, and plot in this science fiction adventure are all top-rate.

### Lesa M. Holstine

SOURCE: A review of *The Lake at the End of the World,* in *Voice of Youth Advocates,* Vol. 12, No. 2, June, 1989, p. 117.

In 2025 at a remote lake in the wilderness, two teenage survivors of the destruction of civilization discover each other and their very different lifestyles and methods of coping with the lack of other civilizations. When the global environment collapsed, Diana and her parents settled on the family property near the lake with the equipment needed for survival. Hector is the last child born to a group of 102 people who moved underground before the environmental disaster, where they are ruled by The Counselor. When the two teenagers discover each other, they are forced to confront their own beliefs about survival and the world's history.

*The Lake at the End of the World* is a thoughtful book to challenge the reader's beliefs about civilization and the environment. It probably moves too slowly for many readers, but it is an enjoyable book for those interested in environmental issues and future worlds.

## Sally Estes

SOURCE: A review of *The Lake at the End of the World,* in *Booklist,* Vol. 85, No. 21, July, 1989, p. 1894.

By the year 2025, chemical pollution and nuclear accidents have virtually wiped out humanity on Earth. Living with her parents at a remote wilderness lake, teenage Diana has never seen any other human beings until, aloft on the wings her dad has made her, she spots Hector, a strange boy with skin "so pale it seemed to shine," skulking in the shadows of some rocks. Mutually distrusting, the two teens find themselves forced to cooperate in order to save the world as they know it from a formidable threat. The lake, which exhibits an aggressively protective attribute, adds a mystical element to the plot and ties it all up rather too neatly. However, told in alternating narratives by Diana and Hector, the story evokes a strong sense of a world denuded of its populace, Diana's family's forced solitary existence above ground, the trauma felt by Hector's despotic underground society, and the developing relationship between Diana and Hector.

## George Hunt

SOURCE: A review of *The Lake at the End of the World,* in *Books for Keeps,* No. 74, May, 1992, p. 19.

Diana and her family have fled to the banks of a semi-mythical lake from an ecological collapse which appears to have wiped out everybody else. Hector is a fugitive from a troglodyte dictatorship which has been isolated underground for 50 years. The story of their meeting and of the coming to terms they force upon their evasive kin is told from alternating viewpoints—a device which emphasises the shifting tensions between them.

This book provides the independent reader with an enthralling adventure story, embellished with eerie folklore and loaded with topical issues.

## 📖 *SPEAKING TO MIRANDA* (1991; U.S. edition, 1992)

## Barbara Sherrard Smith

SOURCE: A review of *Speaking to Miranda,* in *The School Librarian,* Vol. 39, No. 2, May, 1991, pp. 73-4.

The story starts in Australia. Ruby, the eighteen-year-old narrator, has a few weeks to wait before she will know the results of her final school exams. Her childhood, mainly spent with Rob, her adoptive father, has been a happy one. An uncritical ally, he has taken her with him on his consultancy trips, and despite her lack of contemporaries, Ruby has never been lonely. She has an imaginary friend called Miranda, who is sometimes supportive, sometimes critical. Now, Ruby has made up her mind to find out more about her background, and especially about her mother who was drowned when Ruby was a baby. Rob has always been evasive about the past, and his mother can tell Ruby very little. Armed with a few clues and fewer facts, Ruby, driven by her obsession, embarks on her search. It is not until she reaches New Zealand that she uncovers the truth about her mother and about herself. Characterisation is deft and convincing, and the taut spare style is exactly right for the tense absorbing plot. The various strands are skilfully woven together and the reader is as interested in the outcome of Ruby's search as in her self-discovery.

## Marcus Crouch

SOURCE: A review of *Speaking to Miranda,* in *The Junior Bookshelf,* Vol. 55, No. 3, June, 1991, p. 126.

The search for identity has been a common theme in many novels for young adults recently. I have rarely been more moved than by this very remarkable story by a New Zealand writer.

Ruby is eighteen when she begins to tell her story, although she is constantly looking back to her earlier days. She lives with Rob, her adoptive father. She knew that she had been adopted long before he told her; it was one of many secrets revealed by Miranda, her unseen companion, confidante and, sometimes, enemy. As she grows older Miranda drops out of her life. She is no longer needed. Ruby begins to wonder about the mother who had died, heroically, when she was a baby. When at last Rob reluctantly tells her all he knows about Emma—which is very little—Ruby resolves to solve the mystery of her mother's life. The search takes her from Australia to New Zealand (fortunately Rob is very relaxed about the use of his credit cards!) and to a denouement in which the mysteries are stripped away and all identities are changed. Emma was not Emma, Ruby is not Ruby.

This is partly a mystery story, more a self-revelation. In the first-person narrative Ruby reveals herself with complete candour, in all her weakness and strength, her obstinacy and her prejudice. We like her the better for the flaws, although we may spare sympathy for Rob, the tolerant, good-natured father, and give a thought to Kate, Ruby's friend, so rudely abandoned in New Zealand when Ruby's quest hots up. There are some neatly drawn sketches of lesser characters. Where Caroline Macdonald excels is in management of narrative. Whether looking back to a half-remembered past or forcing the pace as the clues come fast, here is a writer firmly in control of her material, her characters and her tone. Many young readers troubled by the problems of their growing maturity will find this both a great story and a guiding light.

### Lucinda Snyder Whitehurst

SOURCE: A review of *Speaking to Miranda,* in *School Library Journal,* Vol. 38, No. 10, October, 1992, p. 144.

At 18, Ruby is no longer satisfied with the fleeting image that her adopted father, Rob, has given her of her long-deceased mother, Emma. She investigates Emma's mysterious past and discovers her real father's identity. Along the way she finds her own direction. This book suffers from abrupt shifts in focus. In the beginning, it is a typical story of an isolated teenager looking for love and a positive self-image. Her closest advisor has been Miranda, an inner voice/imaginary friend who has guided her for years, but who now cannot be trusted. Then the question of "Who was Emma?" takes center stage. Rob is suddenly left behind. Ruby essentially re-creates herself as Emma, cutting herself off from one life to discover a new one. The Australian and New Zealand settings are vividly described, but present some problems. Many slang phrases are unclear in context. Another troubling aspect involves the close relationship between Rob and Ruby. Ruby is accused of not wanting Rob to get married because she wants him for herself. Although nothing is explicit, they do end up together, with Rob breaking his engagement and preparing to become part of Ruby's new life. However, the search for self, the central theme, is well developed and intriguingly realized. Not a first choice, but a book that has a place in larger collections.

### *Publishers Weekly*

SOURCE: A review of *Speaking to Miranda,* in *Publishers Weekly,* Vol. 239, No. 46, October 19, 1992, p. 80.

Australian Ruby Summerton has been constantly haunted by the death of her mother, 17 years earlier, and by Miranda, a voice in her head that is somehow connected to her past. With high school behind her and the only prospect before her to accompany her stepfather, Rob, on construction site visits, Ruby faces an uncertain future. Frustrated by Rob's steadfast refusal to discuss her mother, Ruby begins a quest for the truth that leads her to New Zealand, where past and present finally meet. This intriguing novel moves along slowly as Ruby puzzles through the bits and pieces of her unorthodox upbringing. Although clues about her past are somewhat conveniently presented, this does not detract from Macdonald's narrative—a solidly crafted story that is more intent upon exploring the nature of secrets than on solving a mystery. Ruby is a prickly character and, while readers will be gratified that she finds some answers, the resolution does not end the strangeness of a life lived in half-truths.

### Carolyn Phelan

SOURCE: A review of *Speaking to Miranda,* in *Booklist,* Vol. 89, No. 8, December 15, 1992, p. 731.

In this sensitive, first-person novel, 18-year-old Ruby leaves her boyfriend, travels with her adopted father, and gradually decides to explore the central mysteries of her life: Who was her mother? Who is her family? and, ultimately, Who is she? The quest takes her from her home in Australia to the back roads of New Zealand, where she finds a new home and an unexpected identity for herself and for the inner voice that she has always called Miranda. Touched occasionally with wry humor, the telling is both languid and compelling—just right to describe a thoughtful character who's between childhood and adulthood, sure of herself, yet unsure where she fits in the general framework. While it seems to wind up a bit quickly, this well-written novel, with its memorable characters, will stay with readers for a long time.

### Judy Sasges

SOURCE: A review of *Speaking to Miranda,* in *Voice of Youth Advocates,* Vol. 16, No. 1, April, 1993, p. 27.

Sixteen years ago, Ruby's mother, Emma Blake, drowned in a surfing accident off the Australian coast. Rob, who adopted Ruby soon after the accident, still cannot discuss the mysterious past of the woman he loved and lived with for a year. It is only through Miranda, a phantom voice in her head, that Ruby learns bits and pieces of her early childhood. Now 18, Ruby faces an unfocused future, unable to decide between attending college and following Rob to his construction sites throughout Australia.

With the financial, if not emotional, support of Rob, Ruby searches for the truth about her mother's past. Emma left few traceable clues but, in New Zealand, Ruby uncovers some of her mother's secrets. Even though Ruby discovers facts, Emma's personality remains elusive. Learning about her mother helps Ruby face truths about herself, her future, and the meaning of family. The novel moves slowly but sustains interest as readers identify with Ruby's frustration at the loose ends in her life and her desire to find out about Emma. Ruby is, at times, selfish and irresponsible—in short, she acts like a real person. The Australia/New Zealand setting adds to the hint-of-supernatural atmosphere. This is one novel that does not have a predictable ending.

### HOSTILITIES: NINE BIZARRE STORIES (1991; U.S. edition, 1994)

### Janeen Webb

SOURCE: A review of *Hostilities: Nine Bizarre Stories,* in *Magpies,* Vol. 6, No. 3, July, 1991, p. 4.

Each of the stories in this new collection offers a variation on the theme of interpersonal domestic tensions. Vivienne Goodman's cover illustration, which shows a face torn into distorted pieces, provides a good visual summary of the contents: these are stories portraying aspects of the everyday urban guerilla warfare waged daily between familiar antagonists—bickering parents, adolescents chafing at parental authority, siblings engaging in unfriendly rivalry, conflicting members of extended families, and so on. Caroline Macdonald seeks to reinforce such ordinary human alienation through close encounters with the fantastic, making these commonplace situations provide the settings for the intrusion of hostile supernatural forces into the suburban worlds of her characters. Stories of this kind belong properly to the sub-genre of speculative fiction called Horror: the category that includes ghost stories, supernatural stories, strange and weird tales, thrillers, gothics and such like. As the famous American horror editor David G. Hartwell remarked, the term "horror" "points towards a transaction between the reader and the text": successful horror fiction is not to be identified by the strange elements contained in the text, but rather by the *frisson* experienced by the reader when the safety of the everyday world is invaded by the uncanny to produce a radical disruption of normality. Discussions about the therapeutic value of aesthetic terror have been with us for a long time, and most modern theorists agree that horror literature provides a way in which readers may address the problems that lurk just below the surface of ordinary human relationships.

The idea of enhancing the banality of adolescent *angst* by stressing a connection with the supernatural has a lot of appeal. Indeed, in recent times, there have been some very successful adaptations of this theme, including Suzy Mackee Charnas's short story *Boobs* in which a pubescent girl is transmogrified into a werewolf to take revenge upon a classmate for his relentless teasing about her developing chest. In Macdonald's collection, however, the antagonists are rather more polite, to the extent that the alignment of ordinary teenagers with relatively well-behaved supernatural forces often produces double cliché.

The stories follow a similar structural pattern, in that the protagonists move from city to country settings, there to encounter hostile supernatural elements. The uncanny appears in various guises. Ghostly promptings from beyond the grave inform several stories: a boy's murdered grandfather leads him to the revelation of the victim's skeleton in **"The Dam,"** the most predictable piece in the book; while in **"The Message in the Dust,"** a far future girl archaeologist experiences a supernatural vision which reveals the location of the preserved corpse of a Mayan carver who has experienced and recorded an early communication with space travellers, thus uncovering vital historical information. A different kind of supernatural aid occurs in **"Dandelion Creek,"** when an innocent group of campers is saved from attack by a bike gang because of the warning sound effects that result from a New Year's Eve seance held by a group

of children; while a more sinister girl spirit lures another teenager into a quasi-limbo existence in order to inhabit her body in **"The Thief in the Rocks."** Other stories such as **"At the Old Roxy"** and **"The Greenhouse"** employ less overt, more atmospheric intimations of supernatural agency. . . . The influence of cinema on Macdonald's writing comes through in several of the stories. The title story, **"Hostilities,"** begins very much in the manner of *Duel*, with a menacing encounter between a car and a concrete truck; **"The Thief in the Rocks"** recalls *Picnic at Hanging Rock* in the fashion in which the adolescent girl is lured to destruction; while in **"The Greenhouse,"** an otherwise innocent looking hothouse explodes in flames after producing strangely overripe fruit in an atmosphere reminiscent of *Attack of the Killer Tomatoes*.

All in all, this is a disappointing collection from an award-winning author. The underlying ideas are interesting, and while some of the stories will appeal to young adolescent readers, the collection as a whole offers little that is new. The essence of good horror writing is unpredictability—the text must take the reader by surprise in order to produce the therapeutic thrill that challenges the reader's complacency about the nature of the world. Viewed in this context, Caroline Macdonald's *Hostilities* just aren't scary enough.

### Publishers Weekly

SOURCE: A review of *Hostilities: Nine Bizarre Stories,* in *Publishers Weekly,* Vol. 240, No. 50, December 13, 1993, p. 71.

Macdonald uses her native New Zealand and current homeland of Australia as the backdrops for nine *Twilight Zone*-ish stories that range from spooky to only slightly offbeat. Young heroes and heroines—usually placed in remote locations (campsites, farm houses, etc.)—find themselves on the edge of danger as their notions of reality are challenged. While some of the selections include traditional horrors in the form of seances, soul-switchings and skeletons, other, more subtle stories explore how perceptions are colored by deep emotions. The title story, for example, examines the way a girl's growing resentment of her new half-brother affects her reasoning. **"At the Old Roxy"** traces an adolescent shoplifter's quest for beauty in her crumbling, chaotic world. This book may not leave readers quaking in their boots, but it does offer a number of promising situations and a smattering of surprising conclusions.

### Kirkus Reviews

SOURCE: A review of *Hostilities: Nine Bizarre Stories,* in *Kirkus Reviews,* Vol. LXII, No. 1, January 1, 1994, p. 71.

A delicately macabre ambience infuses these tales from the Australian author of *Speaking to Miranda* (1992): a fugitive finds the story of her own life in an old book;

a boy visiting his aunt's dying farm is haunted by dreams centering around **"The Dam"** and its fetid lake; **"The Thief in the Rocks"** and another malevolent spirit infecting **"The Greenhouse"** behave with chilling malice. The theme of anger also pervades tales of an abused shoplifter who finds someone to cling to **"At the Old Roxy,"** a bed-wetter who finally stops believing his father's **"Lies,"** and the title story, about two warring step-siblings, one of whom gleefully rescues the other from being buried in cement. Hostile indeed, and bizarre. . . .

**Chris Sherman**

SOURCE: A review of *Hostilities: Nine Bizarre Stories,* in *Booklist,* Vol. 90, No. 10, January 15, 1994, p. 919.

Students expecting splatter-punk gore and slashing won't find it in these carefully crafted stories. However, they will find nine unsettling, strange, satisfyingly creepy tales—the kind you don't want to read when you're in the house alone and it's time for bed; the kind you continue to think about hours later. In the title story, a stepsister finds a novel way to get revenge on her stepbrother; in **"The Dam,"** a boy discovers he is living with a murderous aunt; and in **"The Thief in the Rocks,"** a girl's very life is stolen. The Australian slang may occasionally puzzle North American readers, but it won't prevent them from enjoying this eerie collection.

**Deborah L. Earl**

SOURCE: A review of *Hostilities: Nine Bizarre Stories,* in *Voice of Youth Advocates,* Vol. 17, No. 4, October, 1994, p. 210.

Brief, unusual collection of nine short stories involving teens who find their conception of reality threatened as they encounter subtly strange situations. Set in Australia and the author's native New Zealand, the stories are well-framed in these countries' spare, rocky terrain and unusual climate. Although not traditional horror stories, these tales arouse feelings that range from sticky unease to gut-wrenching terror. In the title story, a young woman purposefully almost becomes her new stepbrother's killer, forcing the spoiled boy who hates her to be grateful to her for saving his life. Other stories center around more conventional fears: having one's being invaded by a body snatcher, coping with an out-of-control seance, discovering a relative is a murderer, etc. Fans of Stephen King and R. L. Stine will have to set their sensitivities a notch or so higher to fully appreciate these creative, unsettling yarns, but the stories will stay in their memories much longer than *The Babysitter,* I guarantee: Occasional use of Australian slang does not detract from these spooky tales. Try book-talking these with high school readers who enjoy other-worldly thrills.

## SECRET LIVES (1993; U.S. edition, 1995)

**Tim Rausch**

SOURCE: A review of *Secret Lives,* in *School Library Journal,* Vol. 41, No. 6, June, 1995, p. 131.

Ian, 15, lives with his grandmother in Australia. For a school assignment over the holidays, he must invent and write about a character. He creates Gideon, a mean-spirited, law-breaking youth who displays personality traits similar to Ian's dead father and to his grandfather, who is in prison. Mysteriously, Gideon takes control of Ian's life; soon the boy is involved in a car theft, brutally injures his dog, and burglarizes his maternal grandparents' house. When he makes a vulgar pass at his cousin, he realizes the power that his creation holds over him. He tries to kill Gideon, first by destroying the story he'd written and, when that fails, by inventing a new character to battle the evil one. But the dark and secret side of Ian's personality persists until he realizes that he has the power to control Gideon himself.

Macdonald uses the writing assignment and the emerging psychological Frankenstein to portray the murky side of the human spirit. Unfortunately, the people are unconvincing. Even the real ones seem unreal, and the influence that Gideon exerts on Ian seems contrived. While the introduction of the second fictional character has possibilities, it goes nowhere, and in the end readers will wonder why Ian is suddenly able to dominate his monster. Though this novel paints striking contrasts, it fails to add new insights into the battle of good v. evil.

**Jeanne Triner**

SOURCE: A review of *Secret Lives,* in *Booklist,* Vol. 91, Nos. 19-20, June 1, 1995, p. 1753.

As part of a school assignment, Ian creates Gideon, Ian imaginary rebel, who slowly begins to take over Ian's life. When Ian finds himself at the center of crimes that he doesn't remember committing, he struggles to bring Gideon under control—something he cannot do until he confronts his own past and insecurities. Although the ending is a bit too pat, allowing Ian to escape the consequences of his actions with too few repercussions, the book, overall, is well written.

Ian is believable and complex enough to be worth caring about. The elements of teenage turmoil and horror will make it extremely popular with YA readers, exposing them to structure, style, and characterization that are clearly a cut above what most current books in this semi-horror genre have to offer. A particularly nice touch is the way Macdonald uses Ian to illustrate the importance of loving, human relationships even when Gideon is at his most alienating.

## *Kirkus Reviews*

SOURCE: A review of *Secret Lives,* in *Kirkus Reviews,* Vol. LXIII, No. 12, June 15, 1995, p. 859.

Ian, 15, has a school assignment over the holidays: to write about an imaginary character. He creates Gideon, a rebellious teenager very nearly Ian's total opposite. But this creation asserts himself, forcing Ian's participation in acts of violence and landing him in trouble with just about everyone. When Ian's protestations that Gideon is responsible fall on deaf ears, he admits that the boy is a figment of his imagination. But is he?

Gideon's full-blown malevolence is established well before Ian divulges just how this troublemaker entered his life; it's a brilliant construction that will send readers back through the pages looking for flaws in the logic. There aren't any. Macdonald creates hairpin turns in the plot that force the issues—what is real? what is fiction?—in an explosive narrative. Before Ian can get control of his life, he must regain control of his creature and come to terms with the ghosts of his tortured past. This modern Frankenstein story is suspenseful right to the last, as a troubled teen faces a final confrontation, not with demons, but with himself.

## Sarah A. Hudson

SOURCE: A review of *Secret Lives,* in *Voice of Youth Advocates,* Vol. 18, No. 3, August, 1995, p. 160.

Australian teenager Ian Ganty has a dangerous friend. Gideon holds a certain control over Ian, engaging him in "stupid" behavior. Normally, Ian would not consider joy riding, drinking, or making a move on his friend, Jaz. However, while his grandmother, Lil, is away, Ian begins his self-destructive tendencies, even becoming an unwilling participant in a robbery. Gideon convinces Ian to avoid the police, thereby creating a worse set of problems.

As he learns more about Gideon. Ian reveals more about himself. His birth and childhood were stigmatized by two generations of teenage pregnancy and dysfunctional parenting. After his parents died in an airplane accident, Lil became the stable adult in his life. However, Ian continues to have some unresolved issues concerning his parents' death and his relationship with his maternal grandparents. Ian's psychological state is questionable; Gideon is a character Ian created for a class project. Ian realizes he is in trouble and tries to kill Gideon by creating a good character to overcome evil. It is only by confessing to Lil that he is able to work on his problems.

*Secret Lives* is a difficult novel. It begins with adult Ian introducing the period in his life controlled by Gideon. The action takes place over three or four days, and is revealed by teenage Ian. The plot is fast-paced, but Ian's psychological state makes it hard to keep events clear. Fact and fiction are confused in Ian's mind, which makes

it confused in the reader's mind. However, Macdonald has succeeded in realistically portraying the emotional and mental state of a teenager battling his personal demons. The Australian setting and vernacular may put off some readers, but the cover art and intriguing title may attract browsers.

## *SPIDER MANSION* (1994; U.S. edition, 1996)

### Stephen Matthews

SOURCE: "From the Word Go: Books for Younger Readers," in *Australian Book Review,* No. 165, October, 1994, pp. 66-8.

Caroline Macdonald's touch in **Spider Mansion** is as light as the web traced on the book's seductive cover. And almost surreptitiously the tale weaves such a web of enchantment that my critical faculties might have been immobilised had my disappointment at the end not freed me from the spell.

Fourteen-year-old Chrissie Day has given the nickname Spider Mansion to the remote South Australian homestead where she lives with her parents. Their need to keep up mortgage repayments has led them to offer gourmet weekend holidays. When the Todd family arrives one weekend, they keep finding excuses not to leave, and end up attempting to discredit the Days and drive them away. After her father proves to be ineffectual and her mother succumbs to her fondness for whisky-induced oblivion, Chrissie has to rely on her own resourcefulness to get the Todds to leave.

Macdonald's sharply-observed depiction of the inexorable progress of the Todds' takeover made me wince at times. She makes the Days' combination of unsuspecting cooperativeness, commercial vulnerability and slightly puzzled acceptance of guilt disturbingly believable. What I found less effective was the book's last sequence, which leaves a huge loose end. Perhaps a sequel is planned, but I would have preferred a more conclusive and satisfying ending.

### Marcus Crouch

SOURCE: A review of *Spider Mansion,* in *The Junior Bookshelf,* Vol. 59, No. 3, June, 1995, pp. 113-4.

This paperback original from Australia is not so much thought-provoking as devastating. From early chapters to the open-ended misery of the ending it is designed to harrow the reader, leaving him at the end with no hope. And all for the best of reasons. If the villains (the Todd family) are totally unadmirable, the goodies (the Days) haven't much to commend them; their good points are of a negative kind and goodness and weakness alike leave them vulnerable. In the course of a story in which venom is rampant the Todds take their hosts apart and systematically destroy them.

Godfrey and Brenda Day run Tilvers Homestead (alias Spider Mansion) in a remote part of Australia, offering their guests a short stay with good food and friendly service. What the Todds bring is a hostility so quiet that it is hardly recognised. The Todds are greedy. They also love power, and for power they have to take away the Days' efficiency and eventually their home and all that goes with it. This is at a cost. In the last pages of the book the Todds' son Tiger is bitten by a snake. For complex reasons the Todds have isolated Spider Mansion from the rest of the world, and Tiger cannot be saved without recourse to civilization. So Tiger has to die, and his father, himself injured and in some peril, sees a son's death as a small price to pay for his success in stealing the house and its place in society. Of the Days only the daughter Chrissie has qualities that deserve success. Father and mother are nice folk if left alone. Confronted with a ruthless enemy they go to pieces, Godfrey hiding in the tree-house, his wife turning to drink. Who wins? We are left to our own opinions. At best the Days have lost their business.

Much as one admires this book—and it is written with consistent skill and conviction—it is difficult to enjoy it. The conflict between evil and folly is not one which encourages the taking of sides, and I found even Chrissie only occasionally deserving our sympathy. Nastiness is all. Caroline Macdonald marshalls her forces with great dexterity, and releases them in a series of brilliant and brief chapters.

**David Bennett**

SOURCE: A review of *Spider Mansion,* in *Books for Keeps,* No. 93, July, 1995, p. 13.

Next time an older reader asks for something spooky, reach for this title. The Days' holiday business is progressing well enough until the arrival of the Todds who just won't leave. They are determined to take over the lives and identities of their hosts by a cruelly tenacious, psychological campaign. You can't help but get wrapped up in the battle and feel outrage at the cynical injustice of it all.

### ☐ *THROUGH THE WITCH'S WINDOW* (1996)

**Joan Zahnleiter**

SOURCE: A review of *Through the Witch's Window,* in *Magpies,* Vol. 12, No. 1, March, 1997, p. 10.

One person's trash is another person's treasure. Children love fossicking in tips, given the chance. This is the case with the tip near the Bellaroma Caravan Park where Erana, her brother Stu and Peter and his little sister Yvonne live: the four children fascinated by the activities of a woman in floppy overalls and gumboots. Every few days she pushes her old brown wheelbarrow in to the tip and returns with it laden with assorted junk.

Who is she? What does she do with all that stuff? And more importantly, how is it that she walks with impunity past the ogre who guards the gate of the tip when the notices say plainly KEEP OUT and NO SCAVENGING? Not only that, she stares down their big brash yellow dog Chainsaw so that he runs away, cowed. Or bewitched?

Erana, the eldest, is full of theories about witches and spells. She convinces the children that the mysterious woman is indeed a witch who is putting a spell on Peter. When he develops a sore throat, Erana rests her case.

Meanwhile Rose Tattoo, the sculptor, continues working on her junk totally oblivious of the turmoil she is causing among the four children. She is nonplused when they throw a brick carrying a note—*Take away the spell*—through the window. In attacking the house with a further shower of broken bricks they succeed in frightening the unfortunate Rose Tattoo. When Chainsaw disappears the children decide that she has the upper hand and change their tactics to appeasement.

There are many issues raised here. The children's behaviour is a prime example of Isaac Watts's old adage that . . . Satan finds some mischief still for idle hands to do. Despite the destruction they cause, they are not bad children, rather they are unhappy and alienated at having been uprooted from home by their itinerant parents. With nothing to do but hang around Bellaroma Caravan Park while their parents wait for their dilapidated car to be repaired, boredom takes over and their imaginations run away with them. They perceive the 'different' appearance of Rose Tattoo as a threat and react with hostility. It all gets out of hand so easily. The children learn through their misadventures that cooperation is far better than confrontation, and that 'difference' is just that—difference.

This chapter book for younger readers represents exploration of new territory for Caroline Macdonald whose reputation in writing for older readers is well established. The story will engage the interest of its intended audience, built as it is on the lively activities of children around the age of nine acting with complete independence. In fact their independence of spirit takes them rather too far.

There are a couple of loose ends which may puzzle adults but are not likely to concern children. What is the significance of the name Rose Tattoo? The only link with the play of the same name by Tennessee Williams is the rose tattoo which is on her wrist, not her chest. Nor does Angry Anderson's band come into it either. Tantalising!

The cover of the book, by Mark Sofilas, is deliciously spooky and involves elements of the story. The horror-stricken faces of the children are highlighted, presumably by the glare of the welding torch which also casts sinister shadows around them. The rich colour combinations enhance the eye-catching effect. Throughout the book, Mark Wilson's heavily crosshatched black ink illustrations are in keeping with the mood and action of the story. They capture the dramas of particular events beautifully, e.g. what Yvonne sees through the window. There are also lovely pensive studies of Erana and of Peter. It is a pity that the figure of Rose Tattoo does not emerge more clearly, especially at the end, unless it is the intention to leave her cloaked in mystery.

The spare text which moves at a smart pace and the crisp black-and-white illustrations come together happily in a well produced book which is likely to win even younger followers for Caroline Macdonald.

**Stella Lees**

SOURCE: "Un/Happy Endings," in *Australian Book Review,* No. 189, April, 1997, p. 63.

In **Through the Witch's Window,** four children believe Rose Tattoo (sic), who retrieves junk from the local tip to create metal sculptures, is a witch and casting spells on them. Fear breeds hate, and they attempt retribution by throwing stones at her. One wiser child sees the need for reconciliation and after a few misunderstandings Rose becomes their friend. It's all very predictable, and one has to say, a little unlikely. Which leaves us with the dilemma.

---

Additional coverage of MacDonald's life and career is contained in the following sources published by The Gale Group: *Contemporary Authors,* Vol. 152 and *Something about the Author,* Vol. 86.

# Suzanne Fisher Staples

## 1945-

(Also writes as Suzanne Fisher) American author of fiction; journalist.

Major works include *Shabanu: Daughter of the Wind* (1989), *Haveli* (1993), *Dangerous Skies* (1996; British edition as *Storm*, 1998).

## INTRODUCTION

A compassionate writer concerned with societal change, Staples is known for her compelling coming-of-age stories for young adults that sensitively portray other cultures. Traveling extensively for eight years as a foreign correspondent, primarily in Pakistan and India, Staples brings a strong sense of place to her fiction. Her works expose readers to those different from themselves, as the author tries intently to present her subjects as they truly exist in their own environment. "Masterful at evoking scenery," according to Megan McDonald, Staples creates captivating, exotic settings in her fiction, which is praised by reviewers for its authenticity and wealth of detail. Her works are also acknowledged for their realistic characterizations that often show the not-so-pretty side of humanity. Staples's protagonists are determined young people who rise to new challenges and become stronger persons for doing so. Two of her works, *Shabanu: Daughter of the Wind* and *Haveli*, are set in the Cholistan Desert in Pakistan, and have come under fire by some reviewers and Muslims who have criticized Staples's representation of Islam and the Cholistani culture. While many reviewers have noted that the author accurately captures the place about which she writes, others were skeptical about an "outsider's" presentation of another culture.

In *Bookbird,* Staples expressed that those often taken aback by her works are groups who feel that "someone who has no right to do so 'speaks' for them." She explained that it was never her intent to portray or defend Islam, but to just "write a story about the people of the Cholistan." She further commented in *The ALAN Review,* "During my time in Pakistan, I learned something with my heart that my head already knew: 'different' does not mean 'better' or 'worse'— it just means different." Staples carried this theme into her third novel, *Dangerous Skies*, which examines racism and relationships between two best friends, as well as with their parents and other adults in their community. Despite the exotic locales of Staples's fiction, its themes are completely identifiable to young readers. In a review of *Shabanu*, Megan McDonald pointed out, "[I]t is [Shabanu's] universal struggle to find inner strength and beauty despite the odds around her, that hits home."

**Biographical Information**

Staples was born in 1945 in Philadelphia, Pennsylvania. The daughter of an engineer and a manager, she grew up in a very goal-oriented household. Her love of writing took root at a very young age, and was expressed in journals, diaries, letters, and school newspapers. After graduating from Cedar Crest College in Allentown, Pennsylvania, with a bachelor of arts degree in literature, Staples launched into a career in journalism by working at a small newspaper in Evergreen, Colorado. In 1967, she married Nicholas Green, an American who worked for the Ford Foundation in Asia. In 1974, she decided she wanted to travel, and took a job with Business International in Hong Kong, and then with United Press International in New Delhi. Around this time, Staples and her husband divorced. On her own, she spent a number of years in India and Pakistan, where she carefully observed the culture and took notes, hoping to one day pursue non-journalistic writing. Frustrated with her situation, the reporter felt she was risking her life to write about war-torn countries, only for the story to end up in the "news-in-brief" columns in the U.S. newspapers. She once recalled in *Bookbird,*

"[W]henever I had the chance I reported 'color' features about people's lives. My notebooks were filled with textural details—the color of the sky, the smell of the earth, the feel of the bark of trees."

In 1983, Staples moved back to the United States and took a part-time editorial position at the *Washington Post.* However, her wonderlust returned, and two-years later she traveled to Pakistan as a consultant on an United States Agency for International Development (USAID) project in the Cholistan Desert of the Punjab province. Her focus was on improving the health, nutrition, and housing of poor women and their families in rural areas. Determined not to depend on interpreters, who often distorted the meaning of comments, Staples studied the national language of Urdu for six months. During this time, she worked and lived side by side with the people in the desert and learned of their customs and culture. She also chose to wear, out of respect, women's traditional clothing, which she found not only comfortable, but practical as well. Although she had once viewed the scarf, or *chadr*, worn about the head as a symbol of the repression of women, she found it could be used to haul goods, to create a cradle for a baby in the limbs of a tree, and even for a washcloth. In 1987, after returning to the United States, Staples began writing about what she had experienced in Pakistan. The result was her first novel, *Shabanu: Daughter of the Wind*, which was published in 1989, and was named a Newbery Honor Book.

## Major Works

*Shabanu: Daughter of the Wind* explores the choice between tradition and following one's own desires. In *Something about the Author* (*SATA*), Staples explained that her book was written to describe "the essential human-ness of us all," and also noted that, of the writing that exists of the Islamic world, there is "little or nothing of the poetry and the intellectual, emotional, and general universality we share with Muslims." Narrated by its title character, *Shabanu* is the story of a twelve-year-old Cholistan girl who feels obligated to obey her parents' wishes that she marry an older man of their choosing. Since she has no brothers to tend the family's livestock, Shabanu is responsible for their care. The story recounts the events of the year leading up to the marriage of her older sister Phulan. It had been arranged that the sisters will marry two brothers. However, when the man Phulan is to marry dies, she instead marries Shabanu's fiancé; Shabanu is then matched with a man named Rahim, a rich, old landowner who already has three wives. The novel shows the strength and courage of Shabanu, who is appalled by the marriage but comes to terms with her lot in life and comes to understand that she must listen to her parents and follow her culture. She rises to the challenge and becomes a stronger person in doing so. Betsy Hearne commented, "The richness and tragedy of a whole culture are reflected in the fate of this girl's family, each member of whom is rendered with natural clarity." Hearne concluded, "Through an involving plot Staples has given young

readers insight into lives totally different from their own, but into emotions resoundingly familiar." Although Staples was generally praised for the detail and thoroughness of her descriptions in the story, Barbara Bottner of *The Los Angeles Times Book Review* found that the "sheer detail . . . overwhelms the narrative," but concluded that "Fisher Staples succeeds in establishing the reality of this world and the strict customs and rules that govern it. . . . Shabanu's destiny may be incomprehensible to American readers, but we all are enriched from meeting this undaunted, indomitable nomad girl." Maurya Simon remarked, "It is a pleasure to read a book that explores a way of life profoundly different from our own, and that does so with such sensitivity, admiration and verisimilitude. Ms. Staples . . . has surely accomplished a small miracle in the unfolding of her touching and powerful story."

*Haveli,* a sequel to *Shabanu* written in third person, more closely explains the Pakistani culture and includes a map, a list of characters, and a glossary to help readers comprehend the story. Eighteen-year-old Shabanu, now the fourth wife of Rahim, has a daughter named Mumtaz. Rahim's other three wives, however, do not treat Shabanu or Mumtaz very favorably. Jealous of the attention that Rahim pays to his newest bride, they play dirty tricks on her, leaving a scorpion in her bed, killing her daughter's puppy, and placing a bat in her cupboard. Although Shabanu is Rahim's favorite wife, she is still concerned about the security of her own and her daughter's future in the event of her husband's death. Knowing that having a profession will ensure her daughter's financial independence, Shabanu is determined to provide an education for the girl. Daniyal Mueenuddin, who spent his childhood in Pakistan, favored Staples's "plain and uncluttered prose" that "smoothly mov[es] the narrative forward," but argued that *Haveli* both "exaggerates and naively caricatures the people and the society." Ilene Cooper praised Staples's work, stating, "Staples brews a potent mix here: the issue of a woman's role in a traditional society, page-turning intrigue, tough women characters, and a fluidity of writing that blends it all together. Staples has some very strong things to say about the lack of power some women have over their own lives, but the reader never hears preaching. Rather, as in the best stories, the message comes through the characters, their anguish and their triumphs."

A sharp change of pace from her first two novels, *Dangerous Skies* is a coming-of-age murder-mystery set on the shore of the Chesapeake Bay. The main characters are two twelve-year-old best friends, Buck Smith and Tunes. Buck has grown up with Tunes, the daughter of a black family that has worked on the Smith family farm for generations. The young people hide their friendship at school where Buck is friends with other white students and Tunes prefers to keep to herself. Their lives change forever when Buck finds the body of a Hispanic farm labor manager floating in the river. Convinced that the murderer is Jumbo Rawlin, Buck is horrified when the murder weapon, Tunes's gun, is found and the girl becomes a suspect. Buck encourages Tunes to tell her side of the story, but she disappears. He later discovers that Tunes has been physically and sexually molested by Rawlin, who is a well-respected and prosperous white man. Joyce A. Litton complemented the book: "In a class with Harper Lee's *To Kill a Mockingbird,* Staples's beautifully written and chilling tale of contemporary racism should keep young adult readers turning pages until they reach the heart-breaking end." Although Cindy Darling Codell found some problems with "characterization and voice," she concluded, "Staples has drawn a fascinating picture of an isolated, antiquated way of life along Virginia's Eastern shore. There are many colorful supporting characters, and the author masterfully delineates the way that racism can still divide people who truly care about one another."

**Awards**

*Shabanu: Daughter of the Wind* received the Newbery Honor and the Joan G. Sugarman Children's Book Award, both in 1990, as well as a Best Books for Young Adults citation and a Notable Books for Children citation from the American Library Association. It also was selected as a Notable Book of the Year by *The New York Times* and was regarded as a 1992 Honor List Selection by the International Board on Books for Young People. *Haveli* received a Best Books for Young Adults citation from the American Library Association in 1994, as did *Dangerous Skies* in 1997. *Dangerous Skies* also received a Best Books citation from *Publishers Weekly* in 1996 and a Books for the Teen Age citation from the New York Public Library in 1997.

---

# AUTHOR'S COMMENTARY

### Walter E. Sawyer and Jean C. Sawyer with Suzanne Fisher Staples

SOURCE: "A Discussion with Suzanne Fisher Staples: The Author as Writer and Cultural Observer," in *The New Advocate,* Vol. 6, No. 3, Summer, 1993, pp. 159-69.

[Jean C. Sawyer:] In reading about Shabanu, it is clear that you could not have written the story without being Shabanu in a sense, or developing a kinship with her. The reader experiences and can relate to Shabanu's feelings as she goes through her life and as things change for her. What in your background or experience helped you accomplish this?

[Suzanne Fisher Staples:] Some of that is how I felt about where I grew up. I grew up in the countryside of northeastern Pennsylvania, and I loved it. I loved the mountains, the hills, and the forest. I never wanted to leave it.

I was able to relate to the feelings young girls go through when they're reaching puberty. It becomes much more poignant when the girl is about to be married against her will, and must give up the things she loves. Shabanu is frightened. She is at an age where she is not interested in sex, in moving away from her family, or in losing her freedom. Those are all things from my experience that were transposed to her culture.

[Walter E. Sawyer:] The setting has a profound influence on the story. The depiction of the setting is more subtle than journalistic. There is a distinct view of Shabanu's world even though it is never discussed in great detail. Does a journalism background help you to create such settings?

SS: No. I had to unlearn everything that I had learned as a journalist in order to write fiction. Meticulous attention to detail should be in your notebook as a journalist so that you will know it in case you need to use it later. I remember covering the story of Breshnev (former head of state of the Soviet Union) visiting India. He had been out of the public view for quite awhile. When he landed at the airport all of the ambassadors came. They made several speeches. This happened right after Afghanistan was invaded and everybody was focused on that story. When I had finished writing my story, I received a telephone call from a newspaper in Kansas wanting a physical description of Breshnev. They wanted an article on what Breshnev looked like. I went back to my notebook and constructed it; it was all there. That's the training of a journalist. You notice everything. You record things and filter all of the human emotion out. Fiction, to me, is just the opposite of this. As a journalist I did consciously filter out the emotion.

As a journalist in Asia, it was easy to gauge whether your story would get into the newspaper. It often had to do with whether the World Series was being played or whether the Pope was in the United States. What was happening in the United States was seen as much more important. I realized that I was going out and risking my life for something that often never saw the light of day. I really lost faith in the news media as a vehicle for understanding between people. On the other hand, journalists have a lot of respect for the people living in the places where they themselves are assigned.

When I found out I was going to live in Pakistan, I loved the idea. I love that country. I had been all over it as a political reporter. The idea of going back there and writing about the people was so intriguing to me. I was working for the *Washington Post* at the time, but you are not allowed to report from the country where a member of your immediate family is in the diplomatic corps. Since my husband was in the diplomatic corps, we made the decision to go there based on my decision to leave journalism. I thought it would be interesting to try to reach the people by talking and listening to them. In a sense, journalism influenced what I was trying to do. Paying attention to detail was something I did. Now, I had to learn a new subjective way of expressing thought.

WS: Deciding what details to include or delete is a challenge for any writer. How did you develop the ability to be discriminating about what to include or not include?

SS: I think it's a matter of experience. You learn as you write or even as you grow to appreciate art. The telling detail, a distillation, is what you are after. A telling detail might be when Shabanu's mother is sitting and talking to her as the sun is going down. The sunlight catching in her nosepin tells you more about what the light looks like than if you describe the sky. That's what painters try to do. Instead of telling every little detail, they present one very important detail that tells it all.

I remember discovering this when I was in school. I had gone on a field trip to the Metropolitan Museum in New York and was looking at impressionist paintings. It dawned on me how important it was to capture a tiny bit of the whole thing and have that tiny bit tell the whole story. When I write, I present vignettes that tell more than I am actually putting into words.

JS: In one scene, Shabanu and her father come back from the fair. Her mother wants to hear all about the fair. As they tell her, she is looking off in the distance, reliving her memories through them. It told much about the society. Her mother cannot go to fairs anymore; now she can only try to relive the experience. The reader can picture much from just a line of conversation or from a person's look.

SS: In a way, that is how our minds work. Things that are important to us are the things we tell other people about. When the writer makes the connection with the reader and something rings true, it is very rewarding. Even if we are just talking to friends, we often find that we can strike a common chord so that each knows what the other means. Creativity is related to this. We should demythologize the notion of creativity. It is something that everybody has, but it takes a lot of work to perfect. It takes technique to take a good idea and to execute it well. Some of us can do it in some ways but not in others.

WS: When you used the example of the light shining on the nosepin, your purpose wasn't to describe things literally. Rather, your purpose was to paint a picture with a telling detail. How can beginning writers or those working with developing writers encourage this ability to perceive significant details?

SS: One way might be to look at a slide for just a split second. Ask yourself what sticks in your mind about the picture, and then put that into words.

WS: In schools today there is an increased emphasis on establishing a more realistic balance between the meaningful content and the mechanics of writing.

SS: That's important. I was pleased by the fact that it didn't matter to my publishers how, why, or for whom I had written my book. They were interested in quality literature for young people. I have been reading young people's literature since writing this book. I didn't know anything about this type of literature before. Writing for young people is like having faith that you can talk about another culture because people are fundamentally the same. Children are fundamentally the same as adults. Their thought processes are very similar though perhaps a little bit less developed.

WS: There are many themes in the book . . . duty, parental love, disillusionment, and making one's way in life. How do you establish themes in your writing?

SS: I don't think of **Shabanu** as being filled with themes. I was trying to tell a story in which everything made sense at some level. The finished manuscript, was about 25 percent fuller than it is now. I had to pull some things out, but I was afraid that in the process some things wouldn't make sense. For example, Shabanu's not having brothers makes her more independent. This opens up the question of the place of women in society.

WS: Do you let the themes emerge and then go back to clarify them?

SS: Yes. There were some things that I did have to go back and connect later. There were also some things that I had over-connected; I had to go back and untangle them.

The concepts of creativity, craftsmanship, and thematic writing make writing sound scary. I recall being at Breadloaf with people who talked about these things as though they were real things. I couldn't understand what they were talking about. Even now, when I go into a writer's group I don't understand or even care about those things.

JS: This sometimes happens to the reader as well as the writer. For example, take the notion of the word "choice." The reader learns that Shabanu has no choice about the sale of the camel. Later her aunt uses the word "choice." It came to be related to the inner self. Shabanu has a choice about her inner self and her own thoughts. It wasn't necessarily a theme, but the word came up twice and caused the reader to think about it. Do you consciously keep all of these things in mind as you write?

SS: I don't think I could write that way. One time I came home from Pakistan and attended a birthday party for a friend of mine who had introduced me to my agent. People were talking about things that were being published. These people were all successful writers, publishers, and agents. I became confused and upset by their terms even though I had read most of the things they were talking about. It made me think that I was never going to make it as a fiction writer.

One of the best pieces of advice I ever got about writing was from a writer friend. She said that when something bothers you as a writer, track it down and follow it until it disappears. That really made sense to me. If you can't nail it down, then take it out. You have to learn to trust your own judgment about it. I think you need to trust yourself to know that what makes sense to you is likely to make sense to others. This comes with a certain amount of maturity. You develop the confidence that it is worth writing a book, even if it is just because your family and friends will read about this culture that you have lived in, or because you loved doing it, or because it has helped you express yourself. You have to develop a faith in yourself that it is worthwhile.

JS: Do you read a lot of novels?

SS: I used to, but I don't anymore. It has too great an effect on me. If I'm reading at the same time I am writing, I find myself talking in other people's voices. So, I don't read fiction when I'm writing. It's just too hard for me to do. That disappoints me because I love reading fiction.

Writing is such a personal thing. Why do we tell stories that mean something to us? Everybody does it for a different reason. We need to help young writers get to a stage beyond where they are writing only as an assignment. We need to get them to the point where they hope that someone will identify with their writing.

In writing, you see how much your will can influence events. In my writing, I find distance very helpful. For example, I am writing a sequel to **Shabanu** that deals with her in an urban situation. She is eighteen-years-old, married, and has her own daughter when the book opens. Dealing with adult emotions, things which I might now be experiencing myself, are more difficult for me to write about than things like how she related to her father when she was younger. I can look back and remember my relationship with my father, and associate how I felt emotionally at the time.

I'm having a harder time with this book. For example, Shabanu learns very early on to use her body to please her husband. This is difficult for Western readers to accept and to still see Shabanu as a sympathetic character. Yet, it is so common. It is the way women insure their safety and survival in that part of the world. Everybody is not liberated. We don't realize how different our Western relationships are between women and men. I'm having to work at this book a little bit, go away, and then come back to it. It is very hard to get it right the first time.

WS: What helps you or any other writer to get it right?

SS: A wonderful old UPI editor who still works as a roving world correspondent said that writing is nothing more than clear thinking and that if you can get it down on paper so that it makes sense, then you will be thinking clearly about it. Writing is such a good tool for that reason. The message at the end of my book is that you have to believe in yourself. You have to count on your-

self. The world can be good to you or it can be bad to you. If you have your own inner network in place, things should be okay.

WS: In addition to telling a powerful story, your book effectively captures the essence of another culture. Writers tend to focus on what is familiar to them. You demonstrate the ability to take the unfamiliar and make it meaningful for readers. How did you learn to do this?

SS: It's not easy to write about another culture. Let me share my method of doing research on the people about whom I wrote.

First of all, I learned their language, although I was not really good at it. Fortunately, the desert language was a second language for them as well. It is different from the national language.

Second, I spent as much time with the people as I could. When you spend time with people you get involved in their lives. At the time, there was a terrible drought, the worst in memory for the people who lived in the village.

As we became better acquainted, as my language improved, and as they began to trust me as an outsider, I realized that the important things about people who live on the very edge of survival are important things to us as well.

We laughed at the same things very spontaneously. At the time, I was writing an article about camels and was trying to learn the physiology of mating. We had a long involved uninhibited discussion about it. It was like talking about pickup trucks to them. I was standing by a well one morning and this camel came up and nuzzled my cheek. They said that it thought I was a female camel. We all laughed so hard that one man standing by the well almost fell in.

I found that the things that are fundamental about people are the things that we all have in common. The externals of our lives, however, were so different. The thing that made me feel confident about writing about another culture was a faith that people are fundamentally the same. I made a careful study of their lives, visited the shrines in the desert, and read their mythology. The things I wrote about in my story were things that had happened to them. I did not feel competent to create a story for that culture. I took things from real life and made them happen to one family. I studied, did research, and sat down with an anthropologist and a sociologist who were familiar with the culture. By doing this, I was able to reconstruct the "why" of what was happening. I had also lived in Asia for about twelve years and was familiar with much of the culture.

WS: In other words, we need to become better observers and better listeners about what is happening around us.

SS: Yes, . . . and maybe more empathetic. I think that

writers have to be empathetic. You have to want to be under somebody else's skin to write fiction.

WS: We knew that the people in the story would return to the desert. It seemed so important to them. It is a very subtle concept to understand exactly what is of value to another person. The relationship between Shabanu and her father was both touching and frightening. Shabanu's father, who would never sell their prized camel, all of a sudden does sell the camel. The father who could do no wrong is now, for the right price, selling his daughter as well. Young western readers might be at a similar point in life, perhaps to a less dramatic extent, where they are beginning to see the flaws in the people they previously viewed as the most wonderful people in the world.

SS: Yes, it's disillusionment.

WS: To write about another culture, it would seem that flexibility is especially necessary. When I first worked with families from Pakistan, I was struck by the differences between our cultures and how little I really knew about their culture. Are we capable of truly understanding each other's culture? Why is the ending of *Shabanu* so disturbing to many readers? Is it because of a lack of cultural understanding?

SS: Perhaps we're shocked when we read about a society where a father who loves a daughter so much could do what her father does to her in the name of duty and tradition. I also think that in our society, we would expect that a person who takes a different path but has good motivations will probably succeed. Or, if the person didn't succeed, there would at least be a reward for having tried to do things differently, for having tried to change things.

Things aren't that way in a culture where you constantly bump into tradition. For example, in one scene Shabanu runs into other tribesmen who tell her about the wrongs of the daughter of the man who was leading their search party. The girl had violated a cultural code and then had fled. They explained that when they found the girl, they would kill her. That's what happens. It's very hard for us to accept and understand that this is what happens according to cultural codes.

JS: You mention people who are different but who work hard and are usually rewarded. Sometimes that occurs, and sometimes it takes much time for society to catch up with such people. It sounds like Shabanu's society hasn't changed like that. If you had written this book a hundred years earlier or later would it be the same?

SS: I think change is coming. One of the coming changes, which I just loved, was the communication and travel from village to village. We would be ambling along on our camels and suddenly we would be passed by a camel rider going like a shot because the Pakistani cricket team had just beaten the West Indian team. The rider was like a pony express messenger, going from one

village to the next. Toward the end of my stay there, electricity and television were coming to the outer regions of the desert.

JS: Shabanu is so alone. Everything is uncluttered and sparse. She can't talk to a group of girls, watch television, or read a novel. It all has to be worked out by herself. Women in Pakistani society have the conflict of the new versus the old ways.

SS: Recently I saw a documentary about Pakistani women in jail. Their husbands wanted to get rid of them so they had them thrown in jail. Their families wouldn't take them back because they couldn't afford to feed them. Things like that do exist. I would be the last person to minimize their importance, but people need to recognize that there is joy in people's lives there. Though they are economically disadvantaged and have these very tough traditions and laws, they do have boundaries within which they can operate. Life is very meaningful and rewarding. There is enormous pride, happiness, beauty, respect, affection, and love between men and women. That is what I mean when I say that we are fundamentally the same even though, externally, we are so different.

WS: Were your characters, for instance Aunt Sharma, modeled after people you knew?

SS: There are some very wise older women in Pakistan. They are so oppressed that they have to develop a subtle way to say . . . some things.

JS: Shabanu's father respected the aunt, but he couldn't allow his own daughter to become like her. Is Shabanu an exceptional character? Is she typical of other young girls?

SS: She is exceptional because any family that doesn't have boys is thought to be terribly disadvantaged. The girls in such families have to function as boys. So, Shabanu had a certain amount of independence that most girls do not have. I set her up as an independent character who could conceivably have these things happen to her. She had a leadership role in the family as though she were a boy, yet had the same rules apply to her that applied to all girls.

JS: If Shabanu had an older brother, would this story have happened?

SS: No, I don't think so. Actually the character is based on a little girl I met in the desert. She was an only child of an older woman. She lived with her mother and her grandmother. Her mother was a wise and beautiful woman with leathery skin who was born during the time of Indian independence. That would have been 1946 or 1947. She was younger than I was, but she looked like she was maybe 60. The little girl had been mistreated by the little boys in her village. At one point I saw this girl having her legs whipped by a boy who was much smaller than she. She grabbed him and pushed his face into the dirt. All the boys chased her and she ran home. She had been asking me to come home with her, and that was why these boys had started whipping her legs.

I eventually did go home with her. Her mother's husband lived somewhere else. This was unusual, because most of the desert nomads would not trade the way they lived. When the country was in the middle of the drought, the family left the desert because their animals were dying. Toward the end of the drought, they were working in a city that served as a provincial or district capital. They had television and access to cars, trucks, telephones and radios. Everyone was predicting that when the drought was over they wouldn't go back to the desert. But they did. They saved all their money, gave up their jobs, bought animals, and went back to the desert. They valued that kind of life.

JS: There is a universality to Shabanu's character. Yet if she were in our Western culture, it would all have turned out very differently. If her story had occurred in our culture, how would it have gone for her?

SS: She would probably be a much more mundane character because here there are more opportunities for young women to be independent and creative and to have their minds come alive.

JS: It seemed that some were comfortable with the situation. Her sister accepted the way things transpired. In our society, we do have people who are uncomfortable with the freedom. People sometimes seem mismatched in both worlds.

SS: Well, their world works. The system of arranged marriages works very well there. I have a young friend who has just made the decision to leave his American girl friend and go back and marry the choice of his father in Pakistan. He is going to be a tribal leader. He has chosen that life over life in the United States. One of the things about living in a foreign culture is that you are always stretching to understand. What you need and what you want are always just beyond what you can't quite get your hands on. I think that makes you grow.

JS: Did you start *Shabanu* with the shape of the story in mind, or did it evolve?

SS: I began by being interested in the camels. I thought that those people with this very intense connection between the earth, the animals, and this very marginal existence had wonderful possibilities for storytelling because everything matters. One day without rain can make the difference between life and death.

One day I was riding in a jeep with a friend of mine along the edge of the desert. He was a local politician and a landowner. His real interest, however, was in forming village cooperatives and in organizing women who lived in the desert and came out to work in the cotton fields at harvest time. During our drive, we saw three women walking down the road. The one in the middle was very beautiful and very young. She had her head thrown back and her mouth wide open. She was crying as though she would rather be dead. It was her look that said that she had nothing to live for. We stopped to ask them what was wrong. Her mother and her grandmother were talking fast, so I couldn't understand them. My friend told me what they had said later. The landlord who owned the cotton fields where the girl was working had a hunting party. He invited each of his hunter friends to go into the fields and to pick out a woman. He gave each of the girl's fathers some gold. In this girl's case, her husband was away at school in a nearby city. The landowner gave her father a piece of land and she spent the week with this houseguest of the landowner. When the girl's husband came back from the city where he was living, he wouldn't have her. He threw her out of the home. So this was her mother and her grandmother who had gone to fetch her and to bring her back to her village where she would live, a diminished person by far. Her life was ruined by a man's whim. That was what gave me the idea for Shabanu's story.

### Suzanne Fisher Staples

SOURCE: "Writing about the Islamic World: An American Author's Thoughts on Authenticity," in *Bookbird,* Vol. 35, No. 3, Fall, 1997, pp. 17-20.

I first went to work in an Islamic nation as a news reporter in 1979 in Pakistan, where my novels *Shabanu* and *Haveli* are set. The news in the subcontinent that laid heaviest claim to the attention of Western reporters later that year was about the events that led to the Soviet invasion of Afghanistan on Christmas Eve. We spent weeks at a time in the Kabul Intercontinental Hotel. It was a scary time. Khad, the Soviet-led secret police, was everywhere, and threats to news people and those who associated with us were made openly and violently, if not directly.

A Swiss hotelier in Kabul told me his Afghan driver had not shown up for work in a week. He was worried about his employee, whom he described as a decent and educated man. When the driver finally returned to work one morning he wore a glove on his right hand. The hotelier learned Khad interrogators had torn off the driver's fingernails because they did not believe he had informed completely enough about his boss's contacts and activities. My own contact, a UPI stringer, disappeared completely. His family asked me not to contact them again.

It was in this atmosphere, where I once told my editors "the fear is as thick as the dust on the donkeys," that we reported on events in Afghanistan. Often our dispatches were reduced to a paragraph in "World News in Brief" columns in American newspapers. It was demoralizing. We were risking the welfare of Afghans who helped us to report news of vital significance to Western interests that was getting little attention. A new Afghan Soviet Republic would have given Moscow a good vantage point on the Arabian Gulf, which remains the world's most important petroleum shipping lane. In February of 1980 we were forced to move our base for Afghanistan news coverage to Pakistan.

The reason so many editors seemed not to care what happened in Afghanistan had to do with that nation's remoteness, illiteracy, and poverty, but more significantly, with ignorance on the part of Americans. At around the same time, terrorist acts supported by Iran and the Palestine Liberation Organization appeared on American TV with mind-numbing regularity. The news fostered a perception among Americans that Islam was a brutal religion, and that those who practiced it were dedicated to killing Jews and Christians in general, and Israelis and Americans in particular.

I began to believe the news was not necessarily a good medium for fostering cultural understanding in America—at least news from parts of the world where the way of life is very different from the American one. I also grew increasingly interested in writing fiction. Whenever I had the chance I reported "color" features about people's lives. My notebooks were filled with textural details—the color of the sky, the smell of the earth, the feel of the bark of trees. I began to think in terms of story. But I still had to earn a living, and so I accepted a transfer to Washington, D.C., where I worked first on UPI's national news desk and later at *The Washington Post* as a part-time editor on the foreign news desk. By then I was tired and wanted out of journalism.

My opportunity came in 1985, when I moved back to Pakistan and was hired by the US Agency for International Development to investigate the lives of poor rural women. I studied Urdu, the national language, intensively for six months and began to travel and study women's lives in rural areas of Punjab, on Pakistan's border with India. It was in the course of gathering information for this project that I first visited the Cholistan Desert. There was something about the blue-tiled mosques, the honor and dignity of the people, and the ancient tales they told that made me know I wanted to write a story about this place and these people.

The story of **Shabanu: Daughter of the Wind** took shape slowly. It grew out of real incidents related to me by women around the cooking fires at the end of the day when our work was done, and during long walks to the wells during the dry season. These were stories about their own lives and about the lives of their sisters and cousins. Every scene and chapter in the book was based on a story told to me by a real person.

Over a three-year period I was in the desert or elsewhere in Punjab gathering information for my USAID work, or at the University of the Punjab in Lahore, or the Folk Heritage Institute in Rawalpindi, or interviewing scholars about traditions and culture in Cholistan. Before I submitted the manuscript for **Shabanu** to my publisher I had thirteen scholars and others who knew the area read it for accuracy. Each of them remarked

that I had captured the place, the people, and their lives with a remarkable sense of realism. However, the fact remains that I am not a Muslim. I am not from the Cholistan Desert. I am not a camel herder. Should I have written about these people?

I have come to this subject that has become known as "authenticity" with the advantage of having seen it from more than one angle. When I lived in Asia I was aware of how the news media there portrayed life in the United States. Some Asian reporters based in American cities focused on crime, poverty, and disease in the world's richest nation. Their articles portrayed America as a nation where young people kill each other, where men and women are sexually promiscuous, a place of moral crisis that tries to tell the rest of the world how it should behave. While I did not think these reports were untrue, together they gave an unrealistic, incomplete, and negative impression of what life in the United States is like.

When **Shabanu** and its sequel, **Haveli,** came under fire by some Muslims in the United States, I took it very seriously. I tried without success to find out exactly what it was that people found offensive. In February on a Children's Literature listserve, Jerry Diakiw, a teacher at York University in Ontario (Canada), posted a query in which he said a Pakistani student felt **Shabanu** "selected a very exotic aspect [of] . . . and did not portray her culture fairly." The student went on to say the book is "a subtle example of prevailing anti-Moslem feeling in North America." Diakiw asked if anyone had similar experiences. While a number of respondents said they had heard objections to the book, they did not offer a single concrete example of what was offensive or incorrect or misleading about it.

Last year I was invited to speak to students at the Islamic Academy in Orlando, Florida, where I was living at the time. Before I went into the classroom the principal told me he had found **Shabanu** offensive. When I pressed him to tell me what it was that bothered him he grew agitated. "It is not the story, *per se,* that offends," he said. "What is so hard to swallow is that the rest of the world, if they read such things, will think that all Muslims are backward camel herders." Suddenly I saw a common thread in what other Muslims were saying about **Shabanu** and **Haveli.** The question of authenticity seems to arise when a group of people feels that someone who has no right to do so "speaks" for them.

I did not have in mind a portrayal or defense of Islam when I wrote **Shabanu** and **Haveli.** That is not what story is all about. My intent was to write a story about the people of Cholistan, a very specific subtribe of seminomadic camel herders in the small part of the vast Thar Desert that lies within Pakistan's Punjab province. Their history and culture are unique. That they are Muslim is a fact about them, but that fact is no more central to the stories in these books than the fact that Buck and Tunes in my most recent book, **Dangerous Skies,** are Christian. I tried to write all three books with all the particularity of detail about the lives of individuals that a story must have.

Representation is not what story is meant to do. Story is very particular. It speaks only for the author and the characters the author creates. Its power lies in its focus on the human heart, illumination, and connection. Story is not meant to represent or instruct about or speak for any group of people—and it should not be interpreted in that light.

So when we talk about "authenticity" what are we really talking about? Is it really about how true the author's vision is of made-up events that take place in a culture that is not the author's culture? Or is it a feeling of defensiveness on the part of readers when we cannot control images of our own culture as it comes under scrutiny by people from "outside"? Is the former question an intellectual rationalization of the latter? This is an emotionally charged and complex issue—one that I believe often reflects a mistaken notion of what a story really is.

---

## TITLE COMMENTARY

📖 *SHABANU: DAUGHTER OF THE WIND* (1989; British edition as *Daughter of the Wind,* 1990)

**Betsy Hearne**

SOURCE: A review of *Shabanu: Daughter of the Wind,* in *Bulletin of the Center for Children's Books,* Vol. 43, No. 2, October, 1989, p. 45.

This first novel is, on several counts, one of the most exciting YA books to appear recently. Staples is so steeped in her story and its Pakistani setting that the problematic use of a first-person voice for a desert child rings authentic—the voice is clear, consistent, and convincing, the narrative all the more immediate. An enormous amount of information on nomadic life surfaces in earthy details that move the story along, build a world, and develop a protagonist who is spirited but bound by the ways of her people. Shabanu and her sister Phulan are to marry brothers as soon as they all come of age. It is an ideal match for family and economic reasons, but accumulating the dowries involves selling Shabanu's beloved camel to cruel Afghans. This is Shabanu's first loss of many: she will eventually lose her betrothed and be promised to a wealthy landowner to settle a blood feud. In the end, it is only her innermost strength that she can protect, and we feel this sense of self as if it had crossed a world of distance and traditions to become our own. The richness and tragedy of a whole culture are reflected in the fate of this girl's family, each member of whom is rendered with natural clarity. Scenes of dust storms, camels mating and birthing, the onset of men-

struation that initiates wedding plans, the burial of an honored grandfather, wedding rituals, the carnival atmosphere of an Asian fair, the binding rites of the Muslim faith are all vividly related. Through an involving plot Staples has given young readers insight into lives totally different from their own, but into emotions resoundingly familiar.

**Maurya Simon**

SOURCE: "Desert Flower," in *The New York Times Book Review,* November 12, 1989, p. 32.

Suzanne Fisher Staples's first book, *Shabanu: Daughter of the Wind,* offers young American readers a fascinating glimpse into the alien world of . . . a nomadic family, one headed by a Cholistani named Dalil Abassi. In a voice that's as tremulous and tender as it is defiant and strong, Abassi's 12-year-old daughter, Shabanu, narrates the story of her own coming of age and that of her sister, Phulan. The novel spans the year culminating in Phulan's marriage, and it meticulously documents the rigors and tribulations of nomadic life, as well as the narrator's flowering from a child into a spirited young woman.

Shabanu's role is central to her family, for without brothers to assume the care of livestock, she inherits the duties of maintaining the family's sizable camel herd. Not only must she lead the animals back and forth from the ever-dwindling *toba,* or water hole, but she must also groom them, assist in their births, minister to their wounds and mend their worn saddles and harnesses. Clearly, Shabanu's relationship to her camels is complex, proprietary and proud, for she knows that the animals represent her family's wealth and that, eventually, they will constitute a substantial part of her dowry and Phulan's.

Shabanu's days are exhaustingly full, for besides caring for the camels, she must also help cook and clean, construct makeshift but sturdy shelters, embroider wedding apparel, serve as a scout and act as occasional custodian of her toddler cousins and aged grandfather. Independent and adventurous, she uses her rare free moments to wander from the Abassi enclave in order to bask in the lonely splendor of the desert.

Some of the most affecting and lyrical passages of the book detail the austere beauty of Cholistan, as seen through the young narrator's eyes. She appraises the subtle and ghostly illumination of desert starlight, the rippling daytime mirages, the unexpectedly sweet, scarlet blossoms of the *kharin* plant. Whether she is caught in the midst of a violent windstorm or delighting in a monsoon deluge, Shabanu's astute observations of the desert around her and her responses to it are consistently mesmerizing and instructive.

Shabanu's passion for the desert, however, is equaled by her devotion to her family. Thus, when tragic events related to her sister's betrothal threaten to dishonor and endanger them all, the girl is forced to confront and reconsider both her own rebellious identity and her traditional obligations to those whom she loves. Torn between her unbending willfulness and self-reliance and her allegiance to her family, Shabanu suffers while making choices that teach her ultimately that life is filled with loss, as well as with joy.

It is a pleasure to read a book that explores a way of life profoundly different from our own, and that does so with such sensitivity, admiration and verisimilitude. Ms. Staples, who was a U.P.I. correspondent in Asia and has worked for The Washington Post, has surely accomplished a small miracle in the unfolding of her touching and powerful story. She has managed to present to her readers an engaging and convincing portrait of an adolescent girl who is alternately bewildered and exhilarated by her changing mind and body; at the same time, the author offers rich and provocative insights into a culture so distanced from rock videos and designer jeans as to seem extraplanetary. I hope her readers will gain from it a renewed sense of self and a deep respect for what is other.

## Susan Perren

SOURCE: A review of *Shabanu: Daughter of the Wind,* in *Quill & Quire,* February, 1990, p. 16.

Great novels for ages 12 and up aren't easy to find. Young adolescents are an exacting readership that needs and deserves a good, well-told story, but often has to settle for less. **Shabanu: Daughter of the Wind,** Suzanne Fisher Staples's beautifully told first novel, will go a long way toward filling this void.

This novel is the coming-of-age story of Shabanu, a 12-year-old girl and a member of a family of present-day nomadic camel herders of the Cholistan Desert on the Pakistani-Indian border. Shabanu and her older sister Phulan live in a culture that will seem harsh and overly pragmatic to Westerners; for example there are the financially advantageous marriages that have been arranged for them with two brothers. When the older of the two brothers, the one to whom Phulan is betrothed, is killed, Shabanu learns that her sister will now marry the younger brother to whom Shabanu had been promised. Shabanu is promised instead to a rich man in his 60s for whom she will be one of four wives.

Young readers will share Shabanu's horrified reaction to this arrangement, but will be in awe of her ability to reconcile herself to her fate. She can only obey the dictates of her parents and her culture, but at the same time she resolves to grow within those limitations, to become strong, wise, and very much her own person. Shabanu's story will have resonance for readers because all lives are circumscribed to some degree, no matter the seeming permissiveness of the culture.

The first-person narrative, in Shabanu's voice, and the meticulous piling up of detail about desert life, camels, bazaars, marriage customs, and so on make Staples's novel exceptionally vivid and compelling. More work from this fine writer will be most welcome.

## Megan McDonald

SOURCE: A review of *Shabanu: Daughter of the Wind,* in *The Five Owls,* Vol. 4, No. 4, March-April, 1990, pp. 63-4.

Tending camels. Arranged marriages. Living in thatched mud huts. Thirst. Moving from place to place. Monsoon rains. Enter the world of Shabanu, a world in which parking lots and pollution are replaced by stretches of sand and desert winds. Set in present-day Pakistan's Cholistan Desert, a twelve-year-old girl's nomadic existence is minutely chronicled in this 1990 Newbery Honor book.

As first-person narrator, Shabanu is an intimate observer and recorder of images and events, and it is through her eyes that we, as readers, witness the beauty of a breathtaking opal sunset, the graphic birth of a camel, and the fineness of a gossamer *shatoosh* (shawl). Also through her we experience a wide range of emotions—fear in being forced to marry a man four times her age whom she does not know, grief over the loss of a beloved camel, the death of a grandfather. Hand in hand with Shabanu's joy goes pain, cruelty, and disappointment in a society that permits women to be beaten for disobedience, enslaved in marriage, or stoned to death for looking at another man.

Setting is predominant here, and first-time novelist Staples is masterful at evoking scenery. Strange, exotic surroundings become familiar, even captivating. Clear, descriptive writing is the author's hallmark, and the integration of indigenous words, names, and phrases lends a realistic quality to the language. A helpful glossary is appended, as well as a map and list of characters' names with pronunciations, increasing the story's accessibility.

The novel is not highly plotted, and young adults readers accustomed to plenty of action and drama may find the first half slow-moving. Although the pacing is different, patient readers will be rewarded. The shocking death of Shabanu's sister's betrothed comes late but quickly propels the plot toward its crucial outcome. Will Shabanu surrender her independence and accept the marriage dictated by family and society, or will she choose her own freedom even at the penalty of death?

Her painful decision could not be more difficult nor more deeply felt, as Shabanu grapples with following her own heart and learning "the strength of [her] will and its limits." Self-reflective beyond her years, Shabanu is an intense, sensitive girl who feels "like a child struggling to know what it is to be grown."

Shabanu's situation, surroundings, and story, while completely foreign, will stretch readers beyond limitations of their own geography. But it is her universal struggle to find inner strength and beauty, despite the odds around her, that hits home.

**Ashok Bery**

SOURCE: "No Life for a Nomad," in *The Times Educational Supplement,* No. 3858, June 8, 1990, p. B13.

The Cholistan Desert in Pakistan is the setting of Suzanne Fisher Staples's first novel, which centres on one of the nomadic families inhabiting the region. Phulan, the elder daughter, already engaged to her cousin Hamir, is approaching marriageable age; her sister Shabanu is soon to be betrothed to Hamir's brother Murad. When a local landlord, Nazir Mohammad, attempts to abduct Phulan, her enraged fiancé confronts Nazir Mohammad's entourage, but is killed in the encounter. The family decides that Phulan should marry Shabanu's fiancé, Murad. Partly in order to forestall further hostilities, Shabanu is now offered in marriage to Nazir Mohammad's 55-year-old brother, a well-off local politician called Rahim. Upset by this thwarting of her awakening desire for Murad and repelled by the thought of marriage to a man so much older than she is, Shabanu attempts to run away, but is caught by her father and has to face up to the hard realities of her situation.

As this account might suggest, *Daughter of the Wind* is to a great extent a story of adolescence and of the tensions between individual desires and the demands of the family. Certainly the novel is at its most interesting when it concerns itself with patriarchal domination in the society. But it also aims to portray the lives of the desert people. A large portion of the book is taken up with evoking and describing conditions in the desert: the search for water, the hardships of the nomadic life, the rearing and selling of camels, the harsh sandstorms.

This is adequately done, but largely vitiated by a plot which meanders along episodically until about two thirds of the way through, when the attempted abduction brings about the crisis which decides Shabanu's fate. The failure to generate tension or much sense of progression is compounded by the novel's slack narrative technique and style. Its first-person, present-tense narration (by Shabanu) fosters a lingering, lush texture which eventually becomes cloying. The language flirts throughout with sentimentality, finally succumbing when it arrives at the soggy and hackneyed moral of the story. Phulan is told: "beauty holds only part of a man, and that just for so long. Keep some of yourself hidden . . . the secret is keeping your innermost beauty, the secrets of your soul, locked in your heart so that he must always reach out to you for it." Clichés and archaisms spread like sand. Stars "wink", the desert "shimmers" and "twinkles", hearts lurch into mouths, characters walk with "liquid grace", and say "nay, nay". Out of the sand protrude, like bristling cacti, a few spiky, disconcerting Americanisms: "I soften some and begin to for-

give Dadi's anger"; "I guess"; "I must . . . fix something to eat."

In his poem "Beppo", Byron glances ironically at his own earlier Oriental tales. Had he the art of easy writing, he says, he'd "sell you, mix'd with western sentimentalism / Some samples of the finest Orientalism". Although it has some occasional merits as a piece of reportage, *Daughter of the Wind* does not escape this description; it takes its place in a long and not always particularly distinguished tradition.

**Marie Flay**

SOURCE: A review of *Shabanu: Daughter of the Wind,* in *The School Librarian,* Vol. 38, No. 4, November, 1990, p. 161.

This enchanting, fast-paced story captivated me from the start. In her first novel, Suzanne Fisher Staples provides a fascinating insight into the lives of the desert people of Pakistan. Their complex traditions, social structure and never-ending battle to survive in a hostile environment are brought to life vividly and with love.

Shabanu, wild and free as the winds which sweep her beloved Cholistan Desert, is already betrothed at the age of twelve. In love with her life spent tending her father's camel herd, she strains against the increasing restraint on her freedom as she approaches womanhood. When tragedy wrecks plans for the impending wedding of her elder sister, Phulan, Shabanu is faced with a decision which will change her life forever. She must choose between her dreams and the obligations of her family and her culture.

The author paints a panoramic picture ranging from the minutiae of daily life to the splendour of a wedding. It is immensely interesting and will delight any reader interested in cultures other than our own. It is a must for the school library and I can hardly wait for the paperback edition in order to purchase copies for the classroom.

## HAVELI (1993)

**Ilene Cooper**

SOURCE: A review of *Haveli,* in *Booklist,* Vol. 89, Nos. 19 & 20, June 1 & June 15, 1993, p. 1813.

*Shabanu: Daughter of the Wind,* with its wholly realized characters and its glimpses into another culture, had a presence not easily found in young adult books. It is often difficult for a sequel to generate the same excitement evoked by a first novel from a talented, fresh voice, but that is not the case here. *Haveli* will hold readers with the same rapt attention as its predecessors, and their involvement with the young Pakistani woman, Shabanu, her friends, and family will linger. The story picks up five years later. Shabanu, given in marriage to an elderly, powerful man, has now presented him a daughter, Mumtaz, who means everything to her mother. Though her husband adores Shabanu, he has neither the time nor the inclination to protect her from the various cruelties and intrigues that occur in a household where there are three cultured senior wives who look down on Shabanu as a desert interloper. To protect her daughter, Shabanu is constantly making plans for their safety should her husband die, but when Shabanu becomes involved in a plan to save her only friend from a disastrous marriage and begins having feelings for her husband's nephew, her situation becomes increasingly perilous. Staples brews a potent mix here: the issue of a woman's role in a traditional society, page-turning intrigue, tough women characters, and a fluidity of writing that blends it all together. Staples has some very strong things to say about the lack of power some women have over their own lives, but the reader never hears preaching. Rather, as in the best stories, the message comes through the characters, their anguish and their triumphs.

**Betsy Hearne**

SOURCE: A review of *Haveli*, in *Bulletin of the Center for Children's Books*, Vol. 47, No. 3, November, 1993, p. 73-4.

Suzanne Staples's critically acclaimed first novel, *Shabanu: Daughter of the Wind*, left the twelve-year-old Pakistani protagonist accepting her fate of prearranged marriage with a man forty-two years her elder—yet still determined, as her individualistic aunt has advised, to preserve her inner independence. The sequel, *Haveli*, opens six years later with Shabanu's struggle to maintain dignity for herself and her five-year-old daughter, Mumtaz, in face of hostility from her husband's first three wives, who scorn her nomadic desert background and envy the youthful beauty with which she has "bewitched" their husband. Shabanu's domestic position is precarious enough, but her husband's attempts to consolidate tribal lands through complex intermarriages ultimately lead to a blood feud in which Shabanu and her child's survival depends on constant vigilance, resourceful planning, physical courage, and emotional sacrifice.

Because *Haveli* seems as freshly inspired as its predecessor, it functions more as part of a true set than a sequel, though the opening scenes certainly incorporate enough information—a singular and challenging literary task—to allow the book to stand on its own. As she did in the first volume, Staples has walked a fine line between the outsider's and insider's view. Her respect for a Muslim culture that, from a Western standpoint, renders women powerless (except through their skills at manipulation) resonates in the portrayal of an individual's attempt to balance the best of tradition with fresh new possibilities. On the one hand, Shabanu draws deeply from her family's values; on the other, she rejects the resignation of her best friend—the ill-fated daughter of

her husband's evil youngest brother—who declares, "Duty is not so difficult when there's no alternative."

Supporting the complex social dynamics are vivid details of village and urban settings, all the more immediately rendered through action rather than description. While the intricate cast and unfamiliar terms will send readers scuttling to the list of characters and glossary from time to time, the dramatic plot will bring them breathlessly back to the story. And don't be deceived; in addition to sensitive insights, there's also a realistic strain of sex and violence here. It's never sensationalized and yet will draw YA readers like a magnet. (The focus, by the way, never strays from the teenage mother to her child, which must have required careful control in light of the empathy that naturally centers on a vulnerable naïf.) There is a love story, too, a tragic one that may unsettle those accustomed to television endings. In Shabanu's case, a room of one's own—the rooftop pavilion of a house (*haveli*) in Lahore where she finally finds secret shelter—is lonelier than she could have imagined. Threatening the heroine is an unspeakable villain, one who is perhaps overdrawn in terms of contemporary fiction but who effectively evokes the melodramatic elements of Eastern epics, and more recently, films.

There only remains that niggling question of what audience will read this 260-page saga set somewhere most mall shoppers couldn't locate without a map (which is provided for that purpose). Well, the answer is, whoever reads it will be richly rewarded by going beyond themselves into a new place and persona. And that's enough reason for either a librarian or teacher to expend money and energy on a work of fiction that stretches young adult literature to a new place.

**Daniyal Mueenuddin**

SOURCE: A review of *Haveli*, in *The New York Times Book Review*, November 14, 1993, p. 59.

During my childhood in Pakistan, my family went two or three times each year to the countryside described by Suzanne Fisher Staples in *Haveli* and in her first novel, *Shabanu: Daughter of the Wind*, which was a Newbery Honor Book. . . .

In *Haveli*, Ms. Staples, an American who was a journalist in Asia for many years, has set herself a much more difficult task. When this novel opens, Shabanu is 19 years old and has been married for six years to a rich feudal lord 42 years her senior, the fourth of four wives allowed to him by Muslim law. The senior wives, contemptuous of her humble background and jealous of their common husband Rahim's fascination with her, viciously torment Shabanu, putting a rabid bat in her closet, killing her 4-year-old daughter's puppy. Shabanu carefully plans for the future, knowing that she will not be safe or welcome in her husband's house after his death.

There is much in the novel that is admirable. The prose

is plain and uncluttered, smoothly moving the narrative forward. The texture and dynamics of the relations between the characters are often precisely described, especially the peculiar intimacy that exists between Shabanu and her husband, the delicate threads by which she manipulates him, fueling his hunger by withholding her secret self, carefully gauging when she may press him and when she must remain silent.

But Ms. Staples has tried to describe a much larger slice of Pakistani society than she did in *Shabanu.* That novel represented the life of desert nomads told from the perspective of a simple young girl. *Haveli,* however, is set partly in an enormous village mansion on her husband's lands and partly in the city of Lahore, again in a large household, with a cast of characters ranging from powerful politicians to sweepers. Faced with these complex circumstances, the novel both exaggerates and naively caricatures the people and the society. Depravity, for example, is represented by Nazir, a lecherous drunken landlord straight out of Hollywood; a desert woman, Sharma, dispenses stock medicine-man wisdom.

The portrayal of Shabanu demonstrates another form of misrepresentation, caused by the author's imposing her own Western values on the character. Shabanu's rebellion against the constraints of her chauvinistic society is false not because she would be unlikely to have that impulse but because it would be expressed as the raw struggle for freedom of a fettered being—not, as Ms. Staples presents it, as the expression of an intellectual position.

*Haveli* is suffused with an uninformed romanticism that imposes upon and falsifies the portrayal: slaughters of innocent people, all unpunished as they would not be in reality; trusty retainers tall and glossy-mustachioed, where in fact they would be shuffling and rotund. The hushed and respectful gravity of the tone ultimately becomes lugubrious, as if the author always had a lump in her throat. There is never a moment of irony and, quite remarkably, absolutely no hint of humor. Most readers will be unaware of or undisturbed by the distortions. I missed, however, both the banality and the exuberance of Pakistan's villages and cities.

### Jane Chandra

SOURCE: A review of *Haveli,* in *Voice of Youth Advocates,* Vol. 16, No. 5, December, 1993, p. 302.

In this riveting sequel to Newbery Honor Book *Shanabu: Daughter of the Wind,* eighteen-year-old Shabanu is now the fourth wife of wealthy landowner Rahim, forty-two years her senior, and the mother of a five-year-old daughter, Mumtaz. Cherished by the husband she was forced to marry, Shabanu is looked down upon and mistreated by his other wives and their children, who consider the uneducated daughter of a nomadic camel-raising family inferior.

Marriages in this Pakistani Muslim culture are arranged, often for political expediency and often between cousins to keep land in the family. To this end Rahim's daughter Leyla from his first wife will be married to Omar, the son of Rahim's younger brother, and Leyla's brother Ahmed will be married to Zabo, the beautiful daughter of Rahim's villainous youngest brother. Determined to help her friend Zabo escape from marriage to Ahmed, who is mentally handicapped, Shabanu convinces Rahim to take her and Zabo to the capital, Lahore, where she will ostensibly help Zabo buy the beautiful clothing and jewelry she will need for her wedding, while at the same time plotting Zabo's future and engaging a tutor for Mumtaz and herself. They stay with Rahim's widowed sister in the family's ancestral three-storied mansion in the old city, the *haveli.* There Shabanu meets Omar, who has returned after years of study in America, and they are immediately attracted to each other. Shabanu must juggle her feelings for Omar, her position within the family, her determination to help Zabo, and her love for her daughter. When Rahim is murdered in an ambush by his youngest brother, Shabanu and Zabo escape to the desert, where Zabo also meets a violent death. Shabanu, having left Mumtaz with her parents, allows the world to think that she, too, has died. Instead, she flees to the *haveli,* leaving the door open for a sequel to continue the story of this courageous young woman.

Many characters appear in this novel set in modern Pakistan; Staples helps the reader by providing a list with pronunciations at the beginning of the book. A map puts the story in geographical perspective. The use of terms such as *charpoi, shalwar kameez,* and *tonga* lends authenticity. Explained in context at first, words are defined with pronunciations in a glossary.

High school girls—and adults—will quickly become immersed in this exciting story of a young married woman in love with another man and struggling to live within the confines of her orthodox culture. Readers will feel the heat of the desert, visualize the exquisite fabrics and jewelry, experience village and city life along with Shabanu, and be caught up in the intrigue and eye-for-an-eye justice. *Haveli* stands alone and is for an older audience that *Shabanu.* After reading *Haveli,* however, those who missed *Shabanu* will want to read it to see how the story begins. Booktalk this one since the title and cover alone may not lure readers.

### 📖 DANGEROUS SKIES (1996; British edition as Storm, 1998)

### Kirkus Reviews

SOURCE: A review of *Dangerous Skies,* in *Kirkus Reviews,* Vol. LXIV, No. 13, July 1, 1996, p. 974.

Stubborn naïveté destroys a close interracial friendship in this long, turgid story from the author of *Haveli,* set on Virginia's Eastern Shore. After finding the floating body of a migrant worker, Buck, 12, is horrified when his best friend, Tunes, becomes a suspect. Sure that the real killer is prosperous, respected Jumbo Rawlins, "six foot seven, every inch lean, mean, and ill-intentioned," Buck urges Tunes to tell her side of the story. Instead, Tunes disappears. When Buck tracks her down, he's horrified to learn from her that Rawlins has been abusing her physically and sexually. Tunes tries to tell him that a black girl's word won't carry much weight against that of a white adult, but Buck is so convinced that justice will out that he persuades her to come out of hiding. As predicted, she's arrested and tried while Rawlins remains untouched; though not convicted, Tunes moves away and drops out of Buck's life forever.

In matching smart, resourceful, opaque Tunes to innocent and blindly loyal Buck, Staples creates a telling contrast, but her penchant for explaining characters, relationships, and situations rather than showing them, plus a plot that wanders like the setting's swampy waterways, slows the pace; ambiguities in Tunes's story, plus Buck's disillusioned now-it's-five-years-later-and-life-goes-on finish, are puzzling.

## Cindy Darling Codell

SOURCE: A review of *Dangerous Skies,* in *School Library Journal,* Vol. 42, No. 10, October, 1996, pp. 148-50.

Before leaving for college, Buck Smith recalls the defining moment of his life, which occurred when he was 12. His closest friend, Tunes, is the motherless child of the black family who has served the Smiths since slavery days. When a local Hispanic farm-labor manager is found with a bullet from Tunes's gun in his head, and the richest man in the county swears she was having an affair with the dead man, Buck is convinced that she is innocent. He is stunned when his father refuses to help and counsels him to put distance between himself and Tunes. Even more incomprehensible, her father gives him the same advice. Tunes's running away puts both of the young people in the path of unspeakable evil. Staples has drawn a fascinating picture of an isolated, antiquated way of life along Virginia's Eastern Shore. There are many colorful supporting characters, and the author masterfully delineates the way that racism can still divide people who truly care about one another. Buck comes to believe that life has both beautiful and destructive cycles, just as the Chesapeake Bay does, but that one must survive and forgive. Although it is easy to become enthralled with Staples's ability to convey place, tone, and mood, there are some problems with characterization and voice. The villain seems a bit flat, and it is hard to understand why anyone would believe the sexual accusations he levels at Tunes. Buck's understanding of the story he is relating seems uneven. And, sadly, readers are left wondering if there is any hope of true justice. Not as successful as **Shabanu,** but interesting as a look at a fascinating subculture in a remarkably defined place.

## Joyce A. Litton

SOURCE: A review of *Dangerous Skies,* in *Voice of Youth Advocates,* Vol. 19, No. 5, December, 1996, p. 274.

At twelve, white boy Buck and black girl Tunes Smith are best friends. Buck is descended from English farmers, Tunes from African slaves. Like his ancestors, Tunes's father does farm labor for Buck's dad. The adolescents' idyllic world of fishing and observing nature is shattered when their much older friend Jorge Rodrigues is murdered, and Tunes is accused of the crime. Jumbo Rawlin, a respected white man, says that Tunes and Jorge had a romance which went sour, and Tunes killed him. With much trepidation, Tunes tells Buck that Jumbo has been sexually and physically abusing her. Recently, Jorge rescued her at the cost of his life. When the matter comes before a judge, it is Tunes's word against Jumbo's. Though Tunes is released for lack of evidence, her reputation is ruined, and she leaves town. Buck discovers that he must forgive his father for his inability to believe a black person over a white one. In a class with Harper Lee's *To Kill a Mockingbird* Staples's beautifully written and chilling tale of contemporary racism should keep young adult readers turning pages until they reach the heart-breaking end.

## Cecilin J. Hynes-Higman

SOURCE: A review of *Storm,* in *School Librarian,* Vol. 46, No. 2, Summer, 1998, p. 103.

The review copy comments that accompany **Storm** ensured that my expectations were high as I began this novel, but I was disappointed. I found the writing somewhat overworked and self-consciously aimed at young people. Suzanne Fisher Staples is American and the story is set there, but the imitation Huckleberry Finn style of the narrator soon became intensely irritating. It is unnecessary to use so many adolescent colloquialisms in the narrative, especially as they fade part of the way through. Also, at the end of the novel, we learn that Buck, the narrator, is actually looking back on events and is now on his way to the polytechnic to get an agriculture degree and then get married. This makes the style of the first part even more inappropriate.

In spite of this, the story is of interest, if unoriginal. The author is careful to include the black/white problems in society but in a way that is unconvincing and even puzzling at times. The book would benefit from being shorter and more concentrated in its tale of murder and moral values, bringing with them choices to be made. It boasts, 'a film is in preparation in New York,' so I'd wait for that!

## Robert Dunbar

SOURCE: A review of *Storm,* in *Books for Keeps,* No. 112, September, 1998, p. 25.

'It was dark outside with the storm gathering itself up for another strike, and I felt like there was a darkness inside me, too.' These words, spoken by Buck Smith, the young white narrator of this complex and absorbing novel, capture the ferocity of the elemental and human worlds between which the action moves. We are on the isolated east coast of Virginia, where for generations Buck's ancestors have worked their farm with the help of generations of other Smiths, the descendants of African slaves. Differences of race and colour have never—apparently—been of much significance. But, as Buck painfully comes to realise, this superficial amity covers a multitude of bigotries, even amongst those adults whose notions of right and wrong, truth-telling and lying, he has never before had to question. This is a brilliant contemporary variation on a Romeo and Juliet theme, executed in a style in which anger and compassion are unforgettably combined.

Additional coverage of Staples's life and career is contained in the following sources published by The Gale Group: *Authors and Artists for Young Adults*, Vol. 26; *Contemporary Authors*, Vol. 132; and *Something about the Author*, Vol. 70.

# Kaye Starbird

## 1916-

(Also writes as C. S. Jennison) American author of poetry, fiction, and nonfiction.

Major works include *Speaking of Cows and Other Poems* (1960), *Don't Ever Cross a Crocodile, and Other Poems* (1963), *A Snail's a Failure Socially and Other Poems, Mostly about People* (1966), *The Pheasant on Route Seven* (1968), *The Covered Bridge House and Other Poems* (1979).

## INTRODUCTION

Described by Siddie Joe Johnson as "a master of light verse," Starbird is respected as a poet for children and young adults who combines perceptive views of human nature and the natural world with humor and a smooth, inventive poetic style. She is noted for describing a variety of child and adult characters—several of them unusual or eccentric—with accuracy, insight, and droll wit. Some of these figures, who include such individuals as a dwarf, a bullying child, and an alcoholic, are inhabitants of small New England towns and villages. In addition, Starbird often writes lyrical but unromanticized poems about the beauty of nature, about natural elements such as snowstorms, and about animals and birds. Directing her works to an audience that ranges from the early primary through the upper grades, Starbird is celebrated for her understanding of children and of what appeals to them, as well as for presenting her readers with fresh, childlike observations. She is also credited with creating books of poetry for older children that help to bridge the gap between juvenile and adult literature. As a poet, Starbird is praised for combining an imaginative approach with disciplined form in her works, which range from simple to sophisticated. She writes in a crisp, flowing style that reflects her love of rhythm, rhyme, and wordplay, and she often adds surprise twists and colorful phrasing to her verses. Although Starbird is occasionally criticized for creating poems that are erratic, coy, and inappropriate for children due to their subjects, she is generally commended as the author of entertaining, substantial verse that is notable for its keen assessment of and appreciation for life. Starbird is also the author of two novels for adults; in addition, she has submitted adult poetry, short stories, and essays, as well as poems for children to a number of periodicals.

### Biographical Information

Starbird was born in Fort Sill, Oklahoma, to Alfred A. Starbird, a general in the United States Army, and Ethel Starbird, a homemaker. The poet told *Something about the Author* (*SATA*), "I started writing when I was

eight. . . ." She added, "I never Set Out to Be a Writer. I just started writing." While attending the University of Vermont, Starbird, as she told *SATA*, "started selling verse to magazines like *Good Housekeeping*, . . . going on to magazines like the old *American Mercury* and then satirical verse and essays for the *Atlantic*. After that, I changed to writing books." Starbird has contributed to such newspapers and magazines as *Humpty Dumpty*, the *New York Times*, the *New Yorker*, and the *Saturday Evening Post*; she has also had poems, essays, and stories published in such periodicals as *Cosmopolitan*, *Harper's*, *Ladies' Home Journal*, *McCall's*, *Redbook*, *Vermont Life*, and *Woman's Day*. She married James Dalton, with whom she had two daughters, Kit and Beth. After her husband's death, Starbird married N. E. Jennison, with whom she had a third daughter, Lee, and whose surname she has used occasionally as a pseudonym when writing for adults. Starbird has consistently attempted to introduce young people to the joys of poetry. On the book jacket of *The Pheasant on Route Seven*, she stated that "at 11 or 12 children go into adult reading and should have a bridge to do this and to keep them interested in poetry. Therefore, some of the subjects deal with adult themes as children themselves do at this time." Starbird concluded in *SATA,* "I derive material from experience and also from a galloping imagination that I was born with and for which I claim no credit. . . . Writing is hard work but I am happier doing it than not doing it."

## Major Works

Starbird's first book, *Speaking of Cows and Other Poems,* is a collection of thirty verses for very young children. In this work, the author created, according to Siddie Joe Johnson, "a gay world of rhyme and meter, of cats and cows, lizards and bears, and naughty little girls." Critics noted Starbird's facility with words and knowledge of what children enjoy; Johnson called *Speaking of Cows* "a fit companion for Rachel Field's 'Taxis and Toadstools,'" while Walker Gibson stated, "It seems evident that Miss Starbird has actually *looked* at animals and children in action." In her second volume, *Don't Ever Cross a Crocodile, and Other Poems,* Starbird presents young readers with thirty-two verses that introduce them to humorous characters such as Minnie Morse, a girl who loves horses, and Eat-it-all Elaine while inviting them to look at nature. Anne Izard said that the poems, which are illustrated by the author's daughter Kit Dalton, are "full of imagery, imagination, and insight into the mind and heart of a child." In *A Snail's a Failure Socially and Other Poems Mostly about People,* another title with pictures by Dalton, Starbird continues to present witty character studies in verse. Zena Sutherland observed that the poems are about "animals, weather, human problems, friends, strangers, and relationships" before concluding that the appeal of the book is in "the swinging rhythm, the word play, the humorous concepts, and the rhyme—the latter treated here and there with a cheerful and clearly intentional disrespect." Walker Gibson called *A Snail's a Failure Socially* "a salty joy."

Starbird sets her fourth volume of poetry, *The Pheasant on Route Seven,* in the fictitious New England town of Pleasantport. In describing the town and its inhabitants— "[a]nother smalltown bunch whose foibles you'll recognize and remember," according to a critic in *Kirkus Reviews*—Starbird is credited with presenting shrewd, often amusing observations of her characters and their environment to a more mature audience. Barbara Gibson noted that "the smallest details capture the essence of human individuality," while Zena Sutherland commented that with this work Starbird "has carved a bit deeper her niche in the world of children's poetry." Mary O'Neill claimed that with her poem "The Snowstorm," Starbird "joins the masters of her craft." A critic in *Publishers Weekly* proffered that this visit is one "you won't want to miss, for your guide is Kaye Starbird," and concluded that the characters are "guaranteed to charm and delight, because they so obviously and gaily charm and delight the guide herself." *The Covered Bridge House and Other Poems* is a collection of verses that celebrates New England. Starbird blends evocative nature poems and sensitive lyrics about emotions with long narrative

verses about colorful personalities to create impressions of the land and its people. X. J. Kennedy said, "I always like Miss Starbird's verse portraits of oddballs. . . . With humor and insight she touches on kids' genuine concerns, and she isn't just deft, but also at times deep-going. . . ." Mary M. Burns concluded, "Economically crafted, the poems are appealing not only for their incisive characterization but also for their imaginative wordplay and sense of wonder which . . . transform the mundane into the memorable and the memorable into a transcendent experience." Starbird is also the author of another book for children, *Grandmother Goose's Recycled Rhymes and Permanent Calendar* (1988).

## Awards

Starbird received fellowships from the Bread Loaf Writers' Conference in 1961; the MacDowell Colony in 1966-70, 1972, 1975-76, and 1979; the Helene Wurlitzer Foundation in 1967-68; the Ossabaw Island Project in 1971-73, 1975, 1977-78, and 1980-81; the Virginia Center for Creative Arts, 1971-73 and 1982; and the Rhode Island Creative Arts Center, 1980-82. She also received a grant from the Ella Lyman Cabot Trust in 1971.

---

## TITLE COMMENTARY

### SPEAKING OF COWS AND OTHER POEMS (1960)

#### Siddie Joe Johnson

SOURCE: A review of *Speaking of Cows and Other Poems,* in *Junior Libraries,* Vol. 7, No. 1, September, 1960, pp. 59-60.

The reader moves into a gay world of rhyme and meter, of cats and cows, lizards and bears, and naughty little girls. Kaye Starbird is a master of light verse, the unexpected rhyme, a play on words (but well within the child's comprehension), and a sure knowledge of what interests children. Here is a fit companion for Rachel Field's "Taxis and Toadstools." Parents and teachers will enjoy these verses, too. Rita Fava's drawings on each page are excellent teasers.

#### Walker Gibson

SOURCE: A review of *Speaking of Cows and Other Poems,* in *The New York Times Book Review,* November 13, 1960, p. 56.

[A] book with the title **Speaking of Cows** would seem headed for a low rating. Why not Speaking of School Buses, or Speaking of Space Ships, or, if we must stay down on the farm, Speaking of Manure Spreaders? Actually, though, Kaye Starbird's cows turn out to be no stock pieces of pastoral decor after all."Eyes never blinking, / Jaws always moving, / What are cows thinking! / What are they *proving?*" The familiar rural figures . . . become here convincing, lively and quite unsentimentalized characters: the turtle whose name is Cook County Fair, the crow called Airplane Joe, and the poor toad who "*slowly*" hops off a highway and then "*slowly*" out of the path of a power-mower. It seems evident that Miss Starbird has actually *looked* at animals and children in action. Furthermore, her technical control of rhythm and rhyme, while not spectacular, is absolutely trustworthy. This is her first book, and I hope she will write more; she should move, I think, in the direction of a poem called "The Sea Gull," where beneath the observation and the gay fantasy there lurks something like a serious point.

## Virginia Haviland

SOURCE: A review of *Speaking of Cows and Other Poems,* in *The Horn Book Magazine,* Vol. XXXVI, No. 6, December, 1960, p. 519.

A first book of children's verse by a writer whose poetry has appeared in magazines for adults. Among the thirty lyrics and narratives are many about animals and other small creatures which represent a child's fresh observations, noting, for example, a "yo-yo spider" on "his spider thread," and a bear whose "pantry shelf / Is inside himself," or talking about the "tooth fairies" and a "toad [that] needed a baby sitter." Pleasing rhythms and easy rhymes fill these imaginative and entertaining poems, but they are lacking, however, in memorable lines. One or more lively little sketches are drawn for each selection.

## Margaret Sherwood Libby

SOURCE: A review of *Speaking of Cows and Other Poems,* in *New York Herald Tribune: Lively Arts and Book Review,* Vol. 37, No. 23, January 8, 1961, p. 32.

In the many collections of verses for children there is seldom authentic humor or nonsense, and rarely the combination of acute observation and a musical use of words. Among the thirty verses in Kaye Starbird's collection about animals, birds and children with an occasional elf, all are not of equal quality, but a surprising number are spontaneous and charming as well as tuneful with apt and amusing epithets. We think children will enjoy them. We especially liked her two consecutives, the cows who "mustn't care for new ways of doing, that's what they stare for; that's why they're chewing," and Si, who goes along the "humming highways" steering his course and telling his horse, "these modern ways ain't my ways." Again there are endearing creatures, pets like O'Toole the lizard nobody hugs, the fat little baby cat named Postage Stamp "discussing the world in mews."

## Zena Sutherland

SOURCE: A review of *Speaking of Cows and Other Poems,* in *Bulletin for the Center for Children's Books,* Vol. 14, No. 9, May, 1961, p. 149.

Thirty poems (four of which were previously published in *Humpty Dumpty Magazine*) about people and animals. Some of the rhymes have humor, some have imagery or a fresh phrasing, but the majority are rather heavily coy. Some of the poems are appropriate for young readers: **"The Apple Elf"** or **"The Tooth Fairies"**; others have concepts that are more sophisticated: **"Mrs. Snell,"** for example.

## DON'T EVER CROSS A CROCODILE, AND OTHER POEMS (1963)

### Anne Izard

SOURCE: A review of *Don't Ever Cross a Crocodile, and Other Poems,* in *School Library Journal,* Vol. 10, No. 1, September 15, 1963, p. 122.

With a sure sense of rhythm and lines that never drag or limp, Kaye Starbird has created a new book of poems full of imagery, imagination, and insight into the mind and heart of a child. There are humor, nonsense, and deceptive simplicity in the 32 poems that on the one hand picture such characters as Minnie Morse, Eat-it-all Elaine, and Great-Granny Phipps and on the other take a fresh look at nature. Recommended for all ages to share.

### Margaret W. Brown

SOURCE: A review of *Don't Ever Cross a Crocodile, and Other Poems,* in *The Horn Book Magazine,* Vol. XXXIX, No. 5, October, 1963, p. 502.

The author of ***Speaking of Cows*** writes light verse, which is never trivial, about everyday life. Unlike so many writers of verse for children, she is never sentimental, and her rhyme and meter do not stumble. Take **"Minnie Morse,"** for example, which begins: "Of all the problems no one's solved/ The worst is Minnie Morse's;/ I mean why Minnie's so involved/ With horses." Or **"Horse-Chestnut Time,"** which ends: "I don't *do* much with horse-chestnuts/ Except to make sure I've shined them./ It's just that fall/ Isn't fall at all/ Until I go out and find them." The attractive sketches [by Kit Dalton] remind one of E. H. Shepard's.

### Paul Engle

SOURCE: "There's Every Sort of Poem for Every Kind of Child," in *The New York Times Book Review,* November 10, 1963, p. 2.

The good things in Kaye Starbird's ***Don't Ever Cross a***

*Crocodile* are the quick moments of a poem about a child unable to sleep: "The kitten stamping its paws/The guppies banging their tank." The inadequate things are those lines in which an eagle says "I'm quite the finest thing in feathers," and the poet says "Don't ever lure a lion close/With gifts of steak and suet." For the children of 6 to 10 there is an occasional bright verse such as **"The Hound"**:

> It's funny to look at a hurrying hound,
> Pursuing a scent that's attractive.
> He gallops around
> With his nose to the ground
> And only the back of him active.

The illustrations are ordinary.

 **A SNAIL'S A FAILURE SOCIALLY AND OTHER POEMS, MOSTLY ABOUT PEOPLE (1966)**

**Walker Gibson**

SOURCE: A review of *A Snail's a Failure Socially and Other Poems, Mostly about People,* in *The New York Times Book Review,* November 6, 1966, p. 67.

A final book that deserves the accolade of highly accomplished Light not Slight Verse is one with the simpering title of *A Snail's a Failure Socially.* Once past that coyness, this book by Kaye Starbird, with illustrations by Kit Dalton, is a salty joy, peopled with such characters as "The Widow Fay, who copes, / Goes stalking through the A-and-P/And punching cantaloupes." And "Benny McBlore who's fifty or more / Has rather low I.Q., / Which means he can't do all of the jobs / That fifty-year-olds should do." And Miss Tabor, who is "little and jumpy and thin / And doesn't like joking or joshing / Her home, though it's ugly, is neat as a pin. / And wet from continual washing." Other facets of human nature are shown as well as Nature in various forms, and the illustrations, a little on the E. H. Shephard side, are by the poet's daughter. Salute to Starbird and Company.

**Zena Sutherland**

SOURCE: A review of *A Snail's a Failure Socially and Other Poems, Mostly about People,* in *Bulletin of the Center for Children's Books,* Vol. 20, No. 4, December, 1966, p. 63.

A collection of light verse for the most part, with an occasional poem that sounds a serious note; the small-scale black-and-white illustrations have a good deal of humor and movement. The poems are about animals, weather, human problems, friends, strangers, and relationships—familiar topics, with an occasional odd twist. The appeal of the book, nice to read independently or aloud, is not in the beauty or the originality of the

writing, but in the swinging rhythm, the word play, the humorous concepts, and the rhyme—the latter treated here and there with a cheerful and clearly intentional disrespect.

**Booklist**

SOURCE: A review of *A Snail's a Failure Socially and Other Poems, Mostly about People,* in *Booklist,* Vol. 63, No. 7, December 6, 1966, p. 421.

Thirty original poems about people and about animals, large and small, offer intriguing glimpses into the personalities and activities of rural town life. While varying somewhat in poetic quality, the author's candid and refreshing observations and character studies effectively capture the child's point of view. Small black-and-white sketches complement the text.

**Elizabeth M. Guiney**

SOURCE: A review of *A Snail's a Failure Socially and Other Poems, Mostly about People,* in *School Library Journal,* Vol. 13, No. 5, January 15, 1967, pp. 70-1.

These poems are trite and uninspired and the illustrations are dull. The poet describes several misfits in society: taciturn Mrs. Hanks, Benny McBlore, whose "mind stopped growing when he was young," the pessimistic Gliddens. These are adult judgments of people that children will fail to understand or appreciate. The humorous poems are really not very funny; I doubt that many children would be amused enough to even chuckle.

**THE PHEASANT ON ROUTE SEVEN (1968)**

**The Kirkus Service**

SOURCE: A review of *The Pheasant on Route Seven,* in *The Kirkus Service,* Vol. XXXVI, No. 17, September 1, 1968, p. 993.

On the order of *A Snail's a Failure Socially* another small town bunch whose foibles you'll recognize and remember—like Uncle Gavin Stokes "who lives on dreams and schemes and relatives" or Abigail, a thorn among roses, who "as soon as she teethed . . . bit her nurse." There are eccentric children and sassy senior citizens as well as exceptionally unromanticized animals ("sheep are a bore"). What's best is the uncompromising and forthright treatment of the not so rosy: Auntie before and after her stroke, the dwarf who sees his height as just right for shining shoes, the response to a fix-it man ("I lost a hero, I suppose,/ The day he said he could not fit/ The petals back onto my rose"). A very personal style—humorous and colloquial with offbeat innuendoes.

**Diane Farrell**

SOURCE: A review of *The Pheasant on Route Seven,* in *The Horn Book Magazine,* Vol. XLIV, No. 5, October, 1968, p. 568.

A collection of poems that the reader wants to read straight through—and does—and is left somewhat breathless but well acquainted with a small American town called Pleasantport and its diverse inhabitants. Like "Miss Amos, the poet lady," the author writes "storified verse that sings" about Granny Shriver, who has "always been a strong survivor"; Doctor Ernest Bates, "Who—when he isn't saving lives—/ Is saving paperweights"; Miss Janie Wright, whom sage old Cornelius, the storekeeper, thinks has the best chance of winning the widower, Colonel Kent; Father Spear; the Carey kids; Sheriff Hale; and Banjo Scott, the drunkard. The author's shrewd observations give an added dimension to the lives of ordinary people. For older readers than the author's previous books.

**Eugene M. Rooney**

SOURCE: A review of *The Pheasant on Route Seven,* in *Best Sellers,* Vol. 28, No. 13, October 1, 1968, p. 279.

The author of this book has successfully directed her book toward the eleven-and-twelve-year age level. There is no semblance of sentimentality as she relates poems about the village people of Pleasantport. As she bridges the gap between children and adult reading, she interestingly relates and acquaints the reader of rebel Abigail who writes horror stories, of Captain Carr's return from the sea, of Miss Amos whose fame is recognized outside the village, and does so in a pleasing rhythm of flowing verse. She also interestingly depicts the fox, a snowstorm, and the pheasant in verse form. This book offers delightful reading, as well as a deeper understanding of human nature.

**Barbara Gibson**

SOURCE: A review of *The Pheasant on Route Seven,* in *School Library Journal,* Vol. 15, No. 2, October 15, 1968, p. 160.

Combining light verse with serious intent is a difficult job at best, but Kaye Starbird successfully presents glimpses of human nature which are revealing, poignant, and often highly amusing. In these 33 poems about the people and environs of small-town Pleasantport, the smallest details capture the essence of human individuality. Readers are not likely to forget Abigail ("Among the roses, she was a thorn"), Miss Amos the poetess, Cornelius Proctor the storekeeper, Granny Shriver, or Spence the dwarf. Nature is an integral part of Pleasantport and the imagery in a falling leaf, two robins, or an aging chestnut tree adds to the substance of the poet's message. Enjoyable for readers at almost any age and stage.

**Publishers Weekly**

SOURCE: A review of *The Pheasant on Route Seven,* in *Publishers Weekly,* Vol. 194, No. 17, October 21, 1968, p. 51.

A rhyming visit to a village, a visit you won't want to miss, for your guide is Kaye Starbird, who leads her tourists to the most colorful characters, characters guaranteed to charm and delight, because they so obviously and gaily charm and delight the guide herself. Sign up for the tour—it will be a happy and poetic experience.

**Mary O'Neil**

SOURCE: A review of *The Pheasant on Route Seven,* in *The New York Times Book Review,* October 27, 1968, p. 42.

Like the Poet Lady in this new book, Kaye Starbird writes, "storified verse that sings." And with one poem, **"The Snowstorm,"** she joins the masters of her craft. Her rhymes never falter; her people are real.They gossip, argue, have pretensions and ideals. In this book the village of Pleasantport comes alive. It is an old town, ringed by the sea, the woods and its wildlife, and a modern highway where the pheasant comes to grief.

Perhaps such phrases as, "wine-clear bay," "rue it," "hie me," and, "what fate had put in motion," are still part of the Pleasantport vernacular. But they are disappointing because they shine through the amber of another time. Such usages may partly defeat the book's purpose, defined by the author on the jacket fly leaf: "at 11 or 12 children go into adult reading and should have a bridge to do this and to keep them interested in poetry. Therefore, some of the subjects deal with adult themes as children themselves do at this time."

And, "at this time" children certainly do. But on their own terms, in their own talk. No one is more conscious of the words of now, and in the creation of new expressions, than the adolescents. And to defy them in a book about here and now, is to lose them as readers, however comforting, interesting and pertinent the subject matter. Nevertheless this book has a wild-rose charm. Few cliché types are present. Few rhymes are forced. And the illustrations by Victoria de Larrea are just right.

### THE COVERED BRIDGE HOUSE AND OTHER POEMS (1979)

**Publishers Weekly**

SOURCE: A review of *The Covered Bridge House and Other Poems,* in *Publishers Weekly,* Vol. 216, No. 15, October 8, 1979, p. 71.

Here are no fewer than 52 unpretentious and rewarding

poems, reflecting the appreciative senses of Starbird, who pays tribute to people and things in New England. Some are gentle complaints about mean folk: "Since Beverly likes to frighten kids/ And Beverly's mind is sly,/ I really hated rooming with her/ This summer at Camp Blue Sky." Beverly swings a mouse above the banquet lunch and gets up to other tricks that will remind many a victim of other teases. Other items, however, celebrate special joys including those offered by **"The Covered Bridge House"**; by **"Today,"** with no sign that overdue spring will come except a softness in the air; and by **"The Stranger"** who stopped by a country church and played unforgettable music on the bell. [Jim] Arnosky's strong, decorative ink drawings suit the little volume perfectly.

## X. J. Kennedy

SOURCE: "Rhythm and Rhyme," in *The New York Times Book Review,* November 11, 1979, pp. 53, 68.

Evidently for the larger fry, Kaye Starbird's ***The Covered Bridge House and Other Poems,*** illustrated by Jim Arnosky, is wide-ranging and—with 35 poems—substantial. I always like Miss Starbird's verse portraits of oddballs: This new collection has memorable ones about a boy with a runaway imagination and about a slightly mad old bell-ringer who usurps the local belfry for a rock concert. With humor and insight she touches on kids' genuine concerns, and she isn't just deft, but also at times deep-going: "And suddenly everything listened and glistened, / Each leaf, each vine / And even the numberless needles on every / Steeple-topped pine."

## *Kirkus Reviews*

SOURCE: A review of *The Covered Bridge House and Other Poems,* in *Kirkus Reviews,* Vol. XLVII, No. 22, November 15, 1979, p. 1329.

Predictable rhymes and rhythms and an old-fashioned, very mild sort of humor characterize the light verse collected here. The title poem is a pleasant daydream about living in a covered bridge house, and there are some everyday observations about bird migration, a climbing ant, or clocks stopped in a blizzard—but only the brisk **"The Morning in June"** breaks the monotonous singsong pace of the collection. Many of the selections are ditties about the salient characteristics of named individuals, mostly kids. Ruth who broke a tooth insists on the truth—and thus objects to the dentist's saying "our tooth" instead of "your tooth"; pesky Beverly plagues her roommate at Camp Blue Sky; Heather has lots of luxuries but no friends; Loring is a walking encyclopedia (but one thing even he doesn't know is why he goes on storing up information); Eddie is never ready—and so gets left behind; Miss Casper has (by the punch line) a two-cow garage; and so it goes, unobjectionably but without much snap.

## Barbara Elleman

SOURCE: A review of *The Covered Bridge House and Other Poems,* in *Booklist,* Vol. 76, No. 7, December 1, 1979, p. 560.

Droll wit and keen perception give mobility to Starbird's poetic eye as she translates impressions of emotions, personalities, and events into imaginative verse. The focus sharpens when she gives her attention to children's capricious capers such as Heather's nasty disposition in **"Jump Rope Song,"** Ruth's altercation with a dentist in **"Ruth,"** Hugh's problem of spelling *kangaroo* in **"The Spelling Test,"** a young boy's active imagination in **"Artie,"** and Beverly's antics at camp in **"Watch Out!"** The rhyme, which trips smoothly along, is used more for structure than for sound, giving a fullness to the cadence. Black-and-white line drawings accented with silhouettes decorate the pages. A collection to smile and ponder over, equally suited for reading alone or aloud.

## Zena Sutherland

SOURCE: A review of *The Covered Bridge,* in *Bulletin of the Center for Children's Books,* Vol. 33, No. 5, January, 1980, p. 102.

Deft little lozenge-framed black or silhouette pictures illustrate a collection of poems that, with a few exceptions, fall into two categories: lyric poems, usually about some facet of natural beauty, and narrative poems, which tend to be long and very funny. The lyric poetry is often moving and evocative, the narrative poems occasionally seem self-consciously comic; it's a nice mix, however, and there's little question that the humor and action of the longer poems will appeal to children.

## Daisy Kouzel

SOURCE: A review of *The Covered Bridge House and Other Poems,* in *School Library Journal,* Vol. 26, No. 5, January, 1980. p. 61.

These 35 poems, while not of a moving, or introspective, or lyrical character, and not always observant of measures, are consistently great fun to read, and that's not saying little. Whether Starbird tells about "Artie Dole/ (who) can't seem to control/ His busy imagination," or Joe Malloy the corner newsman, cheerfulness intact in the fierce December cold, or Little Lenore who dreams of a Coke machine within easy reach, or a blizzard, or the birds, or a morning in June, young readers will be easily captivated by the gentle humor, the easy musicality of the rhymes, and the upbeat windup of each poem. Everybody, from Slim Slater who lives in a camper, to Miss Flynn who has 30 cats, to the nameless would-be possessor of the covered bridge house of the title, seems content with their lot. The small black-and-white scratchboard illustrations punctuating several pages are as unobtrusive as they are attractive. As the British would say, jolly good.

**Mary M. Burns**

SOURCE: A review of *The Covered Bridge House and Other Poems,* in *The Horn Book Magazine,* Vol. LVI, No. 1, February, 1980, p, 70.

As in her earlier collections—for example, **The Pheasant on Route Seven** and **A Snail's a Failure Socially,** the poet deftly works within the strictures of rhyme and rhythm imposed by familiar poetic forms to create a gallery of remarkable individuals as well as to de-

scribe various aspects of nature with fresh insight. Susie Skinner, along with Grace, **"The World's Best Hopper,"** and Beverly, *enfant terrible* of the summer camp, are all originals; while city-bred Nate and the farm boy Evan are contemporary proponents of the attitudes in the fable **"The Town Mouse and the Country Mouse."** Economically crafted, the poems are appealing not only for their incisive characterization but also for their imaginative wordplay and sense of wonder which, as in **"That Morning in June,"** transform the mundane into the memorable and the memorable into a transcendent experience. Attractively produced with black-and-white decorative illustrations, the thirty-five poems offer both variety and substance.

---

**Additional coverage of Starbird's life and career is contained in the following sources published by The Gale Group:** *Contemporary Authors New Revision Series,* **Vol. 38;** *Major Authors and Illustrators for Children and Young Adults;* **and** *Something about the Author,* **Vol. 6.**

# Theresa Tomlinson

## 1946-

English author of fiction.

Major works include *The Flither Pickers* (1987), *Riding the Waves* (1990), *The Rope Carrier* (1991), *The Forest-wife* (1993), *The Cellar Lad* (1995).

## INTRODUCTION

Tomlinson's young adult novels, mainly set in her native Yorkshire, explore the social and economic conditions of the working poor, as well as the personal past of the individual. Using these different facets of history, Tomlinson emphasizes the important roles of both the individual and the community and shows how individuals can come to understand themselves better, find a purpose for joining together, and have courage in the face of daily hardship. She told *Something about the Author* (*SATA*), "Resilience is what I admire most in human beings." Although many of Tomlinson's historical novels are set in Sheffield, they are regional only in location, while their themes cross borders and continents. Several take place around the turn of the century, including *The Flither Pickers, The Rope Carrier, The Herring Girls* (1994), and *The Cellar Lad*, and generally feature strong female protagonists. Praised by reviewers for their historical accuracy, these novels tell of the impoverished workers who were, in one way or another, affected by the Industrial Revolution and the rise of the unions in the steel industry. Tomlinson also has written fiction with contemporary settings and themes, dealing with issues ranging from intergenerational relationships to fighting cancer. Her works are character-driven, featuring young people who explore their own histories as they grow into adults. In such works as *Summer Witches* (1989), *Dancing through the Shadows* (1997), and the highly commended *Riding the Waves*, Tomlinson's protagonists gain understanding of their own lives by listening to the stories told by their elders about their own lives and the local histories that surround them.

When writing about the more distant past, Tomlinson turns to legend. She has written three books—*The Forest-wife, Child of the May* (1998), and *The Path of the She-wolf* (1999)—based on the stories of Robin Hood, but with a modern twist. These works feature female protagonists, and treat Robin Hood more as a hot-headed adventurer than a romantic hero. Tomlinson's versions emphasize themes of communal cooperation and the competence of independent females. Although these stories stray from the reality of the Middle Ages, they are regarded as entertaining and insightful for young readers, particularly girls. Tomlinson told *SATA*, "I think that it is important to find exciting ways of passing a sense of history to our children. A knowledge of the

resilience of ordinary people who have lived before us can inspire modern children and help them with their own struggles and decisions." From the angst of a frustrated surfer to the exploits of Maid Marian in the forests of Sherwood, Tomlinson's novels engage young readers on several levels and generally end with an upbeat message delivered not with a sledgehammer but with a smile.

### Biographical Information

Tomlinson was born in the North Yorkshire county of Sussex in 1946. As a child, she wanted to be a ballet dancer, not a writer, but her parents read to her and encouraged a love of books in the young girl. Tomlinson married and had three children. When her children were young, she made little picture books for them, and as they grew older and the stories became longer, she found that she enjoyed the pastime very much. She took a creative writing course led by Helen Cresswell and Lynne Reid Banks and offered them the manuscript of *The Water Cat* (1988). Both were so moved by the story that they cried, and Cresswell commented that she wished she had written it herself. Encouraged, Tomlinson sent the manuscript for publication, and it was accepted within the year. With a flourishing literary career ahead of her, Tomlinson was diagnosed later with breast cancer. Her struggles inspired her novel *Dancing through the Shadows*. "When faced with a long period of treatment," Tomlinson told *SATA*, "I felt that it would be beneficial to try to keep writing, so I decided to use what was happening to me as the theme for a novel." Tomlinson, now recovered, has continued to write, turning out over a dozen novels about ordinary men and women who, simply by living their daily lives, have helped to shape the world.

## Major Works

Illustrated with photographs of real people taken by Frank Sutcliffe at the turn of the century, Tomlinson's first book, *The Flither Pickers*, is set in Yorkshire among the poor fishing folk of Sheffield village. Based on true accounts, but with fictional characters, *The Flither Pickers* chronicles the lives of the women who gathered shellfish bait and waited for their men to return from the sea, exhausted by harsh labor and terrible poverty. Lisa, the protagonist and narrator of the story, has the opportunity to better herself by education. But Lisa is torn between loyalty to her family and her desire to become a writer. *The Flither Pickers* was greeted as a refreshing, honest, and distinguished recreation of history, and an understanding depiction of a young woman growing up. Marcus Crouch noted that Tomlinson "has written a most distinguished novel which is also a convincing piece of historical reconstruction," and also observed that the narration rendered by Lisa had a "rough eloquence . . . which strikes exactly the right note."

Intergenerational friendship is the theme of *Riding the Waves*. Set in a small English coastal town, the novel deals with the dreams of Matt, who desperately wants to be part of a group of surfers. As his history homework, he has to interview an old family friend, Florrie, and almost against his will, he becomes friends with her. As she tells him about the history of his home, he grows fascinated by her stories of smugglers, bathing machines, and of her life before World War I, including the out-of-wedlock child she had to put up for adoption. Matt helps Florrie face her fear of leaving her house, and upbraids her when he thinks she is giving up on herself during a hospital stay that has gone on too long. In return, Florrie introduces Matt to the surfers, who remember her warmly from the days when she owned a chip shop, and encourages him as he learns to surf in the cold North Sea. Applauding Tomlinson's well-crafted characters, Sheila Allen observed, "There are so many aspects of this book to absorb and encourage the reader. . . . Surfing, history, adoption, care of and respect for the elderly, are all woven into this very readable tale."

*The Rope Carrier*, with its unusual, but authentic setting, features eighteenth-century rope-makers who live in a subterranean village in Derbyshire near Sheffield. Times are difficult, but life in the cities is harder. When Minnie Dakin, an experienced rope-maker at nine, leaves her underground cottage to help her sister in Sheffield, she finds her sister's family in desperate circumstances. Her brother-in-law is thrown into debtor's prison, but is released during public riots over the closing of the public lands. Eventually they all return to their underground village, which is their home. Marcus Crouch noted, "This is social and industrial history with a human face, and very convincing it is . . . a most absorbing and attractive book, of great educational value but likely to be read with interest for its moving story and its vividly realized characters."

Tomlinson moved further back into history in *The Forestwife*. This version of the Robin Hood legend features Maid Marian as its central character. Escaping an unwanted marriage to an elderly man, young Mary de Holt runs away to Sherwood Forest, and is followed by her faithful nurse, Agnes. When they come to the cottage of the Forestwife, the legendary healer of the region, they find her dead, and Agnes becomes the new Forestwife, renaming her young charge, Marian, and taking her on as an assistant. The forest becomes a refuge for a group of renegade nuns, as well as for many disenfranchised people of the surrounding country, most of them women, who have been abused by Norman and Saxon lords. Agnes's son Robert appears intermittently with his band of "merrie men," pursuing unrealistic political ideals, but eventually giving Marian his respect and love. Tomlinson followed *The Forestwife* with two sequels, *Child of the May* and *The Path of the She-wolf*. While reviewers complained about the book's somewhat self-righteous social agenda, which weighed down the story and made it seem more New Age than Middle Ages, others praised the competent, honest, and hardworking heroine, whose concern is for the safety of the people.

Set in Sheffield, *The Cellar Lad* revolves around the Chartist campaign for universal male suffrage and the rise of the unions in the steel industry. Ben works with his father in Dyson's Yard where, like all those in his class, he spends long hours at a dangerous job and receives little compensation. Ben's home life is warm and, although there are scenes of poverty and misery, the book depicts a family whose struggles are mitigated by their close relationship. Some critics welcomed the details of daily life worked into the settings and praised the historical accuracy of time and place, while others found the story uninvolving with an imperfect plot. Marcus Crouch observed that with all the difficulties facing the characters in this novel, "it would have been easy to lay on the suffering with a trowel, but here is a writer who sees her subject whole."

## Awards

Tomlinson has had two books on the Carnegie Medal Short List of the British Library Association, *Riding the Waves* in 1991 and *Meet Me by the Steelmen* in 1998.

## GENERAL COMMENTARY

### David Bennett

SOURCE: "David Bennett on the Novels of Theresa Tomlinson," in *Books for Keeps,* No. 81, July, 1993, p. 32.

Theresa Tomilson has published five books with a sixth, *The Forestwife,* due this month. Readers might be forgiven for thinking that her first book was *The Water Cat* which came out in 1988, but in fact a small publisher had produced *The Flither Pickers* in 1987, and that was later re-packaged by Walker.

Helen Cresswell and Lynne Reid Banks were leading an Arvon creative writing course when a very shy and diffident Theresa offered them a story to read. Both cried and both were highly impressed. Helen told me later that it was a story she wished she had written herself and felt so confident about it that she offered to bet £1,000 that *The Water Cat* would be accepted within the year. The novel was indeed published but I can't discover whether Theresa took Helen up on the bet.

The story is a fantasy that combines fact and fiction as ancient local lore imprints itself on a present, which is Coronation Year, 1953. As with all of Theresa's books the places are real and part of her own experience. Using real places, usually around Sheffield or the North Yorkshire coast, enables her to concentrate on the story and not worry too much about background. At the centre of *The Water Cat* is the legend of the merman, Catterstyn. His friendship with Enid, the girl who rescued him from death, and his role in the relief of a village famine when a ship full of carlins was washed up on the coast, are told in a story that ebbs and flows between the real world, the past world and the fantasy world. Underpinning all of this is the sense that what modern man's 'magic', i.e. steel-making, has created is at odds with the benign magics of the past, toxic more than potent.

Old magic featured in the next book, *The Secret Place,* a short novel where two friends playing in an abandoned bomb shelter discover that two little girls, Rose and Lily, played there before them and one was the seemingly strange old lady whom that they are now convinced is a witch. Circumstances forced the friends to assist Miss Lily in a time of need and they discover that behind her strangeness is her inability to speak or hear and a great weight of guilt surrounding her own mother's death in a bombing raid. Their prejudices and fears about someone who is simply different melt away and they start to learn from her a closeness to the earth that we should respect and care for, not fill with rubbish and pollution.

> "But did they have magic?" Susanna asked. "Only the magic that's all around us. The magic that brings the sun and fresh shoots each spring. I think that they saw each season as magical. We seem to take it all for granted now."

This is a modern version of the village wise woman. Reviled by many, yet talented and clever beyond the understanding of most. She is frightening and fascinating, shunned and yet vital to the community in which she lives.

This theme is picked up again in *The Forestwife,* which has Maid Marian as its heroine. Theresa Tomlinson seems concerned to look back and to see what strengths women had in the past and to afford them due acknowledgement in the present. There is perhaps a notion that, forgetting the likes of Nightingale and Curie, women, ordinary women, had a negative or passive share in events. In fact their lives are dominated by the very basic but absolutely vital events of birth, life and death and the all importance of love. This love is not reserved for the family alone but also for the community in which they live.

*The Flither Pickers* demonstrates this in a very compelling, unsentimental way as it leads us into the harrowingly harsh lives of North Yorkshire womenfolk who gathered their flithers to bait the lines of their menfolk. They were the ones who supported each other as each fought to stave off grinding poverty and waited with stoic patience for their husbands and sons to return from the sea, or not, depending on the vagaries of weather and tide. In 1901 a group of such women were the only ones who could launch a lifeboat off the beach at Runswick Bay when all their men were caught out at sea in a storm. Their lives were captured by Frank Meadow Sutcliffe, the Whitby photographer, whose photos accompany the text and inspired Theresa to write the novel. The juxtaposition of story and pictures makes up one of the best produced and affecting paperbacks I've come across in the twelve years I've been reviewing fiction for young people.

Scrupulous research goes into Theresa's work and undoubtedly enables her to write so vividly. She has come to a passion for History later on in life. She attends a local History Workshop one morning per week in Sheffield, where she lives, and often spends one other day a week in the Local Studies Library researching her novels. *The Rope Carrier* came out of her studies of the file cutters and ropemakers of the eighteenth century, who lived around Castleton, Derbyshire. The latter actually inhabited a subterranean village inside the Peak Cavern, visited by Queen Victoria in 1842, when she was entertained by three old women, the last residents. With increasing skill and maturity of style since the earlier books, Theresa has blended all of the historical detail into her story with striking compassion and has succeeded in not producing an historical novel laden down with the facts of the past. This one picks up the earlier themes and concerns and yet manages to be freshly up to date for modern readers. Minni Daykin is an ordinary/extraordinary girl, positive and resourceful whatever fate and man might try to do with her. In a male-orientated environment she determines to take control of her own destiny against the odds. We are relieved that she succeeds. Contemporary drawings accompany the text and make this an impressive companion to *The Flither Pickers.*

*Riding the Waves* saw a return to the northeast coast and earned a commendation for the Carnegie Medal. Research for this was closer at home. Of her three teenage children two are adopted. Together the family decided that a storybook was due about modern, ordinary kids who are adopted in relatively ordinary circumstances. *Anne of Green Gables, Pollyanna* and the like were Theresa's favourite reading when she was young but they don't have too much that is ordinary about them for today's readers. Matt's story emerges not without humour from the pen of an assured and confident writer. The important adoption theme is overlaid with the relationship of the young to the old. It was a school History project that brought Matt and Florrie together into a relationship that didn't start well but was to prove mutually beneficial. We have again the old woman with a secret guilt and she's a wise old bird, who can solve deep wounds as she advises her troubled friend from her own experience:

> "You mustn't give up. You have to sort yourself out, get yourself together and start all over again."

As ever the characterisation and motivation are surefooted and the dialogue convincing whilst the background and supporting detail is sketched in fully, though not heavy-handedly.

Theresa tells me that she writes remembering how she felt about books when she was young. She liked books that had action, were interesting, about the basic things in life and above all weren't too long to cope with. That memory has helped her to produce an impressive range and collection of work so far. The only way to find out is to go forth, read and see if you agree.

---

# TITLE COMMENTARY

## THE FLITHER PICKERS (1987)

### Marcus Crouch

SOURCE: A review of *The Flither Pickers,* in *The Junior Bookshelf,* Vol. 54, No. 6, December, 1990, p. 302.

Theresa Tomlinson, a writer new to me, has written a most distinguished novel which is also a convincing piece of historical reconstruction.

The 'flither pickers' of the title are the womenfolk of Yorkshire fishermen who gather shellfish bait in all weathers, a gruelling operation. It is altogether a hard life for Lisa Welford and her family and friends, one

which at the best of times is maintained not much above subsistence level and desperate when, as happens often, a breadwinner is drowned. There is an additional irony if one of the family, like Lisa, has the capacity to break out of the mould and better herself by education. Lisa suffers a conflict of loyalties as she weighs her duties towards home and parents against her love of school and her yearnings to be a writer. She, like the author, is painfully honest. There is no contrivance in her story. There are hard decisions to be made, and Ms. Tomlinson, like her tough little heroine, looks for no easy way out.

The story is inspired by the author's knowledge and love of the Yorkshire coast and its people and also by the work of Frank Sutcliffe, a photographer around the turn of the century who recorded the harsh beauty of the scene and the buoyant spirits of the fisherfolk. Sutcliffe himself appears in the story, and Lisa and her friend Mary Jane are the subject of one of his pictures which make effective illustrations.

Lisa's story is told by herself, and the tone of a young girl, candid and innocent, is maintained throughout. There is a rough eloquence in the narrative which strikes exactly the right note.

The photographic illustrations are integrated with the text. Consequently the whole is printed on coated paper, the sheen from which makes difficult reading. A pity, but there is no satisfactory alternative. One might quarrel more justifiably with the jacket design; it is beautifully drawn, but the cute and very clean blonde is very far from the reader's mental image of hard-working Lisa after a spell of 'mucking the lines'.

### Sandra Kemp

SOURCE: A review of *The Flither Pickers,* in *The Times Educational Supplement,* No. 3883, December 7, 1990, p. 30.

"So bursting with sauciness, but frozen still, we had our picture made." The two impish little girls, posed rakishly on the rocks against the backdrop of the sea, laugh out at us from the doublespread centrepiece photo of *The Flither Pickers* with irrepressible energy and delight.

Theresa Tomlinson's new novel is a peculiarly effective play of fiction and reality. The fictional narrative of the cycle of family life in a Victorian fishing village incorporates an incident based on a true story. In 1901, when all the men were caught out at sea in a storm, the women of Runswick Bay launched the lifeboat with a scratch crew led by an old coxswain. The author of the novels given to the child narrator is based on the character of Mary Linskill, the Victorian novelist from Whitby. At the same time, the story itself is counterpointed by the real-life photos of Frank Meadow Sutcliffe which bear no literal relation to its fictional characters. Vivid, stark and stoical, most of the photos are of women. Old and young, their poses and expressions betray the harshness of existence. The intense black and white of the photos seems to highlight the tragic back-drop of the sea, and to blend them more strongly with the story:

"There's plenty of the fishermen carry the stones, though it wasn't talked about much. They live in fear of a long struggling death if they're thrown overboard, so they don't learn to swim—and they carry heavy stones in their pockets so as to make sure they'll sink straight down. . . . I hated to think of John with his pockets full of dogger. He must have gone off up the coast deliberate-like, looking for the heavy egg-shaped iron-stones, for they're only found where the Cleveland iron seam meets the sea."

The story unfolds like one of Grandad's "slow rare smiles". The exactly measured pace matches the selec-tive telling. The local wise-woman Miriam cautions the child-narrator: "I'll tell what I think I should, but I'll not tell all." So, the story of the narrator's brother Billy, whose double, or alter-ego, Mam's little brother, drowned when Mam was meant to be looking after him, only emerges bit by bit. Other family stories—Irene's unmarried pregnancy, grandad's recovery from gran's death—and the story of the picture-man and of the Whitby author, are also told in fragments.

*The Flither Pickers* has all the ingredients of chil-dren's fiction: sibling rivalry, difficulty with parents—"Mam's hard shell was as strong as the flithers"—and so on. The narrative reflects the familiar slow process of understanding and of a particular kind of growth. But there is no formula here. Like the lives that centre round the old life-boat, *The Flither Pickers* is ballasted by a Woolfian sense of the commonality of readers and writers, of feelings and experiences that reach beyond a particular time and place. The story ends with the child's poignant recognition of her kinship with the author of the books given to her by the picture-man: "a thin lady, writing at a desk, with no boots for her feet."

### David Bennett

SOURCE: A review of *The Flither Pickers,* in *Books for Keeps,* No. 74, May, 1992, pp. 20-1.

The backbreaking, daily drudgery of the fishermen's wives in turn-of-the-century North Yorkshire is recount-ed in this short novel that was inspired by the photo-graphs of Frank Meadow Sutcliffe, which illustrate the text.

The community of women for whom life is always over-shadowed by the spectre of 'the sea takes those it wants' is realised vividly and compassionately, with an unerring sense of sharing and concern for the welfare of each other, climaxing in the courageous launching by the

women of the Sandwick Lifeboat. A beautiful produc-tion worth recommending.

## 📖 *THE WATER CAT* (1988)

### Deborah Singmaster

SOURCE: A review of *The Water Cat,* in *The Times Literary Supplement,* No. 4479, February, 1988, p. 120.

Carlingford, a steel-manufacturing town in the north of England, is integral to the plot of Theresa Tomlinson's novel *The Water Cat.* From her new home Jane looks out on a dramatic landscape: "The sky on the far side was lit with a rosy glow, but it wasn't the dawn, just the white hot slag, turning red, on the tip beyond the vil-lage." Carlingford's past is linked to the present by the merman, Mr. Catterstyn (the Water Cat of the title in his preferred "shape-change"), who once saved the village when it was threatened with famine but is now held prisoner by the steelworks: steel is kryptonite to Catterstyn's Superman and the mining works are blocking his return route to the sea. Tomlinson produces the occasional fine image. She is also good on period: it is 1952, the year of the Coronation, and television is such a novelty that the children "even watched the morning programmes that were meant for testing the sets". Her handling of the central fantasy element is less successful; Mr. Catterstyn is a wooden charac-ter who talks in olde English ("You are clever, fair youth") and fails to generate an aura of mystery suffi-ciently powerful to eclipse his realistic industrial sur-roundings. This reservation apart, *The Water Cat* is an exciting tale for younger readers and a promising first novel.

### Margery Fisher

SOURCE: A review of *The Water Cat,* in *Growing Point,* Vol. 27, No. 5, January, 1989, pp. 5087-93.

It is never difficult to apportion magical powers to cats, those reserved and mysterious dwellers on the fringe of our domestic life. *The Water Cat* is set in a Northern steel-working town where an incoming brother and sister pull a bedraggled cat out of the marsh and try to dry it, without success. Puzzled by this, they are receptive enough when they find the cat is in fact a shape-changer, a merman who has been cut off from the sea by the hostile metal of the steel workings. In plain prose which is circumstantial enough to deny disbelief the author describes the practical contrivances by which Jane and Tom manage to carry the merman/cat past the metal barrier, helped by seagulls and pigeons which put up a diversion. A slender story-line is supported by satisfying concrete detail and by a strong contrast between technol-ogy and water-magic, a contrast easily accepted by two lively children exploring a new habitat and hardly sur-prised to find it unusual.

📖　***SUMMER WITCHES* (1989; also as *The Secret Place,* 1990)**

**Ilene Cooper**

SOURCE: A review of *Summer Witches,* in *Booklist,* Vol. 87, No. 13, March 1, 1991, p. 1389.

Tomlinson sets her story in northern England and writes of the commonalities and differences that shape relationships. Sarah and her friend Susanna are delighted with the old air-raid shelter in Sarah's back yard. They will refurbish it and use it as a meeting place. The girls realize the shelter was used during World War II, but what they do not know is that two elderly sisters who live near by, Lily and Rose, used the shelter as girls. Sarah has always been afraid of Miss Lily, who is deaf and uses sign language to communicate. When the girls learn of Lily's tragedy during the war (Lily still feels guilty that her mother left the shelter to get her some water and died when a bomb struck), Sarah's feelings change. Happily, as the relationship between the two young girls and the women grows, Sarah and Susanna are able to banish the ghosts that haunt Miss Lily. There are several elements here that may concern some readers. . . . [T]his contains many Briticisms, though Tomlinson does explain some of them in an introduction. More significantly, there is what some may consider problematic—the introduction of witchcraft into the plot. Sarah, disturbed by what she perceives as Miss Lily's oddness, has called her a witch. A few readers, primarily adults, may be bothered by the fact that there is some truth to this perception. Lily has a way with plants, herbs, and healing, and Rose is an expert on white witchcraft. Most readers, though, will appreciate the story for what it is—a thoughtful story of banished prejudices and friendship between generations.

*Kirkus Reviews*

SOURCE: A review of *Summer Witches,* in *Kirkus Reviews,* Vol. LIX, No. 8, April 15, 1991, p. 540.

Sarah's discovery that new neighbor Susanna has the makings of a fine friend despite her clunky shoes presages more complex realizations about the unusual woman.

Sarah has enjoyed pretending that old Lily is a witch; after all, she's deaf and can't hear the jibes. But after the two girls cement their friendship while transforming the bomb shelter in Sarah's garden into their private place, Sarah finds a child's secret note tucked away there. The girls learn that Lily was the note's author, and that a terrible experience during WW II thwarted her learning to speak; they also get to know her as a productive, caring person. Meanwhile, Lily's sister Rose (the local librarian) has led them to consider the ancient, destructive witch stereotype and contrast it with the reality that Lily exemplifies: a wise woman, skilled with herbs and healing, whose differences may provoke distrust.

With admirable skill, Tomlinson weaves her serious theme into an appealing, accessible story with likable, well-individualized characters and a neatly satisfying conclusion: the girls coax Lily into visiting the shelter for the first time since her trauma, thus themselves becoming the sort of witches whose "magic" is healing. This fine American debut is introduced by an eminently sensible note explaining some of the British terms and giving readers credit for the ability to figure the others out.

**Virginia Golodetz**

SOURCE: A review of *Summer Witches,* in *School Library Journal,* Vol. 37, No. 5, May, 1991, p. 95.

Two British schoolgirls discover an old secret document and other surprises when they clean out the 50-year-old World War II air-raid shelter in Sarah's backyard. Sarah and her friend Susanna want to fix it up as a den, but discovering the document and the signs that someone else had used the shelter makes them feel uncomfortable. Sarah also feels spooky about Miss Lily, an older neighbor who is deaf. The woman makes strange movements with her arms and face, and often the girls see her watching them. Sarah is convinced she is a witch. Despite their fears, a bomb scare at Miss Lily's house compels them to come to her rescue. When the emergency is over, they visit her and some of the secrets connected with the shelter begin to unravel. They come to know and respect this gentle, artistic woman who shares with them her extensive knowledge of herbs. Their curiosity about witches continues, and with the help of the local librarian they learn the difference between fairy-tale witches and real ones. This warm, well-written story of friendship between those of different ages and abilities is balanced with enough mystery to keep readers involved.

**Martha V. Parravano**

SOURCE: A review of *Summer Witches,* in *The Horn Book Magazine,* Vol. LXVII, No. 3, May-June, 1991, p. 332.

When Sarah and her friend Susanna decide to clean out an old wartime air-raid shelter in Sarah's back garden and secretly turn it into a private den for themselves, they discover cheerful vestiges of earlier inhabitants. Through a cryptic note found hidden in their now-cozy hideaway, the girls make friends with Miss Lily, a deaf neighbor, and learn that it was Lily and her sister, Rose, who used the shelter as children in World War II. Sadly, Lily has not been near her old house since the night her mother was killed—hit by a bomb when she went out of the shelter to get Lily a drink. In the past, Sarah had been frightened of Miss Lily, calling her an old witch, but the girls' fascination with Lily's affinity with growing things leads them to an understanding of who witches really were—healers and wise women who dealt in "the magic that's all around us . . . that brings the sun and fresh green shoots each spring." Sarah and Susanna transform their hideaway into a witch's den, adorning it with bundles of herbs and symbols of nature and dressing as witches themselves in big-pocketed aprons and wreaths for their hair. With newly acquired intuition they realize that the moment is right to invite Miss Lily into the shelter, driving away the guilt and terrible memories it holds for her. "'You two witches have really done a bit of healing, a bit of magic,'" Rose tells them proudly. Middle-grade girls will be hooked immediately by the private hideaway with a sense of mystery surrounding it, and the story that unfolds lives up to its enticing premise. The British setting is not in the least off-putting, thanks to the universality of the story and a helpful explanatory note to the reader.

## RIDING THE WAVES (1990; U.S. edition, 1993)

### Sheila Allen

SOURCE: A review of *Riding the Waves,* in *School Library Journal,* Vol. 39, No. 1, February, 1991, p. 33.

There are so many aspects to this book to absorb and encourage the reader. Matt's heroes are the surf-riders who ride the huge waves as they come pounding to the shore, but he can only watch when he longs to join them. He befriends, almost against his will, Florrie, an elderly lady who knew his granny and whom he interviewed for his history homework. Matt learns much about Florrie and himself as he becomes ever more fascinated by life in his seaside town some thirty odd years ago. It is Florrie who helps Matt to realise his dream, but he finds surfing a very tough sport.

The subject of adoption is a key theme and it is treated most sensitively. Matt is adopted and he learns how much anguish is involved when a young woman decides to give her baby for adoption. His mother tells Matt of the law which will enable him to try to trace his real mother later on. Surfing, history, adoption, care of and respect for the elderly, are all woven into this very readable tale. And Theresa Tomlinson's characters are no cardboard cut-outs but real people.

### A. R. Williams

SOURCE: A review of *Riding the Waves,* in *The Junior Bookshelf,* Vol. 55, No. 3, June, 1991, p. 123.

It is not quite accurate or fair to describe Miss Tomlinson's close-knit saga of events in a small seaside resort as an exercise in local history via nostalgia but the young Matt's homework projects certainly lead to some highly interesting revelations about Seaburn Bay and its inhabitants. Matt's (originally) reluctant visits to Aunt Florrie, a feisty senior citizen and a connection of his family, provide him with ample material for his

school tasks with recollections of well-dressed pre-war visitors, dances, pierrots, bathing-machines and smugglers, for all of which there are present-day links and some personal involvements. Florrie does not live entirely in the past and so far as health permits takes a practical interest in Matt's desire for knowledge as well as enabling him to fulfill his constant ambition of joining the carefree surfing crowd. Theresa Tomlinson recreates the past without condescension and uses the threads of private lives to bind her small community into an organic unit. As a painless guide to the way we were it has the pointedness of Picture Post. As an adopted child of local parents Matt is gradually, but only gradually, made aware of the facts of his birth. Gentle revelation is probably the secret of the story's charm.

### Steven Engelfried

SOURCE: A review of *Riding the Waves,* in *School Library Journal,* Vol. 39, No. 5, May, 1993, p. 110.

A strong novel about the surprising relationship that evolves between a boy and an elderly woman. Matt lives in a small seaside town in England, and dreams of joining a group of surfers, who have all the glamour of film stars in his eyes. They seem unattainable, however, until he is forced by a class project to pay a visit to Florrie, an old friend of his deceased grandmother's. After an awkward start, the pair find they have a lot to offer one another. Her stories of her youth in Seaburn actually interest and inspire him, while his problems and frustrations give her something to live for. When she asks the boy to accompany her to the beach, he fears she'll embarrass him in front of his surfing idols. In a neat twist, Florrie turns out to be a favorite of the surfing gang, and her presence helps him make the new friends he'd hoped for. Natural dialogue and deft insight into the characters' feelings raise this book above its fairly conventional plot. Matt's problem with learning to surf works as an unobtrusive metaphor for his other struggles and for Florrie's as well. The conclusion is particularly satisfying. She has not won her battle with ill health, but, inspired by Matt, is determined to keep trying. Low-keyed but thoroughly enjoyable.

### Deborah Abbott

SOURCE: A review of *Riding the Waves,* in *Booklist,* Vol. 89, No. 17, May 1, 1993, p. 1593.

Matt discovers on his first school assignment "charity visit" that his supposedly prim "client" Auntie Florrie (his deceased grandmother's lifelong friend) is a strong-minded woman who craves gossip about their English seaside village. Matt also finds that Auntie's long, fascinating life holds its share of sad secrets, including the birth of an out-of-wedlock son given up for adoption. For Matt, also adopted, this common tie strengthens their relationship. With Matt's help, Auntie Florrie, a recluse, rediscovers her community. And it is Auntie who introduces Matt to the surfing crowd (which knows her from the days of her chip shop) that Matt has secretly envied for months. How these two characters affect each other as well as the community results in a well-paced novel that has an upbeat and satisfying ending. A startlingly refreshing story about an intergenerational friendship.

### Kirkus Reviews

SOURCE: A review of *Riding the Waves,* in *Kirkus Reviews,* Vol. LXI, No. 9, May 1, 1993, p. 605.

The author of the well-received **Summer Witches** offers another complex, satisfying intergenerational relationship. Forced by school assignments to interview frail "Auntie" Florrie, Matt finds in the old woman not only a source of colorful town history but also a sturdy friend. Discovering that he's been enviously watching the local surfers, she takes him to the beach, introduces him, and cheers him on as he stubbornly tries to learn the sport; moreover, she helps him with his feelings about being adopted by sharing memories of her lover, killed at Dunkirk, and the child she bore and gave away. In return, Matt helps Auntie Florrie overcome her fear of leaving her house, and later sneaks into the hospital to visit her. When he sees that she's letting herself go, he administers an effective tonic by furiously chewing her out for ignoring her own self-reliant philosophy. Tomlinson gives Matt stable, sensitive parents and a sense of self-worth that's echoed and strengthened by his spirited older neighbor. A rich story, embellished with strong sentiment, genuine-sounding voices, and the pleasure of personal goals reached.

### 📖 THE ROPE CARRIER (1991)

### Marcus Crouch

SOURCE: A review of *The Rope Carrier,* in *The Junior Bookshelf,* Vol. 55, No. 6, December, 1991, p. 269.

Rope carriers, like flither pickers (the subject of Theresa Tomlinson's last novel) and nicker peckers (which make their appearance halfway through this one), may seem esoteric subjects for a children's novel, but don't worry. Ms. Tomlinson describes these forgotten crafts in terms of flesh-and-blood people and forces the reader to become involved in their fortunes. *The Rope Carrier* opens in the heart of the Peak of Derbyshire, where a whole village of rope-makers is established in the great cavern of Castleton. Minnie Dakin is born in the cave, and her dying Great Grandma predicts that she will carry the ropes, and walk for ever.' Certainly it seems that the fate of her sisters and herself will be to live and die in the ancient craft, but Netty leaves the cave to marry and Minnie follows her when Netty falls sick and a strong girl is needed to help her and her husband Josh, who is a nicker-pecker (a maker of files). The old hand craft is dying and Sheffield is in the throes of industrial revolution, aggravated by the enclosure of common lands.

The little country girl shows her strength in these turbulent times and even wins the reluctant goodwill of Josh's hard mother. When all seems lost, it is Minnie who comes up with the life-saving idea.

This is social and industrial history with a human face, and very convincing it is. The main characters are invented, but all the details of the story are supported by historical evidence and Ms. Tomlinson captures the atmosphere of change and stress. *The Flither Pickers* enjoyed a great advantage by using illustrations from the work of a contemporary photographer of genius. *The Rope Carrier* has reproductions from old topographical engravings, beautifully printed and attractive in themselves, but lacking human interest and insufficiently varied to serve as effective illustrations. This is nevertheless a most absorbing and attractive book, of great educational value but likely to be read with interest for its moving story and its vividly realized characters.

### Margery Fisher

SOURCE: A review of *The Rope Carrier,* in *Growing Point,* Vol. 30, No. 5, January, 1992, pp. 5641-642.

In a cave complex near Sheffield a whole settlement and a whole industry were contained, a life underground which attracted astonished visitors from a more prosperous world than the harsh subsistence life of the Dakins and their neighbours as they worked in cold and wet to prepare hemp with primitive machinery. The careful concrete detail of the book, backed by prints that take one straight back to the 1780s, is integrated in a narrative which concerns the Dakin family and in particular young Minnie, curious about the outside world and about a certain young man whom she guided through the lamp-lit mazes of the underground village. When Minnie was finally privileged to travel to Sheffield with her father and with the pack mules bearing their goods, the curiosity of childhood turned to something more bitter and difficult as she was forced to realise how grossly the working classes were exploited and how cruelly their search for justice could be punished. Riots halted by dragoons, prison and hunger, domestic service and family gatherings, are woven together in a terse, finely planned and vigorously expressed tale which gives an unforgettable picture of Derbyshire two centuries ago and of an extraordinary mode of life based on a specialised craft which depended on the impersonal facts of geology and climate and the abiding energy and tenacity of human beings.

### Geoff Dubber

SOURCE: A review of *The Rope Carrier,* in *School Library Journal,* Vol. 40, No. 1, February, 1992, p. 33.

This is another excellent read from the pen of Theresa Tomlinson. Set in the North Derbyshire/South Yorkshire area in the late eighteenth century, it is a story of artisan deprivation, economic and social hardships, and family loyalty. Minnie Dakin's family are skilled rope-makers living in the caves of the Castleton district, where whole families lived in cottages underground. The opening chapters draw on the atmosphere of these subterranean caverns and will capture the interest of the reader immediately. The story follows the fortunes and fortitudes of Minnie and her sister Netty, after Netty's marriage to Josh Eyre, when the two sisters find themselves in the dust and dirt of the developing metal industries of Sheffield.

Clearly and carefully written, based loosely on real people, and interspersed with some excellent contemporary lithographs of the area, this story will have wide appeal. The descriptive passages create an excellent atmosphere (one can almost smell the stench and filth of the debtor's prison). The main characters are well developed, and the plot moves along at an enjoyable pace. Recommended reading for the top classes of the junior school and the lower classes of the secondary school, and a good buy for the school library.

## 📖 THE FORESTWIFE (1993; U.S. edition, 1995)

### Publishers Weekly

SOURCE: A review of *The Forestwife*, in *Publishers Weekly*, Vol. 242, No. 7, February 13, 1993, p. 79.

Readers who wish to see Maid Marian as more than a glorified moll to the Merry Men will find much to relish in this ambitious, albeit flawed reworking of the Robin Hood legends. On the run from an arranged marriage, Mary de Holt is led by her devoted nurse Agnes to the isolated cottage of the dreaded Forestwife. As it happens, the old Forestwife—a skilled healer with vague connections to pre-Christian traditions—has recently died and Agnes takes on her job, with Mary (renamed Marian) as her assistant. The book teems with wholesomely rough-hewn details in the style of Brian Jacques's Redwall series: the inherited girdle of the Forestwife, for example, is "rich with the forest dyes of madder, blackberry, sorrel, and marigold." Also included are less photogenically folksy period particulars, such as the use of "scold's bridles" to muzzle outspoken women. Almost immediately, once-sheltered Marian becomes a sort of feminist guerilla leader, enlisting an evergrowing band of (mostly female) friends to fight injustice. She also finds the time to carry on a troubled romance with Robert of Loxley (who turns out to be old Agnes's son) and to make a none-too-startling discovery about her own parentage as well. Unfortunately, the tale never quite takes off; the spark of storytelling is overwhelmed by a heavy-handed and somewhat self-righteous social agenda.

### Deborah Stevenson

SOURCE: A review of *The Forestwife*, in *Bulletin of the Center for Children's Books*, Vol. 48, No. 7, March, 1995, pp. 252-53.

When Mary de Holt's uncle commands Mary to enter into an arranged marriage with "an elderly widower, who had rotten black stumps of teeth and smelled of sour ale and saddle grease," she rebels and runs away to live in the forest. Soon she is joined by her beloved old nurse, Agnes, and a few other strays—a pregnant local girl, a bevy of nuns—who find that the cruel economy and class structure of twelfth-century England have left them without any other place to go. Agnes becomes the Forestwife, a position of healer and wise woman handed down over the generations, and she renames Mary "Marian"; Marian feels herself challenged by but drawn to Agnes' son, Robert, who, with his fellow outcasts, fights against the oppressive landowners who crush the poor. Readers won't find the traditional Robin Hood and Maid Marian romance here, as Tomlinson's story focuses on the community of women and their relationship with nature; Marian, in fact, acknowledges that her destiny as Forestwife prevents her from marrying Robert. Tomlinson has romanticized the story in a different way: the idealized portrait of the nature-connected women, although attractive, is sentimental and more New Age than Middle Ages, the characters are flat and uncomplicatedly good or evil (and there's not a bad woman among them), and the plot owes much to melodrama (especially the revelation of the identity of Marian's mother). This is . . . an atmospheric read about a durable heroine.

### Susan L. Rogers

SOURCE: A review of *The Forestwife*, in *School Library Journal*, Vol. 41, No. 3, March, 1995, pp. 225-26.

Mary de Holt, 15, runs away from her uncle's manor to avoid marrying the elderly widower he has chosen for her, and her nurse, Agnes, follows. They take refuge in the endless, forbidding forest, and Mary finds it teeming with life—wretched folk on the run, defrocked nuns, and a mysterious prophetess, among others. Local lore tells of a fearsome witch, the Forestwife, who in truth is a woman skilled in herbs and potions who provides assistance to all those desperate enough to seek it. Agnes and Mary find her, but too late; she has died, and they soon take over her role. As Mary becomes more self-sufficient and assimilated into the forest, Agnes renames her Marian. Agnes's son, an outlaw who comes to them for healing and returns their kindness with poached game and stolen goods, becomes Robin Hood. . . . Tomlinson uses imagined details and historical facts and settings to create a . . . moving and believable story with a strong, competent heroine. In her afterword, she describes her research, the places and events linked to the legends, and the records concerning women's lives in medieval England. Plot elements involving the activities of King Richard the Lionhearted and his quarrelsome brother John give the story a place in time, while the occasional use of middle English words add to the ambiance.

## Mary L. Adams

SOURCE: A review of *The Forestwife,* in *Voice of Youth Advocates,* Vol. 18, No. 2, June, 1995, p. 100.

In Medieval England, Mary de Holt rebels at her uncle's order to marry an elderly, toothless, wealthy man so he can pay King Richard's taxes. She runs away blindly with little plan or preparation. She is followed and rescued by her old nurse, Agnes, who has foreseen this day and prepared for it. They flee to Barnsdale Forest in Sheffield where the myth of the terrible Forestwife protects all comers. They arrive just after the Forestwife's death, bury her, and Agnes assumes her title and role. The Forestwife is an herbalist, healer, and protector of all in the forest, good, not evil. Mary works hard and gains a well deserved reputation for saving people on the edge of the forest from wealthy landowners. The only thorn in their forest is Robert, Agnes's son who visits whenever he has become too wanted by King John's men or too hurt to harass them in King Richard's name. Jealousy turns to love, but Mary must assume the role of Forestwife on Agnes's death, and the Forestwife must never marry.

This exciting book is based on Medieval folk tales of the Green Lady and Green Man and Robin Hood. The premise of Maid Marian as a strong, capable, intelligent woman working hard, rescuing her people and Robin is well developed and makes a great tale. The book is full of strong, memorable characters, action, and vivid descriptions with an underlying love story. Mary is decisive, responsible, and honorable, yet adventurous and romantic. Girls will like her. Highly recommended.

## THE HERRING GIRLS (1994)

### George Hunt

SOURCE: A review of *The Herring Girls,* in *Books for Keeps,* No. 98, May, 1996, p. 13.

In a good, honest, unadorned voice reminiscent of that of Laura Ingalls Wilder, Dory Lythe, a nineteenth-century villager from the Yorkshire coast, recounts her experiences as a 13-year-old herring gutter. She's forced by family tragedy to work alongside the gangs of formidably tough Scottish girls who descend on Whitby every season. The story in itself is fascinating, but what makes the book indispensable (and wonderful value for money) are the reproductions of contemporary photographs of fishing village life taken by Frank Meadow Sutcliffe, the 'picture man' who also appears in the story. Very highly recommended for readers and browsers of all ages.

### S. M. Ashburner

SOURCE: A review of *The Herring Girls,* in *The Junior Bookshelf,* Vol. 60, No. 3, June, 1996, p. 126.

This historical novel is set around the turn of the last century; there is a wealth of social history detail. The story is set in Whitby and its neighbourhood, and focuses on a thirteen year old girl, Dory (Dorothy) who has to become a 'herring girl', to save her family from going to the workhouse.

The writer presents a world that has gone forever, vividly recreating the economic hardships which then faced the poor. Yet there is optimism in the togetherness of friends and neighbours. The text is supported by real photographs of the time. In fact, the characters in the book are inspired by the people photographed.

The characterisation and descriptions of scenes are good, and the plot is reasonably fast-moving. This is probably, however, a book only for the enthusiastic reader, because there is little excitement or humour.

## THE CELLAR LAD (1995)

### Marcus Crouch

SOURCE: A review of *The Cellar Lad,* in *The Junior Bookshelf,* Vol. 59, No. 3, June, 1995, pp. 110-11.

Theresa Tomlinson has made the fictional interpretation of the English industrial revolution her own, and this new story serves to reinforce an already impressive reputation. As always reality and invention are closely interwoven. In an introduction and a concluding note the author helps us to sort things out, identifying minor figures in history and separating them from others, creations of the writer, which carry equal conviction. Contemporary illustrations and quotations from sources of the time reinforce the message. A local poet of the time provides the chapter headings.

This time Tomlinson's scene is Sheffield in the days of the Chartists. Sheffield steel is not yet fully mechanized, but the craftsmen and labourers whose skill and courage make production possible are badly paid and treated. Still work is work, and Ben, who is intelligent and thoughtful, is glad to join his father as Cellar Lad at Dyson's Yard. Here he is a shrewd witness to the activities of workers and bosses; here he puts his mind to the mystery of 'Mary Ann' who acts for the workers in their fight for freedom and the vote. It would have been easy to lay on the suffering with a trowel, but here is a writer who sees her subject whole. Ben has fun as well as aggression. In time he will marry his Ruth and carry on family traditions in a society which makes progress very slowly.

Ms. Tomlinson's integrity is beyond question. Here, as in her earlier books, she is inclined to be historian first, novelist second, and this is perhaps the right choice. The story is strong and true. The players are somewhat lacking in individuality, historical symbols rather than persons. I admire and respect the book even while I, and some young readers, take less pleasure from the reading than from other, less authentic, historical novels.

## Linda Saunders

SOURCE: A review of *The Cellar Lad,* in *School Librarian,* Vol. 43, No. 3, August, 1995, p. 119.

It is easy to forget just how hard working people had to fight to establish the rights we now take for granted, for instance, the right to vote or to more humane working conditions. Most children also started working very young and for long hours at physically demanding jobs. Theresa Tomlinson's new novel brings this situation to life through the story of Ben Sterndale and his family who find themselves caught up in the fight to have only union labour employed, at reasonable rates, and the Chartist campaign for universal male suffrage. Her pictures of life in the middle of the nineteenth century are full of detail and very convincing.

Ben and his father live with his grandmother; his sister's husband, who is a grinder, knows he will die young and his sister fights a losing battle to keep her family going; young William is left an orphan when both his parents die; Ruth and her mother Jess struggle on together because her father was also a grinder and also died young. Each scene is vividly realised with lots of detail—wet washing, rag rugs, straw beds—that will help children get a feel for what life was like then. Anyone teaching nineteenth-century history could make great use of this book for reading extracts to children from 8 or 9 upwards. I am not so sure, however, that the book hangs together as a whole. The dialogue is not always convincing and the plot failed to involve. Eleven-year-olds and over who are into historical novels might enjoy it but it lacks the feeling of drama that makes such books so exciting.

## David Buckley

SOURCE: A review of *The Cellar Lad,* in *The Times Educational Supplement,* No. 4128, August 11, 1995, p. 17.

The year is 1842, and in the opening chapter of *The Cellar Lad,* young Ben Sterndale is enjoying his last day of freedom roaming through Ecclesall Woods before going to join his father in the steelworks. His friends the charcoal burners are still free spirits with an opportunity to roam and, as it turns out, agitate for the Chartists.

Despite this sense of loss, Ben enjoys his work at Dyson's Yard, where his father is the potman baking the clay crucibles for the molton steel. But then Ben is a good lad, at home among the camaraderie of men and women doing dangerous work and happy to be sent hither and thither.

Dyson's Yard is now Abbeydale Industrial Hamlet in the leafy southwest of Sheffield and Tomlinson is accurate with her local history. Her real subject is the rise of Chartism and the determination of the unions to protect their closed shop.

The book is something of a history lesson. The author doesn't avoid the horrors of the workhouse, and the debilitating diseases and shortened lifespans the steelworkers had to endure. The grinders, particularly, seemed doomed, inhaling a lethal dust and risking the grinding wheel exploding in their faces. With so little to look forward to, the grinders were the fiercest and most fearless in their battles with employers.

It is odd, then, that there is a strangely sanitised feel to this wholly worthy novel for children in late primaryearly secondary years. This is partly because Ben is so good, his home life so warm, and he is such a good child carer when his father and grandma take in a young waif destined for the workhouse.

It's also because the point of view is so firmly fixed in the workers' own perspective, there is a lack of conflicting opinion. When Ben's grandma, watching a Chartist procession, declares "They're decent hardworking folk . . . Why should they not have the vote?" there's no one to argue with her.

Poor Old Dyson setting on two non-union grinders and facing the destruction of his grinding hull is a fleshless victim and feeble enemy never brought to life.

Tomlinson does, however, present a strong sense of community, and handles pathos well. *The Cellar Lad—* helped by the inclusion of 19th-century etchings— succeeds in putting history on its feet.

## DANCING THROUGH THE SHADOWS (1997)

### Kirkus Reviews

SOURCE: A review of *Dancing through the Shadows,* in *Kirkus Reviews,* Vol. LXV, No. 18, September 15, 1997, p. 1464.

Ellen's mother has breast cancer, and Ellen (a British teenager), like her father and brother, is trying her very best to be supportive, even though her own worry is often overwhelming. Woven into the account of the mother's lumpectomy, chemotherapy, and radiation treatments is the story of the discovery of an ancient spring beneath a muddy, trash-strewn bank on the grounds of Ellen's school. Ellen and her best friend, Laura, begin helping Miss Corrigan, their history teacher (and, it turns out, a breast-cancer survivor), restore the site. "Corrie" believes that the site was once a sacred spot where travelers and those in search of healing drank and left offerings for "Ellen of the Ways," a pagan goddess later identified with the Christian St. Helen. As her family copes with the ups and downs of the protracted cancer treatment, Ellen finds solace at the well. The book ends with a ceremony marking the restoration of the spring and a family holiday celebrating the end of the treatments—and the hope that Ellen's mother is well. Gracefully avoiding didacticism, Tomlinson makes regular reference to the many sources of healing, finding it not only in modern medicine, but in ancient wisdom, the mind and imagination, and in the love and support of family and friends. Readers will be borne along by the lively pace and the first-person, dialogue-heavy style.

## Rosalyn Pierini

SOURCE: A review of *Dancing through the Shadows* in *School Library Journal,* Vol. 43, No. 11, November, 1997, p. 124.

One young woman's odyssey through adolescence after her mother is diagnosed with breast cancer is the subject of this British novel. Ellen is a prickly, but fundamentally normal teenager whose solipsistic universe is rocked by her mother's illness. The family's ordeal is realistically depicted as the woman first undergoes a lumpectomy and then must undergo both chemotherapy and radiation treatment. The family's stages of denial, grief, and acceptance are well drawn. Ellen finds the strength to face her mother's illness and mortality through her loving and supportive family, her friends, and her involvement in her school's dance program. A subplot has Ellen and a friend helping their eccentric history teacher unearth an ancient well near their school. Dubious about the project at first, Ellen finds it to be an important distraction. She learns that natural wells in the British countryside have historically been regarded as sources of life and renewal and were purported to have healing powers. The well becomes a life-affirming symbol for both the teen and her mother. This is a quiet, thoughtful story, and readers who have experienced a serious illness in their family will respond to Ellen's fears and uncertainties. The nicely interwoven archaeology and dance elements may also attract additional readers.

## *Publishers Weekly*

SOURCE: A review of *Dancing through the Shadows,* in *Publishers Weekly,* Vol. 244, No. 45, November 3, 1997, p. 86.

Themes of courage, survival and rebirth are explored in this story of a teenager coping with her mother's illness. Ellen's excitement over her year-end dance recital and summer vacation at the beach is cut short the day she learns her mother has breast cancer. Later that day, she discovers another secret: her history teacher, Miss Corrigan (Corrie) has found the site of an ancient, sacred well behind the school and has begun to unearth the remains. Tomlinson counterpoints lofty lore about the well and its healing powers with earthbound, sometimes blunt dialogues about the progression of Ellen's mother's disease ("The truth is, it's not really the thought of

feeling sick or tired that bothers me. It's not even the thought of my hair falling out. It's the needles! Lots of injections. That's my real dread," says Ellen's mother). The author's subtlety allows readers to draw their own conclusions from the parallels between the excavation of the well (in which Ellen takes part) and the resurrection of the heroine's lagging spirits and her mother's gradual recovery. Tomlinson addresses painful truths about the progression of cancer and at the same time celebrates the resiliency of body and spirit.

## Nancy Thackaberry

SOURCE: A review of *Dancing through the Shadows,* in *Voice of Youth Advocates,* Vol. 20, No. 6, February, 1998, pp. 391-92.

Ellen lovingly and courageously comforts her mother who is beginning a fight with breast cancer, and Ellen's father consoles them both when tensions arise during chemotherapy treatments and after a missed dance recital. Ellen also confronts her mixed emotions about boys, drinking, and her classmate, Laura, who is beginning to show more promise in the art of dance than Ellen had anticipated she would.

When Ellen's problems are too much to bear, she retreats to an ancient Celtic well that is being unearthed by a teacher from her school, where Ellen is in her second year. As she spends more time at the well helping in the digging, she learns that her teacher is a breast cancer survivor. Meanwhile, Ellen's family's bond strengthens as they challenge breast cancer together. Their love for one another becomes an additional, ethereal character that intertwines itself with the increasingly clearing water from the well.

What a relief to read a compassionate young adult novel that allows teens to test their adult emotions and responsibilities, without any sitcom-type, forced plot or joking. Some British terms and dialogue might confuse younger readers, but not enough to impede the story.

## CHILD OF THE MAY (1998)

### Kay Ecclestone

SOURCE: A review of *Child of the May,* in *School Librarian,* Vol. 46, No. 3, Autumn, 1998, p. 159.

A story of a young girl living in the forest at the time of King John, and her involvement with Robin Hood and his fellows. The author states in her note that the book is 'a strange mixture of ideas from the earliest Robin Hood ballads, life at the time of King John and my own special interest in women's history.' It may be a strange mixture but it works well. The main characters of the Robin Hood legends are here but seen from the viewpoint of Magda, an orphan brought up by the forestwife (Marian) who, obviously, does not see them as legends but merely as people who are a part of her life. Although I found myself trying to identify the 'Robin Hood' characters and tales, it is the portrayal of life in Sherwood Forest at this time that is the strength of this book. The characters, minor and major, interweave to create a true picture of this rural society. The author obviously knows her background well and has produced an engrossing tale that transports you into the past. Definitely a purchase for the secondary school library, and it made me hasten to obtain a copy of Theresa Tomlinson's earlier book on this theme, *The Forestwife.* Is there a better recommendation than that?

### Kirkus Reviews

SOURCE: A review of *Child of the May,* in *Kirkus Reviews,* Vol. LXVI, No. 19, October 1, 1998, p. 1465.

Revisiting the scene of **The Forestwife,** Tomlinson continues to recast the Robin Hood legend from the perspectives of strong women who play major roles in the action.

Magda, 15, is a Child of the May—conceived at the May festival by John and her mother, Emma, the latter of whom was murdered by an evil mercenary. She is bored and wants to see a world beyond the forest clearing where she lives with the elderly Marian, a healer and the woman who loves Robert, a moody, hooded hero who moves mysteriously through the country, and who delights in plots and plans to defeat his enemies. Magda gets her wish when John lets her masquerade as a boy, on a mission to bring home two ladies held for ransom at the sheriff's castle. Danger and unpredictability follow; Magda soon longs for the warmth and quiet of home, but as adventures ensue, she is a crucial cog in the fight for noble ladies and against the fearful mercenaries. She misreads some people and situations: subtle hints point out that she is mistaken to fear an ill, abandoned boy, and that she is sure to end up with Tom, her brave and patient suitor. She overcomes these mistakes and joyfully fulfills her destiny of becoming, someday, the forestwife. Tomlinson's language creates a powerful mood; readers will hope for more news of Magda, with her courage, strength, and skills.

### Cheri Estes

SOURCE: A review of *Child of the May,* in *School Library Journal,* Vol. 44, No. 11, November, 1998, p. 131.

This exciting sequel to **The Forestwife** features John and Emma's daughter Magda. A prologue explains that Emma has just been murdered by the evil mercenary Fitz-Ranulf, and John and Robert, the Hooded One, have taken the infant to Marian, the Forestwife, for care. The action then shifts to some 15 years later. The forest dwellers have been enlisted to help their friend Isabel, her mother, and a nun who have been imprisoned because of Isabel's refusal to marry FitzRanulf. When the men go to seek additional help, the forestwomen fear that they won't return in time and hatch a plan to save the women themselves. In the process, Magda kills FitzRanulf, avenging the death of her mother. A subplot involves a budding romance between Magda and Tom, a character featured in the earlier novel. Readers unfamiliar with the first book may initially be confused but once the action gets going, this story stands on its own. However, the swift climax and resolution are a bit unsatisfying, mostly because the author has created characters whom readers want to know more about. The epilogue hints at a sequel. This novel will please fans of Karen Cushman's *The Midwife's Apprentice* and send them looking for the prequel to this story if they haven't already read it.

### Anne Deifendeifer St. John

SOURCE: A review of *Child of the May,* in *The Horn Book Magazine,* Vol. LXXIV, No. 6, November-December, 1998, p. 742.

This sequel to **The Forestwife** is a coming-of-age story about motherless Magda, who was brought to the Forestwife's clearing as a baby. At fifteen, Magda finds life in the clearing full of drudgery, a succession of endless chores required to care for the ill and needy who flock there. She longs to seek adventure with her father and the rest of the band of outlaws living in the forest. Her wish is fulfilled when a crisis draws the outlaws to Nottingham Castle, and her father takes her along, disguised as a boy. Although the plot is well constructed, the novel's strength is in its fully realized setting and cast of strong-willed characters. At times sullen and stubborn, Magda is not always likable. When the young man she likes takes on the burden of caring for a leper boy, Magda objects, because her fear of the disease is greater than her compassion. But when she and several other women barricade themselves in Langden Manor in order to care for elderly Lady Matilda and her daughter Isabel, who have been imprisoned there without food or water by the king's mercenaries, Magda faces danger bravely and lifts her bow to defend another without hesitation. Inspired by the legend of Robin Hood, the novel characterizes Robert, the Hooded One, as a brooding, enigmatic man; John as a loyal fighter with a loving heart; and Marian as a pragmatic healer. Although a fine tale in its own right, the novel will be best appreciated by those who know **The Forestwife.**

Additional coverage of Tomlinson's life and career is contained in the following source published by The Gale Group: *Something about the Author,* Vol. 103.

# Mark Twain

## 1835-1910

(Pseudonym of Samuel Langhorne Clemens) American author of fiction, nonfiction, and plays; journalist.

Major works include *The Innocents Abroad; or, The New Pilgrims' Progress* (1869; British edition as Volume 1: *Innocents Abroad* and Volume 2: *The New Pilgrims' Progress,* 1870), *The Adventures of Tom Sawyer* (1876), *The Prince and the Pauper* (1881), *The Adventures of Huckleberry Finn, Tom Sawyer's Comrade* (1884), *A Connecticut Yankee in King Arthur's Court* (British edition as *A Yankee at the Court of King Arthur,* 1889).

Major works about the author include *The Innocent Eye: Childhood in Mark Twain's Fiction* (by Albert E. Stone, 1961*), Mark Twain: The Development of a Writer* (by Henry Nash Smith, 1962), *The Art of Mark Twain* (by William R. Gibson, 1976), *The Authentic Mark Twain: Literary Biography* (by Everett H. Emerson, 1984), *Satire or Evasion? Black Perspectives on Huckleberry Finn* (edited by James S. Leonard, Thomas A. Tenney, and Thadious M. Davis, 1992).

The following entry presents criticism on *The Adventures of Huckleberry Finn.*

## INTRODUCTION

Considered Mark Twain's masterpiece and one of America's greatest novels, *The Adventures of Huckleberry Finn* is also regarded as the first significant American work to break with European literary traditions. The novel's semiliterate narrator, vernacular dialogue, forthright depiction of the hypocrisy and brutality of American life, and unrefined frontier humor were sufficiently radical at the time of its publication to warrant the novel's banishment from numerous libraries as "the veriest trash." Though Twain would contend that *Huckleberry Finn* was an adult novel, its close association with *The Adventures of Tom Sawyer*—which Twain also considered an adult work, but which had been published as a book for boys—practically guaranteed that many young people would read it. Many critics took issue with this, as few felt the actions of a pipe-smoking, barefooted truant were worthy of the adulation or respect such a character could engender. An early review of the book in *Life* sarcastically noted such "hilarious results" as "an elevating and laughable description of how Huck killed a pig, smeared its blood on an axe and mixed in a little of his own hair, and then ran off, setting up a job on the old man and the community, and leading them to believe him murdered. This little joke can be repeated by any smart boy for the amusement of his fond parents." These very improprieties, however, eventually became the basis for critical acclaim and initiated the divergence of the

American novel from European conventions. *Huckleberry Finn* soon became prized for its re-creation of the Antebellum South, its insights into slavery, its depiction of adolescent life, and, throughout, its irreverence and compassion. Ernest Hemingway contended, "All modern American literature comes from one book by Mark Twain called *Huckleberry Finn* . . . . There was nothing before. There has been nothing as good since."

### Biographical Information

Born Samuel Langhorne Clemens in Florida, Missouri, in 1835, Twain grew up with his family of three brothers and two sisters in Hannibal, a small town on the Mississippi River. When Twain was twelve, the death of his father put an end to his formal education and he set to work as a printer's apprentice in the office of a local newspaper. But life was not all tragedy in Hannibal; much of it was an idyll of youth that Twain would replay the rest of his life through his fiction. Young Twain used the river and its banks as his playground, constructing rafts and discovering swimming holes. In 1857, he began an apprenticeship as a riverboat pilot, and earned his pilot's license two years later. He joined the Confederate Army during the Civil War, and by 1862, he began writing humourous pieces, as well as conventional news for various newspapers. Throughout the 1860s, Twain continued traveling and writing and publishing comic tales and sketches, many of which were collected and printed in books such as *The Celebrated Jumping Frog of Calaveras County, and Other Sketches* (1867), *The Innocents Abroad,* and *Roughing It* (1872). Twain published his first solo novel for boys, *The Adventures of Tom Sawyer,* in 1876. Regarded as a childhood classic, the novel and its eponymous youth quickly entered the American idiom.

Twain began writing *The Adventures of Huckleberry Finn* immediately after the publication of *Tom Sawyer. Huckleberry Finn* was intended as a sequel to the popular children's book, which chronicled the adventures of a mischievous but good-hearted boy and his companions in a Mississippi Valley town modeled after Twain's boyhood home of Hannibal. According to Twain, Huck, a minor figure in the earlier story, was inspired by real-life Tom Blankenship, and Twain's description of Tom in his *Autobiography* could serve equally well for Huck: "He was ignorant, unwashed, insufficiently fed; but he had as good a heart as ever any boy had. His liberties were totally unrestricted. He was the only really independent person—boy or man—in the community." Twain rapidly completed about four hundred pages of the narrative in the summer of 1876. He then lost interest in the story and set it aside, writing to his friend and editor William Dean Howells: "I like it only tolerably well, as far as I have got, and may possibly pigeonhole or burn the ms. when it is done." The novel remained unfinished for the next seven years while Twain devoted the bulk of his creative energy to *A Tramp Abroad* (1880), *The Prince and the Pauper,* and numerous minor literary projects. In 1883, Twain's enthusiasm for *Huckleberry Finn* suddenly returned, perhaps prompted by an 1882 visit to Hannibal, and he completed the novel in a few months, commenting, "modesty compels me to say it's a rattling good one." Dissatisfied with his previous publishers, Twain resolved to publish *Huckleberry Finn* himself in time for the Christmas season of 1884. British publication proceeded on schedule in early December, but American publication was delayed until the following February by the discovery of an obscene alteration to one of the illustrations. The incident was widely publicized and, according to Michael Patrick Hearn, "tainted the novel's reputation long before its official publication."

Initial reception of *Huckleberry Finn* was mixed, but most commentators agreed with the *Springfield Republican* that "the trouble with Mr. Clemens is that he has no reliable sense of propriety." The public library of Concord, Massachusetts, banned the novel "as rough, coarse, and inelegant, dealing with a series of experiences not elevating, the whole book being more suited to the slums than to intelligent, respectable people." Commentators note that although Twain was hurt by the typically vicious tone of critical response, he professed

to be undisturbed by the reviews and by the Concord Library's well-publicized banishment, which he called "a rattling tip-top puff" that "will sell 25,000 copies for us sure." His lack of concern proved well-founded; critical opinion had no effect on the novel's popular success, which was overwhelming. *Huckleberry Finn* became the best-selling book of Twain's career, and has remained one of the most popular American novels ever written.

## Plot and Major Characters

*Huckleberry Finn* records Huck's adventures as he accompanies Jim, an escaped slave, down the Mississippi in a quest for freedom. Amid abundant social satire, the narrative focuses on Huck's developing moral independence from the teachings of his society, and critics concur that *Huckleberry Finn* far surpasses *Tom Sawyer* in the depth of both its main character and its themes. The opening of the novel finds Huck having somewhat adapted to the "sivilizin'" influences of Widow Douglas and even attending school. But one day Huck learns that his alcoholic father, Pap, who he had not seen for a year, has returned to St. Petersburg. Fearful that his father will take his share of the treasure recovered by him and Tom Sawyer (in *Tom Sawyer*), Huck entrusts his portion with Judge Thatcher. True to form, Pap does take Huck off to the woods where he beats him, but Huck manages to escape, making it look as though he is dead. The rest of the book is an elegy to the river and the freedom it represents. On the island where Huck has escaped to, he discovers Jim, a runaway slave belonging to Widow Douglas's sister, Miss Watson. They stay there together for a few days and then Huck returns to the mainland in disguise to learn that his, Huck's, death has been attributed to Jim. Returning to the island, Huck tells the events to Jim, who decides to escape to the North. Huck accompanies him on a raft, but it is not long before they crash into a riverboat. Jim disappears as Huck saves himself. On shore, Huck is taken in by the Grangerford family, representatives of the old debased southern aristocracy, who are continually feuding with their neighbors, the Sheperdsons. Huck once again discovers Jim, hiding in the woods, and together the two escape to the river again, leaving the feuding families shooting at each other on shore. More adventures ensue when the duo encounter the Duke and the King, two con-artist carpetbaggers who are hoping to swindle a family's inheritance by posing as the deceased's long-lost brother. Ultimately the Duke turns Jim in for reward money, but Huck once again plans to help him escape. This time, however, Tom Sawyer is called in to help. Tom develops a convoluted scheme to set Jim free, a scheme made unnecessary when Miss Watson grants Jim his freedom on her deathbed. They also learn that Huck's father, too, has died. In the end, Tom's Aunt Sally offers to adopt Huck, but he realizes that the process of becoming civilized is not an enjoyable one.

Though they start with Huck's life with Widow Douglas and some Tom Sawyer tomfoolery, Huck's adventures really begin when he stages own murder in order to escape from his abusive father. Huck learns that Jim has run away from his owner because she agreed to sell him to a slave trader from New Orleans. Huck and Jim's journey is generally considered a symbolic repudiation of the corrupt society of the Mississippi Valley, and the novel as a whole is often regarded as a condemnation of civilization. At the start of their journey to a hoped-for freedom for Jim, Huck's attitudes toward the escaped slave are those of the prevailing white majority. He considers Jim his intellectual and social inferior and has little conception of him as a human being. Through a series of episodes strengthening Huck's awareness of Jim as an individual, however, Huck progresses from uncritical acceptance of traditional attitudes and morals to an independent moral stance in direct defiance to social conventions. Huck ruminates on the religious implications of what he has done, that is, setting free someone else's "property," and decides he would rather "go to hell for Jim" than see his friend lose his freedom. It is only when the plot veers from this progress toward the end that some critics feel the story suffers. The concluding chapters, in which Jim is captured and locked up at the Phelps' farm and Tom Sawyer returns to the story to mastermind his escape, have fueled a seemingly endless controversy over Twain's intention. Critical dissatisfaction generally centers on the novel's abrupt change of tone: Huck and Jim's quest for freedom is suddenly superceded by a farcical parody of romantic literature, as Tom designs an elaborate escape based on such adventure stories as *The Count of Monte Cristo*. The action is dominated by Tom, whose values are distinctly those of the society against which Huck and Jim have rebelled, and their journey is rendered pointless by the deathbed repentance of Miss Watson, who grants Jim's freedom.

## Critical Reception

Critical reaction to *Huckleberry Finn* has gradually evolved from initial hostility to nearly universal acclaim. Several decades after the book's publication, critical opinion began to swing more strongly in its favor. In 1919, the novelist and critic Waldo Frank characterized the work as "a voice of American chaos, the voice of a precultural epoch," and dubbed its protagonist "the American epic hero." That same year, H. L. Mencken called *Huckleberry Finn* "one of the great masterpieces of the world." He continued, "I believe that it will be read by human beings of all ages, not as a solemn duty but for the honest love of it, and over and over again, long after every book written in America between the years 1800 and 1860 . . . has disappeared entirely. . . ." Modern critics generally agree that the artistry of *Huckleberry Finn* far surpasses that of Twain's other works, which were more highly admired during his lifetime. Although the book lacks a formal structure, being composed of a series of loosely connected episodes, the narrative achieves a high degree of unity through the repetition and interplay of various themes and motifs. Many critics find Huck's narrative voice to be the nov-

el's most unique and distinctive aspect. Huck's naïve, unadorned observations provide much of the book's characteristic humor and irony, and through Huck's innocent eyes, Twain was able to present a fresh vision of American life.

Some debate has continued over whether or not the work is considered appropriate for younger audiences, particularly because of the controversy over its racial implications and the rebelliousness of its young protagonist. John H. Wallace contended that *Huckleberry Finn* "is the most grotesque example of racist trash ever written," and that it continues to cause black children "embarrassment about their heritage." He continued, "It contributes to their feelings of low self esteem and to the white students' disrespect for black people. . . . *Huckleberry Finn* is an American classic for no other reason than that it ridicules blacks to a greater extent than any other book given our children to read." Julius Lester found the book parlous not only for its denigration of black people, but also for its false portrayal of adolescence: "There is no more powerful evocation in American literature of the eternal adolescent than *Adventures of Huckleberry Finn*. It is fantasy adolescence, however. Not only is it free of the usual adolescent problems caused by awakening sexuality, but also Huck has a verbal cleverness, beyond the capability of an actual fourteen-year-old. In the person of Huck, the novel exalts verbal cleverness, lying and miseducation." Lester concluded that the novel is ultimately "a dismal portrait of the white male psyche." Margery Fisher took a two-fold approach to the work: "Read as an allegory of questing man, it is not a children's book; read as a funny, touching, rambling, shrewd and honest story of boyhood, it is."

A frequent topic of critical discussion is the role played by Jim in Twain's novel. Although it is generally agreed that Jim's emancipation from slavery is of secondary importance in the narrative to Huck's emancipation from society, critics disagree over Jim's exact function in the novel. Several critics have argued that Jim's purpose is solely to provide opportunities for the development of Huck's character; it is Jim's place in society as an escaped slave that precipitates Huck's moral crisis, as he attempts to reconcile his knowledge of Jim as a human being with the teachings of his society. Other critics have contended that one of the book's dominant themes is Huck's search for a father figure, and that through their travels Jim gradually becomes Huck's father-surrogate. The figure of Jim has prompted further controversy in recent years by critics who have argued that *Huckleberry Finn* is replete with racial stereotypes and that Jim in particular is portrayed as a "comic stage Negro" similar to the ignorant and gullible characters in nineteenth-century minstrel shows. Frederick Woodard and Donnarae MacCann wrote: "The depiction of Blacks in *Huck Finn* matches those of numerous minstrel plays in which Black characters are portrayed as addlebrained, boastful, superstitious, childish and lazy. These depictions are not used to poke fun at white attitudes about Black people; Jim is portrayed as a kindly comic who *does* act foolishly." The African-American novelist Ralph Ellison noted that Jim was "a white man's inadequate portrait of a slave." Twain apologists have countered that Jim is one of the few adults in the novel portrayed in a favorable light, and that his exhibition of such qualities as compassion, logic, and self-sacrifice forms a distinct and obvious contrast to the callousness, gullibility, and greed demonstrated by the novel's white characters.

The book's conclusion provides as much difficulty for some critics as the race issue does for others. Although such critics as Lionel Trilling and T. S. Eliot have defended the conclusion as formally appropriate, Bernard DeVoto has asserted that "in the whole reach of the English novel there is no more abrupt or chilling descent." One of the most vehement detractors of the novel's conclusion has been Leo Marx, who has maintained that the ending "jeopardizes the significance of the entire novel." In submitting to Tom's childish sense of adventure, Marx argued, Huck and Jim lose the dignity and individuality that they had developed on the river. Furthermore, as Miss Watson is an outstanding example of the hypocrisy of valley society, her freeing of Jim "accomplishes a vindication of persons and attitudes symbolically repudiated when [Huck and Jim] set forth downstream." Marx considered the conclusion a failure on the part of Twain, who, "having revealed the tawdry nature of the great valley, yielded to its essential complacency." Other critics have attributed less significance to the concluding sequence, maintaining that the entire episode is merely a technical device allowing Twain both to further his attack on romanticism and to conclude the novel, and that Huck's final decision to "light out for the Territory" signals his successful emancipation from conventional society. Many critics, however, have agreed with James M. Cox, who considered Huck's initiation into society, rather than his escape from it, to be the book's dominant theme, and therefore found "an inexorable and crushing logic inherent in the ending."

While scholars debate the philosophical issues and themes raised in what they consider one of the masterpieces of American literature, the novel's popularity continues. Justin Kaplan, in *The New York Times Book Review*, wrote, "No other major book has been so vigorously challenged, and over so many years, as *Adventures of Huckleberry Finn*. Yet it manages somehow, through its humor, lyricism and distinctive, even revolutionary narrative voice, not only to survive but to transcend its author's definition of a classic: 'A book that people praise but don't read.'"

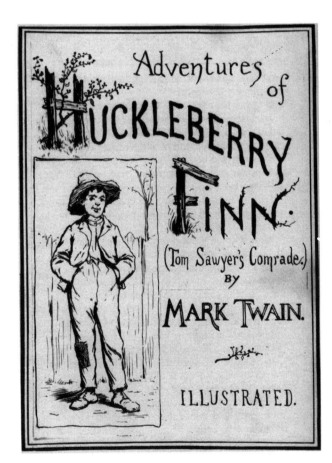

*Cover illustration from the first edition of* The Adventures of Huckleberry Finn, *written by Mark Twain, 1884. Illustrated by E. W. Kemble.*

## COMMENTARY

### Mark Twain

SOURCE: A letter to W. D. Howells, July 21, 1883, in *The Adventures of Huckleberry Finn: An Authoritative Text, Backgrounds and Sources, Criticism, Second Edition,* edited by Sculley Bradley, Richmond Croom Beatty, E. Hudson Long, and Thomas Cooley, W. W. Norton & Company, Inc., 1977, p. 283.

[*Twain began writing* **The Adventures of Huckleberry Finn** *in 1867 at Quarry Farm near Elmira, NY. Yet, with half the book written, Twain was dissatisfied, and stated, 'I like it only tolerably well, as far as I have got, and may possibly pigeonhole or burn the ms when it is done." He became involved in other projects until 1882, when he returned to the* **Huckleberry Finn** *manuscript. In the following letter written to writer and friend W. D. Howells on July 21, 1883, Twain discusses his enthusiasm for writing* **Huckleberry Finn**. *The book was finished by the Spring, 1884. The book was first published in England in December, 1884. The first U.S. edition appeared in February, 1885.*]

I haven't piled up MS so in years as I have done since we came here to the farm three weeks & a half ago. Why, it's like old times, to step straight into the study, damp from the breakfast table, & sail right in & sail right on, the whole day long, without thought of running short of stuff or words. I wrote 4000 words to-day & I touch 3000 & upwards pretty often, & don't fall below 2600 on any working day. And when I get fagged out, I lie abed a couple of days & read & smoke, & then go it again for 6 or 7 days. I have finished one small book, & am away along in a big one that I half-finished two or three years ago. I expect to complete it in a month or six weeks or two months more. And *I* shall *like* it, whether anybody else does or not. It's a kind of companion to Tom Sawyer. There's a raft episode from it in second or third chapter of Life on the Mississippi.

## Mark Twain

SOURCE: A letter to W. D. Howells in Boston, April 8, 1884, in *Mark Twain's Letters,* Vol. II, arranged with comment by Albert Bigelow Paine, Harper & Brothers Publishers, 1917, pp. 442-43.

[*Twain wrote the following letter to Howells, who agreed to read the proofs of* **The Adventures of Huckleberry Finn.** *After reading the proofs, Howells later responded, "If I had written half as good a book as* **Huck Finn** *I shouldn't ask anything better than to read the proofs; even as it is, I don't, so send them on; they will always find me somewhere."*]

My Dear Howells,—It took my breath away, and I haven't recovered it yet, entirely—I mean the generosity of your proposal to read the proofs of **Huck Finn.**

Now if you *mean* it, old man—if you are in *earnest*—proceed, in God's name, and be by me forever blest. I cannot conceive of a rational man deliberately piling such an atrocious job upon himself; but if there is such a man and you be that man, why then *pile it on.* It will cost me a pang every time I think of it, but this anguish will be eingebüsst to me in the joy and comfort I shall get out of the not having to read the verfluchtete proofs myself. But if you have repented of your augenblicklichen Tobsucht and got back to calm cold reason again, I won't hold you to it unless I find I have got you down in writing somewhere. Herr, I would not read the proof of one of my books for any fair and reasonable sum whatever, if I could get out of it.

The proof-reading on the P & P cost me the last rags of my religion.

## William Ernest Henley

SOURCE: A review of *The Adventures of Huckleberry Finn,* in *The Critical Response to Mark Twain's "Huckleberry Finn,"* edited by Laurie Champion, Greenwood Press, 1991, p. 21.

[*The following review was originally published in* Athenaeum, *December 27, 1884.*]

For some time past Mr. Clemens has been carried away by the ambition of seriousness and fine writing. In **Huckleberry Finn** he returns to his right mind, and is again the Mark Twain of old time. It is such a book as he, and he only, could have written. It is meant for boys; but there are few men (we should hope) who, once they take it up, will not delight in it. It forms a companion, or sequel, to *Tom Sawyer.* Huckleberry Finn, as everybody knows, is one of Tom's closest friends; and the present volume is a record of the adventures which befell him soon after the event which made him a person of property and brought Tom Sawyer's story to a becoming conclusion. They are of the most surprising and delightful kind imaginable, and in the course of them we fall in with a number of types of character of singular freshness and novelty, besides being schooled in half a dozen extraordinary dialects—the Pike County dialect in all its forms, the dialect of the Missouri negro, and "the extremest form of the backwoods South-Western dialect," to wit. Huckleberry, it may be noted, is stolen by his disreputable father, to escape from whom he contrives an appearance of robbery and murder in the paternal hut, goes off in a canoe, watches from afar the townsfolk hunting for his dead body, and encounters a runaway negro—Miss Watson's Jim—an old particular friend of Tom Sawyer and himself. With Jim he goes south down the river, and is the hero of such scrapes and experiences as make your mouth water (if you have ever been a boy) to read of them. We do not purpose to tell a single one; it would be unfair to author and reader alike. We shall content ourselves with repeating that the book is Mark Twain at his best, and remarking that Jim and Huckleberry are real creations, and the worthy peers of the illustrious Tom Sawyer.

## Brander Matthews

SOURCE: A review of *The Adventures of Huckleberry Finn,* in *The Critical Response to Mark Twain's "Huckleberry Finn,"* edited by Laurie Champion, Greenwood Press, 1991, pp. 22-4.

[*The following review was originally published in* the London Saturday Review, *January 31, 1885.*]

The boy of to-day is fortunate indeed, and of a truth, he is to be congratulated. While the boy of yesterday had to stay his stomach with the unconscious humour of *Sanford and Merlon,* the boy of to-day may get his fill of fun and of romance and of adventures in *Treasure Island* and in *Tom Brown* and in **Tom Sawyer,** and now in a sequel to **Tom Sawyer,** wherein Tom himself appears in the very nick of time, like a young god from the machine. Sequels of stories which have been widely popular are not a little risky. **Huckleberry Finn** is a sharp exception to this general rule. Although it is a sequel, it is quite as worthy of wide popularity as **Tom Sawyer.** An American critic once neatly declared that the late G. P. P. James hit the bull's-eye of success with his first shot, and that for ever thereafter he went on firing through the same hole. Now this is just what Mark Twain has not done. **Huckleberry Finn** is not an attempt to do *Tom Sawyer* over again. It is a story quite as unlike its predecessor as it is like. Although Huck Finn appeared first in the earlier book, and although Tom Sawyer reappears in the later, the scenes and the characters are otherwise wholly different. Above all, the atmosphere of the story is different. *Tom Sawyer* was a tale of boyish adventure in a village in Missouri, on the Mississippi river, and it was told by the author. *Huckleberry Finn* is autobiographic; it is a tale of boyish adventure along the Mississippi river told as it appeared to Huck Finn. There is not in *Huckleberry Finn* any one scene quite as funny as those in which Tom Sawyer gets his friends to whitewash the fence for him, and then uses the spoils thereby acquired to attain the highest situation of the Sunday school the next morning. Nor is there any distinction quite as thrilling as that awful moment in the cave when the boy and the girl are lost in the darkness, and when Tom Sawyer suddenly sees a human hand bearing a light, and then finds that the hand is the hand of Indian Joe, his one mortal enemy; we have always thought that the vision of the hand in the cave in *Tom Sawyer* is one of the very finest things in the literature of adventure since Robinson Crusoe first saw a single footprint in the sand of the seashore. But though *Huckleberry Finn* may not quite reach these two highest points of *Tom Sawyer,* we incline to the opinion that the general level of the later story is perhaps higher than that of the earlier. For one thing, the skill with which the character of Huck Finn is maintained is marvellous. We see everything through his eyes—and they are his eyes and not a pair of Mark Twain's spectacles. And the comments on what he sees are his comments—the comments of an ignorant, superstitious, sharp, healthy boy, brought up as Huck Finn had been brought up; they are not speeches put into his mouth by the author. One of the most artistic things in the book—and that Mark Twain is a literary artist of a very high order all who have considered his later writings critically cannot but confess—one of the most artistic things in *Huckleberry Finn* is the sober self-restraint with which Mr. Clemens lets Huck Finn set down, without any comment at all, scenes which would have afforded the ordinary writer matter for endless moral and political and sociological disquisition. We refer particularly to the account of the Grangerford-Shepherdson feud, and of the shooting of Boggs by Colonel Sherburn. Here are two incidents of the rough old life of the South-Western States, and of the Mississippi Valley forty or fifty years ago, of the old life which is now rapidly passing away under the influence of advancing civilization and increasing commercial prosperity, but which has not wholly disappeared even yet, although a slow revolution in public sentiment is taking place. The Grangerford-Shepherdson feud is a vendetta as deadly as any Corsican could wish, yet the parties to it were honest, brave, sincere, good Christian people, probably people of deep religious sentiment. Not the less we see them taking their guns to church, and, when occasion serves, joining in what is little better than a general massacre. The killing of Boggs by Colonel Sherburn is told with equal sobriety and truth; and the later scene in which Colonel Sherburn cows and lashes the mob which has set out to lynch him is one

of the most vigorous bits of writing Mark Twain has done.

In *Tom Sawyer* we saw Huckleberry Finn from the outside; in the present volume we see him from the inside. He is almost as much a delight to any one who has been a boy as was Tom Sawyer. But only he or she who has been a boy can truly enjoy this record of his adventures, and of his sentiments and of his sayings. Old maids of either sex will wholly fail to understand him or to like him, or to see his significance and his value. Like Tom Sawyer, Huck Finn is a genuine boy; he is neither a girl in boy's clothes like many of the modern heroes of juvenile fiction, nor is he a "little man," a full-grown man cut down; he is a boy, just a boy, only a boy. And his ways and modes of thought are boyish. As Mr. F. Anstey understands the English boy, and especially the English boy of the middle classes, so Mark Twain understands the American boy, and especially the American boy of the Mississippi Valley of forty or fifty years ago. The contrast between Tom Sawyer, who is the child of respectable parents, decently brought up, and Huckleberry Finn, who is the child of the town drunkard, not brought up at all, is made distinct by a hundred artistic touches, not the least natural of which is Huck's constant reference to Tom as his ideal of what a boy should be. When Huck escapes from the cabin where his drunken and worthless father had confined him, carefully manufacturing a mass of very circumstantial evidence to prove his own murder by robbers, he cannot help saying, "I did wish Tom Sawyer was there, I knowed he would take an interest in this kind of business, and throw in the fancy touches. Nobody could spread himself like Tom Sawyer in such a thing as that." Both boys have their full share of boyish imagination; and Tom Sawyer, being given to books, lets his imagination run on robbers and pirates and genies, with a perfect understanding with himself that, if you want to get fun out of this life, you must never hesitate to make believe very hard; and, with Tom's youth and health, he never finds it hard to make believe and to be a pirate at will, or to summon an attendant spirit, or to rescue a prisoner from the deepest dungeon 'neath the castle moat. But in Huck this imagination has turned to superstition; he is a walking repository of the juvenile folklore of the Mississippi Valley— a folklore partly traditional among the white settlers but largely influenced by intimate association with the negroes. When Huck was in his room at night all by himself waiting for the signal Tom Sawyer was to give him at midnight, he felt so lonesome he wished he was dead:

> The stars was shining and the leaves rustled in the woods ever so mournful; and I heard an owl, away off, who-whooing about somebody that was dead, and a whippowill and a dog crying about somebody that was going to die; and the wind was trying to whisper something to me, and I couldn't make out what it was, and so it made the cold shivers run over me. Then away out in the woods I heard that kind of a sound that a ghost makes when it wants to tell about something that's on its mind and can't make

itself understood, and so can't rest easy in its grave, and has to go about that way every night grieving. I got so downhearted and scared I did wish I had some company. Pretty soon a spider went crawling up my shoulders, and I flipped it off and it lit in the candle; and before I could budge it was all shrivelled up. I didn't need anybody to tell me that that was an awful bad sign and would fetch me some bad luck, so I was scared and most shook the clothes off me. I got up and turned around in my tracks three times and crossed my breast every time; and then I tied up a little lock of my hair with a thread to keep witches away. But I hadn't no confidence. You do that when you've lost a horse-shoe that you've found, instead of nailing it up over the door, but I hadn't ever heard anybody say it was any way to keep off bad luck when you'd killed a spider.

The romantic side of Tom Sawyer is shown in most delightfully humorous fashion in the account of his difficult devices to aid in the easy escape of Jim, a runaway negro. Jim is an admirably drawn character. There have been not a few fine and firm portraits of negroes in recent American fiction, of which Mr. Cable's Bras-Coupé in the *Grandissimes* is perhaps the most vigorous, and Mr. Harris's Mingo and Uncle Remus and Blue Dave are the most gentle. Jim is worthy to rank with these; and the essential simplicity and kindliness and generosity of the Southern negro have never been better shown than here by Mark Twain. Nor are Tom Sawyer and Huck Finn and Jim the only fresh and original figures in Mr. Clemens's new book; on the contrary, there is scarcely a character of the many introduced who does not impress the reader at once as true to life—and therefore as new, for life is so varied that a portrait from life is sure to be as good as new. That Mr. Clemens draws from life, and yet lifts his work from the domain of the photograph to the region of art, is evident to any one who will give his work the honest attention which it deserves. . . . No one, we venture to say, who reads this book will readily forget the Duke and the King, a pair of as pleasant "confidence operators" as one may meet in a day's journey, who leave the story in the most appropriate fashion, being clothed in tar and feathers and ridden on a rail. Of the more broadly humorous passages—and they abound—we have not left ourselves space to speak; they are to the full as funny as in any of Mark Twain's other books; and, perhaps, in no other book has the humorist shown so much artistic restraint, for there is in *Huckleberry Finn* no mere "comic copy," no straining after effect; one might almost say that there is no waste word in it. Nor have we left ourselves room to do more than say a good word for the illustrations, which, although slight and unpretending, are far better than those to be found in most of Mark Twain's books. For one thing, they actually illustrate—and this is a rare quality in illustrations nowadays. They give the reader a distinct idea of the Duke and the King, of Jim and of Colonel Sherburn, of the Shepherdsons and the Grangerfords. They are all by one artist, Mr. E. W. Kemble, hitherto known to us only as the illustrator of the *Thompson Street Poker Club,* an amusing romance of highly-coloured life in New York.

## Robert Bridges

SOURCE: "Mark Twain's Blood-Curdling Humor," in *The Merrill Studies in Huckleberry Finn,* compiled by John C. Gerber, Charles E. Merrill Publishing Company, 1971, pp. 7-8.

*[The following review was originally published in* Life *magazine, February 26, 1885.]*

Mark Twain is a humorist or nothing. He is well aware of this fact himself, for he prefaces the *Adventures of Huckleberry Finn* with a brief notice, warning persons in search of a moral, motive or plot that they are liable to be prosecuted, banished or shot. This is a nice little artifice to scare off the critics—a kind of "trespassers on these grounds will be dealt with according to law."

However, as there is no penalty attached, we organized a search expedition for the humorous qualities of this book with the following hilarious results:

A very refined and delicate piece of narration by Huck Finn, describing his venerable and dilapidated "pap" as afflicted with delirium tremens, rolling over and over, "kicking things every which way," and "saying there was devils ahold of him." This chapter is especially suited to amuse the children on long, rainy afternoons.

An elevating and laughable description of how Huck killed a pig, smeared its blood on an axe and mixed in a little of his own hair, and then ran off, setting up a job on the old man and the community, and leading them to believe him murdered. This little joke can be repeated by any smart boy for the amusement of his fond parents.

A graphic and romantic tale of a Southern family feud, which resulted in an elopement and from six to eight choice corpses.

A polite version of the "Giascutus" story, in which a nude man, striped with the colors of the rainbow, is exhibited as "The King's Cameleopard; or, The Royal Nonesuch." This is a good chapter for Lenten parlor entertainments and church festivals.

A sidesplitting account of a funeral, enlivened by a "sick melodeum," a "long-legged undertaker," and a rat episode in the cellar.

## *Boston Transcript*

SOURCE: An excerpt from *The Merrill Studies in Huckleberry Finn,* compiled by John C. Gerber, Charles E. Merrill Publishing Company, 1971, p. 8.

*[Shortly after its publication in America,* **The Adventures of Huckleberry Finn** *sparked controversy*

*in Concord, Massachusetts, where it was removed from the shelves of the Concord Public Library. The following notice appeared in the* Boston Transcript, *March 17, 1885.*]

The Concord (Mass.) Public Library committee has decided to exclude Mark Twain's latest book from the library. One member of the committee says that, while he does not wish to call it immoral, he thinks it contains but little humor, and that of a very coarse type. He regards it as the veriest trash. The librarian and the other members of the committee entertain similar views, characterizing it as rough, coarse and inelegant, dealing with a series of experiences not elevating, the whole book being more suited to the slums than to intelligent, respectable people.

## Mark Twain

SOURCE: A letter to Charles Webster, March 18, 1885, in *The Critical Response to Mark Twain's "Huckleberry Finn,"* edited by Laurie Champion, Greenwood Press, 1991, p. 15.

[*In response to Concord Public Library's banning of* **Huckleberry Finn** *in March, 1885, Twain wrote the following letter, dated March 18, 1885, to his friend and publisher Charles Webster.*]

Dear Charley—

The committee of the Public Library of Concord, Mass., have given us a rattling tip-top puff which will go into every paper in the country. They have expelled Huck from their library as "trash and suitable only for the slums." That will sell 25,000 copies for us, sure.

## Boston Commonwealth

SOURCE: "Twain Laughs in His Sleeves," in *The Critical Response to Mark Twain's "Huckleberry Finn,"* edited by Laurie Champion, Greenwood Press, 1991, p. 15.

[*The following article was originally published March 21, 1885.*]

The Concord Library managers have pronounced **Huckleberry Finn** (Mark Twain's latest book) as trivial, of a low wit, immoral, and all that, and have withdrawn it from circulation. But why don't these good people do all this quietly, without getting into the newspapers with their disapprobation? We venture to say every boy and girl in Concord will make a point to get that book and read it. They will want to know if it is indeed an improper book. As for Twain himself, he is probably laughing in his sleeves at the advertisement his book has received in Concord, with every newspaper referring to it. There are some things best accom-

plished by quiet suppression, and a bad book is one of them.

## The Critic

SOURCE: An excerpt from *The Merrill Studies in Huckleberry Finn,* compiled by John C. Gerber, Charles E. Merrill Publishing Company, 1971, pp. 8-9.

[*The following article was reprinted in the Spring-field* Republican *as quoted in* The Critic, *March 28, 1885.*]

The Concord Public Library committee deserves well of the public by their action in banishing Mark Twain's new book, **Huckleberry Finn,** on the ground that it is trashy and vicious. It is time that this influential pseudonym should cease to carry into homes and libraries unworthy productions. Mr. Clemens is a genuine and powerful humorist, with a bitter vein of satire on the weaknesses of humanity which is sometimes wholesome, sometimes only grotesque, but in certain of his works degenerates into a gross trifling with every fine feeling. The trouble with Mr. Clemens is that he has no reliable sense of propriety. His notorious speech at an *Atlantic* dinner, marshalling Longfellow and Emerson and Whittier in vulgar parodies in a Western miner's cabin, illustrated this, but not in much more relief than the ***Adventures of Tom Sawyer*** did, or these Huckleberry Finn stories, do. . . . They are no better in tone than the dime novels which flood the blood-and-thunder reading population. Mr. Clemens has made them smarter, for he has an inexhaustible fund of 'quips and cranks and wanton wiles,' and his literary skill is, of course, superior; but their moral level is low, and their perusal cannot be anything less than harmful.

## Mark Twain

SOURCE: A letter to Charles Webster, April 4, 1885, in *The Critical Response to Mark Twain's "Huckleberry Finn,"* edited by Laurie Champion, Greenwood Press, 1991.

Dear Charley—

The *Advertiser* and the *Republican* still go for me daily. All right, we may as well get the benefit of such advertising as can be drawn from it.

So, if the idea seems good to you, add this new page—this "Prefatory Remark," and insert it right after the copyright page in all future editions [of **Huck Finn**]. I would bind up a . . . few copies immediately and send to all the New York and Boston papers, and to a scattering few western ones—and don't *mark* them; but when you are ready to ship them get W. McKay [Mackay] Laffan (go to see him at Harper & Bros.) to drop the Prefatory Remark into the *Sun*, with a mere quiet editorial comment to the effect that we are inserting this in deference to a generally expressed curiosity on the part of the public to know whether Huck is a real or imaginary character.

You might bring a proof of the P.R. and hand it to Laffan for publication *immediately* (before Gen Grant dies and absorbs all newspaper interest,) without waiting to bind up and send off the books.

Ys
S L C

*Prefatory Remark*

Huckleberry Finn is not an imaginary person. He still lives; or rather *they* still live; for Huckleberry Finn is two persons in one—namely, the author's two uncles, the present editors of the Boston *Advertiser* and the Springfield *Republican.* In character, language, clothing, education, instinct, and origin, he is the painstakingly and truthfully drawn photograph and counterpart of these two gentlemen as they were in the time of their boyhood, forty years ago. The work has been most carefully and conscientiously done, and is exactly true to the originals, in even the minutest particulars, with but one exception, and that a trifling one: this boy's language has been toned down and softened, here and there, in deference to the taste of a more modern and fastidious day.

## Thomas Sergeant Perry

SOURCE: "The First American Review," in *The Adventures of Huckleberry Finn: An Authoritative Text, Backgrounds and Sources, Criticism, Second Edition,* edited by Sculley Bradley, Richmond Croom Beatty, E. Hudson Long, and Thomas Cooley, W. W. Norton & Company, Inc., 1977, pp. 289-90.

[*Perry is credited with writing the first significant review of* **Huckleberry Finn** *in the United States, originally published in* Century, *May, 1885.*]

*Huckleberry Finn* has the great advantage of being written in autobiographical form. This secures a unity in the narration that is most valuable; every scene is given, not described; and the result is a vivid picture of Western life forty or fifty years ago. While **Tom Sawyer** is scarcely more than an apparently fortuitous collection of incidents, and its thread is one that has to do with murders, this story has a more intelligible plot. Huckleberry, its immortal hero, runs away from his worthless father, and floats down the Mississippi on a raft, in company with Jim, a runaway negro. This plot gives great opportunity for varying incidents. The travelers spend some time on an island; they outwit every one they meet; they acquire full knowledge of the hideous fringe of civilization that then adorned that valley; and the book is a most valuable record of an important part of our motley American civilization.

What makes it valuable is the evident truthfulness of the

narrative, and where this is lacking and its place is taken by ingenious invention, the book suffers. What is inimitable, however, is the reflection of the whole varied series of adventures in the mind of the young scapegrace of a hero. His undying fertility of invention, his courage, his manliness in every trial, are an incarnation of the better side of the ruffianism that is one result of the independence of Americans, just as hypocrisy is one result of the English respect for civilization. The total absence of morbidness in the book—for the *mal du siècle* has not yet reached Arkansas—gives it a genuine charm; and it is interesting to notice the art with which this is brought out. The best instance is perhaps to be found in the account of the feud between the Shepherdsons and the Grangerfords, which is described only as it would appear to a semi-civilized boy of fourteen, without the slightest condemnation or surprise,—either of which would be bad art,—and yet nothing more vivid can be imagined. That is the way that a story is best told, by telling it, and letting it go to the reader unaccompanied by sign posts or directions how he shall understand it and profit by it. Life teaches its lessons by implication, not by didactic preaching; and literature is at its best when it is an imitation of life and not an excuse for instruction.

As to the humor of Mark Twain, it is scarcely necessary to speak. It lends vividness to every page. The little touch in **Tom Sawyer,** where, after the murder of which Tom was an eye-witness, it seemed "that his schoolmates would never get done holding inquests on dead cats and thus keeping the trouble present to his mind," and that in the account of the spidery six-armed girl of Emmeline's picture in **Huckleberry Finn,** are in the author's happiest vein. Another admirable instance is to be seen in Huckleberry Finn's mixed feelings about rescuing Jim, the negro, from slavery. His perverted views regarding the unholiness of his actions are most instructive and amusing. It is possible to feel, however, that the fun in the long account of Tom Sawyer's artificial imitation of escapes from prison is somewhat forced; everywhere simplicity is a good rule, and while the account of the Southern *vendetta* is a masterpiece, the caricature of books of adventure leaves us cold. In one we have a bit of life; in the other Mark Twain is demolishing something that has no place in the book.

Yet the story is capital reading, and the reason of its great superiority to **Tom Sawyer** is that it is, for the most part, a consistent whole. If Mark Twain would follow his hero through manhood, he would condense a side of American life that, in a few years, will have to be delved out of newspapers, government reports, county histories, and misleading traditions by unsympathetic sociologists.

## *The Summary*

SOURCE: An excerpt from *The Merrill Studies in Huckleberry Finn,* compiled by John C. Gerber, Charles E. Merrill Publishing Company, 1971, pp. 9-10.

*[The following article was originally printed in* The Summary, *a weekly journal published for the New York State Reformatory. It was reprinted by* The Critic, *May 30, 1885.]*

We clip the following from *The Summary,* a weekly journal published in the interests of the New York State Reformatory:—Some time ago the Concord Library purchased Mark Twain's *Huckleberry Finn,* and was grieved to find that it was an 'irreligious' book. The local newspapers took up the story and passed it round, each adding its own embellishment, until at last it was proclaimed that Mark Twain's day as a humorist was over. The Reformatory Library also procured *Huckleberry Finn,* was similarly impressed, and the fact came under the notice of Professor Sanborn when he was visiting us. In a letter of last week this gentleman writes to the Superintendent: 'I have read *Huckleberry Finn,* and I do not see any reason why it should not go into your Reference Library, at least, and form the subject of a debate in your Practical Morality Class. I am serious in this.' This at least suggests an adequate apology for the general toleration of *Huckleberry Finn.*

### Joel Chandler Harris

SOURCE: "To the Editors of *The Critic,*" in *The Merrill Studies in Huckleberry Finn,* compiled by John C. Gerber, Charles E. Merrill Publishing Company, 1971, pp. 12-13.

*[The following review was originally published in* The Critic, *November 28, 1885, in celebration of Twain's fiftieth birthday.]*

[Twain] has put his youth in his books, and there it is perennial. His last book is better than his first, and there his youth is renewed and revived. I know that some of the professional critics will not agree with me, but there is not in our fictive literature a more wholesome book than *Huckleberry Finn.* It is history, it is romance, it is life. Here we behold human character stripped of all tiresome details; we see people growing and living; we laugh at their humor, share their griefs; and, in the midst of it all, behold we are taught the lesson of honesty, justice and mercy.

### Andrew Lang

SOURCE: "The Art of Mark Twain," in *The Illustrated London News,* Vol. XCVIII, No. 2704, February 14, 1891, p. 222.

*[A prolific magazine critic, Lang was also a key figure in the late nineteenth century revival of romance literature. In the excerpt below, Lang discusses Twain's strengths and weaknesses as a writer both of humorous and serious work.]*

I have no hesitation in saying that Mark Twain is one among the greatest of contemporary makers of fiction. For some reason, which may perhaps be guessed, he has only twice chosen to exercise this art seriously, in *Tom Sawyer* and in *Huckleberry Finn.* The reason, probably, is that old life on the Mississippi is the only form of life in which Mark Twain finds himself so well versed that he can deal with it in seriousness. Again, perhaps his natural and cultivated tendency to extravagance and caricature is only to be checked by working on the profound and candid seriousness of boyhood. These are unlucky limitations, if they really exist, for they have confined him, as a novelist, to a pair of brief works, masterpieces which a fallacious appearance has confounded with boys' books and facetiae. Of the two, by an unheard-of stroke of luck, the second, the sequel, is by far the better.

### Laurence Hutton

SOURCE: A review of *The Adventures of Huckleberry Finn,* in *Harper's New Monthly Magazine,* Vol. XCIII, No. DLVI, September, 1896, pp. 1-2.

*[The following is a review of the second edition of* **Huckleberry Finn,** *published in 1896.]*

It is by no means an easy matter, at this late day, to say anything new or fresh about Huckleberry Finn. We first made his acquaintance, as the son of the town-drunkard in *Life on the Mississippi,* more than twenty years ago, when he started to run away from his persecuting father, and from a persecuting, good widow who wished to make a nice, truth-telling, respectable boy of him; we saw a good deal more of him as the comrade of his immortal friend Tom Sawyer, a year or two later; and the present volume, entirely devoted to the narration of his adventures and experiences, first appeared in 1884. He is one of the most original and the most delightful juvenile creations of fiction; and to millions of persons, all over the world, he is as real as is the Maid of Orleans. The conductor of this Department of the *Harper's New Monthly Magazine* carried him, in his satchel, to the North Cape, where he read him by the light of the Midnight Sun; and he has heard him quoted by a donkey-boy, as an allegory on the banks of the Nile. The name of that donkey-boy's donkey, by-the-way, was "Markie Twainie!"

Huckleberry Finn in his new dress—new types, new plates, new size, new binding—appeals to two distinct classes of readers: to those who are perfectly familiar with him, and with all his doings, with all the dialects he hears and utters; and to those who are yet to be introduced to him. Happy the boy, of any age, who is to read *Huckleberry Finn* for the first time. It is safe to say that he will run the risk of prosecution in order to discover its motive; that he will take the chances of banishment rather than miss its moral; and, if he is anything of a mildly profane boy, "he'll be shot if he don't find its plot."

## William Lyon Phelps

SOURCE: "Mark Twain," in *Essays on Modern Novelists,* The Macmillan Company, 1910, pp. 99-114.

Although Mark Twain has the great qualities of the true humorist—common sense, human sympathy, and an accurate eye for proportion—he is much more than a humorist. His work shows high literary quality, the quality that appears in first-rate novels. He has shown himself to be a genuine artist. He has done something which many popular novelists have signally failed to accomplish—he has created real characters. His two wonderful boys, Tom Sawyer and Huckleberry Finn, are wonderful in quite different ways. The creator of Tom exhibited remarkable observation; the creator of Huck showed the divine touch of imagination. Tom is the American boy— he is "smart." In having his fence whitewashed, in controlling a pool of Sabbath-school tickets at the precise psychological moment, he displays abundant promise of future success in business. Huck, on the other hand, is the child of nature, harmless, sincere, and crudely imaginative. His reasonings with Jim about nature and God belong to the same department of natural theology as that illustrated in Browning's *Caliban.*

Mark Twain has so much dramatic power that, were his literary career beginning instead of closing, he might write for us the great American play that we are still awaiting. The story of the feud between the Grangerfords and the Shepherdsons is thrillingly dramatic, and the tragic climax seizes the heart. The shooting of the drunken Boggs, the gathering of the mob, and its control by one masterful personality, belong essentially to true drama, and are written with power and insight. The pathos of these scenes is never false, never mawkish or overdone; it is the pathos of life itself. Mark Twain's extraordinary skill in descriptive passages shows, not merely keen observation, but the instinct for the specific word—the one word that is always better than any of its synonyms, for it makes the picture real—it creates the illusion, which is the essence of all literary art.

*Tom Sawyer* and *Huckleberry Finn* are prose epics of American life. The former is one of those books—of which *The Pilgrim's Progress, Gulliver's Travels,* and *Robinson Crusoe* are supreme examples—that are read at different periods of one's life from very different points of view; so that it is not easy to say when one enjoys them the most—before one understands their real significance or after. Nearly all healthy boys enjoy reading *Tom Sawyer,* because the intrinsic interest of the story is so great, and the various adventures of the hero are portrayed with such gusto. Yet it is impossible to outgrow the book. The eternal Boy is there, and one cannot appreciate the nature of boyhood properly until one has ceased to be a boy. The other masterpiece, *Huckleberry Finn,* is really not a child's book at all. Children devour it, but they do not digest it. It is a permanent picture of a certain period of American history, and this picture is made complete, not so much by the striking portraits of individuals placed on the huge canvas, as by the vital

unity of the whole composition. If one wishes to know what life on the Mississippi really was, to know and understand the peculiar social conditions of that highly exciting time, one has merely to read through this powerful narrative, and a definite, coherent, vivid impression remains.

## Albert Bigelow Paine

SOURCE: "Huck Finn Comes into His Own," in *Mark Twain, a Biography: The Personal and Literary Life of Samuel Langhorne Clemens, Vol. II,* Harper & Brothers Publishers, 1912, pp. 793-98.

[*Paine was Twain's secretary and the author or editor of six books on Twain's life and works. Paine is credited with recording a great deal of first-hand information on Twain that might otherwise have been lost. In the following excerpt, Paine discusses some of the qualities that make* **Huckleberry Finn** *a superior work of literature.*]

The story of *Huck Finn* will probably stand as the best of Mark Twain's purely fictional writings. A sequel to *Tom Sawyer,* it is greater than its predecessor; greater artistically, though perhaps with less immediate interest for the juvenile reader. In fact, the books are so different that they are not to be compared—wherein lies the success of the later one. Sequels are dangerous things when the story is continuous, but in *Huckleberry Finn* the story is a new one, wholly different in environment, atmosphere, purpose, character, everything. The tale of Huck and Nigger Jim drifting down the mighty river on a raft, cross-secting the various primitive aspects of human existence, constitutes one of the most impressive examples of picaresque fiction in any language. It has been ranked greater than *Gil Blas,* greater even than *Don Quixote;* certainly it is more convincing, more human, than either of these tales. Robert Louis Stevenson once wrote, "It is a book I have read four times, and am quite ready to begin again to-morrow."

It is by no means a flawless book, though its defects are trivial enough. The illusion of Huck as narrator fails the least bit here and there; the "four dialects" are not always maintained; the occasional touch of broad burlesque detracts from the tale's reality. We are inclined to resent this. We never wish to feel that Huck is anything *but* a real character. We want him always the Huck who was willing to go to hell if necessary, rather than sacrifice Nigger Jim; the Huck who watched the river through long nights, and, without caring to explain why, felt his soul go out to the sunrise.

Take the story as a whole, it is a succession of startling and unique pictures. The cabin in the swamp which Huck and his father used together in their weird, ghastly relationship; the night adventure with Jim on the wrecked steamboat; Huck's night among the towheads; the Grangerford-Shepherdson battle; the killing of Boggs—to name a few of the many vivid presentations—these are of no time or literary fashion and will never lose their flavor nor their freshness so long as humanity itself does not change. The terse, unadorned Grangerford-Shepherdson episode—built out of the Darnell-Watson feuds [in *Life on the Mississippi*]—is simply classic in its vivid casualness, and the same may be said of almost every incident on that long river-drift; but this is the strength, the very essence of picaresque narrative. It is the way things happen in reality; and the quiet, unexcited frame of mind in which Huck is prompted to set them down would seem to be the last word in literary art. To Huck, apparently, the killing of Boggs and Colonel Sherburn's defiance of the mob are of about the same historical importance as any other incidents of the day's travel. When Colonel Sherburn threw his shotgun across his arm and bade the crowd disperse Huck says:

> The crowd washed back sudden, and then broke all apart and went tearing off every which way, and Buck Harkness he heeled it after them, looking tolerable cheap. I could a staid if I'd a wanted to, but I didn't want to.

> I went to the circus, and loafed around the back side till the watchman went by, and then dived in under the tent.

That is all. No reflections, no hysterics; a murder and a mob dispersed, all without a single moral comment. And when the Shepherdsons had got done killing the Grangerfords, and Huck had tugged the two bodies ashore and covered Buck Grangerford's face with a handkerchief, crying a little because Buck had been good to him, he spent no time in sentimental reflection or sermonizing, but promptly hunted up Jim and the raft and sat down to a meal of corn-dodgers, buttermilk, pork and cabbage, and greens. . . .

Able critics have declared that the psychology of Huck Finn is the book's large feature: Huck's moral point of view—the struggle between his heart and his conscience concerning the sin of Jim's concealment, and his final decision of self-sacrifice. Time may show that as an epic of the river, the picture of a vanished day, it will rank even greater. The problems of conscience we have always with us, but periods once passed are gone forever. Certainly Huck's loyalty to that lovely soul Nigger Jim was beautiful, though after all it may not have been so hard for Huck, who could be loyal to anything. Huck was loyal to his father, loyal to Tom Sawyer of course, loyal even to those two river tramps and frauds, the King and the Duke, for whom he lied prodigiously, only weakening when a new and lovelier loyalty came into view—loyalty to Mary Wilks.

The King and the Duke, by the way, are not elsewhere matched in fiction. The Duke was patterned after a journeyman-printer Clemens had known in Virginia City, but the King was created out of refuse from the whole human family—"all tears and flapdoodle," the very ultimate of disrepute and hypocrisy—so perfect a specimen that one must admire, almost love, him. "Hain't we all the fools in town on our side? and ain't that a big enough majority in any town?" he asks in a critical moment—a remark which stamps him as a philosopher of classic rank. We are full of pity at last when this pair of rapscallions ride out of the history on a rail and feel some of Huck's inclusive loyalty and all the sorrowful truth of his comment: "Human beings *can* be awful cruel to one another."

The "poor old king" Huck calls him, and confesses how he felt "ornery and humble and to blame, somehow," for the old scamp's misfortunes. "A person's conscience ain't got no sense," he says, and Huck is never more real to us, or more lovable, than in that moment. Huck is what he is because, being made so, he cannot well be otherwise. He is a boy throughout—such a boy as Mark Twain had known and in some degree had been. One may pettily pick a flaw here and there in the tale's construction if so minded, but the moral character of Huck himself is not open to criticism. And indeed any criticism of this the greatest of Mark Twain's tales of modern life would be as the mere scratching of the granite of an imperishable structure. *Huck Finn* is a monument that no puny pecking will destroy. It is built of indestructible blocks of human nature; and if the blocks do not always fit, and the ornaments do not always agree, we need not fear. Time will blur the incongruities and moss over the mistakes. The edifice will grow more beautiful with the years.

### H. L. Mencken

SOURCE: "Credo," in *A Mencken Chrestomathy*, Alfred A. Knopf, Inc., 1924, p. 485.

[*Mencken's essay was first published in* The Smart Set, *February, 1913.*]

I believe that **Huckleberry Finn** is one of the great masterpieces of the world, that it is the full equal of *Don Quixote* and *Robinson Crusoe*, that it is vastly better than *Gil Blas, Tristram Shandy, Nicholas Nickleby* or *Tom Jones.* I believe that it will be read by human beings of all ages, not as a solemn duty but for the honest love of it, and over and over again, long after every book written in America between the years 1800 and 1860, with perhaps three exceptions, has disappeared entirely save as a classroom fossil. I believe that Mark Twain had a clearer vision of life, that he came nearer to its elementals and was less deceived by its false appearances, than any other American who has ever presumed to manufacture generalizations. I believe that, admitting all his defects, he wrote better English, in the sense of cleaner, straighter, vivider, saner English, than either Irving or Hawthorne. I believe that four of his books—**Huck, Life on the Mississippi, Captain Stormfield's Visit to Heaven,** and *A Connecticut Yankee*—are alone worth more, as works of art and as criticisms of life, than the whole output of Cooper, Irving, Holmes, Mitchell, Stedman, Whittier and Bryant. I believe that he ranks well above Whitman and certainly not below

Poe. I believe that he was the true father of our national literature, the first genuinely American artist of the blood royal.

## Waldo Frank

SOURCE: "The Land of the Pioneer," in *Our America,* Boni and Liveright, Publishers, 1919, pp. 13-58.

[*Huckleberry Finn*] must go down in history, not as the expression of a rich national culture like the books of Chaucer, Rabelais, Cervantes, but as the voice of American chaos, the voice of a precultural epoch. Mark Twain kept this book long at his side. Ostensibly, it was the sequel to *The Adventures of Tom Sawyer* which appeared in 1875. *Huck* came nine years later. In it for once, the soul of Mark Twain burst its bonds of false instruction and false ideal, and found voice. Mark Twain lived twenty-six years longer. That voice never spoke again.

*Huckleberry Finn* is the simple story of a young white lad, born on the banks of the Mississippi who, with an escaped slave named Jim, builds a raft and floats down the mighty current. Mark Twain originally had meant it to be nothing else: had meant it for the mere sequel of another tale. But his theme was too apt a symbol. Into it he poured his soul.

Huck is a candid ignorant courageous child. He is full of the cunning and virtue of the resilient savage. He wears the habiliments of the civilization from which he comes, loosely, like trinkets about his neck. He and his companion build a raft and float. At night they veer their craft into the shallows or sleep on land. They have many adventures. The adventures that Huck has are the material of pioneering life. He always *happens* upon them. At times, he is a mere spectator: at times enforced accessory. Always, he is passive before a vaster fact. Huck is America. And Huck *floats* down the current of a mighty Stream.

Huckleberry Finn is the American epic hero. Greece had Ulysses. America must be content with an illiterate lad. He expresses our germinal past. He expresses the movement of the American soul through all the sultry climaxes of the nineteenth century.

The Mississippi with its countless squalid towns and its palatial steamboats was a ferment of commingled and insoluble life. All the elements of the American East and all the elements of Europe seethed here, in the hunt of wealth. A delirium of dreams and schemes and passions, out of which shaped our genius for invention and exploitation. The whole gamut of American beginnings ran with the river. And Huck along. One rises from the book, lost in the beat of a great rhythmic flow: the unceasing elemental march of a vast life, cutting a continent, feeding its soil. And upon the heaving surface of this flood, a human child: ignorant, joyous and courageous. The American soul like a bridge upon the tide of a world.

## Carl Van Doren

SOURCE: "Mark Twain," in *The American Novel,* The Macmillan Company, 1921, pp. 157-87.

In richness of life *Tom Sawyer* cannot compare with [*Huckleberry Finn*]. The earlier of the two books keeps close home in one sleepy, dusty village, illuminated only, at inconvenient moments, by Tom Sawyer's whimsies. But in *Huckleberry Finn* the plot, like Mark Twain's imagination, goes voyaging. Five short chapters and Huck leaves his native village for the ampler world of the picaresque. An interval of captivity with his father—that unpleasant admonitory picture of what Huck may someday become if he outgrows his engaging youthful fineness—and then the boy slips out upon the river which is the home of his soul. There he realizes every dream he has ever had. He has a raft of his own. He has a friend, the negro Jim, with the strength of a man, the companionableness of a boy, and the fidelity of a dog. He can have food for the fun of taking it out of the water or stealing it from along the shore. He sleeps and wakes when he pleases. The weather of the lower Mississippi in summer bites no one. At the same time, this life is not too safe. Jim may be caught and taken from his benefactor. With all his craft, Huck is actually, as a boy, very much at the mercy of the rough men who infest the river. Adventure complicates and enhances his freedom. And what adventure! It never ceases, but flows on as naturally as the river which furthers the plot of the story by conveying the characters from point to point. Both banks are as crowded with excitement, if not with danger, as the surrounding forest of the older romances. Huck can slip ashore at any moment and try his luck with the universe in which he moves without belonging to it. Now he is the terrified and involuntary witness of a cruel murder plot, and again of an actual murder. Now he strays, with his boy's astonished simplicity, into the Grangerford-Shepherdson vendetta and sees another *Romeo and Juliet* enacted in Kentucky. In the undesired company of the "king" and the "duke," certainly two as sorry and as immortal rogues as fiction ever exhibited, Huck is initiated into degrees of scalawaggery which he could not have experienced, at his age, alone; into amateur theatricals as extraordinary as the Royal Nonesuch and frauds as barefaced as the impostures practised upon the camp-meeting and upon the heirs of Peter Wilks. After sights and undertakings so Odyssean, the last quarter of the book, given over to Tom Sawyer's romantic expedients for getting Jim, who is actually free already, out of a prison from which he could have been released in ten minutes, is preserved from the descent into anticlimax only by its hilarious comic force. As if to make up for the absence of more sizable adventures, this mimic conspiracy is presented with enough art and enough reality in its genre studies to furnish an entire novel. That, in a way, is the effect of *Huckleberry Finn* as a whole: though the hero, by reason of his youth, cannot entirely take part in the action, and the action is therefore not entirely at first hand, the picture lacks little that could make it more vivid or veracious.

In the futile critical exercise of contending which is the greatest American novel, choice ordinarily narrows down at last to *The Scarlet Letter* and **Huckleberry Finn**—a sufficiently antipodean pair and as hard to bring into comparison as tragedy and comedy themselves. Each in its department, however, these two books do seem to be supreme. *The Scarlet Letter* offers, by contrast, practically no picture; **Huckleberry Finn,** no problem. Huck undergoes, it is true, certain naggings from the set of unripe prejudices he calls his conscience; and once he rises to an appealing unselfishness when, in defiance of all the principles he has been taught to value, he makes up his mind that he will assist the runaway slave to freedom. But in the sense that *The Scarlet Letter* poses problems, **Huckleberry Finn** poses none at all. Its criticism of life is of another sort. It does not work at the instigation of any doctrine, moral or artistic, whatever. As Hawthorne, after long gazing into the somber dusk over ancient Salem, had seen the universal drama of Hester and Dimmesdale and Chillingworth being transacted there, and had felt it rising within him to expression, so Mark Twain, in the midst of many vicissitudes remembering the river of his youthful happiness, had seen the panorama of it unrolling before him and also had been moved to record it out of sheer joy in its old wildness and beauty, assured that merely to have such a story to tell was reason enough for telling it. Having written *Life on the Mississippi* he had already reduced the river to his own language; having written *Tom Sawyer,* he had got his characters in hand. There wanted only the moment when his imagination should take fire at recollection and rush away on its undogmatic task of reproducing the great days of the valley. Had Mark Twain undertaken to make another and a greater **Gilded Age** out of his matter, to portray the life of the river satirically on the largest scale, instead of in such dimensions as fit Huck's boyish limitations of knowledge, he might possibly have made a better book, but he would have had to be another man. Being the man he was, he touched his peak of imaginative creation not by taking thought how he could be a Balzac to the Mississippi but by yarning with all his gusto about an adventure he might have had in the dawn of his days. Although he did not deliberately gather riches, riches came.

## Mark Twain

SOURCE: "Mark Twain's Autobiography," in *The Adventures of Huckleberry Finn: An Authoritative Text, Backgrounds and Sources, Criticism, Second Edition,* edited by Sculley Bradley, Richmond Croom Beatty, E. Hudson Long, and Thomas Cooley, W. W. Norton & Company, Inc., 1977, pp. 279-81.

[*In the following excerpt from* **Mark Twain's Autobiography,** *1924, Twain discusses his model for the character of Huck Finn, as well as one source for the farm setting in the novel.*]

In **Huckleberry Finn** I have drawn Tom Blankenship exactly as he was. He was ignorant, unwashed, insufficiently fed; but he had as good a heart as ever any boy had. His liberties were totally unrestricted. He was the only really independent person—boy or man—in the community, and by consequence he was tranquilly and continuously happy, and was envied by all the rest of us. We liked him; we enjoyed his society. And as his society was forbidden us by our parents, the prohibition trebled and quadrupled its value, and therefore we sought and got more of his society than of any other boy's. I heard, four years ago, that he was justice of the peace in a remote village in Montana, and was a good citizen and greatly respected.

My uncle, John A. Quarles, was a farmer, and his place was in the country four miles from Florida. He had eight children and fifteen or twenty negroes, and was also fortunate in other ways, particularly in his character. I have not come across a better man than he was. I was his guest for two or three months every year, from the fourth year after we removed to Hannibal till I was eleven or twelve years old. I have never consciously used him or his wife in a book, but his farm has come very handy to me in literature once or twice. In **Huck Finn** and in **Tom Sawyer, Detective** I moved it down to Arkansas. It was all of six hundred miles, but it was no trouble; it was not a very large farm—five hundred acres, perhaps—but I could have done it if it had been twice as large. And as for the morality of it, I cared nothing for that; I would move a state if the exigencies of literature required it.

It was a heavenly place for a boy, that farm of my uncle John's. . . .

## Ernest Hemingway

SOURCE: In *Green Hills of Africa,* Charles Scribner's Sons, 1953, p. 22.

[*Hemingway's* Green Hills of Africa *was first published in 1935.*]

All modern American literature comes from one book by Mark Twain called **Huckleberry Finn.** If you read it you must stop where the nigger Jim is stolen from the boys. This is the real end. The rest is just cheating. But it's the best book we've had. All American writing comes from that. There was nothing before. There has been nothing as good since.

## F. Scott Fitzgerald

SOURCE: A commentary on *The Adventures of Huckleberry Finn,* in *Twentieth Century Interpretations of Adventures of Huckleberry Finn,* edited by Claude M. Simpson, Prentice-Hall, Inc., 1968, p. 107.

[*The following commentary was written in 1935 on the occasion of the centenary of Mark Twain's birth. It was printed in* Fitzgerald Newsletter, *Winter, 1960.*]

Huckleberry Finn took the first journey *back.* He was the first to look *back* at the republic from the perspective of the west. His eyes were the first eyes that ever looked at us objectively that were not eyes from overseas. There were mountains at the frontier but he wanted more than mountains to look at with his restless eyes—he wanted to find out about men and how they lived together. And because he turned back we have him forever.

## Asa Don Dickinson

SOURCE: "*Huckleberry Finn* Is Fifty Years Old—Yes; But Is He Respectable?" in *The Critical Response to Mark Twain's "Huckleberry Finn,"* edited by Laurie Champion, Greenwood Press, 1991, pp. 31-5.

[*The following excerpt is taken from Dickinson's essay, originally published in* Wilson Bulletin for Librarians, *November, 1935.*]

The honor of being the original Huck has been claimed for more than one of Sam Clemens's boyhood friends in Hannibal, Missouri. But Mark has explicitly stated that Huck is an exact portrait of Tom Blankenship, son of the Hannibal town drunkard. "He was ignorant, unwashed, insufficiently fed; but he had as good a heart as ever any boy had. . . . He was the only really independent person—boy or man—in the community, and by consequence he was tranquilly and continuously happy and was envied by all the rest of us." It may be noted that in later life Blankenship became a respected citizen of Montana and a justice of the peace. What would Miss Watson say to that?

From his fourth to his twelfth year little Sam Clemens spent his summers at the farm of his uncle, John A. Quarles, near Florida, Missouri. This became the Phelps farm in *Huckleberry Finn.* "I moved it down to Arkansas," he tells us. "It was all of six hundred miles, but it was no trouble; it was not a very large farm—five hundred acres perhaps—but I could have done it if it had been twice as large. And as for the morality of it, I cared nothing for that; I would move a state if the exigencies of literature required it."

On this farm Mark made the acquaintance of "Uncle Dan'l," the original of Jim. He was "a middle-aged slave whose head was the best one in the Negro quarters, whose sympathies were wide and warm, and whose heart was honest and simple and knew no guile."

There can be no doubt that Clemens wrote the stories of Huck and Tom not primarily for the edification of youth, but rather to please himself, and incidentally to earn a living. At the same time he was a good wholesome man, a lover of children, and the father of a family. When squeamish librarians, as they did now and then, saw in him a corrupter of youth, and excluded his books from their children's collections, Mark did not like it. His feelings were hurt. Were not his books much less out-rageous than this gentle wild man would naturally have written them? Had he not, raging but dutiful, always submitted them to the home censor? Listen to his little daughter, Susy:

> Ever since papa and mama were married papa has written his books and then taken them to mama in manuscript, and she has expergated [*sic*] them. Papa read **Huckleberry Finn** to us. . . . He would leave parts of it with mama to expergate, while he went off to the study to work, and sometimes Clara and I would be sitting with mama while she was looking the manuscript over, and I remember so well, with what pangs of regret we used to see her turn down the leaves of the pages, which meant that some delightfully terrible part must be scratched out.

Poor Mark! Was ever roaring lion so forced to content himself with a diet of prunes and prisms? . . .

In 1905 I attended a meeting of children's librarians in Brooklyn and—because of my own great love and admiration for Huck—begged that he be allowed a place on the shelves of the children's rooms. It was no use. The good ladies assured me in effect that Huck was a deceitful boy; that he not only itched but scratched; and that he said *sweat* when he should have said *perspiration.* But my fervor amused them and they graciously gave me permission to plead his cause again at a later meeting if I wanted to. In desperation I wrote Mr. Clemens for help and promptly received the following reply:

> Dear Sir:
>
> I am greatly troubled by what you say. I wrote **Tom Sawyer** and **Huck Finn** for adults exclusively, and it always distresses me when I find that boys and girls have been allowed access to them. The mind that becomes soiled in youth can never again be washed clean; I know this by my own experience, and to this day I cherish an unappeasable bitterness against the unfaithful guardians of my young life, who not only permitted but compelled me to read an unexpurgated Bible through before I was 15 years old. None can do that and ever draw a clean sweet breath again this side of the grave. Ask that young lady—she will tell you so.
>
> Most honestly do I wish I could say a softening word or two in defense of Huck's character, since you wish it, but really in my opinion it is no better than God's (in the Ahab chapter and 97 others) and those of Solomon, David, Satan, and the rest of the sacred brotherhood.
>
> If there is an unexpurgated in the Children's Department, won't you please help that young woman remove Huck and Tom from that questionable companionship?
>
> Sincerely yours,
>
> (signed) S. L. Clemens.
>
> I shall not show your letter to anyone—it is safe with me.

## Clifton Fadiman

SOURCE: "Lead-Ins: A Note on *Huckleberry Finn*," in *Party of One,* World Publishing Company, 1955, pp. 129-31.

[*In the following excerpt, originally published as an introduction to the 1940 Heritage Press edition of* Huckleberry Finn, *Fadiman examines the aspects of the novel that make it a uniquely American work.*]

This is the book with which we as a literary people begin. Two thousand years from now American professors of literature—if such still exist—will speak of **Huckleberry Finn** as English professors of literature now speak of Chaucer. For **Huckleberry Finn** is our Chaucer, our Homer, our Dante, our Virgil. It is the source of the stream, the seed-bed, the book which, read or unread, has influenced a thousand American writers, the first great mold within which the form and pattern of our speech were caught. It has spawned both Hemingway and Mickey Spillane.

First-rate writers existed on this continent before **Huckleberry Finn.** But **Huckleberry Finn** is the first important work written out of a simple, vast unconsciousness of the existence of any country except ours. It is not traditionless, but its traditions all have their roots in the Mississippi Valley. It is the nearest thing we have to a national epic.

And what an extraordinary national epic it is! It has its Achilles, but he is a fourteen-year-old boy. The hero has his Patroclus, but Patroclus is an illiterate Negro. It has its Kings and Dukes, but they are frauds and through them the whole principle of aristocracy (a principle upon which national epics rest) is ridiculed. It has its voyages and explorations, but they are undertaken on a raft. Its central episode is not some feat of high emprise, upon which rests the fate of a people, but an elaborate hoax involving the unnecessary freeing of a Negro slave. And the tone of this epic! Not a heroic phrase, no elevation, no invocation to the Muses. On the contrary, a style casual, conversational, the first completely unliterary style to appear on the American continent. "I sing of arms and the man" begins the noble Virgilian strain. And how does our *Aeneid* begin? "You don't know about me without you have read a book by the name of ***The Adventures of Tom Sawyer;*** but that ain't no matter. That book was made by Mr. Mark Twain, and he told the truth, mainly. There was things which he stretched, but mainly he told the truth." These sentences announce the birth of a literature.

Yes, from one point of view, its language is the most important thing about **Huckleberry Finn,** more important than its humor, its characters, its story. For its language *is* in a way the humor, the characters, the story. Just as the Declaration of Independence (let us hope) contains in embryo our whole future history as a nation, so the language of **Huckleberry Finn** (another declaration of independence) expresses our popular char-

acter, our humor, our slant. This is the way we talk and think in those moods when we are most remote from our European or African beginnings. The smoking-car conversation, the Rotary Club address, the talk at a church social, the spiel of the traveling salesman, the lingo of Broadway—whatever is uniquely of this country has a smack, a tang, a flow, an accent, a rhythm, that go back to the language of **Huckleberry Finn.** For its language is not merely a comic device intended to convey the character of a rather unevenly educated boy of fourteen. It has in it the casual drawl of the frontier, the irreverent intonation of the democratic idea, and an innocent disregard of all the traditions of European writing. When Huck, complaining over the widow's preference for cooking each kind of food by itself says, "In a barrel of odds and ends it is different; things get mixed up, and the juice kind of swaps around, and the things go better," when he says this, we know we are listening to the idiom of a separate civilization.

Perhaps the word civilization is a bad one, for this book—and here lies its troubling appeal to us—is an epic of rebellion against civilization. We have become a people of cities and motorcars and vacuum cleaners and two-week vacations and commutation tickets. But that is not the way we began, and despite our childish delight in gadgetry, we have a deep hankering for the forest, the river, the rifle out of which this country came. **Huckleberry Finn** is our most typical novel precisely because it expresses this hankering. The typical novels of France or England or Russia are novels of civilization. They assume the permanence of certain sophisticated societal relations. **Huckleberry Finn,** on the contrary, is a book about primitive things: small boys and food and weather and murders and darkness. Though produced in the century of Balzac, Tolstoy, and Thackeray it is more akin to the *Odyssey* or the Norse myths than to any of the representative great novels of the European tradition.

Here, in this rambling tale about the unimportant adventures of a boy who will probably not amount to much when he grows older (except that he will never grow older) are the matters, the myths, the deep conflicts of the American people: the influence of the frontier, the unresolved problem of the Negro, the revolt against city-convention, the fascinated absorption in deeds of violence, the immense sense of a continent cut in two by a vast river, the type-figure of the self-sufficient frontiersman, the passion for exploration, the love of the hoax, the exaggeration, and the practical joke, the notion of basic social equality, the enskying of youth.

## V. S. Pritchett

SOURCE: "Current Literature: Books in General," in *The New Statesman and Nation,* Vol. XXII, No. 545, August 2, 1941, p. 113.

Out of the mess which Twain made of his life, amid the awful pile of tripe which he wrote, there does rise one book which has the serenity of a thing of genius. *Huckleberry Finn* takes the breath away. Knowing Mark Twain's life, knowing the hell of vulgarity from which the book has ascended, one dreads as one turns from page to page the seemingly inevitable flop. How can a low comedian, so tortured and so angry, refrain from blackguarding God, Man and Nature for the narrow boredom of his early life, and ruining the perfect comedy and horror of this story? But imaginative writers appear to get at least one lucky break in their careers; for a moment the conflicts are assimilated, the engine ceases to work against itself. *Huckleberry Finn* does not flop. America gets its first truly indigenous masterpiece. The small boyhood of Huck Finn is the small boyhood of a new culture.

## T. S. Eliot

SOURCE: "An Introduction to Huckleberry Finn," in *The Adventures of Huckleberry Finn: An Authoritative Text, Backgrounds and Sources, Criticism, Second Edition,* edited by Sculley Bradley, Richmond Croom Beatty, E. Hudson Long, and Thomas Cooley, W. W. Norton & Company, Inc., 1977, pp. 328-35.

[*T. S. Eliot wrote the following introduction to the 1950 British edition of* **The Adventures of Huckleberry Finn.**]

*The Adventures of Huckleberry Finn* is the only one of Mark Twain's various books which can be called a masterpiece. I do not suggest that it is his only book of permanent interest; but it is the only one in which his genius is completely realized, and the only one which creates its own category. There are pages in *Tom Sawyer* and in *Life on the Mississippi* which are, within their limits, as good as anything with which one can compare them in *Huckleberry Finn;* and in other books there are drolleries just as good of their kind. But when we find one book by a prolific author which is very much superior to all the rest, we look for the peculiar accident or concourse of accidents which made that book possible. In the writing of *Huckleberry Finn* Mark Twain had two elements which, when treated with his sensibility and his experience, formed a great book: these two are the Boy and the River.

*Huckleberry Finn* is, no doubt, a book which boys enjoy. I cannot speak from memory: I suspect that a fear on the part of my parents lest I should acquire a premature taste for tobacco, and perhaps other habits of the hero of the story, kept the book out of my way. But *Huckleberry Finn* does not fall into the category of juvenile fiction. The opinion of my parents that it was a book unsuitable for boys left me, for most of my life, under the impression that it was a book suitable only for boys. Therefore it was only a few years ago that I read for the first time, and in that order, *Tom Sawyer* and *Huckleberry Finn.*

*Tom Sawyer* did not prepare me for what I was to find

its sequel to be. *Tom Sawyer* seems to me to be a boys' book, and a very good one. The River and *the* Boy make their appearance in it; the narrative is good; and there is also a very good picture of society in a small mid-Western river town (for St. Petersburg is more Western than Southern) a hundred years ago. But the point of view of the narrator is that of an adult observing a boy. And Tom is the ordinary boy, though of quicker wits, and livelier imagination, than most. Tom is, I suppose, very much the boy that Mark Twain had been: he is remembered and described as he seemed to his elders, rather than created. Huck Finn, on the other hand, is the boy that Mark Twain still was, at the time of writing his adventures. We look at Tom as the smiling adult does: Huck we do not look at—we see the world through his eyes. The two boys are not merely different types; they were brought into existence by different processes. Hence in the second book their roles are altered. In the first book Huck is merely the humble friend—almost a variant of the traditional valet of comedy; and we see him as he is seen by the conventional respectable society to which Tom belongs, and of which, we feel sure, Tom will one day become an eminently respectable and conventional member. In the second book their nominal relationship remains the same; but here it is Tom who has the secondary role. The author was probably not conscious of this, when he wrote the first two chapters: *Huckleberry Finn* is not the kind of story in which the author knows, from the beginning, what is going to happen. Tom then disappears from our view; and when he returns, he has only two functions. The first is to provide a foil for Huck. Huck's persisting admiration for Tom only exhibits more clearly to our eyes the unique qualities of the former and the commonplaceness of the latter. Tom has the imagination of a lively boy who has read a good deal of romantic fiction: he might, of course, become a writer—he might become Mark Twain. Or rather, he might become the more commonplace aspect of Mark Twain. Huck has not imagination, in the sense in which Tom has it: he has, instead, vision. He sees the real world; and he does not judge it—he allows it to judge itself.

Tom Sawyer is an orphan. But he has his aunt; he has, as we learn later, other relatives; and he has the environment into which he fits. He is wholly a social being. When there is a secret band to be formed, it is Tom who organizes it and prescribes the rules. Huck Finn is alone: there is no more solitary character in fiction. The fact that he has a father only emphasizes his loneliness; and he views his father with a terrifying detachment. So we come to see Huck himself in the end as one of the permanent symbolic figures of fiction; not unworthy to take a place with Ulysses, Faust, Don Quixote, Don Juan, Hamlet and other great discoveries that man has made about himself.

It would seem that Mark Twain was a man who—perhaps like most of us—never became in all respects mature. We might even say that the adult side of him was boyish, and that only the boy in him, that was Huck Finn, was adult. As Tom Sawyer grown up, he wanted success and applause (Tom himself always needs an audience). He wanted prosperity, a happy domestic life of a conventional kind, universal approval, and fame. All of these things he obtained. As Huck Finn he was indifferent to all these things; and being composite of the two, Mark Twain both strove for them, and resented their violation of his integrity. Hence he became the humorist and even clown: with his gifts, a certain way to success, for everyone could enjoy his writings without the slightest feeling of discomfort, self-consciousness or self-criticism. And hence, on the other hand, his pessimism and misanthropy. To be a misanthrope is to be in some way divided; or it is a sign of an uneasy conscience. The pessimism which Mark Twain discharged into *The Man That Corrupted Hadleyburg* and *What is Man?* springs less from observation of society, than from his hatred of himself for allowing society to tempt and corrupt him and give him what he wanted. There is no wisdom in it. But all this personal problem has been diligently examined by Mr. Van Wyck Brooks; and it is not Mark Twain, but *Huckleberry Finn,* that is the subject of this introduction.

You cannot say that Huck himself is either a humorist or a misanthrope. He is the impassive observer: he does not interfere, and, as I have said, he does not judge. Many of the episodes that occur on the voyage down the river, after he is joined by the Duke and the King (whose fancies about themselves are akin to the kind of fancy that Tom Sawyer enjoys) are in themselves farcical; and if it were not for the presence of Huck as the reporter of them, they would be no more than farce. But, seen through the eyes of Huck, there is a deep human pathos in these scoundrels. On the other hand, the story of the feud between the Grangerfords and the Shepherdsons is a masterpiece in itself: yet Mark Twain could not have written it so, with that economy and restraint, with just the right details and no more, and leaving to the reader to make his own moral reflections, unless he had been writing in the person of Huck. And the *style* of the book, which is the style of Huck, is what makes it a far more convincing indictment of slavery than the sensationalist propaganda of *Uncle Tom's Cabin.* Huck is passive and impassive, apparently always the victim of events; and yet, in his acceptance of his world and of what it does to him and others, he is more powerful than his world, because he is more *aware* than any other person in it.

Repeated readings of the book only confirm and deepen one's admiration of the consistency and perfect adaptation of the writing. This is a style which at the period, whether in America or in England, was an innovation, a new discovery in the English language. Other authors had achieved natural speech in relation to particular characters—Scott with characters talking Lowland Scots, Dickens with cockneys: but no one else had kept it up through the whole of a book. Thackeray's Yellowplush, impressive as he is, is an obvious artifice in comparison. In *Huckleberry Finn* there is no exaggeration of grammar or spelling or speech, there is no sentence or phrase to destroy the illusion that these are Huck's own words.

It is not only in the way in which he tells his story, but in the details he remembers, that Huck is true to himself. There is, for instance, the description of the Grangerford interior as Huck sees it on his arrival; there is the list of the objects which Huck and Jim salvaged from the derelict house:

> We got an old tin lantern, and a butcher-knife without any handle, and a bran-new Barlow knife worth two bits in any store, and a lot of tallow candles, and a tin candlestick, and a gourd, and a tin cup, and a ratty old bed quilt off the bed, and a reticule with needles and pins and beeswax and buttons and thread and all such truck in it, and a hatchet and some nails, and a fish-line as thick as my little finger, with some monstrous hooks on it, and a roll of buckskin, and a leather dog-collar, and a horseshoe, and some vials of medicine that didn't have no label on them; and just as we was leaving I found a tolerable good curry-comb, and Jim he found a ratty old fiddle-bow, and a wooden leg. The straps was broke off of it, but barring that, it was a good enough leg, though it was too long for me and not long enough for Jim, and we couldn't find the other one, though we hunted all round.

> And so, take it all round, we made a good haul.

This is the sort of list that a boy reader should pore over with delight; but the paragraph performs other functions of which the boy reader would be unaware. It provides the right counterpoise to the horror of the wrecked house and the corpse; it has a grim precision which tells the reader all he needs to know about the way of life of the human derelicts who had used the house; and (especially the wooden leg, and the fruitless search for its mate) reminds us at the right moment of the kinship of mind and the sympathy between the boy outcast from society and the negro fugitive from the injustice of society.

Huck in fact would be incomplete without Jim, who is almost as notable a creation as Huck himself. Huck is the passive observer of men and events, Jim the submissive sufferer from them; and they are equal in dignity. There is no passage in which their relationship is brought out more clearly than the conclusion of the chapter in which, after the two have become separated in the fog, Huck in the canoe and Jim on the raft, Huck, in his impulse of boyish mischief, persuades Jim for a time that the latter had dreamt the whole episode.

> . . . my heart wuz mos' broke bekase you wuz los', en I didn' k'yer no mo' what become er me en de raf'. En when I wake up en fine you back agin', all safe en soun', de tears come en I could a got down on my knees en kiss' yo' foot, I's so thankful. En all you wuz thinkin' 'bout wuz how you could make a fool uv ole Jim wid a lie. Dat truck dah is *trash;* en trash is what people is dat puts dirt on de head er dey fren's en makes 'em ashamed.' . . .

> It was fifteen minutes before I could work myself up to go and humble myself to a nigger—but I done it, and I warn't ever sorry for it afterwards, neither.

*Nook Farm, Mark Twain's home in Connecticut.*

This passage has been quoted before; and if I quote it again, it is because I wish to elicit from it one meaning that is, I think, usually overlooked. What is obvious in it is the pathos and dignity of Jim, and this is moving enough; but what I find still more disturbing, and still more unusual in literature, is the pathos and dignity of the boy, when reminded so humbly and humiliatingly, that his position in the world is not that of other boys, entitled from time to time to a practical joke; but that he must bear, and bear alone, the responsibility of a man.

It is Huck who gives the book style. The River gives the book its form. But for the River, the book might be only a sequence of adventures with a happy ending. A river, a very big and powerful river, is the only natural force that can wholly determine the course of human peregrination. At sea, the wanderer may sail or be carried by winds and currents in one direction or another; a change of wind or tide may determine fortune. In the prairie, the direction of movement is more or less at the choice of the caravan; among mountains there will often be an alternative, a guess at the most likely pass. But the river with its strong, swift current is the dictator to the raft or to the steamboat. It is a treacherous and capricious dictator. At one season, it may move sluggishly in a channel so narrow that, encountering it for the first time at that point, one can hardly believe that it has travelled already for hundreds of miles, and has yet many hundreds of miles to go; at another season, it may obliterate

the low Illinois shore to a horizon of water, while in its bed it runs with a speed such that no man or beast can survive in it. At such times, it carries down human bodies, cattle and houses. At least twice, at St. Louis, the western and the eastern shores have been separated by the fall of bridges, until the designer of the great Eads Bridge devised a structure which could resist the floods. In my own childhood, it was not unusual for the spring freshet to interrupt railway travel; and then the traveller to the East had to take steamboat from the levee up to Alton, at a higher level on the Illinois shore, before he could begin his rail journey. The river is never wholly charitable; it changes its pace, it shifts its channel, unaccountably; it may suddenly efface a sand-bar, and throw up another bar where before was navigable water.

It is the River that controls the voyage of Huck and Jim; that will not let them land at Cairo, where Jim could have reached freedom; it is the River that separates them and deposits Huck for a time in the Grangerford household; the River that re-unites them, and then compels upon them the unwelcome company of the King and the Duke. Recurrently we are reminded of its presence and its power.

> When I woke up, I didn't know where I was for a
> minute. I set up and looked around, a little scared.
> Then I remembered. The river looked miles and miles
> across. The moon was so bright I could a counted the

drift-logs that went a-slipping along, black and still, hundreds of yards out from shore. Everything was dead quiet, and it looked late, and *smelt* late. You know what I mean—I don't know the words to put it in.

It was kind of solemn, drifting down the big still river, laying on our backs looking up at the stars, and we didn't ever feel like talking loud, and it warn't often that we laughed, only a little kind of a low chuckle. We had mighty good weather as a general thing, and nothing ever happened to us at all, that night, nor the next, nor the next.

Every night we passed towns, some of them away up on black hillsides, nothing but just a shiny bed of lights, not a house could you see. The fifth night we passed St. Louis, and it was like the whole world lit up. In St. Petersburg they used to say there was twenty or thirty thousand people in St. Louis, but I never believed it till I see that wonderful spread of lights at two o'clock that still night. There warn't a sound there; everybody was asleep.

We come to understand the River by seeing it through the eyes of the Boy; but the Boy is also the spirit of the River. *Huckleberry Finn,* like other great works of imagination, can give to every reader whatever he is capable of taking from it. On the most superficial level of observation, Huck is convincing as a boy. On the same level, the picture of social life on the shores of the Mississippi a hundred years ago is, I feel sure, accurate. On any level, Mark Twain makes you see the River, as it is and was and always will be, more clearly than the author of any other description of a river known to me. But you do not merely see the River, you do not merely become acquainted with it through the senses: you experience the River. Mark Twain, in his later years of success and fame, referred to his early life as a steamboat pilot as the happiest he had known. With all allowance for the illusions of age, we can agree that those years were the years in which he was most fully alive. Certainly, but for his having practised that calling, earned his living by that profession, he would never have gained the understanding which his genius for expression communicates in this book. In the pilot's daily struggle with the River, in the satisfaction of activity, in the constant attention to the River's unpredictable vagaries, his consciousness was fully occupied, and he absorbed knowledge of which, as an artist, he later made use. There are, perhaps, only two ways in which a writer can acquire the understanding of environment which he can later turn to account: by having spent his childhood in that environment—that is, living in it at a period of life in which one experiences much more than one is aware of; and by having had to struggle for a livelihood in that environment—a livelihood bearing no direct relation to any intention of writing about it, of *using* it as literary material. Most of Joseph Conrad's understanding came to him in the latter way. Mark Twain knew the Mississippi in both ways: he had spent his childhood on its banks, and he had earned his living matching his wits against its currents.

Thus the River makes the book a great book. As with

Conrad, we are continually reminded of the power and terror of Nature, and the isolation and feebleness of Man. Conrad remains always the European observer of the tropics, the white man's eye contemplating the Congo and its black gods. But Mark Twain is a native, and the River God is his God. It is as a native that he accepts the River God, and it is the subjection of Man that gives to Man his dignity. For without some kind of God, Man is not even very interesting.

Readers sometimes deplore the fact that the story descends to the level of *Tom Sawyer* from the moment that Tom himself re-appears. Such readers protest that the escapades invented by Tom, in the attempted "rescue" of Jim, are only a tedious development of themes with which we were already too familiar—even while admitting that the escapades themselves are very amusing, and some of the incidental observations memorable. But it is right that the mood of the end of the book should bring us back to that of the beginning. Or, if this was not the right ending for the book, what ending would have been right?

In *Huckleberry Finn* Mark Twain wrote a much greater book than he could have known he was writing. Perhaps all great works of art mean much more than the author could have been aware of meaning: certainly, *Huckleberry Finn* is the one book of Mark Twain's which, as a whole, has this unconsciousness. So what seems to be the rightness, of reverting at the end of the book to the mood of *Tom Sawyer,* was perhaps unconscious art. For Huckleberry Finn, neither a tragic nor a happy ending would be suitable. No worldly success or social satisfaction, no domestic consummation would be worthy of him; a tragic end also would reduce him to the level of those whom we pity. Huck Finn must come from nowhere and be bound for nowhere. His is not the independence of the typical or symbolic American Pioneer, but the independence of the vagabond. His existence questions the values of America as much as the values of Europe; he is as much an affront to the "pioneer spirit" as he is to "business enterprise"; he is in a state of nature as detached as the state of the saint. In a busy world, he represents the loafer; in an acquisitive and competitive world, he insists on living from hand to mouth. He could not be exhibited in any amorous encounters or engagements, in any of the juvenile affections which are appropriate to Tom Sawyer. He belongs neither to the Sunday School nor to the Reformatory. He has no beginning and no end. Hence, he can only disappear; and his disappearance can only be accomplished by bringing forward another performer to obscure the disappearance in a cloud of whimsicalities.

Like Huckleberry Finn, the River itself has no beginning or end. In its beginning, it is not yet the River; in its end, it is no longer the River. What we call its headwaters is only a selection from among the innumerable sources which flow together to compose it. At what point in its course does the Mississippi become what the Mississippi *means?* It is both one and many; it is the Mississippi of this book only after its union with the Big

Muddy—the Missouri; it derives some of its character from the Ohio, the Tennessee and other confluents. And at the end it merely disappears among its deltas: it is no longer there, but it is still where it was, hundreds of miles to the North. The River cannot tolerate any design, to a story which is its story, that might interfere with its dominance. Things must merely happen, here and there, to the people who live along its shores or who commit themselves to its current. And it is as impossible for Huck as for the River to have a beginning or end—a *career*. So the book has the right, the only possible concluding sentence. I do not think that any book ever written ends more certainly with the right words:

> But I reckon I got to light out for the Territory ahead of the rest, because Aunt Sally she's going to adopt me and civilize me, and I can't stand it. I been there before.

## Leo Marx

SOURCE: "Mr. Eliot, Mr. Trilling, and *Huckleberry Finn*," in *The Adventures of Huckleberry Finn: An Authoritative Text, Backgrounds and Sources Criticism, Second Edition,* edited by Sculley Bradley, Richmond Croom Beatty, E. Hudson Long, and Thomas Cooley, W. W. Norton & Company, Inc., 1977, pp. 336-49.

[*Marx's essay originally appeared in* The American Scholar, *1953.*]

**The Adventures of Huckleberry Finn** has not always occupied its present high place in the canon of American literature. When it was first published in 1885, the book disturbed and offended many reviewers, particularly spokesmen for the genteel tradition. In fact, a fairly accurate inventory of the narrow standards of such critics might be made simply by listing epithets they applied to Clemens's novel. They called it vulgar, rough, inelegant, irreverent, coarse, semi-obscene, trashy and vicious. So much for them. Today (we like to think) we know the true worth of the book. Everyone now agrees that **Huckleberry Finn** is a masterpiece: it is probably the one book in our literature about which highbrows and lowbrows can agree. Our most serious critics praise it. Nevertheless, a close look at what two of the best among them have recently written will likewise reveal, I believe, serious weaknesses in current criticism. Today the problem of evaluating the book is as much obscured by unqualified praise as it once was by parochial hostility.

I have in mind essays by Lionel Trilling [in the "The Greatness of Huckleberry Finn"] and T. S. Eliot. Both praise the book, but in praising it both feel obligated to say something in justification of what so many readers have felt to be its great flaw: the disappointing "ending," the episode which begins when Huck arrives at the Phelps place and Tom Sawyer reappears. There are good reasons why Mr. Trilling and Mr. Eliot should feel the need to face this issue. From the point of view of scope alone, more is involved than the mere "ending"; the episode comprises almost one-fifth of the text. The prob-

lem, in any case, is unavoidable. I have discussed **Huckleberry Finn** in courses with hundreds of college students, and I have found only a handful who did not confess their dissatisfaction with the extravagant mock rescue of Nigger Jim and the denouement itself. The same question always comes up: "What went wrong with Twain's novel?" Even Bernard De Voto, whose wholehearted commitment to Clemens's genius is well known, has said of the ending that "in the whole reach of the English novel there is no more abrupt or more chilling descent." Mr. Trilling and Mr. Eliot do not agree. They both attempt, and on similar grounds, to explain and defend the conclusion.

Of the two, Mr. Trilling makes the more moderate claim for Clemens's novel. He does admit that there is a "falling off" at the end; nevertheless he supports the episode as having "a certain formal aptness." Mr. Eliot's approval is without serious qualification. He allows no objections, asserts that "it is right that the mood of the end of the book should bring us back to the beginning." I mean later to discuss their views in some detail, but here it is only necessary to note that both critics see the problem as one of form. And so it is. Like many questions of form in literature, however, this one is not finally separable from a question of "content," of value, or, if you will, of moral insight. To bring **Huckleberry Finn** to a satisfactory close, Clemens had to do more than find a neat device for ending a story. His problem, though it may never have occurred to him, was to invent an action capable of placing in focus the meaning of the journey down the Mississippi.

I believe that the ending of **Huckleberry Finn** makes so many readers uneasy because they rightly sense that it jeopardizes the significance of the entire novel. To take seriously what happens at the Phelps farm is to take lightly the entire downstream journey. What is the meaning of the journey? With this question all discussion of **Huckleberry Finn** must begin. It is true that the voyage down the river has many aspects of a boy's idyl. We owe much of its hold upon our imagination to the enchanting image of the raft's unhurried drift with the current. The leisure, the absence of constraint, the beauty of the river—all these things delight us. "It's lovely to live on a raft." And the multitudinous life of the great valley we see through Huck's eyes has a fascination of its own. Then, of course, there is humor—laughter so spontaneous, so free of bitterness present almost everywhere in American humor that readers often forget how grim a spectacle of human existence Huck contemplates. Humor in this novel flows from a bright joy of life as remote from our world as living on a raft.

Yet along with the idyllic and the epical and the funny in **Huckleberry Finn,** there is a coil of meaning which does for the disparate elements of the novel what a spring does for a watch. The meaning is not in the least obscure. It is made explicit again and again. The very words with which Clemens launches Huck and Jim upon their voyage indicate that theirs is not a boy's lark but a quest for freedom. From the electrifying moment when

Huck comes back to Jackson's Island and rouses Jim with the news that a search party is on the way, we are meant to believe that Huck is enlisted in the cause of freedom. "Git up and hump yourself, Jim!" he cries. "There ain't a minute to lose. They're after us!" What particularly counts here is the *us*. No one is after Huck; no one but Jim knows he is alive. In that small word Clemens compresses the exhilarating power of Huck's instinctive humanity. His unpremeditated identification with Jim's flight from slavery is an unforgettable moment in American experience, and it may be said at once that any culmination of the journey which detracts from the urgency and dignity with which it begins will necessarily be unsatisfactory. Huck realizes this himself, and says so when, much later, he comes back to the raft after discovering that the Duke and the King have sold Jim:

> After all this long journey . . . here it was all come to nothing, everything all busted up and ruined, because they could have the heart to serve Jim such a trick as that, and make him a slave again all his life, and amongst strangers, too, for forty dirty dollars.

Huck knows that the journey will have been a failure unless it takes Jim to freedom. It is true that we do discover, in the end, that Jim is free, but we also find out that the journey was not the means by which he finally reached freedom.

The most obvious thing wrong with the end, then, is the flimsy contrivance by which Clemens frees Jim. In the end we not only discover that Jim has been a free man for two months, but that his freedom has been granted by old Miss Watson. If this were only a mechanical device for terminating the action, it might not call for much comment. But it is more than that: it is a significant clue to the import of the last ten chapters. Remember who Miss Watson is. She is the Widow's sister whom Huck introduces in the first pages of the novel. It is she who keeps "pecking" at Huck, who tries to teach him to spell and to pray and to keep his feet off the furniture. She is an ordent proselytizer for piety and good manners, and her greed provides the occasion for the journey in the first place. She is Jim's owner, and he decides to flee only when he realizes that she is about to break her word (she cannot resist a slave trader's offer of eight hundred dollars) and sell him down the river away from his family.

Miss Watson, in short, is the Enemy. If we except a predilection for physical violence, she exhibits all the outstanding traits of the valley society. She pronounces the polite lies of civilization that suffocate Huck's spirit. The freedom which Jim seeks, and which Huck and Jim temporarily enjoy aboard the raft, is accordingly freedom *from* everything for which Miss Watson stands. Indeed, the very intensity of the novel derives from the discordance between the aspirations of the fugitives and the respectable code for which she is a spokesman. Therefore, her regeneration, of which the deathbed freeing of Jim is the unconvincing sign, hints a resolution of the novel's essential conflict. Perhaps because this device most transparently reveals that shift in point of view which he could not avoid, and which is less easily discerned elsewhere in the concluding chapters, Clemens plays it down. He makes little attempt to account for Miss Watson's change of heart, a change particularly surprising in view of Jim's brazen escape. Had Clemens given this episode dramatic emphasis appropriate to its function, Miss Watson's bestowal of freedom upon Jim would have proclaimed what the rest of the ending actually accomplishes—a vindication of persons and attitudes Huck and Jim had symbolically repudiated when they set forth downstream.

It may be said, and with some justice, that a reading of the ending as a virtual reversal of meanings implicit in the rest of the novel misses the point—that I have taken the final episode too seriously. I agree that Clemens certainly did not intend us to read it so solemnly. The ending, one might contend, is simply a burlesque upon Tom's taste for literary romance. Surely the tone of the episode is familiar to readers of Mark Twain. The preposterous monkey business attendant upon Jim's "rescue," the careless improvisation, the nonchalant disregard for common-sense plausibility—all these things should not surprise readers of Twain or any low comedy in the tradition of "Western humor." However, the trouble is, first, that the ending hardly comes off as burlesque: it is *too* fanciful, *too* extravagant; and it is tedious. For example, to provide a "gaudy" atmosphere for the escape, Huck and Tom catch a couple of dozen snakes. Then the snakes escape.

> No, there warn't no real scarcity of snakes about the house for a considerable spell. You'd see them dripping from the rafters and places every now and then; and they generly landed in your plate, or down the back of your neck. . . .

Even if this were *good* burlesque, which it is not, what is it doing here? It is out of keeping; the slapstick tone jars with the underlying seriousness of the voyage.

*Huckleberry Finn* is a masterpiece because it brings Western humor to perfection and yet transcends the narrow limits of its conventions. But the ending does not. During the final extravaganza we are forced to put aside many of the mature emotions evoked earlier by the vivid rendering of Jim's fear of capture, the tenderness of Huck's and Jim's regard for each other, and Huck's excruciating moments of wavering between honesty and respectability. None of these emotions are called forth by the anticlimactic final sequence. I do not mean to suggest that the inclusion of low comedy per se is a flaw in *Huckleberry Finn.* One does not object to the shenanigans of the rogues; there is ample precedent for the place of extravagant humor even in works of high seriousness. But here the case differs from most which come to mind: the major characters themselves are forced to play low comedy roles. Moreover, the most serious motive in the novel, Jim's yearning for freedom, is made the object of nonsense. The conclusion, in short, is farce, but the rest of the novel is not.

That Clemens reverts in the end to the conventional manner of Western low comedy is most evident in what happens to the principals. Huck and Jim become comic characters; that is a much more serious ground for dissatisfaction than the unexplained regeneration of Miss Watson. Remember that Huck has grown in stature throughout the journey. By the time he arrives at the Phelps place, he is not the boy who had been playing robbers with Tom's gang in St. Petersburg the summer before. All he has seen and felt since he parted from Tom has deepened his knowledge of human nature and of himself. Clemens makes a point of Huck's development in two scenes which occur just before he meets Tom again. The first describes Huck's final capitulation to his own sense of right and wrong: "All right, then, I'll *go* to Hell." This is the climactic moment in the ripening of his self-knowledge. Shortly afterward, when he comes upon a mob riding the Duke and the King out of town on a rail, we are given his most memorable insight into the nature of man. Although these rogues had subjected Huck to every indignity, what he sees provokes this celebrated comment:

> Well, it made me sick to see it; and I was sorry for them poor pitiful rascals, it seemed like I couldn't ever feel any hardness against them any more in the world. It was a dreadful thing to see. Human beings can be awful cruel to one another.

The sign of Huck's maturity here is neither the compassion nor the skepticism, for both had been marks of his personality from the first. Rather, the special quality of these reflections is the extraordinary combination of the two, a mature blending of his instinctive suspicion of human motives with his capacity for pity.

But at this point Tom reappears. Soon Huck has fallen almost completely under his sway once more, and we are asked to believe that the boy who felt pity for the rogues is now capable of making Jim's capture the occasion for a game. He becomes Tom's helpless accomplice, submissive and gullible. No wonder that Clemens has Huck remark, when Huck first realizes Aunt Sally has mistaken him for Tom, that "it was like being born again." Exactly. In the end, Huck regresses to the subordinate role in which he had first appeared in *The Adventures of Tom Sawyer*. Most of those traits which made him so appealing a hero now disappear. He had never, for example, found pain or misfortune amusing. At the circus, when a clown disguised as a drunk took a precarious ride on a prancing horse, the crowd loved the excitement and danger; "it warn't funny to me, though," said Huck. But now, in the end, he submits in awe to Tom's notion of what is amusing. To satisfy Tom's hunger for adventure he makes himself a party to sport which aggravates Jim's misery.

It should be added at once that Jim doesn't mind too much. The fact is that he has undergone a similar trans-

formation. On the raft he was an individual, man enough to denounce Huck when Huck made him the victim of a practical joke. In the closing episode, however, we lose sight of Jim in the maze of farcical invention. He ceases to be a man. He allows Huck and "Mars Tom" to fill his hut with rats and snakes, "and every time a rat bit Jim he would get up and write a line in his journal whilst the ink was fresh." This creature who bleeds ink and feels no pain is something less than human. He has been made over in the image of a flat stereotype: the submissive stage-Negro. These antics divest Jim, as well as Huck, of much of his dignity and individuality.

What I have been saying is that the flimsy devices of plot, the discordant farcical tone, and the disintegration of the major characters all betray the failure of the ending. These are not aspects merely of form in a technical sense, but of meaning. For that matter, I would maintain that this book has little or no formal unity independent of the joint purpose of Huck and Jim. What components of the novel, we may ask, provide the continuity which links one adventure with another? The most important is the unifying consciousness of Huck, the narrator, and the fact that we follow the same principals through the entire string of adventures. Events, moreover, occur in a temporal sequence. Then there is the river; after each adventure Huck and Jim return to the raft and the river. Both Mr. Trilling and Mr. Eliot speak eloquently of the river as a source of unity, and they refer to the river as a god. Mr. Trilling says that Huck is "the servant of the river-god." Mr. Eliot puts it this way: "The River gives the book its form. But for the River, the book might be only a sequence of adventures with a happy ending." This seems to me an extravagant view of the function of the neutral agency of the river. Clemens had a knowledgeable respect for the Mississippi and, without sanctifying it, was able to provide excellent reasons for Huck's and Jim's intense relation with it. It is a source of food and beauty and terror and serenity of mind. But above all, it provides motion; it is the means by which Huck and Jim move away from a menacing civilization. They return to the river to continue their journey. The river cannot, does not, supply purpose. That purpose is a facet of their consciousness, and without the motive of escape from society, *Huckleberry Finn* would indeed "be only a sequence of adventures." Mr. Eliot's remark indicates how lightly he takes the quest for freedom. His somewhat fanciful exaggeration of the river's role is of a piece with his neglect of the theme at the novel's center.

That theme is heightened by the juxtaposition of sharp images of contrasting social orders: the microcosmic community Huck and Jim establish aboard the raft and the actual society which exists along the Mississippi's banks. The two are separated by the river, the road to freedom upon which Huck and Jim must travel. Huck tells us what the river means to them when, after the Wilks episode, he and Jim once again shove their raft into the current: "It *did* seem so good to be free again and all by ourselves on the big river, and nobody to bother us." The river is indifferent. But its sphere is relatively uncontaminated by the civilization they flee, and so the river allows Huck and Jim some measure of freedom at once, the moment they set foot on Jackson's Island or the raft. Only on the island and the raft do they have a chance to practice that idea of brotherhood to which they are devoted. "Other places do seem so cramped and smothery," Huck explains, "but a raft don't. You feel mighty free and easy and comfortable on a raft." The main thing is freedom.

On the raft the escaped slave and the white boy try to practice their code: "What you want, above all things, on a raft, is for everybody to be satisfied, and feel right and kind towards the others." This human credo constitutes the paramount affirmation of *The Adventures of Huckleberry Finn,* and it obliquely aims a devastating criticism at the existing social order. It is a creed which Huck and Jim bring to the river. It neither emanates from nature nor is it addressed to nature. Therefore I do not see that it means much to talk about the river as a god in this novel. The river's connection with this high aspiration for man is that it provides a means of escape, a place where the code can be tested. The truly profound meanings of the novel are generated by the impingement of the actual world of slavery, feuds, lynching, murder, and a spurious Christian morality upon the ideal of the raft. The result is a tension which somehow demands release in the novel's ending.

But Clemens was unable to effect this release and at the same time control the central theme. The unhappy truth about the ending of *Huckleberry Finn* is that the author, having revealed the tawdry nature of the culture of the great valley, yielded to its essential complacency. The general tenor of the closing scenes, to which the token regeneration of Miss Watson is merely one superficial clue, amounts to just that. In fact, this entire reading of *Huckleberry Finn* merely confirms the brilliant insight of George Santayana, who many years ago spoke of American humorists, of whom he considered Mark Twain an outstanding representative, as having only "half escaped" the genteel tradition. Santayana meant that men like Clemens were able to "point to what contradicts it in the facts; but not in order to abandon the genteel tradition, for they have nothing solid to put in its place." This seems to me the real key to the failure of *Huckleberry Finn.* Clemens had presented the contrast between the two social orders but could not, or would not, accept the tragic fact that the one he had rejected was an image of solid reality and the other an ecstatic dream. Instead he gives us the cozy reunion with Aunt Polly in a scene fairly bursting with approbation of the entire family, the Phelpses included.

Like Miss Watson, the Phelpses are almost perfect specimens of the dominant culture. They are kind to their friends and relatives; they have no taste for violence; they are people capable of devoting themselves to their spectacular dinners while they keep Jim locked in the little hut down by the ash hopper, with its lone window boarded up. (Of course Aunt Sally visits Jim to see if he is "comfortable," and Uncle Silas comes in "to pray

with him.") These people, with their comfortable Sunday-dinner conviviality and the runaway slave padlocked nearby, are reminiscent of those solid German citizens we have heard about in our time who tried to maintain a similarly *gemütlich* way of life within virtual earshot of Buchenwald. I do not mean to imply that Clemens was unaware of the shabby morality of such people. After the abortive escape of Jim, when Tom asks about him, Aunt Sally replies: "Him? . . . the runaway nigger? . . . They've got him back, safe and sound, and he's in the cabin again, on bread and water, and loaded down with chains, till he's claimed or sold!" Clemens understood people like the Phelpses, but nevertheless he was forced to rely upon them to provide his happy ending. The satisfactory outcome of Jim's quest for freedom must be attributed to the benevolence of the very people whose inhumanity first made it necessary.

But to return to the contention of Mr. Trilling and Mr. Eliot that the ending is more or less satisfactory after all. As I have said, Mr. Trilling approves of the "formal aptness" of the conclusion. He says that "some device is needed to permit Huck to return to his anonymity, to give up the role of hero," and that therefore "nothing could serve better than the mind of Tom Sawyer with its literary furnishings, its conscious romantic desire for experience and the hero's part, and its ingenious schematization of life. . . ." Though more detailed, this is essentially akin to Mr. Eliot's blunt assertion that "it is right that the mood at the end of the book should bring us back to that of the beginning." I submit that it is wrong for the end of the book to bring us back to that mood. The mood of the beginning of *Huckleberry Finn* is the mood of Huck's attempt to accommodate himself to the ways of St. Petersburg. It is the mood of the end of *The Adventures of Tom Sawyer,* when the boys had been acclaimed heroes, and when Huck was accepted as a candidate for respectability. That is the state in which we find him at the beginning of *Huckleberry Finn.* But Huck cannot stand the new way of life, and his mood gradually shifts to the mood of rebellion which dominates the novel until he meets Tom again. At first, in the second chapter, we see him still eager to be accepted by the nice boys of the town. Tom leads the gang in re-enacting adventures he has culled from books, but gradually Huck's pragmatic turn of mind gets him in trouble. He has little tolerance for Tom's brand of make-believe. He irritates Tom. Tom calls him a "numbskull," and finally Huck throws up the whole business:

> So then I judged that all that stuff was only just one of Tom Sawyer's lies. I reckoned he believed in the A-rabs and the elephants, but as for me I think different. It had all the marks of a Sunday school.

With this statement, which ends the third chapter, Huck parts company with Tom. The fact is that Huck has rejected Tom's romanticizing of experience; moreover, he has rejected it as part of the larger pattern of society's make-believe, typified by Sunday school. But if he cannot accept Tom's harmless fantasies about the A-rabs, how are we to believe that a year later Huck is capable of awestruck submission to the far more extravagant fantasies with which Tom invests the mock rescue of Jim?

After Huck's escape from his "pap," the drift of the action, like that of the Mississippi's current, is *away* from St. Petersburg. Huck leaves Tom and the A-rabs behind, along with the Widow, Miss Watson, and all the pseudo-religious ritual in which nice boys must partake. The return, in the end, to the mood of the beginning therefore means defeat—Huck's defeat; to return to that mood *joyously* is to portray defeat in the guise of victory.

Mr. Eliot and Mr. Trilling deny this. The overriding consideration for them is form—form which seems largely to mean symmetry of structure. It is fitting, Mr. Eliot maintains, that the book should come full circle and bring Huck once more under Tom's sway. Why? Because it begins that way. But it seems to me that such structural unity is *imposed* upon the novel, and therefore is meretricious. It is a jerry-built structure, achieved only by sacrifice of characters and theme. Here the controlling principle of form apparently is unity, but unfortunately a unity much too superficially conceived. Structure, after all, is only one element—indeed, one of the more mechanical elements—of unity. A unified work must surely manifest coherence of meaning and clear development of theme, yet the ending of *Huckleberry Finn* blurs both. The eagerness of Mr. Eliot and Mr. Trilling to justify the ending is symptomatic of that absolutist impulse of our critics to find reasons, once a work has been admitted to the highest canon of literary reputability, for admiring every bit of it.

What is perhaps most striking about these judgments of Mr. Eliot's and Mr. Trilling's is that they are so patently out of harmony with the basic standards of both critics. For one thing, both men hold far more complex ideas of the nature of literary unity than their comments upon *Huckleberry Finn* would suggest. For another, both critics are essentially moralists, yet here we find them turning away from a moral issue in order to praise a dubious structural unity. Their efforts to explain away the flaw in Clemens's novel suffer from a certain narrowness surprising to anyone who knows their work. These facts suggest that we may be in the presence of a tendency in contemporary criticism which the critics themselves do not fully recognize.

Is there an explanation? How does it happen that two of our most respected critics should seem to treat so lightly the glaring lapse of moral imagination in *Huckleberry Finn*? Perhaps—and I stress the conjectural nature of what I am saying—perhaps the kind of moral issue raised by *Huckleberry Finn* is not the kind of moral issue to which today's criticism readily addresses itself. Today our critics, no less than our novelists and poets, are most sensitively attuned to moral problems which arise in the sphere of individual behavior. They are deeply aware of sin, of individual infractions of our culture's Christian ethic. But my impression is that they are, possibly because of the strength of the reaction against the mechanical sociological criticism of the thirties, less sensitive to questions of what might be called social or political morality.

By social or political morality I refer to the values implicit in a social system, values which may be quite distinct from the personal morality of any given individual within the society. Now *The Adventures of Huckleberry Finn,* like all novels, deals with the behavior of individuals. But one mark of Clemens's greatness is his deft presentation of the disparity between what people do when they behave as individuals and what they do when forced into roles imposed upon them by society. Take, for example, Aunt Sally and Uncle Silas Phelps, who consider themselves Christians, who are by impulse generous and humane, but who happen also to be staunch upholders of certain degrading and inhuman social institutions. When they are confronted with an escaped slave, the imperatives of social morality outweigh all pious professions.

The conflict between what people think they stand for and what social pressure forces them to do is central to the novel. It is present to the mind of Huck and, indeed, accounts for his most serious inner conflicts. He knows how he feels about Jim, but he also knows what he is expected to do about Jim. This division within his mind corresponds to the division of the novel's moral terrain into the areas represented by the raft on the one hand and society on the other. His victory over his "yaller dog" conscience therefore assumes heroic size: it is a victory over the prevailing morality. But the last fifth of the novel has the effect of diminishing the importance and uniqueness of Huck's victory. We are asked to assume that somehow freedom can be achieved in spite of the crippling power of what I have called the social morality. Consequently the less importance we attach to that force as it operates in the novel, the more acceptable the ending becomes.

Moreover, the idea of freedom, which Mr. Eliot and Mr. Trilling seem to slight, takes on its full significance only when we acknowledge the power which society exerts over the minds of men in the world of *Huckleberry Finn.* For freedom in this book specifically means freedom from society and its imperatives. This is not the traditional Christian conception of freedom. Huck and Jim seek freedom not from a burden of individual guilt and sin, but from social constraint. That is to say, evil in *Huckleberry Finn* is the product of civilization, and if this is indicative of Clemens's rather too simple view of human nature, nevertheless the fact is that Huck, when he can divest himself of the taint of social conditioning (as in the incantatory account of sunrise on the river), is entirely free of anxiety and guilt. The only guilt he actually knows arises from infractions of a social code. (The guilt he feels after playing the prank on Jim stems from his betrayal of the law of the raft.) Huck's and Jim's creed is secular. Its object is harmony among men, and so Huck is not much concerned with his own salvation. He repeatedly renounces prayer in favor of pragmatic solutions to his problems. In other words, the central insights of the novel belong to the tradition of the Enlightenment. The meaning of the quest itself is hardly reconcilable with that conception of human nature embodied in the myth of original sin. In view of the current fashion of reaffirming man's innate depravity, it is perhaps not surprising to find the virtues of *Huckleberry Finn* attributed not to its meaning but to its form.

But "if this was not the right ending for the book," Mr. Eliot asks, "what ending would have been right?" Although this question places the critic in an awkward position (he is not always equipped to rewrite what he criticizes), there are some things which may justifiably be said about the "right" ending of *Huckleberry Finn.* It may be legitimate, even if presumptuous, to indicate certain conditions which a hypothetical ending would have to satisfy if it were to be congruent with the rest of the novel. If the conclusion is not to be something merely tacked on to close the action, then its broad outline must be immanent in the body of the work.

It is surely reasonable to ask that the conclusion provide a plausible outcome to the quest. Yet freedom, in the ecstatic sense that Huck and Jim knew it aboard the raft, was hardly to be had in the Mississippi Valley in the 1840s, or, for that matter, in any other known human society. A satisfactory ending would inevitably cause the reader some frustration. That Clemens felt such disappointment to be inevitable is borne out by an examination of the novel's clear, if unconscious, symbolic pattern. Consider, for instance, the inferences to be drawn from the book's geography. The river, to whose current Huck and Jim entrust themselves, actually carries them to the heart of slave territory. Once the raft passes Cairo, the quest is virtually doomed. Until the steamboat smashes the raft, we are kept in a state of anxiety about Jim's escape. (It may be significant that at this point Clemens found himself unable to continue work on the manuscript, and put it aside for several years.) Beyond Cairo, Clemens allows the intensity of that anxiety to diminish, and it is probably no accident that the fainter it becomes, the more he falls back upon the devices of low comedy. Huck and Jim make no serious effort to turn north, and there are times (during the Wilks episode) when Clemens allows Huck to forget all about Jim. It is as if the author, anticipating the dilemma he had finally to face, instinctively dissipated the power of his major theme.

Consider, too, the circumscribed nature of the raft as a means of moving toward freedom. The raft lacks power and maneuverability. It can only move easily with the current—southward into slave country. Nor can it evade the mechanized power of the steamboat. These impotencies of the raft correspond to the innocent helplessness of its occupants. Unresisted, the rogues invade and take over the raft. Though it is the symbolic locus of the novel's central affirmations, the raft provides an uncertain and indeed precarious mode of traveling toward freedom. This seems another confirmation of Santayana's perception. To say that Clemens only half escaped

the genteel tradition is not to say that he failed to note any of the creed's inadequacies, but rather that he had "nothing solid" to put in its place. The raft patently was not capable of carrying the burden of hope Clemens placed upon it. (Whether this is to be attributed to the nature of his vision or to the actual state of American society in the nineteenth century is another interesting question.) In any case, the geography of the novel, the raft's powerlessness, the goodness and vulnerability of Huck and Jim, all prefigure a conclusion quite different in tone from that which Clemens gave us. These facts constitute what Hart Crane might have called the novel's "logic of metaphor," and this logic—probably inadvertent—actually takes us to the underlying meaning of *The Adventures of Huckleberry Finn.* Through the symbols we reach a truth which the ending obscures: the quest cannot succeed.

Fortunately, Clemens broke through to this truth in the novel's last sentences:

> But I reckon I got to light out for the territory ahead of the rest, because Aunt Sally she's going to adopt me and civilize me, and I can't stand it. I been there before.

Mr. Eliot properly praises this as "the only possible concluding sentence." But one sentence can hardly be advanced, as Mr. Eliot advances this one, to support the rightness of ten chapters. Moreover, if this sentence is right, then the rest of the conclusion is wrong, for its meaning clashes with that of the final burlesque. Huck's decision to go west ahead of the inescapable advance of civilization is a confession of defeat. It means that the raft is to be abandoned. On the other hand, the jubilation of the family reunion and the proclaiming of Jim's freedom create a quite different mood. The tone, except for these last words, is one of unclouded success. I believe this is the source of the almost universal dissatisfaction with the conclusion. One can hardly forget that a bloody civil war did not resolve the issue.

Should Clemens have made Huck a tragic hero? Both Mr. Eliot and Mr. Trilling argue that that would have been a mistake, and they are very probably correct. But between the ending as we have it and tragedy in the fullest sense, there was vast room for invention. Clemens might have contrived an action which left Jim's fate as much in doubt as Huck's. Such an ending would have allowed us to assume that the principals were defeated but alive, and the quest unsuccessful but not abandoned. This, after all, would have been consonant with the symbols, the characters, and the theme as Clemens had created them—and with history.

Clemens did not acknowledge the truth his novel contained. He had taken hold of a situation in which a partial defeat was inevitable, but he was unable to—or unaware of the need to—give imaginative substance to that fact. If an illusion of success was indispensable, where was it to come from? Obviously Huck and Jim could not succeed by their own efforts. At this point

Clemens, having only half escaped the genteel tradition, one of whose preeminent characteristics was an optimism undaunted by disheartening truth, returned to it. *Why* he did so is another story, having to do with his parents and his boyhood, with his own personality and his wife's, and especially with the character of his audience. But whatever the explanation, the faint-hearted ending of *The Adventures of Huckleberry Finn* remains an important datum in the record of American thought and imagination. It has been noted before, both by critics and non-professional readers. It should not be forgotten now.

To minimize the seriousness of what must be accounted a major flaw in so great a work is, in a sense, to repeat Clemens's failure of nerve. This is a disservice to criticism. Today we particularly need a criticism alert to lapses of moral vision. A measured appraisal of the failures and successes of our writers, past and present, can show us a great deal about literature and about ourselves. That is the critic's function. But he cannot perform that function if he substitutes considerations of technique for considerations of truth. Not only will such methods lead to errors of literary judgment, but beyond that, they may well encourage comparable evasions in other areas. It seems not unlikely, for instance, that the current preoccupation with matters of form is bound up with a tendency, by no means confined to literary quarters, to shy away from painful answers to complex questions of political morality. The conclusion to *The Adventures of Huckleberry Finn* shielded both Clemens and his audience from such an answer. But we ought not to be as tender-minded. For Huck Finn's besetting problem, the disparity between his best impulses and the behavior the community attempted to impose upon him, is as surely ours as it was Twain's.

### F. R. Leavis

SOURCE: A review of *The Adventures of Huckleberry Finn,* in *Twentieth Century Interpretations of Adventures of Huckleberry Finn,* edited by Claude M. Simpson, Prentice-Hall, Inc., 1968, pp. 109-11.

[*The following is an excerpt from Leavis's introduction to the 1955 edition of* Pudd'nhead Wilson.]

*Huckleberry Finn,* by general agreement Mark Twain's greatest work, is supremely the American classic, and it is one of the great books of the world. The significance of such a work doesn't admit of exhaustive recognition in a simple formula, or in several. Mark Twain himself was no simple being, and the complexity of his make-up was ordinarily manifested in strains, disharmonies, and tormenting failures of integration and self-knowledge. These, in his supreme masterpiece, can be seen to provide the creative drive. There is of course the aspect of return to boyhood, but the relation to complexity and strain represented by *Huckleberry Finn* is not one of escape from them—in spite of the qualities that have established the book as a classic for children (and

in spite of Mark Twain's conviction, at times, that appeal should be as such). It is true that the whole given through Huck, the embodiment of that Weste vernacular, or of the style created out of that, in whi the book is written. But that style, perfectly as it rende the illiterate Huck, has been created by a highly soph ticated art to serve subtle purposes, and Huck himself of course not merely the naïve boyish consciousness so successfully enacts; he is, by one of those triumpha sleights or equivocations which cannot be judiciou contrived, but are proof of inspired creative possessi the voice of deeply reflective maturity—of a life's ex rience brooded on by an earnest spirit and a fine in ligence. If Mark Twain lacked art in Arnold Benne sense (as Arnold Bennett pointed out), that only sho how little art in Arnold Bennett's sense matters, in c parison with art that is the answer of creative genius the pressure of a profoundly felt and complex expe ence. If *Huckleberry Finn* has its examples of the intelligence that may accompany the absence of s tained critical consciousness in an artist, even a g one, nevertheless the essential intelligence that preva and from the poetic depths informs the work, comp our recognition—the intelligence of the whole enga psyche; the intelligence that represents the integrity this, and brings to bear the wholeness. . . .

The book is a profound study of civilized man. about its attitude towards civilization as represented the society depicted in it there is nothing simple simplifying, either in a "frontier" spirit or in a spiri reductive pessimism. It is not to the point to add such private utterances of Mark Twain's as: "We h no real morals, but only artificial ones—morals cre and preserved by the forced suppression of natural healthy instinct." "Never trust the artist; trust the ta Lawrence's dictum might have been addressed to M Twain's case. *Huckleberry Finn,* the tale, gives u wholeness of attitude that transcends anything ordina attainable by the author. The liberation effected by memories of youth and the Mississippi was, for creative genius at his greatest, not into irresponsib but the reverse. The imaginatively recovered vitalit youth ministered, in sum, no more to the spiri "Pudd'nhead Wilson's Calendar" than to nostalgi daydream, but to the attainment of a sure and profo moral maturity. That is, to call *Huckleberry Fin* great work is not an exaggeration.

### William Van O'Connor

SOURCE: "Why *Huckleberry Finn* Is Not the G American Novel," in *College English,* Vol. 17, No October, 1955, pp. 6-10.

The critical acumen of [T.S.] Eliot and [Lionel] Tril notwithstanding, there are a number of flaws in *Hu leberry Finn,* some of them attributable to Twain's fusal to respect the "work of art" and others attributa to his imperfect sense of tone. The downstream mo ment of the story (theme as well as action) runs cou

*From* The Adventures of Huckleberry Finn, *written by Mark Twain. Illustrated by E. W. Kemble.*

to Jim's effort to escape. Life on the raft may indeed be read as implied criticism of civilization—but it doesn't get Jim any closer to freedom. One may also ask (it has been asked before) why it never occurred to Jim, or to Huck, to strike out for the Illinois shore and freedom. It is possible that Twain felt Tom's highjinks were necessary not merely to prepare for the disappearance of Huck but to shift attention away from his conflicting themes.

For the downward movement of the novel, of course, the picaresque form serves its subject very well, allowing for innumerable and rapid adventures, afloat and ashore, and for the sort of ponderings that are peculiar to Huck. The picaresque form is also a clue to the kind of unity the book does have, a melodramatic mixture of reality and unreality and of comedy and horror. It is frequently theatrical in a good sense of the word. But the unity depends on Huck's mind, and too often there are bits of action, dialogue, and observation which are not appropriate to him. There are two sorts of theatricality in the novel, melodrama and claptrap.

Huck's relationship with his father is melodrama. So is the shooting of Boggs, or the tar and feathering of the Duke and King. A proof of their being melodrama is the

ease with which one moves from a scene of violence to a humorous dialogue. For example, the encounter of Huck and Jim with the thieves and murderers aboard the *Walter Scott* is followed by the minstrel show, end-men sort of humor of "Was Solomon Wise?" Verisimilitude offers no problem when reality merges with unreality or horror dissolves innocently into comedy, but sometimes Twain's sense of proper distance, the degree and nature of the stylization he is employing, fails him and the action becomes gruesomely real. An instance of this is Huck's telling of the murders in "Why Harney Rode Away for His Hat." The starkness is too unrelieved. The scene does not respect the premises nor the general tone of the novel, and, even though it might work in another novel, it does not work here.

A good deal is made, quite justly, of Huck's affection for Jim, and the example commonly given is Huck's apology to Jim after having tormented him with a lie about there having been no storm. "It was fifteen minutes," Huck says, "before I could work myself up to go and humble myself to a nigger, but I done it, and I warn't sorry for it afterwards neither." But Twain sometimes loses sight of Huck's moral sensitivity. An instance is in Chapters XVII and XVIII.

Near the close of Chapter XVI the raft is run over by an upstream steamboat. In the darkness, after he and Jim have dived into the water, Huck cannot see Jim and his calls go unanswered. Huck then strikes out for shore. The following chapter, "The Grangerfords Take Me In," is a humorous introduction to the Grangerford family. Huck stays with the Grangerfords for many days, perhaps weeks, getting involved in their affairs, notably as courier between the lovers Miss Sophia Grangerford and Harney Shepherdson. No thought about Jim enters Huck's head! It doesn't occur to him to search for the old Negro. Jack, Huck's "nigger servant," finally invites him to see a "stack o' water-moccasins" in a swamp, a trick for leading him to the spot where Jim is hiding. "I poked into the place a ways and come to a little open patch as big as a bedroom all hung round with vines, and found a man lying there asleep—and, by jingo, it was my old Jim!" There is not much indication that Huck is greatly relieved or moved at finding Jim alive: "I waked him up, and I reckoned it was going to be a grand surprise to him to see me again. . . . He nearly cried he was so glad. . . ." Huck says nothing about being glad himself. Perhaps we are to read this passage ironically, as an instance of a boy's self-centeredness and believe that true affection lies beneath it. This might be so, but it doesn't explain away Huck's absence of grief over Jim's "death," or his failure to search for him if alive, or his general indifference to Jim's fate.

Technically, too, the device for getting rid of Jim so that Huck can move into the Grangerford-Shepherdson world is awkward and unconvincing. Jim tells Huck he had heard him call for him when they were swimming toward shore but hadn't answered for fear of being detected. Presumably one reply would have quieted Huck and made detection much less likely. And if Huck had been

allowed to help Jim hide, or even to maintain some awareness of him, he would be the Huck known to us in "Fooling Old Jim."

Huck's parody (Chapter XVII) of the activities of Emmeline Grangerford, poetess, is extremely amusing, but the "voice" is more nearly Twain's than Huck's. Many other things are put into the mouth of the twelve or thirteen year old Huck that, sometimes only weakly humorous themselves, are Twain himself speaking. This, for example, from a boy with almost no schooling:

> Look at Henry the Eight; this 'n' a Sunday-school Superintendent to *him*. And look at Charles Second, and Louis Fourteen, and Louis Fifteen, and James Second, and Edward Second, and Richard Third, and forty more; besides all them Saxon heptarchies that used to rip around so in oldtimes and raise Cain. . . .

There are other witticisms about kings, a theme appropriate enough to *Huckleberry Finn,* but Twain might have found some other way of introducing them. In "An Arkansas Difficulty," where Twain is giving a sense of life in a small river-town, he makes Huck relate an observation on "chawing tobacker" that one would expect to find as "filler" in a nineteenth-century newspaper or magazine. Most incongruous of all, perhaps, is Huck's account of the Duke's rendition of Hamlet's soliloquy.

A more self-conscious artist would not have allowed such discrepancies to mar the tone of his novel. The truth is that Twain, however gifted a raconteur, however much genius he had as an improviser, was not, even in *Huckleberry Finn,* a great novelist.

## Richard Chase

SOURCE: In *The American Novel and Its Tradition,* by Richard Chase, Doubleday & Company, Inc., 1957, pp. 144-45.

The departures from and returns to the river as Huck goes through his adventures approximate the *rite de passage* which in religious cult introduces a boy into manhood, so that in this respect one thinks of *Huckleberry Finn* in relation to the book of [James Fenimore] Cooper's Mark Twain most disliked—*Deerslayer,* as well as in relation to *The Red Badge of Courage,* Hemingway's *In Our Time,* and Faulkner's *The Bear.* Actually, however, this myth is present in *Huckleberry Finn* only dimly, as a kind of abstract framework or unrealized possibility. This is typical of American literature. Generally speaking, it is not a literature in which the classic actions of the soul as traditionally depicted in myth, religion, and tragedy are carried through. Only in *Deerslayer* and *The Bear* is the drama of initiation rendered with any fullness. Characters in American fiction who seem to be, because of their situation and prospects,

candidates for initiation do not usually change much under the pressure of what happens to them and when the author ascribes to his character, as in *The Red Badge of Courage,* a new manhood, new courage, new tragic awareness of life, it sounds unmistakably like "the moral"—in short, an afterthought—and we do not feel that the theme of initiation has been dramatically realized. In looking for the typical American candidates for initiation, one finds either that, sensitive, suffering, and intelligent as they may be, they turn out like Christopher Newman in James's *The American* to be impervious to transformation and tragic awareness or, like Huck Finn himself (or Frederic Henry in *A Farewell to Arms*), they are already initiated, they already know the real world with a tragic awareness. There is no real change in Huck Finn during the course of the book, except that he comes to adopt, as he reflects on his duty to Jim, a morality based on New Testament ethic rather than the convention of his time and place. This is a great achievement but it doesn't make a myth of initiation. What we have is only some of the abstract framework of this myth and some of its poetic awareness of the presence of deity in nature.

## Margery Fisher

SOURCE: "Who's Who in Children's Books: Tom Sawyer," in *Who's Who in Children's Books: A Treasury of the Familiar Characters of Childhood,* Holt, Rinehart and Winston, 1975, p. 361.

Many do not consider [*Huckleberry Finn*] to be a children's book. It takes up the story of the two boys after their help in the capture of Injun Joe has brought them each a substantial reward. When Huck's father hears of this he returns to try to get his son's money, and Huck, already weary of life with the Widow Douglas, who has undertaken to civilize him, runs away with black Jim, who mistakenly believes that Miss Watson is planning to 'sell him down the river'. Although during the boat journey down the Mississippi Huck Finn is introduced to some extremely unpleasant aspects of human nature (for which even life with his Pap has not prepared him) and though first-person narrative imposes a certain air of maturity on him, he is as much of a child as Tom Sawyer is. He is confused by finding he has no consistent opinion of the two confidence tricksters he is involved with, and no certain idea of how far his own responsibility for Jim goes. His grumbling criticism of Tom's absurdly elaborate plans for releasing Jim from captivity shows not the practical scorn of an adult but the incomprehension of a boy who has had no chance to live out of books.

Generations of readers have approached *Huckleberry Finn,* a seminal book in American literature, with their own interpretation of Mark Twain's facetious admonition at the beginning, 'persons attempting to find a motive in this narrative will be persecuted; persons attempting to find a moral in it will be banished . . .' Read as an allegory of questing man, it is not a children's book:

read as a funny, touching, rambling, shrewd and honest story of boyhood, it is.

## Thomas Cooley

SOURCE: A preface to *The Adventures of Huckleberry Finn: An Authoritative Text, Backgrounds and Sources, Criticism, Second Edition,* edited by Sculley Bradley, Richmond Croom Beatty, E. Hudson Long, and Thomas Cooley, W. W. Norton & Company, Inc., 1977, pp. ix-xi.

Mark Twain was a great writer who never wrote a great book. *Adventures of Huckleberry Finn,* so this argument runs, is Mark Twain's masterpiece; yet it is seriously flawed by a weak ending—the last ten or a dozen chapters, in which the author fails to sustain the tone and vitality of the long central section. If "great" is defined as "technically perfect," this argument is probably correct. Yet it is equally true, as Ernest Hemingway once said of the novel, that "all modern American literature comes from one book by Mark Twain called *Huckleberry Finn* . . . it's the best book we've had. All American writing comes from that."

Mark Twain began *Huckleberry Finn* as a sequel to *Tom Sawyer,* intending "to take a boy of twelve and run him on through life"; Huck's "autobiography" was to be a story of growing up. In the book Mark Twain actually wrote, however, Huck never reaches manhood. Though his age seems to waver between twelve (or ten or eight) and fourteen (or sixteen or thirty), it is not easy to say whether his knowledge of the world grows in any consistent way. Huck's narrative might properly be viewed as a sequence of assaults upon his innocence rather than a sure progress toward a healthy maturity. By brilliantly portraying the hazards of a journey that constantly forces Huck to alter his parentage, name and, therefore, his identity, Mark Twain helped guide American fiction toward its characteristic search for self. "Would you say that the search for identity is primarily an American theme?" novelist Ralph Ellison was once asked by an interviewer. "It is *the* American theme," he replied.

The geography of *Huckleberry Finn,* dominated by the great river, is another of the triumphs of the book, and it conveys a tension between the individual and society that has also been called typically American. In the nineteenth century, some British readers charged that American literature was basically antisocial. Its heroes lived only in remote regions—the dark forest, a whaling ship at sea, the distant Walden Pond of Henry David Thoreau's imagination; seldom did they thrive within the ordered society of town, city, or court. When the raft serves Huck as a free and easy refuge from the cruelty of the shore, it provides the solitude American literature has been said to require for the fullest expression of the self. When, however, the river delivers Huck upon its banks or makes him collide with such agents of "civilization" as the duke and the king or the steamboat in Chapter XVI, we should recall that the typical "hero" of American fiction makes his "separate peace" (the phrase is Hemingway's) in order to return whole to the challenge of living in groups. Mark Twain's satire of shore life, like all good satire, exposes to correct. Moreover, by using as the principal vehicle of his satire the mighty river (always eating away at the puny foundations of the St. Petersburgs and Bricksvilles lining its shore), Mark Twain paid homage to those unruly forces of nature which can overwhelm both self and society at almost any time in American literature.

It was largely because of Huck's colloquial language, most critics agree, however, that Hemingway credited Mark Twain with giving that literature a distinctive modern turn. Here, for example, is a passage describing Huck's separation from Jim in a dense fog:

> I throwed the paddle down. I heard the whoop again; it was behind me yet, but in a different place; it kept coming, and kept changing its place, and I kept answering, till by-and-by it was in front of me again and I knowed the current had swung the canoe's head down stream and I was all right, if that was Jim and not some other raftsman hollering. I couldn't tell nothing about voices in a fog, for nothing don't look natural nor sound natural in a fog.

This is the language of speech, and it is very different from the language in which most American literature was written before 1885. The language of Irving, Emerson, Thoreau, Hawthorne, and even Melville was a formal, "literary" language; at its worst, it was sometimes inflated into what Mark Twain called "the showiest kind of book-talk." Mark Twain's greatest achievement, perhaps, was to make a spoken language do everything a literary language alone could do before him. Nothing is lost when Huck describes his panic in the fog, or the coming of a storm, or Pap's malice, or Jim's kindness—all in the vocabulary and syntax of the uneducated son of the town drunk, whose special way of seeing beyond conventional prejudices required an unconventional way of speaking. Nothing was lost, and a great deal was gained for a literature which is so often *told* in the first person by narrators whose innocence is the highest knowledge.

## Michael Patrick Hearn

SOURCE: "Expelling Huck Finn," in *The Nation,* Vol. 235, No. 4, August 7-14, 1982, p. 117.

"All modern American literature comes from one book by Mark Twain called *Huckleberry Finn,*" said Hemingway. "There was nothing before it. There has been nothing as good since." This opinion is now being challenged in the classrooms of Davenport, Iowa; Warrington, Pennsylvania; Houston, Texas; Montgomery County, Maryland; and in the courts as well. The loudest condemnation of *Huckleberry Finn* has come from something called the Human Relations Committee of Mark Twain Intermediate School in Fairfax County, Virginia. According to a spokesman for the racially balanced group, which demanded the removal of the book from the school's curriculum, *Huckleberry Finn* "is poison. It is anti-American; it works against the melting pot theory of our country; it works against the 14th Amendment of the Constitution and against the Preamble that guarantees all men life, liberty and the pursuit of happiness." Wow! Is it possible that the *Huckleberry Finn* taught in Fairfax County is the same *Huckleberry Finn* that describes how a poor white boy befriends a runaway slave in his flight down the Mississippi?

The current controversy is a perfect example of how one can read a book and not really *read* the book. Anyone who labels *Huckleberry Finn* "racist trash" does not recognize that the principal purpose of the novel was to describe an ignorant 14-year-old boy's awakening to the injustices of slavery. No work of American literature exposes the corruption of the "peculiar institution" more eloquently than does Mark Twain's novel. Twain courageously described the slave system as it was, introducing all the stupidities and sad prejudices of its ideology. Yes, Huck does use the word "nigger." He is a child of his time; one can hardly expect him to refer to slaves as "Afro-Americans."

Twain chose as his hero the lowest of the low: Huck Finn is poor white trash, the son of the town drunkard, and he has been reared in Missouri, a slave state—as was Twain himself. "In my schoolboy days," Twain confessed in his *Autobiography,* "I had no aversion to slavery. I was not aware that there was anything wrong about it. No one arraigned it in my hearing; the local papers said nothing against it; the local pulpit taught us that God approved it . . . if the slaves themselves had an aversion to slavery they were wise and said nothing." Twain was a reformed Southerner, and in *Huckleberry Finn* he expressed his shame for the way his race had treated another. "Human beings *can* be awful cruel to one another," says Huck.

What redeems the boy is his good heart. Twain once described the chief conflict in the novel as that in which "a sound heart and a deformed conscience come into collision and conscience suffers defeat." For Twain, the conscience is the repository of society's rules and prejudices. What Huck suffers throughout his travels with Jim down the Mississippi is the moral conflict between the teachings of slave society and the workings of his own better nature. Fate has thrown the two fugitives together. Huck has escaped from his drunken father and Jim from his owner, who wants to sell him South, and the two conspire to flee together by raft. Most likely the poor white would have had little to do with the slave back in St. Petersburg, Missouri, but out in the wilderness Huck needs Jim, who proves to be an able protector, skilled in the ways of the wilderness, and a true friend.

The raft is the great equalizer: each learns to depend on the other. As Huck admits, "You want, above all things, on a raft, is for everybody to be satisfied, and feel right and kind towards the others." Slowly (and sometimes

painfully) the boy realizes the humanity and dignity of his companion. The harmony on the river is disrupted only when the fugitives encounter civilization. To others, Jim is just a piece of property; they want to capture him, to chain him up, to sell him. Huck quickly learns to lie, cheat and steal to protect his friend.

Why should this poor white risk everything to help a runaway slave? Huck cannot go home again; he would be labeled a "nigger-stealer," considered by some at the time to be worse than a murderer. In his flight with Jim, Huck denies everything—his people, his country, his God. Finally, to protect himself when Jim is captured, Huck tries to write to Jim's owner and confess all. But he cannot mail the letter. He can think only of "Jim before me, all the time, in the day, and the night-time, sometimes moonlight, sometimes storms, and we afloating along, talking, and singing, and laughing. But somehow I couldn't seem to strike no places to harden me against him, but only the other kind. I'd see him . . . always call me honey, and pet me, and do everything he could think of for me, and how good he always was. . . ." What child, black or white, however hardened by its parents' prejudices, can remain unmoved by Huck's affection for Jim? Huck is Jim's only friend; Jim is Huck's only friend. Huck tears up the letter. He must free Jim. At least this boy believes that there are laws greater than men's laws. Like Dr. Martin Luther King Jr., Huck concludes that if a law be unjust, one has the right to break it. If Huck Finn is a racist, then God help the country.

Because of the recent public outcry, Fairfax County has ruled that *Huckleberry Finn* may be taught, but only with "appropriate planning." One wonders how it must have been presented before this ruling. The problem is the teaching, not the novel. How could anyone assign the book and not place it within its proper historical context? Should any class fail to discuss the humanity of Mark Twain's novel, then the school board should keep *Huckleberry Finn* and chuck the teacher.

### Robert B. Brown

SOURCE: "One Hundred Years of Huck Finn," in *American Heritage,* Vol. 35, No. 4, June-July, 1984, pp. 81-5.

"By and By," Mark Twain wrote to William Dean Howells in 1875, "I shall take a boy of twelve and run him through life (in the first person) but not Tom Sawyer—he would not be a good character for it." A month later he knew that the boy would be Huck, and he began work; by midsummer of 1876 Twain was well under way. But something went wrong. He gave up the notion of carrying Huck on into adulthood and told Howells of what he had written thus far: "I like it only tolerably well, and may possibly pigeonhole or burn the ms. when it is done."

Twain did put the book aside for seven years, during

which time he produced *A Tramp Abroad, The Prince and the Pauper,* and *Life on the Mississippi*. It was his return to the great river that enabled Twain to return to Huck: he knew that the river was the structural center of the book and its life's blood; now all went well. He reported to his family: "I am piling up manuscript in a really astonishing way. I believe I shall complete, in two months, a book which I have been going over for 7 years. This summer it is no more trouble to me to write than it is to lie." And to Howells, in August of 1883, he wrote: "I have written eight or nine hundred manuscript pages in such a brief space of time that I mustn't name the number of days; I shouldn't believe it myself, and of course couldn't expect you to. I used to restrict myself to four and five hours a day and five days in the week, but this time I have wrought from breakfast till 5:15 P.M. six days in the week, and once or twice I smouched a Sunday when the boss wasn't looking. Nothing is half so good as literature hooked on Sunday, on the sly."

A few months later he gave the manuscript to Charles L. Webster (his nephew by marriage), whom Twain had set up as head of his own publishing company. When Twain saw the illustrations he had commissioned by E. W. Kemble, an artist whose work he had admired in *Life,* he urged him to make Huck look less "ugly" and less "Irishy." Kemble obeyed.

The book was to be sold by subscription. "Keep it diligently in mind," Twain wrote to Webster, "that we don't issue until we have made a *big sale.* Get at your canvassing early and drive it with all your might, with an intent and purpose of issuing on the 10th or 15th of next December (the best time in the year to tumble a big pile into the trade); but if we haven't 40,000 subscriptions we simply postpone publication till we've got them."

Publication was postponed, but not for lack of subscriptions. While the book was being printed, someone added a few lines to Kemble's drawing of Uncle Silas on page 283; the lines emerging from Silas's groin were clearly obscene. The culprit was never discovered, although Webster immediately offered a reward of five hundred dollars to anyone who could name—and prove the guilt of—the man who did it. According to Webster, "250 copies left the office, I believe, before the mistake was discovered. Had the first edition been run off our loss would have been $25,000. Had the mistake not been discovered, Mr. Clemens's credit for decency and morality would have been destroyed." The printer, J. J. Little, was more succinct: "This cost me plenty."

Because of the delay Webster missed the Christmas target date, and what is perhaps the greatest American novel was published first in England by Chatto & Windus on December 10, 1884. The first American edition appeared on February 18, 1885. (According to the title page of both the manuscript and Webster's edition, the correct title is *Adventures of Huckleberry Finn.* The word *the* was added by the publishers to the running heads and by Kemble in his illustrations. Sales were

good. Webster's figures show that he had 9,000 orders by September 2, 1884, and over 40,000 by April of 1885. He planned to print 50,000. On May 6 he noted, "I have already sold 51,000 of Huck." A century later the Twain scholar Walter Blair estimates that, the world over, about twenty million copies have been sold, with sales still going strong.

Glad as he was about the book's commercial success, Twain was disheartened by its reception. The *Century Magazine,* which had serialized three excerpts from the novel, ran a generally favorable review by Thomas Sergeant Perry, who spoke of Huck as the "immortal hero"—but the review did not appear until three months after the book's publication. The newspapers were silent or, for the most part, negative: in Boston the book was attacked by both the *Advertiser* and the *Transcript,* the latter finding it "so flat, as well as coarse, that nobody wants to read it after a taste in the *Century."* Robert Bridges gave it a sarcastic review in *Life:* "a . . . delicate piece of narration by Huck Finn, describing his venerable and dilapidated 'pap' as afflicted with delirium tremens . . . is especially suited to amuse children on long, rainy afternoons . . . ."

It is, of course, impossible that so great a novel should have been misconstrued by everyone. Howells knew right away: "If I had written half as good a book as Huck Finn, I shouldn't ask anything better than to read the proofs [which he did]. . . ." It was called the "great American novel" as early as 1891 by the English writer Andrew Lang, and nine years after that a Harvard professor wrote that it was the "most admirable work of literary art as yet produced on this continent." Twain did not live to see *Adventures of Huckleberry Finn* assume the unshakable place in the literary firmament it holds today, but there is no doubt he knew its worth. And yet what held his increasingly bitter attention—almost from the moment the book appeared—was the controversy into which it was born.

In March of 1885 there occurred one of the great ironies of our literary history; *Adventures of Huckleberry Finn* was banned by a committee of the Public Library in Concord, Massachusetts, the town of Emerson and Thoreau, which had been the brightest center of intellect the country had ever known. The committee found the book too crude and had it removed from the public bookshelves. Louisa May Alcott expressed the committee members' views: "If Mr. Clemens cannot think of something better to tell our pure-minded lads and lasses he had best stop writing for them."

Twain thus was probably the first American writer to gain advantage by being banned in (or around) Boston. As he wrote to Webster: "The Committee of the Public Library of Concord, Mass., have given us a rattling tip-top puff which will go into every paper in the country. . . . That will sell 25,000 copies for us sure." In his notebook for April 15 he observed: "Those idiots in Concord are not a court of last resort, and I am not disturbed by their moral gymnastics. No other book of mine has sold so many copies within 2 months after issue as this one has done."

The "moral gymnastics"—as American as the book itself—have now continued for one hundred years and show no sign of abating.

The first objections to Huck arose merely from notions of gentility: literature was to be high-toned and elevating. Even Emerson, who had noted again and again that ordinary speech had its own power and poetry, thought it necessary to keep it out of his printed *Essays.* But in his journal entry for October 5, 1840, Emerson wrote: "What a pity that we cannot curse and swear in good society. . . . It is the best rhetoric and for a hundred occasions these forbidden words are the only good ones." In addition to the language, there was the problem of Huck's character: he told lies, defied his elders, was shiftless. Not a good example for young people.

So widespread was this genteel recoiling that in 1907 E. L. Pearson, a librarian, complained that Tom and Huck were being "turned out of some library every year." Pearson went on to conjure up the attitudes of a censorious children's librarian: "No, no," she says, "Tom Sawyer, and you, you *horrid* Huckleberry Finn, you mustn't come here. All the boys and girls in here are good and pious; they have clean faces, they go to Sun-day-school, and they love it, too. . . . But you—you naughty, bad boys, your faces aren't washed, and your clothes are all covered with dirt. I do not believe either of you brushed his hair this morning. . . . As for you, Huckleberry, you haven't any shoes or stockings at all, and every one knows what your father is." Yet what is literature, asks Pearson, but a "record of people doing the things they should not do."

During the last forty-odd years the objections have shifted to other grounds. Now it is the treatment of Jim, the presence of the word *nigger,* and what seems to some readers a degree of ambiguity in Huck's (and Twain's) attitude toward the man. Others cannot even see ambiguity. The book is the "most grotesque example of racism I've ever seen in my life," said a school administrator in Virginia in 1982. His post was at the Mark Twain Intermediate School.

Mark Twain wrote his own sad projections about Huck in 1891, when he planned a sequel: "Huck comes back, 60 years old, from nobody knows where—and crazy. Thinks he is a boy again, and scans always every face for Tom and Becky, etc. Tom comes at last from . . . wandering the world and tends Huck, and together they talk the old times, both are desolate, life has been a failure, all that was lovable, all that was beautiful, is under the mold. They die together." He never wrote the book, and Tom and Huck probably will live forever.

*Revised manuscript page from*
The Adventures of Huckleberry Finn.

**Allison R. Ensor**

SOURCE: "The Illustrating of *Huckleberry Finn*: A Centennial Perspective," in *One Hundred Years of Huckleberry Finn: The Boy, His Book, and American Culture,* edited by Robert Sattelmeyer and J. Donald Crowley, University of Missouri Press, 1985, pp. 255-81.

What did Huckleberry Finn look like? Since the novel is a first-person narrative, Huck gives no description of himself, and few if any clues are provided by what he reports the other characters as saying. We can, of course, use our imaginations, and there are those who would argue that this is best. One can do little else with the familiar Riverside, Bantam, Signet, Penguin, or Norton Critical editions used in so many classrooms, for they contain no illustrations beyond those on their covers. When the novel's text appears in an anthology of American literature, there are usually no pictures at all. But if one reads **Huckleberry Finn** in an illustrated edition, as everyone did one hundred years ago, then his imagination is directed, supplemented, by pictures revealing the artist's conception of Huck, Jim, Tom Sawyer, the Grangerfords, the King and the Duke, the Wilks girls, Aunt Sally and Uncle Silas Phelps. And in most instances the artist depicts these characters in action against the backgrounds of the places where that action occurred: St. Petersburg, the Grangerford house, the Wilks place, the Phelps farm, and, above all, the Mississippi River.

Beginning with Edward Winsor Kemble (1861-1933),

the illustrator chosen by Samuel Clemens and his publisher, Charles Webster, for the first edition, artist after artist has assumed the task of depicting the adventures of Huckleberry Finn. The approaches and techniques used have varied widely. Some have drawn a great many pictures, others relatively few. Some made black-and-white pen-and-ink drawings; others produced full-color oil paintings. Some pictures are highly realistic and vividly detailed; others are so impressionistic that out of context one would be unlikely to connect them with the novel at all. Some artists have worked with a good deal of knowledge of the Mississippi valley; others have had none at all. Some artists have emphasized the darker, more violent moments of the novel; others have ignored these almost entirely. Even Clemens himself apparently wanted the illustrations to blink at some of the realities that the text portrayed.

How many illustrated editions of **Huckleberry Finn** have there been? It is not an easy question to answer. Michael Patrick Hearn lists forty-five "notable" editions of the novel; of these, twenty-three were illustrated by eighteen different artists. One is illustrated with stills from a film version of the novel, a procedure that several publishers domestic and foreign have followed. The **Huckleberry Finn** collection at the Buffalo and Erie County Public Library contains about sixty editions in English, plus over seventy-five foreign-language editions. Well over half of these are illustrated. Besides the standard editions of the novel, there have been profusely illustrated abridged and simplified children's editions, including a "Better Little Book" with pictures on every other page and two quite different *Classics Illustrated* comic books.

Clearly, among artists who illustrated **Huckleberry Finn** the best known were Norman Rockwell and Thomas Hart Benton. Neither Howard Pyle nor N. C. Wyeth attempted **Huckleberry Finn,** though they did illustrate other books by Clemens. Certain of Rockwell's pictures are well known today, though more for their appearance in books devoted to Rockwell's work than for their presence in the original Heritage Press edition. The Rockwell paintings are almost certainly better known to the American public than any other illustrations of the novel. Benton's drawings are, in contrast, not widely known. They are seldom reproduced, and the limited edition in which they were published is not easily found. More accessible is his depiction of Huck and Jim in part of a mural for the Missouri state capitol; it has been reproduced several times. The original Kemble drawings have appeared in more editions, American and foreign, than any other and are still readily available, as in ***The Annotated Huckleberry Finn,*** the 1979 Franklin Library edition, and in the forthcoming Iowa-California edition of the novel.

To attempt to deal with every illustrated edition of **Huckleberry Finn** is clearly beyond the scope of this essay. What can be done is to look at some of the most significant illustrated editions—those of Kemble, Rockwell, Benton, and certain lesser-known artists—and to consider the various approaches they have taken as they tried to aid the reader in visualizing the characters and action of this major American novel.

The story of the illustrating of the first edition of **Huckleberry Finn** has been told several times—by the illustrator himself, by his model, and by recent scholars. Certain parts of it must necessarily be recounted here.

After brief consideration of an artist named Hooper whose services could be obtained rather cheaply, Clemens turned to E. W. Kemble, son of the founder and publisher of the *San Francisco Alta California,* the paper that printed many of Clemens's 1867 letters from Europe and the Holy Land. Kemble, now in the East, had done work for *Harper's Bazaar,* the *New York Graphic,* and *Life.* He would later recall that Clemens's attention was attracted to him by a *Life* drawing of a little boy being stung by a bee, a boy who matched Clemens's mental image of Huck Finn. Clemens's letter to his publisher of 31 March 1884, however, mentions a different *Life* drawing: "There *is* a Kemble on *Life,*" he wrote, "but is he the man who illustrated the applying of electrical protectors to door knobs, door-mats &c & electrical hurriers to messengers, waiters, &c, 4 or 5 weeks ago. *That* is the man I want to try." The drawing in question, "Some Uses for Electricity," had appeared in *Life's* issue of 13 March 1884 and included a picture Clemens understandably failed to mention, of a book agent being shocked by an electrified doormat. Kemble was contacted and an agreement worked out whereby he would produce about 175 illustrations for a fee of $1,200. In some respects Kemble might have seemed poorly qualified: he was only twenty-three years old, he had been drawing professionally for only two years, he had never had a contract for book illustrations before, and he had never seen the Mississippi River valley or the South. As he candidly admitted latter, "I had up to that time, never been further south than Sandy Hook."

Undaunted by his lack of firsthand information concerning the setting of the new novel, Kemble set about illustrating it as best he could from the chapters of the manuscript he had been given. As his model for Huck Finn he selected a sixteen-year-old boy named Courtland P. Morris but usually called Cort. Young Morris was a native of New Jersey living in the Bronx at the time Kemble asked him to pose, offering the boy four dollars a week. As Kemble later recalled, Morris was "a bit tall for the ideal boy, but I could jam him down a few pegs in my drawing and use him for the other characters." And that is just what Kemble did: Morris served as model not only for Huck Finn but also for every character, male or female, white or black, in the entire book. Kemble made use of a variety of costumes—an old sunbonnet and faded skirt for Mrs. Judith Loftus, an old frock coat and padded waistline for the King.

Clemens was in the meantime getting impatient. "I sent the MS. to-day," he wrote Webster on 12 April. "Let Kemble rush–time is already growing short." Such pressure would not seem an ideal situation for an artist, and

Kemble's predicament was worsened by conditions at his house. He wrote Webster on 1 May, "We all have the moving craze & are experiencing such little delights as eating our meals from off the mantle [*sic*] piece, bathing in a coal scuttle behind a fire screen &c &c. I have tried to work but cannot make it go." He included a sketch labeled "A faint idea of my condition," which depicts the artist seated on a barrel that is resting on a box, his pad leaned against a stepladder, as a passing worker casts an eye over Kemble's shoulder. Another difficulty Kemble had to deal with was lack of access to the entire manuscript. At one point he asked Webster to "send me the manuscript from the XIII chapter on, as there are illustrations here & there which are described very minutely & I am afraid to touch them without the reading matter to refer to."

Kemble did manage to get some of his illustrations finished, and they were passed on to Clemens. The author was not enthusiastic. "All right & good, & will answer," he told Webster on 7 May, after having seen the proposed cover for the book, "although the boy's mouth is a trifle more Irishy than necessary." On 24 May, Clemens had a more detailed objection to make:

> Some of the pictures are good, but none of them are very *very* good. The faces are generally ugly, & wrenched into over-expression amounting sometimes to distortion. As a rule (though not always) the people in these pictures are forbidding and repulsive. Reduction will modify them, no doubt, but it can hardly make them pleasant folk to look at. An artist shouldn't follow a book too literally, perhaps—if this is the necessary result. And mind you, much of the drawing, in these pictures is careless & bad.
>
> The pictures will *do*—they will just barely do—& that is the best I can say for them.
>
> The frontispiece has the usual blemish—an ugly, ill-drawn face. Huck Finn is an exceedingly good-hearted boy, & should carry a good & good-looking face.
>
> Don't dishearten the artist—show him where he has *improved,* rather than where he has failed, & punch him up to improve more.

The theory of illustration that Clemens espouses here is interesting and perhaps surprising: that an illustrator should not follow the text too closely, that the pictures should not tell as much truth as the text. Clemens made exactly this point again in a letter to Webster on 11 June. Now much better satisfied, he declared, "I *knew* Kemble had it *in* him, if he would only modify his violence & come down to careful, painstaking work. This batch of pictures is most rattling good. They please me exceedingly." Having said this, he went on to object to a particular picture. "But you must knock out one of them," he declared, "—the lecherous old rascal kissing the girl at the camp meeting. It is powerful good, but it mustn't go in—don't forget it. Let's not make *any* pictures of the camp meeting. The subject won't *bear* illustrating. It is a disgusting thing, & pictures are sure to

tell the truth about it too plainly." One is reminded of Clemens's statement to Dan Beard, the illustrator of **A Connecticut Yankee**, about five years later: "I have endeavored to put in all the coarseness and vulgarity . . . that is necessary and rely upon you for all the refinement and delicacy of humor your facile pen can depict." Accordingly, the offending illustration was omitted, and the only camp meeting picture that survives is one of two young people "courting on the sly." Kemble apparently needed no advice from Clemens to avoid portraying Huck and Jim in the state of nudity Huck says they were often in. And there is certainly nothing risqué about Kemble's picture of the King enacting the "Royal Nonesuch." Even so, the caption diverts our attention with the word *Tragedy.*

The only further objection Clemens made to Kemble's pictures concerned a matter of riverboat knowledge. In drawing a wrecked steamboat, Kemble (who, we remember, did not always have as much of the manuscript as he needed) placed on it the name *Texas,* apparently assuming from mention of the texas deck that this was the boat's name. Clemens pointed out that "*every* boat" had a texas and that "that word had better be removed from that pilot house—that is where a boat's *name* is put, & that particular boat's name was, Walter Scott." Clemens raised no objections to other errors that have been noted: the King was given a black hat in the Wilks episode, when the text specifically says he wore a white beaver hat; Joanna Wilks, according to the text about the same age as Huck, is shown considerably older. Huck himself hardly looks a consistent fourteen throughout the book.

Clemens appears to have made no comment about what must appear rather striking to anyone studying the work of a variety of illustrations: Kemble's inclination to illustrate purely imaginary scenes. In only one instance do these scenes involve the main characters. At the beginning of Chapter 15, Kemble shows Huck and Jim in Cairo, Illinois, trying to sell their raft. Huck and Jim of course missed Cairo entirely; selling the raft there was something they only intended to do. Among the most capricious drawings are those showing the distressed parents of young Stephen Dowling Bots, the boy memorialized in Emmeline Grangerford's poem; the King as the pirate he claims to have been; Henry VIII tossing tea into Boston harbor, one of Huck's historical mistakes; Hanner Proctor with the mumps, which Huck claims she has; witches, apparently as imagined by the slave who brings Jim's food to him; a prisoner about to cut off his hand, as Tom says some of "the best authorities" have done in order to escape; and finally a picture labeled "One of His Ancestors," in which Kemble plays with the ambiguity of Huck's statement that Uncle Silas's warming pan "belonged to one of his ancestors with a long wooden handle that came over from England with William the Conqueror." Kemble depicts the ancestor with both a long-handled warming pan and a long wooden leg. Mention might also be made of the satirical drawing at the conclusion of the chapter in which the King and the Duke appear for the first time: in it the emblems of royalty intermingle with the whiskey bottle and satchel of the two frauds.

Most of the 174 drawings in the first edition are of a different nature, of course, for they simply depict the action of the book. Except for the frontispiece, none occupies a full page, and many are surrounded by text on three sides. Since there were to be so many drawings, it was necessary for Kemble to depict virtually every scene of importance in the book. Kemble did not decline to picture some of the novel's harsher realities: Jim Turner menaced by the men on the *Walter Scott,* the Grangerford-Shepherdson feud (though no dead bodies are shown), the shooting of Boggs by Colonel Sherburn (we see Boggs from the rear), the King and the Duke ridden out of town on a rail (the caption calls it "Traveling by Rail," thus inviting a laugh at what is for Huck a moment of pity and sadness). Nevertheless, as we will see, Kemble did miss certain scenes that have been great favorites with later illustrators. Kemble's pictures were considerably reduced in size for publication, as they were originally something like six and a half by eight inches. The originals are now scattered; Vassar College, Poughkeepsie, New York, has thirty-seven of them, plus the original design for the cover.

One of Kemble's illustrations was initially reproduced in a form different from that in which Kemble drew it. For the last picture of Chapter 32, Kemble showed Huck standing before an irate Uncle Silas and a grinning Aunt Sally, as the latter asks her husband, "Who do you reckon it is?" Apparently some mischievous person in the printing establishment found the expressions on the faces suggestive; it may have looked to him as if Huck had suddenly come upon some intimate scene. At any rate, he proceeded to alter the original drawing by adding a penis protruding from Uncle Silas's trousers. The change was discovered before any books were issued, but one would like to know what choice profanities escaped Clemen's lips when he first learned that this particular bit of mischief would cause his new book to miss the Christmas trade of 1884. The British and Canadian editions were able to appear in December, but the American had to wait until February of the next year.

On the whole Clemens seems to have been satisfied with Kemble's work, particularly in the last part of the book. "Kemble's pictures are mighty good, now," he wrote Webster on 1 July, and in another letter later in the year he seems to take pride in the *Century*'s Richard Watson Gilder having described Kemble as "a gem of an artist." It is not surprising that in August 1887, as he was planning his *Library of Humor,* he wrote Fred Hall and Webster: "I suggest that you get *Kemble* as artist; and that you get him right away, if he is getable." Kemble was, in fact, paid $2,000 for the 204 illustrations in the *Library of Humor.* In time, though, Clemens became disenchanted with Kemble's work; in reference to the illustrating of *A Connecticut Yankee,* he said:

> I prefer this time to contract for the very best an artist can do. This time I want pictures, not black-

board outlines and charcoal sketches. If Kemble illustrations for my last book were handed me today, I could understand how tiresome to me that sameness would get to be, when distributed through a whole book, and I would put them promptly in the fire.

It is scarcely surprising, then, that Clements did not call upon Kemble to illustrate either of the sequels to *Huckleberry Finn* published in Clemens's lifetime, *Tom Sawyer Abroad* and *Tom Sawyer, Detective.*

Kemble may well have supposed that he was done with Huck and his adventures after 1884. In fact he was to produce eight more illustrations based on the novel. For the Autograph Edition of 1899 Kemble did four pen-and-wash pictures, and these were used as full-page illustrations in various editions of later years, including the widely available Author's National Edition, which used as a frontispiece Kemble's 1899 picture of Huck arriving at the Phelps farm to be met by a large black woman with three small children peeping out from behind her. Also in 1899 Kemble drew three illustrations for the *New York World* of 10 December, when its comic supplement ran a special Mark Twain number. Kemble's final drawing, made in 1932, the year before his death, shows Huck, Tom, and Jim reading about themselves in a copy of *Huckleberry Finn.* The drawing was done at George Macy's request and placed on the title page of the Limited Editions Club edition of the novel.

Whatever second thoughts Clemens may have had about Kemble's ability as an artist, the verdict of posterity has been favorable. Thomas Hart Benton declared in 1942, "Kemble was a good illustrator and he did a particularly good job with Huck's adventures. . . . No illustrator who has tackled the book since has in any way approached his delicate fantasy, his pat humor, or his ability to produce an atmosphere of pathos." Much more recently, Michael Patrick Hearn declared that no artist—Benton and Norman Rockwell included—has outdone Kemble. With perhaps some exaggeration, he found that "Huck Finn himself is remembered as much for Kemble's image of the good-hearted boy as for Twain's description." It was, Hearn concludes, "a perfect marriage of author and illustrator." There has, however, been some dissent about Kemble's ability as an artist. Joel Chandler Harris, some of whose work was illustrated by Kemble, commented, "For a man who has no conception whatever of human nature, Kemble does very well. But he is too doggoned flip to suit me." Thomas Hart Benton complained that Kemble "was not much of a designer. . . . he didn't know how to lay out a space and set up a clean finished structure therein. His pictures came to no pictorial conclusion. They just ended." Benton also objected to Kemble's "monotonous pen-and-ink methods" and particularly to the fact that most of the Mississippi River characters looked like "Connecticut Yankees."

The Kemble illustrations were used repeatedly in subsequent editions of the novel. Occasionally all of them appeared, but more often only a few were chosen. Leo

Marx's edition for Bobbs-Merrill (1967), for instance, used only five and made them all into full-page illustrations. The Franklin Library edition (1979) used many of the Kemble drawings, with some as full-page illustrations and others printed the same size as in the first edition. Kemble's pictures have also appeared in a number of foreign-language editions, including Danish, Lettish, Russian, Swedish, and Ukranian. Furthermore, according to Kemble, his illustrations were used as a basis for the first (1920) film version of the novel. The director, Kemble recalled, "took a copy of the original edition and made his characters fit my drawings."

Apparently the second American to illustrate **Huckleberry Finn** was Worth Brehm (1883-1928), an Indiana native whose pictures of life in that state were published in *Outing* magazine and thus came to the attention of Harper's. The firm commissioned Brehm to illustrate first **Tom Sawyer** and then its sequel. His **Huckleberry Finn** appeared in 1923. Brehm's approach was entirely different from Kemble's. Instead of a great many drawings, Brehm prepared only nine, including a color frontispiece of Huck alone, fishing. Each picture occupied a full page and included much fuller detail than Kemble's had. . . .

As Brehm's was the most notable illustrated **Huck Finn** of the 1920s, the most notable of the 1930s was an edition illustrated by A. S. Forrest. This time there were seventeen illustrations, beginning with a frontispiece showing the by now familiar scene of Jim cowering before what he believes is the ghost of Huck Finn. As in Brehm's edition, the frontispiece was in color, while all the rest were black-and-white full-page drawings. Except for this frontispiece, Forrest seems to have sought to avoid following too closely in the footsteps of Kemble and Brehm.

The 1940s brought to the illustrating of **Huckleberry Finn** both Norman Rockwell and Thomas Hart Benton. Rockwell had already done **Tom Sawyer** for the Heritage Press edition of 1936, a task for which he must have seemed eminently suitable, in view of his many *Saturday Evening Post* covers depicting boys who might well have been characters in **Tom Sawyer** or **Huckleberry Finn**. To acquire a sense of the actual place where some of the novels' adventures occurred, Rockwell made a trip to Hannibal, Missouri, where he visited all the appropriate sites and acquired a lot of old clothes to take back to the East with him. It has been said that though Rockwell was "perfect" for the **Tom Sawyer** illustrations, he "failed to capture the bitter satire" of **Huck Finn**. . . .

Rockwell did a remarkable job of avoiding almost all of the darker side of **Huckleberry Finn,** its terror, violence, and death. The Grangerford-Shepherdson feud was left out entirely, as were the scene on the *Walter Scott,* the shooting of Boggs, and the tarring and feathering of the King and the Duke. In fact, the frontispiece presents the only really frightening moment depicted: Huck comes into his room at the Widow Douglas's to find Pap reared

back in his chair waiting for him. Yet even here Rockwell's treatment minimizes the sinister quality that Benton and others were to bring out very strongly. . . .

Benton's pictures are much less explicit, more "suggestive," to use his word. They are not oil paintings, for one thing; they are ink and sepia wash, with some outlining in black. Typical of Benton's work, there is a kind of rumpled quality to the bodies and clothing, an exaggeration of facial features, an elongation of form.

Benton prepared a great many drawings for his edition, though not nearly so many as Kemble. Each chapter begins with a small picture, and there are forty-five full-page illustrations. Having forty-five instead of Rockwell's eight, Benton obviously had more opportunity to illustrate different scenes from the book. Unlike Rockwell, Benton does not shrink from showing us some unpleasant moments: Pap chasing Huck with a knife and threatening to kill him, Jim's discovery of Pap's body (with several choice four-letter words partly visible on the wall of the floating house), some of the actual shooting in the Grangerford-Shepherdson feud. The killing of Boggs is dramatically depicted (Benton lets us see Boggs's face, as Kemble does not), and we see the King and the Duke being ridden on a rail. We have then a much closer look at the novel's harsh realities; we see life pretty much as it is, without any romantic coloring. . . .

A notable British edition of the 1950s is that of C. Walter Hodges. There are four full-page color illustrations, beginning with the frontispiece, a big crowd scene in which the "opposition line," the rival claimants to the fortune of Peter Wilks, arrives to confront the King and the Duke. The second color illustration, of Huck alone with a rifle on Jackson's Island, would have been a more traditional frontispiece. Other color scenes include the steamboat bearing down on Huck and Jim's raft (not nearly so frightening as Burra's or Powers's version) and an extensive river view in which we have the raft in the foreground, a steamboat in the middle distance, and then the river receding far into the background. In addition to the color plates, Hodges did fourteen black-and-white line drawings, none of them occupying a full page. These in particular seem rather British and might well be illustrating a story by Dickens.

Perhaps the most interesting American illustrations of the 1960s are those of John Falter. . . . Some of Falter's detailed, quite realistic scenes are familiar: Jim before Huck when he thinks Huck is a ghost, Jim and Huck leaping overboard as the steamboat approaches the raft (Falter's picture is striking, as he makes the steamboat appear like a monster about to devour them), the Duke reciting Shakespeare on the raft, Huck about to reveal to Mary Jane the truth about the "uncles," and Aunt Sally besieged by the rats. All of these themes had been used time and again, though Falter does them very well. In some instances, Huck and Mary Jane, for example, a scene so much like Rockwell's, Falter is somehow more appealing, more convincing—despite the fact that the picture is in black and white and the background is not filled in. . . .

The late 1970s saw the appearance of two American editions that deserve attention here. Warren Chappell illustrated the novel for Harper and Row's "Centennial Edition" of *The Complete Adventures of Tom Sawyer and Huckleberry Finn* in 1978. Instead of doing full-page pictures, Chappell produced a series of smaller drawings in black and white, with some green added. More suggestive than realistic, the drawings provide little specific detail. A few squiggles often represent the background. The view of the King enacting the Royal Nonesuch is more explicit than usual, although he is not any rival to Uncle Silas in the "obscene" illustration in the first edition.

The Franklin Library issued in 1978 a volume of **Huck Finn** with twelve full-page black-and-white pictures by Barnett Plotkin. The treatment is considerably more realistic than Chappell's and is indeed more like the work of John Falter, though there is more filling in of the background here. The frontispiece perhaps goes back to Worth Brehm for its inspiration, for it shows Huck alone, fishing. We get Huck and Pap, but in the hut in the woods, not at the widow's; Jim and Huck on the island; Huck and Jim seeing the wreck of the *Walter Scott.* An unusual scene not often illustrated is that of Huck deceiving the men who are looking for runaway slaves. The Shepherdson-Grangerford feud is missing, but the King and the Duke turn up; we have, in fact, the King preaching at the camp meeting, one of those scenes Clemens would not allow Kemble to depict. Generally, one might say that Plotkin stays away from the violent and the unpleasant (though he does show Pap in the throes of the D.T.s). Perhaps the most dramatic scene is the often-used raising of the coffin of Peter Wilks as an eager crowd looks on and lightning streaks the sky.

A few words must be said about the foreign-language editions of **Huckleberry Finn.** There have been a great many, far more than there have been editions in English, and a high proportion of them have been illustrated in some way. Some have used movie stills; others have reprinted (sometimes rather poorly) illustrations from American editions; most have employed their own artists. These last have used a wide variety of techniques. There are Italian editions, for instance, with full-color, full-page plates almost like Rockwell's in their concern for detail (though one doubts that the artists spent much time in Hannibal, Missouri). Particularly notable in this regard is the work of Didone for a 1953 Milan edition. It is a little surprising, however, to see both Jim and the King completely bald and the King sporting a beard that extends downward to left and right from his mustache but does not cover his chin. More often the illustrations are in black and white, sometimes covering an entire page, sometimes smaller. Many of the scenes most frequently found in editions in English appear here too. Thus, the German artist Horst Lemke depicts Huck and Jim standing on their raft a moment before jumping to escape the approaching steamboat, and a similar scene

appears—far more impressionistically—in a Bulgarian edition of 1963. Huck flees from the cemetery where Peter Wilks's body has just been exhumed in Didone's Italian edition and in a full-page color illustration for a Japanese edition. Perhaps the main faults that American readers might complain of are that the characters often do not look American—the Huck on the title page of the 1963 Bulgarian edition looks almost Vietnamese—and foreign artists are more likely to resort to caricature, especially in regard to Jim. Most of the pictures in a Hungarian edition of 1956 look like cartoons, and Jim's huge eyes and lips dominate his face. In one scene, in Jim's cabin at the Phelps farm, he is surrounded by comical snakes, mice, and a spider hanging by a long thread from its web high above. The artist suggests that the reader need not take the situation of Jim's imprisonment seriously. Of course, many of the foreign illustrations are quite good; among the most praised are those of Eric Palmquist for a 1957 Swedish edition, which has many black-and-white illustrations and an occasional double-page illustration such as that of the King and the Duke tarred and feathered.

We have now considered the work of some fifteen artists who have wrestled with the task of illustrating one of the greatest works of American fiction. Presumably all had in mind a similar goal, to help readers visualize the characters and incidents of the book. No doubt many a reader—especially a young reader—has had his perception of the novel shaped by the illustrations, and no doubt many still visualize the characters in accord with how they looked in the pictures accompanying the edition in which they first encountered Huck, Jim, the King and the Duke, the Grangerfords, the Shepherdsons, and the Phelpses. To look at several sets of illustrations, one might find it hard to believe that all the artists are illustrating the same novel. While one finds it a sunny, happy story in which nothing too serious happens, another finds it a grim, bleak novel filled with unsavory characters and frightening incidents. Such differences occur for a variety of reasons: the intended audience (children or adults), the personality of the artist, the artist's interpretation of the novel. In Kemble's case, one has to add the personality and desires of the author as well. In the end, we perhaps ought to look at the illustrations as we would at printed critical interpretations, choosing those that most appeal to us, that seem to come closest to our own views of the text. That there can be so many varied interpretations in art as in written criticism is further testimony to the richness of **Huckleberry Finn.**

**Margery Fisher**

SOURCE: "Learning the Land," in *The Bright Face of Danger,* The Horn Book, Inc., 1986, pp. 267-292.

When Huck Finn decamps from St. Petersburg it is not primarily to escape from domestic constraints, however irksome these may seem to him, but to avoid a confrontation with his father, who has come to reclaim him on hearing of the money invested for him; although Huck has a shrewdness and resource beyond his years, he still lacks the experience to stand up to a determined and ruthless adult. Jackson's Island is not his goal, but the starting point for a journey downriver on a raft which takes him deep into the South and brings danger and problems far beyond most of the cliché-adventures which Tom contrives from books. All the same, *The Adventures of Huckleberry Finn* belongs in the same category as *The Adventures of Tom Sawyer.* Indeed, it seems a pity that the close scrutiny given to 'the greatest American novel' by so many critics has made it hard to read the book as a story, with the same expectations that one had as a child.

Psychiatric comment on Mark Twain's dislike of being labelled as a comic writer, 'a buffoon' as he put it, makes one almost embarrassed at enjoying the rich humour of the book, even when one takes in also the irony and melancholy, the lurking distaste, the farcical sordidness of some of the characters—the skull beneath the comic skin. As a story claimed by children, as well as by adults, the book has been read first of all as a sequel to *Tom Sawyer;* Mark Twain gave it the subtitle 'Tom Sawyer's Comrade' and it can be approached with the same anticipation of role-playing and retribution which are satisfied by the earlier book. The idea of a boy escaping the shackles of domestic propriety is immediately appealing to young readers and so is the method of escape. Whatever symbols an adult interpretation may attach to Huck's raft, to a child it is part of the dream of freedom and independence in which he can avoid the uncomfortable fact that home-made rafts tend to collapse.

None-the-less, the beguiling action and idiom of *Huckleberry Finn* contain layers of meaning, clusters of imagery, which work on the imagination even though young readers, held by incidents and scenes, are not consciously aware of the moral complexities and the trenchant social comment in Huck's adventures—indeed, they may be bored or puzzled by such parts of the story as the crazy obligations of the feud between the Grangerfords and the Shepherdsons or the tortuous schemes of the confidence tricksters self-styled the Duke of Bilgewater (sic) and the exiled King of France.

Accepting Huck Finn as a boy-hero, children are able to regard as perfectly natural the way he sees through the pretensions of villains while still remaining with them. They will understand in simple terms the difficult decision Huck has to make, whether to do his civic duty and betray Jim, the runaway slave who has joined him on his journey, or whether to keep his secret in loyalty to a friend.

They may well feel less ill at ease than adults do with the change towards the end of the book from a harsh, sardonic description of corrupt people to a farcical return to boyish fantasy, when Tom reappears to plan the elaborate, book-oriented and totally unnecessary rescue of Jim (who, as Tom knows perfectly well, has already

been freed by his owner). They may sense that Huck, though he too is an escaper, keeps his lifeline to civilisation: the raft is his home, his point of reference on the river and his link with the town he is unwilling entirely to give up. The raft, in fact, is from the point of view of a young reader the significant centre of the book. For an adult it is the river, impersonal and outside civilisation but admitting to its banks a succession of imperfect, greedy and sordid men, which is the true centre, the concrete embodiment of Mark Twain's assertion of the creative, natural world which he has seen threatened in the name of progress. Huck Finn, lay about and free soul though he is, is not the mouthpiece of a philosophy of nature. . . . It is the author, speaking through description, through the innocent common sense and honesty of his central character, through the breadth of Huck's involuntary experience, who expresses his theme.

### John H. Wallace

SOURCE: "The Case Against Huck Finn," in *Satire or Evasion? Black Perspectives on Huckleberry Finn,* edited by James S. Leonard, Thomas A. Tenney, and Thadious M. Davis, Duke University Press, 1992, pp. 16-24.

*The Adventures of Huckleberry Finn,* by Mark Twain, is the most grotesque example of racist trash ever written.

For the past forty years, black families have trekked to schools in numerous districts throughout the country to say, "This book is not good for our children," only to be turned away by insensitive and often unwittingly racist teachers and administrators who respond, "This book is a classic." Classic or not, it should not be allowed to continue to cause our children embarrassment about their heritage.

Louisa May Alcott, the Concord Public Library, and others condemned the book as trash when it was published in 1885. The NAACP and the National Urban League successfully collaborated to have *Huckleberry Finn* removed from the classrooms of the public schools of New York City in 1957 because it uses the term "nigger." In 1969 Miami-Dade Junior College removed the book from its classrooms because the administration believed that the book creates an emotional block for black students which inhibits learning. It was excluded from the classrooms of the New Trier High School in Winnetka, Illinois, and removed from the required reading list in the state of Illinois in 1976.

My own research indicates that the assignment and reading aloud of *Huckleberry Finn* in our classrooms is humiliating and insulting to black students. It contributes to their feelings of low self-esteem and to the white students' disrespect for black people. It constitutes mental cruelty, harassment, and outright racial intimidation to force black students to sit in the classroom with their white peers and read *Huckleberry Finn.* The attitudes

*From* The Adventures of Huckleberry Finn, *1884. Illustrated by E. W. Kemble.*

developed by the reading of such literature can lead to tensions, discontent, and even fighting. If this book is removed from the required reading lists of our schools, there should be improved student-to-student, student-to-teacher, and teacher-to-teacher relationships. . . .

When "authorities" mention the "historical setting" of *Huckleberry Finn,* they suggest that it is an accurate, factual portrayal of the way things were in slavery days. In fact, the book is the outgrowth of Mark Twain's memory and imagination, written twenty years after the end of slavery. Of the two main characters depicted, one is a thief, a liar, a sacrilegious corn-cob-pipe-smoking truant; the other is a self-deprecating slave. No one would want his children to emulate this pair. Yet some "authorities" speak of Huck as a boyhood hero. Twain warns us in the beginning of *Huckleberry Finn,* "Persons attempting to find a motive in this narrative will be prosecuted; persons attempting to find a moral in it will be banished; persons attempting to find a plot in it will be shot." I think we ought to listen to Twain and stop feeding this trash to our children. It does absolutely nothing to enhance racial harmony. The prejudice that existed then is still very much apparent today. Racism against blacks is deeply rooted in the American culture and is continually reinforced by the schools, by concern for socioeconomic gain, and by the vicarious ego enhancement it brings to those who manifest it.

*Huckleberry Finn* is racist, whether its author intended it to be or not. The book implies that black people are not honest. For example, Huck says about Jim: "It most froze me to hear such talk. He wouldn't ever dared to talk such talk in his life before. Just see what a difference it made in him the minute he judged he was about free. It was according to the old saying, 'give a nigger an inch and he'll take an ell.' Thinks I, this is what comes of my not thinking". And in another section of the book, the Duke, in reply to a question from the King, says: "Mary Jane'll be in mourning from this out; and the first you know the nigger that does up the rooms will get an order to box these duds up and put 'em away; and do you reckon a nigger can run across money and not borrow some of it?"

*Huckleberry Finn* also insinuates that black people are less intelligent than whites. In a passage where Huck and Tom are trying to get the chains off Jim, Tom says: "They couldn't get the chain off, so they just cut their hand off and shoved. And a leg would be better still. But we got to let that go. There ain't necessity enough in this case; and, besides, Jim's a nigger, and wouldn't understand the reason for it." On another occasion, when Tom and Huck are making plans to get Jim out of the barn where he is held captive, Huck says: "He told him everything. Jim, he couldn't see no sense in most of it, but he allowed we was white folks and knowed better than him; so he was satisfied, and said he would do it all just as Tom said." . . .

*Huckleberry Finn* even suggests that blacks are not human beings. When Huck arrives at Aunt Sally's house, she asks him why he is late:

"We blowed a cylinder head."

"Good gracious! anybody hurt?"

"No'm. Killed a nigger."

"Well, it's lucky; because sometimes people do get hurt."

There are indications that the racist views and attitudes implicit in the preceding quotations are as prevalent in America today as they were over one hundred years ago. *Huckleberry Finn* has not been successful in fighting race hate and prejudice, as its proponents maintain, but has helped to retain the status quo. . . .

It is difficult to believe that Samuel Clemens would write a book against the institution of slavery; he did, after all, join a Confederate army bent on preserving that peculiar institution. Also, he could not allow Huck to help Jim to his freedom. It seems he was a hodge-podge of contradictions.

*Huckleberry Finn* is an American classic for no other reason than that it ridicules blacks to a greater extent than any other book given our children to read. The book and racism feed on each other and have withstood the test of time because many Americans insist on preserving our racist heritage. . . .

## Julius Lester

SOURCE: "Morality and *Adventures of Huckleberry Finn*," in *Satire or Evasion? Black Perspectives on Huckleberry Finn,* edited by James S. Leonard, Thomas A. Tenney, and Thadious M. Davis, Duke University Press, 1992, pp. 199-207.

I don't think I'd ever read *Adventures of Huckleberry Finn.* Could that be? Every American child reads it, and a child who read as much as I did must have.

As carefully as I search the ocean floor of memory, however, I find no barnacle-encrusted remnant of Huckleberry Finn. I may have read *Tom Sawyer*, but maybe I didn't. Huckleberry Finn and Tom Sawyer are embedded in the American collective memory like George Washington (about whom I know I have never read). Tom and Huck are part of our American selves, a mythologem we imbibe with our mother's milk.

I do have an emotional memory of going to Hannibal, Missouri, with my parents when I was eight or nine, and visiting the two-story white frame house where Mark Twain lived as a boy—where Huck and Tom lived as boys. In the American collective memory, Twain, Huck, and Tom merge into a paradigm of boyhood which shines as poignantly as a beacon, beckoning, always beckoning to us from some paradise lost, albeit no paradise we (or they) ever had.

I remember that house, and I remember the white picket fence around it. Maybe it was my father who told me the story about Tom Sawyer painting the fence (if it was Tom Sawyer who did), and maybe he told me about Huckleberry Finn, too. But it occurs to me only now to wonder if my father ever read Twain's books—my father born in Mississippi when slavery still cast a cold shadow at brightest and hottest noon. And if he did not read Twain, is there any Lester who did? Probably not, and it doesn't matter. In the character of Huckleberry Finn, Twain evoked something poignant and real in the American psyche, and now, having read the novel, I see that it is something dangerously, fatally seductive. . . .

I am grateful that among the many indignities inflicted on me in childhood, I escaped *Huckleberry Finn.* As a black parent, however, I sympathize with those who want the book banned, or at least removed from required reading lists in schools. While I am opposed to book banning, I know that my children's education will be enhanced by not reading *Huckleberry Finn.* It is, in John Gardner's phrase, a "well-meant, noble sounding error" that "devalue[s] the world."

That may sound harsh and moralistic, but I cannot separate literature, no matter how well written, from morality. By morality I do not mean bourgeois mores, which seek to govern the behavior of others in order to create (or coerce) that conformity thought necessary for social cohesion. The truly moral is far broader, far more difficult, and less certain of itself than bourgeois morality, because it is not concerned with the "what" of behavior but with the spirit we bring to our living, and, by implication, to literature. . . .

It is in this sense, then, that morality can and should be one of the criteria for assessing literature. It must be if a book is to "serve as the axe for the frozen sea within us," as Kafka wrote. *Adventures of Huckleberry Finn* is not the axe; it is the frozen sea, immoral in its major premises, one of which demeans blacks and insults history.

Twain makes an odious parallel between Huck's being "enslaved" by a drunken father who keeps him locked in a cabin and Jim's legal enslavement. Regardless of how awful and wrong it is for a boy to be held physically captive by his father, there is a profound difference between that and slavery. By making them into a parallelism, Twain applies a veneer to slavery which obscures the fact that, by definition, slavery was a horror. Such a parallelism also allowed Twain's contemporaries to comfortably evade responsibility and remorse for the horror they had made.

A boy held captive by a drunken father is not in the same category of human experience as a man enslaved. Twain willfully refused to understand what it meant to be legally owned by another human being and to have that legal ownership supported by the full power of local, state, and federal government enforcement. Twain did not take slavery, and therefore black people, seriously.

Even allowing for the fact that the novel is written from the limited first-person point of view of a fourteen-year-old boy (and at fourteen it is not possible to take anything seriously except oneself), the author must be held responsible for choosing to write from that particular point of view. If the novel had been written before emancipation, Huck's dilemma and conflicting feelings over Jim's escape would have been moving. But in 1884 slavery was legally over. Huck's almost Hamlet-like interior monologues on the rights and wrongs of helping Jim escape are not proof of liberalism or compassion, but evidence of an inability to relinquish whiteness as a badge of superiority. "I knowed he was white inside," is Huck's final assessment of Jim.

Jim does not exist with an integrity of his own. He is a childlike person who, in attitude and character, is more like one of the boys in Tom Sawyer's gang than a grown man with a wife and children, an important fact we do not learn until much later. But to Twain, slavery was not an emotional reality to be explored extensively or with love.

The novel plays with black reality from the moment Jim runs away and does not immediately seek his freedom. It defies logic that Jim did not know Illinois was a free state. Yet Twain wants us not only to believe he didn't, but to accept as credible that a runaway slave would drift *south* down the Mississippi River, the only route to freedom he knew being at Cairo, Illinois, where the

Ohio River meets the Mississippi. If Jim knew that the Ohio met the Mississippi at Cairo, how could he not have known of the closer proximity of freedom to the east in Illinois or north in Iowa? If the reader must suspend intelligence to accept this, intelligence has to be dispensed with altogether to believe that Jim, having unknowingly passed the confluence of the Ohio and Mississippi Rivers, would continue down the river and go deeper and deeper into the heart of slave country. A century of white readers have accepted this as credible, a grim reminder of the abysmal feelings of superiority with which whites are burdened.

The least we expect of a novel is that it be credible—if not wholly in fact, then in emotion; for it is emotions that are the true subject matter of fiction. As Jim floats down the river farther and farther into slave country, without anxiety about his fate and without making the least effort to reverse matters, we leave the realm of factual and emotional credibility and enter the all-too-familiar one of white fantasy in which blacks have all the humanity of Cabbage Patch dolls.

The novel's climax comes when Jim is sold and Tom and Huck concoct a ridiculous scheme to free him. During the course of the rescue, Tom Sawyer is shot. Huck sends the doctor, who cannot administer to Tom alone. Jim comes out of hiding and aids the doctor, knowing he will be recaptured. The doctor recounts the story this way:

> so I says, I got to have *help,* somehow; and the minute I says it, out crawls this nigger from somewheres, and says he'll help, and he done it, too, and done it very well. Of course I judged he must be a runaway nigger, and there I *was!* and there I had to stick, right straight along, all the rest of the day, and all night. . . . *I never see a nigger that was a better nuss or faithfuller* [emphasis added], and yet he was resking his freedom to do it, and was all tired out, too, and I see plain enough he'd been worked main hard, lately. I liked the nigger for that; I tell you, gentlemen, a nigger like that is worth a thousand dollars—and kind treatment, too. . . . there I *was,* . . . and there I had to stick, till about dawn this morning; then some men in a skiff come by, and as good luck would have it, the nigger was setting by the pallet with his head propped on his knees, sound asleep; so I motioned them in, quiet, and they slipped up on him and grabbed him and tied him before he knowed what he was about, and we never had no trouble. . . . the nigger never made the least row nor said a word, from the start. He ain't no bad nigger, gentlemen; that's what I think about him.

This depiction of a black "hero" is familiar by now since it has been repeated in countless novels and films. It is a picture of the only kind of black that whites have ever truly liked—faithful, tending sick whites, not speaking, not causing trouble, and totally passive. He is the archetypal "good nigger," who lacks self-respect, dignity, and a sense of self separate from the one whites want him to have. A century of white readers have accepted this characterization because it permits their own "humanity" to shine with more luster.

The depth of Twain's contempt for blacks is not revealed fully until Tom Sawyer clears up something that has confused Huck. When Huck first proposed freeing Jim, he was surprised that Tom agreed so readily. The reason Tom did so is because he knew all the while that Miss Watson had freed Jim when she died two months before.

Once again credibility is slain. Early in the novel Jim's disappearance from the town coincided with Huck's. Huck, having manufactured "evidence" of his "murder" to cover his escape, learned that the townspeople believed that Jim had killed him. Yet we are now to believe that an old white lady would free a black slave suspected of murdering a white child. White people may want to believe such fairy tales about themselves, but blacks know better.

But this is not the nadir of Twain's contempt, because when Aunt Sally asks Tom why he wanted to free Jim, knowing he was already free, Tom replies: "Well that *is* a question, I must say; and *just* like women! Why, I wanted the *adventure* of it." Now Huck understands why Tom was so eager to help Jim "escape."

Tom goes on to explain that his plan was "for us to run him down the river, on the raft, and have adventures plumb to the mouth of the river." Then he and Huck would tell Jim he was free and take him "back up home on a steamboat, in style, and pay him for his lost time." They would tell everyone they were coming and "get out all the niggers around, and have them waltz him into town with a torchlight procession and a brass band, and then he would be a hero, and so would we."

There is no honor here; there is no feeling for or sense of what Gardner calls that which "is necessary to humanness." Jim is a plaything, an excuse for "the *adventure* of it," to be used as it suits the fancies of the white folk, whether that fancy be a journey on a raft down the river or a torchlight parade. What Jim clearly is not is a human being, and this is emphasized by the fact that Miss Watson's will frees Jim but makes no mention of his wife and children.

Twain doesn't care about the lives the slaves actually lived. Because he doesn't care, he devalues the world.

> Every hero's proper function is to provide a noble image for men to be inspired by and guided by in their own actions; that is, the hero's business is to reveal what the gods require and love. . . . [T]he hero's function . . . is to set the standard in action . . . the business of the poet (or "memory" . . . ) is to celebrate the work of the hero, pass the image on, keep the heroic model of behavior fresh, generation on generation. [Gardner]

Criticizing **Adventures of Huckleberry Finn** because of Twain's portrayal of blacks is almost too easy, and, some would add sotto voce, to be expected from a black writer. But a black writer accepts such arrogant dismissals before he or she sits down to write. We could not write otherwise.

But let me not be cynical. Let me allow for the possibility that what I have written may be accepted as having more than a measure of truth. Yet doesn't **Huckleberry Finn** still deserve to be acknowledged as an American classic, eminently deserving of being read?

The Council on Interracial Books for Children, while highly critical of the book, maintains "that much can be learned from this book—not only about the craft of writing and other issues commonly raised when the work is taught, but also about racism. . . . Unless **Huck Finn**'s racist *and* anti-racist messages are considered, the book can have racist results." While it is flattering that the council goes on to recommend one of my books, *To Be a Slave,* as supplementary reading to correct Twain's portrayal of slavery, racism is not the most insidious and damaging of the book's flaws. In its very essence the book offends that morality which would give "a noble image . . . to be inspired and guided by." If it is the hero's task "to reveal what the gods require and love," what do we learn from *Adventures of Huckleberry Finn*?

The novel's major premise is established in the first chapter: "The widow Douglas, she took me for her son, and allowed she would sivilize me; but it was rough living in the house all the time, considering how dismal regular and decent the widow was in all her ways; so when I couldn't stand it no longer, I lit out. I got into my old rags, and my sugar-hogshead again, and was free and satisfied." Civilization is equated with education, regularity, decency, and being "cramped up," and the representatives of civilization are women. Freedom is old clothes and doing what one wants to do. "All I wanted was a change, I warn't particular."

The fact that the novel is regarded as a classic tells us much about the psyche of the white American male, because the novel is a powerful evocation of the *puer,* the eternal boy for whom growth, maturity, and responsibility are enemies. There is no more powerful evocation in American literature of the eternal adolescent than *Adventures of Huckleberry Finn.* It is a fantasy adolescence, however. Not only is it free of the usual adolescent problems caused by awakening sexuality, but also Huck has a verbal adroitness and cleverness beyond the capability of an actual fourteen-year-old. In the person of Huck, the novel exalts verbal cleverness, lying, and miseducation. The novel presents, with admiration, a model we (men) would and could be if not for the pernicious influence of civilization and women.

In its lyrical descriptions of the river and life on the raft, the novel creates an almost primordial yearning for a life of freedom from responsibility:

> It was kind of solemn, drifting down the big still river, laying on our backs looking up at the stars, and we didn't ever feel like talking loud, and it warn't often that we laughed, only a little kind of low chuckle.

We had mighty good weather, as a general thing, and nothing ever happened to us at all.

> Sometimes we'd have that whole river all to ourselves for the longest time. Yonder was the banks and the islands, across the water; and maybe a spark—which was a candle in a cabin window—and sometimes on the water you could see a spark or two—on a raft or a scow, you know; and maybe you could hear a fiddle or a song coming over from one of them crafts. It's lovely to live on a raft. We had the sky, up there, all speckled with stars, and we used to lay on our backs and look up at them, and discuss about whether they was made, or only just happened.

It is in passages such as these that the book is most seductive in its quiet singing of the "natural" life over the life of "sivilization," which is another form of slavery for Huck. It is here also that the novel fails most profoundly as moral literature.

Twain's notion of freedom is the simplistic one of freedom from restraint and responsibility. It is an adolescent vision of life, an exercise in nostalgia for the paradise that never was. Nowhere is this adolescent vision more clearly expressed than in the often-quoted and much-admired closing sentences of the book: "But I reckon I got to light out for the Territory ahead of the rest, because aunt Sally she's going to adopt me and sivilize me, and I can't stand it. I been there before."

That's just the problem, Huck. You haven't "been there before." Then again, neither have too many other white American males, and that's the problem, too. They persist in clinging to the teat of adolescence long after only blood oozes from the nipples. They persist in believing that freedom from restraint and responsibility represents paradise. The eternal paradox is that this is a mockery of freedom, a void. We express the deepest caring for this world and ourselves only by taking responsibility for ourselves and whatever portion of this world we make ours.

Twain's failure is that he does not care until it hurts, and because he doesn't, his contempt for humanity is disguised as satire, as humor. No matter how charming and appealing Huck is, Twain holds him in contempt. And here we come to the other paradox, the critical one that white Americans have so assiduously resisted: it is not possible to regard blacks with contempt without having first so regarded themselves.

To be moral. It takes an enormous effort of will to be moral, and that's another paradox. Only to the extent that we make the effort to be moral do we grow away from adolescent notions of freedom and begin to see that the true nature of freedom does not lie in "striking out for the territory ahead" but resides where it always has—in the territory within.

Only there does one begin to live with oneself with that seriousness from which genuine humor and satire are born. Twain could not explore the shadowy realms of slavery and freedom with integrity because he did not risk becoming a person. Only by doing so could he have achieved real compassion. Then Jim would have been a man and Huck would have been a boy, and we, the readers, would have learned a little more about the territory ahead which is always within.

*Adventures of Huckleberry Finn* is a dismal portrait of the white male psyche. Can I really expect white males to recognize that? Yet they must. All of us suffer the consequences as long as they do not.

## Donald A. Barclay

SOURCE: "Mark Twain," in *Children's Books and Their Creators,* edited by Anita Silvey, Houghton Mifflin Company, 1995, pp. 656-57.

*Huckleberry Finn* has attracted young readers who delight in Huck, the book's picaresque narrator, as well as his adventures. Huck's adventures are amusing and thrilling enough to hold the attention of young readers, while his journey down the Mississippi strikes a deeper chord by representing the delightful—and terrifying—possibilities inherent in any attempt to escape the tyranny of adult society. Besides attracting young readers, *The Adventures of Huckleberry Finn* has attracted debate over its suitability for children. Certainly its irony eludes many young readers, and the book's plot includes such "unsuitable" elements as theft, murder, running away from home, child abuse, human slavery, and mob violence. Furthermore, the text is spiced with dialect speech that many younger readers have trouble deciphering and contains language that many children and adults find offensive. The book's language has generated accusations of racism. These accusations have, in turn, generated hot denials from those readers who see the book as a testament to racial tolerance. Although there is no denying that some of Huck's words are racially offensive, he does, however, avow that he will "go to hell" rather than see his friend Jim remain enslaved. Despite this, the controversy over *Huckleberry Finn* continues to swirl like a Mississippi back eddy, just as the book itself continues to roll on with all the force of Huck's "monstrous big" river. Having appeared in over 850 editions published in some sixty-five languages, *The Adventures of Huckleberry Finn* remains a reading rite of passage for much of the literate world.

Twain's image as an author for children has been shaped not only by his own talent for writing about children but also by the various ways in which his works have been packaged. For years publishers have abridged, bowdlerized, and illustrated Twain's work expressly for the children's market. His work has also been packaged for children via feature films, television programs, stage plays, musicals, animated films, and comic books. Frequently, such child-oriented packaging has resulted in many freckle-faced and barefoot interpretations that omit or gloss over Twain's darker intentions.

Despite Louisa May Alcott's unfriendly recommendation that the coarse Mark Twain should not write for children, the fact is that most often Twain's intended audience was the entire family, not just its younger nor just its older members. Like all popular writers of his time and station, Twain tried (if not always successfully) to observe those nineteenth-century standards of taste and decorum that held that good writing should be fit for consumption by men, women, and children alike. So conscious of these standards was Twain that he willingly allowed his upright and proper wife, Olivia, to censor from his work anything that might prove offensive to young or old.

That Twain could successfully write for both young and old at the same time is as much a mark of his greatness as the fact that his work is as popular now, among both young and old, as it was when first published. And while the list of those who write for children but manage to appeal to adults is long, Twain is among the very few writers who have managed to find an audience of children without writing specifically for them.

## Jane Smiley

SOURCE: "Say It Ain't So, Huck; Second Thoughts on Mark Twain's 'Masterpiece'," in *Harper's Magazine,* Vol. 292, No. 1748, January, 1996, pp. 61-7.

So I broke my leg. Doesn't matter how—since the accident I've heard plenty of broken-leg tales, and, I'm telling you, I didn't realize that walking down the stairs, walking down hills, dancing in high heels, or stamping your foot on the brake pedal could be so dangerous. At any rate, like numerous broken-legged intellectuals before me, I found the prospect of three months in bed in the dining room rather seductive from a book-reading point of view, and I eagerly got started. Great novels piled up on my table, and right at the top was *The Adventures of Huckleberry Finn,* which, I'm embarrassed to admit, I hadn't read since junior high school. The novel took me a couple of days (it was longer than I had remembered), and I closed the cover stunned. Yes, stunned. Not, by any means, by the artistry of the book but by the notion that this is the novel all American literature grows out of, that this is a great novel, that this is even a serious novel.

Although Huck had his fans at publication, his real elevation into the pantheon was worked out early in the Propaganda Era, between 1948 and 1955, by Lionel Trilling, Leslie Fiedler, T. S. Eliot, Joseph Wood Krutch, and some lesser lights, in the introductions to American and British editions of the novel and in such journals as *Partisan Review* and *The New York Times Book Review.* The requirements of *Huck*'s installation rapidly revealed themselves: the failure, of the last twelve chapters (in which Huck finds Jim imprisoned on the Phelps plantation and Tom Sawyer is reintroduced and elaborates a cruel and unnecessary scheme for Jim's liberation) had to be diminished, accounted for, or forgiven; after that, the novel's special qualities had to be placed in the context first of other American novels (to their detriment) and then of world literature. The best bets here seemed to be Twain's style and the river setting, and the critics invested accordingly: Eliot, who had never read the novel as a boy, traded on his own childhood beside the big river, elevating Huck to the Boy, and the Mississippi to the River God, therein finding the sort of mythic resonance that he admired. Trilling liked the river god idea, too, though he didn't bother to capitalize it. He also thought that Twain, through Huck's lying, told truths, one of them being (I kid you not) that "something . . . had gone out of American life after the [Civil War], some simplicity, some innocence, some peace." What Twain himself was proudest of in the novel—his style—Trilling was glad to dub "not less than definitive in American literature. The prose of *Huckleberry Finn* established for written prose the virtues of American colloquial speech. . . . He is the master of the style that escapes the fixity of the printed page, that sounds in our ears with the immediacy of the heard voice, the very voice of unpretentious truth." The last requirement was some quality that would link *Huck* to other, though "lesser," American novels such as Herman Melville's *Moby-Dick,* that would possess some profound insight into the American character. Leslie Fiedler obligingly provided it when he read homoerotic attraction into the relationship between Huck and Jim, pointing out the similarity of this to such other white man-dark man friendships as those between Ishmael and Queequeg in *Moby-Dick* and Natty Bumppo and Chingachgook in James Fenimore Cooper's *Last of the Mohicans.*

The canonization proceeded apace: great novel (Trilling, 1950), greatest novel (Eliot, 1950), world-class novel (Lauriat Lane Jr., 1955). Sensible naysayers, such as Leo Marx, were lost in the shuffle of propaganda. But, in fact, *The Adventures of Huckleberry Finn* has little to offer in the way of greatness. There is more to be learned about the American character from its canonization than through its canonization.

Let me hasten to point out that, like most others, I don't hold any grudges against Huck himself. He's just a boy trying to survive. The villain here is Mark Twain, who knew how to give Huck a voice but didn't know how to give him a novel. Twain was clearly aware of the story's difficulties. Not finished with having revisited his boyhood in *Tom Sawyer,* Twain conceived of a sequel and began composition while still working on *Tom Sawyer*'s page proofs. Four hundred pages into it, having just passed Cairo and exhausted most of his memories of Hannibal and the upper Mississippi, Twain put the manuscript aside for three years. He was facing a problem every novelist is familiar with: his original conception was beginning to conflict with the implications of the actual story. It is at this point in the story that Huck and Jim realize two things: they have become close friends, and they have missed the Ohio River and drifted into what for Jim must be the most frightening territory of all—down the river, the very place Miss Watson was going to sell him to begin with. Jim's putative savior,

Huck, has led him as far astray as a slave can go, and the farther they go, the worse it is going to be for him. Because the Ohio was not Twain's territory, the fulfillment of Jim's wish would necessarily lead the novel away from the artistic integrity that Twain certainly sensed his first four hundred pages possessed. He found himself writing not a boy's novel, like *Tom Sawyer,* but a man's novel, about real moral dilemmas and growth. The patina of nostalgia for a time and place, Missouri in the 1840s (not unlike former President Ronald Reagan's nostalgia for his own boyhood, when "Americans got along,") had been transformed into actual longing for a timeless place of friendship and freedom, safe and hidden, on the big river. But the raft had floated Huck and Jim, and their author with them, into the truly dark heart of the American soul and of American history: slave country.

Twain came back to the novel and worked on it twice again, once to rewrite the chapters containing the feud between the Grangerfords and the Shepherdsons, and later to introduce the Duke and the Dauphin. It is with the feud that the novel begins to fail, because from here on the episodes are mere distractions from the true subject of the work: Huck's affection for and responsibility to Jim. The signs of this failure are everywhere, as Jim is pushed to the side of the narrative, hiding on the raft and confined to it, while Huck follows the Duke and the Dauphin onshore to the scenes of much simpler and much less philosophically taxing moral dilemmas, such as fraud. Twain was by nature an improviser, and he was pleased enough with these improvisations to continue. When the Duke and the Dauphin finally betray Jim by selling him for forty dollars, Huck is shocked, but the fact is neither he nor Twain has come up with a plan that would have saved Jim in the end. Tom Sawyer does that.

Considerable critical ink has flowed over the years in an attempt to integrate the Tom Sawyer chapters with the rest of the book, but it has flowed in vain. As Leo Marx points out, and as most readers sense intuitively, once Tom reappears, "[m]ost of those traits which made [Huck] so appealing a hero now disappear. . . . It should be added at once that Jim doesn't mind too much. The fact is that he has undergone a similar transformation. On the raft he was an individual, man enough to denounce Huck when Huck made him the victim of a practical joke. In the closing episode, however, we lose sight of Jim in the maze of farcical invention." And the last twelve chapters are boring, a sure sign that an author has lost the battle between plot and theme and is just filling in the blanks.

As with all bad endings, the problem really lies at the beginning, and at the beginning of *The Adventures of Huckleberry Finn* neither Huck nor Twain takes Jim's desire for freedom at all seriously; that is, they do not accord it the respect that a man's passion deserves. The sign of this is that not only do the two never cross the Mississippi to Illinois, a free state, but they hardly even consider it. In both *Tom Sawyer* and *Huckleberry Finn,* the Jackson's Island scenes show that such a crossing, even in secret, is both possible and routine, and even though it would present legal difficulties for an escaped slave, these would certainly pose no more hardship than locating the mouth of the Ohio and then finding passage up it. It is true that there could have been slave catchers in pursuit (though the novel ostensibly takes place in the 1840s and the Fugitive Slave Act was not passed until 1850), but Twain's moral failure, once Huck and Jim and link up, is never even to account for their choice to go down the river rather than across it. What this reveals is that for all his lip service to real attachment between white boy and black man, Twain really saw Jim as no more than Huck's sidekick, homoerotic or otherwise. All the claims that are routinely made for the book's humanitarian power are, in the end, simply absurd. Jim is never autonomous, never has a vote, always finds his purposes subordinate to Huck's, and, like every good sidekick, he never minds. He grows ever more passive and also more affectionate as Huck and the Duke and the Dauphin and Tom (and Twain) make ever more use of him for their own purposes. But this use they make of him is not supplementary; it is integral to Twain's whole conception of the novel. Twain thinks that Huck's affection is a good enough reward for Jim.

The sort of meretricious critical reasoning that has raised Huck's paltry good intentions to a "strategy of subversion" [says David L. Smith] and a "convincing indictment of slavery" [says T. S. Eliot] precisely mirrors the same sort of meretricious reasoning that white people use to convince themselves that they are not "racist." If Huck feels positive toward Jim, and loves him, and thinks of him as a man, then that's enough. He doesn't actually have to act in accordance with his feelings. White Americans always think racism is a feeling, and they reject it or they embrace it. To most Americans, it seems more honorable and nicer to reject it, so they do, but they almost invariably fail to understand that how they feel means very little to black Americans, who understand racism as a way of structuring American culture, American politics, and the American economy. To invest *The Adventures of Huckleberry Finn* with "greatness" is to underwrite a very simplistic and evasive theory of what racism is and to promulgate it, philosophically, in schools and the media as well as in academic journals. Surely the discomfort of many readers, black and white, and the censorship battles that have dogged *Huck Finn* in the last twenty years are understandable in this context. No matter how often the critics place in context Huck's use of the word "nigger," they can never excuse or fully hide the deeper racism of the novel—the way Twain and Huck use Jim because they really don't care enough about his desire for freedom to let that desire change their plans. And to give credit to Huck suggests that the only racial insight Americans of the nineteenth or twentieth century are capable of is a recognition of the obvious—that blacks, slave and free, are human.

Ernest Hemingway, thinking of himself, as always, once said that all American literature grew out of *Huck Finn.*

It undoubtedly would have been better for American literature, and American culture, if our literature had grown out of one of the best-selling novels of all time, another American work of the nineteenth century, *Uncle Tom's Cabin,* which for its portrayal of an array of thoughtful, autonomous, and passionate black characters leaves *Huck Finn* far behind. *Uncle Tom's Cabin* was published in 1852, when Twain was seventeen, still living in Hannibal and contributing to his brother's newspapers, still sympathizing with the South, nine years before his abortive career in the Confederate Army. *Uncle Tom's Cabin* was the most popular novel of its era, universally controversial. In 1863, when Harriet Beecher Stowe visited the White House, Abraham Lincoln condescended to remark to her, "So this is the little lady who made this great war." . . .

The very heart of nineteenth-century American experience and literature, the nature and meaning of slavery, is finally what Twain cannot face in *The Adventures of Huckleberry Finn.* As Jim and Huck drift down Twain's beloved river, the author finds himself nearing what must have been a crucial personal nexus: how to reconcile the felt memory of boyhood with the cruel implications of the social system within which that boyhood was lived. He had avoided this problem for the most part in *Tom Sawyer:* slaves hardly impinge on the lives of Tom and the other boys. But once Twain allows Jim a voice, this voice must speak in counterpoint to Huck's voice and must raise issues that cannot easily be resolved, either personally or culturally. . . .

[Stowe's] views about many issues were brilliant, and her heart was wise. She gained the respect and friendship of many men and women of goodwill, black and white, such as Frederick Douglass, the civil-rights activist Mary Church Terrill, the writer and social activist James Weldon Johnson, and W. E. B. Du Bois. What she did was find a way to talk about slavery and family, power and law, life and death, good and evil, North and South. She truly believed that all Americans together had to find a solution to the problem of slavery in which all were implicated. When her voice, a courageously public voice—as demonstrated by the public arguments about slavery that rage throughout *Uncle Tom's Cabin*—fell silent in our culture and was replaced by the secretive voice of Huck Finn, who acknowledges Jim only when they are alone on the raft together out in the middle of the big river, racism fell out of the public world and into the private one, where whites think it really is but blacks know it really isn't.

Should *Huckleberry Finn* be taught in the schools? The critics of the Propaganda Era laid the groundwork for the universal inclusion of the book in school curriculums by declaring it great. Although they predated the current generation of politicized English professors, this was clearly a political act, because the entry of *Huck Finn* into classrooms sets the terms of the discussion of racism and American history, and sets them very low: all you have to do to be a hero is acknowledge that your poor sidekick is human; you don't actually have to act in the interests of his humanity. Arguments about censorship have been regularly turned into nonsense by appeals to **Huck's** "greatness." Moreover, so much critical thinking has gone into defending **Huck** so that he can be great, so that American literature can be found different from and maybe better than Russian or English or French literature, that the very integrity of the critical enterprise has been called into question. That most readers intuitively reject the last twelve chapters of the novel on the grounds of tedium or triviality is clear from the fact that so many critics have turned themselves inside out to defend them. Is it so mysterious that criticism has failed in our time after being so robust only a generation ago? Those who cannot be persuaded that *The Adventures of Huckleberry Finn* is a great novel have to draw some conclusion.

I would rather my children read *Uncle Tom's Cabin,* even though it is far more vivid in its depiction of cruelty than **Huck Finn,** and this is because Stowe's novel is clearly and unmistakably a tragedy. No whitewash, no secrets, but evil, suffering, imagination, endurance, and redemption—just like life. Like little Eva, who eagerly but fearfully listens to the stories of the slaves that her family tries to keep from her, our children want to know what is going on, what has gone on, and what we intend to do about it. If "great" literature has any purpose, it is to help us face up to our responsibilities instead of enabling us to avoid them once again by lighting out for the territory.

### Justin Kaplan

SOURCE: "Selling 'Huck Finn' Down the River," in *The New York Times Book Review,* March 10, 1996, p. 27.

[*The following essay is Kaplan's response to Jane Smiley's disavowal of* **Huckleberry Finn** *as a great American masterpiece.*]

Harriet Beecher Stowe's novel portrays "thoughtful, autonomous and passionate black characters," Ms. Smiley writes, while Mark Twain's Jim is merely a sidekick for Huck, who, moreover, fails to take Jim's quest for freedom seriously. **Huckleberry Finn** promotes a "simplistic and evasive theory" of racism as a problem to be alleviated through feeling rather than action. A truly responsible writer, she seems to be saying, would not have been satisfied with Huck's recognition of Jim's humanity and dignity but would have evolved Huck into John Brown and Jim into Nat Turner, two people who, indeed, "did" something about racism instead of just having a feeling about it.

The issue here, in part, is whether you want certainty or conflict in the literature you value—closure or risk, instruction or exploration, right-mindedness or free-mindedness. Writing **Uncle Tom's Cabin** in 1850-51, a decade before the argument about slavery boiled over into the Civil War, Stowe was dealing with a clear and present

evil for which, as she believed, abolition and an aroused public were the sole remedy. In **Huckleberry Finn,** started in 1876, by which time slavery was no longer a present fact, Mark Twain was writing a historical, not a reformist, novel. Instead of being issue-driven, a cry for action, as Stowe's book was, his was autobiographical and nostalgic. Perhaps he had set out to do something not altogether possible, to meld a tenderly remembered boyhood with a profoundly troubled adult recognition that the same white, riverine society that allowed Huck his brief rafting idyll was also heartless and greedy, a league of swindlers, drunks, hypocrites, lunkheads, bounty hunters and trigger-happy psychopaths. To praise (as Ms. Smiley does) Stowe's reformist novel for its "clarity of both . . . style and substance" while faulting Mark Twain's quite different sort of book for its conflictiveness and "secretive voice" is to sell stylistic innovation, humor and imaginative literature down the river.

Inevitably, given the rhetorical thrust and focus of much discussion these days, the issue comes down to one of "correctness," but even on this dismal level Ms. Smiley's praise of the one book to the virtual stigmatization

*From* The Adventures of Huckleberry Finn, *1884.*
*Illustrated by E. W. Kemble.*

of the other doesn't make much sense. *Huckleberry Finn* is in constant trouble with teachers, librarians and parents because of its iterations of "nigger," a word that has a pre-emptive force today that it did not have in Huck Finn's Mississippi Valley of the 1840s. As far as I can tell, there have been no comparable objections to the frequent use, again by black characters as well as whites, of the word in *Uncle Tom's Cabin.*

For all its undisputed power, moral outrage and a literary brilliance too easily overshadowed by message, Stowe's novel comes with serious problems of attitude for contemporary readers: the same "deeper racism" Ms. Smiley finds in *Huckleberry Finn.* This begins with the stereotypical portrayal of Uncle Tom presiding over a family evening in his cabin and affects lesser characters like Black Sam, so called from his being "three shades blacker than any other son of ebony on the place," and shown hitching up his pantaloons, "his regularly organized method of assisting his mental perplexities." Other problems that afflict this book are organic and structural, reflecting the belief, held by Stowe and other abolitionists, that blacks were genetically unadaptable to both the climate and the advanced society of the United States. Repatriation to a gentler haven far away appeared to be the only answer. Lucy, one of Stowe's black characters, commits suicide; Prue becomes a drunk and a thief; George Harris and Eliza leave for Liberia; Tom is beaten to death. This generalized hopelessness, in Stowe's vision representing the tragedy inherent not only in slavery as an institution but in blacks as an uprooted race, is alien to *Huckleberry Finn,* where Jim's future as a free man reunited with his family at least remains an open question.

No other major American book has been so vigorously challenged, and over so many years, as *Adventures of Huckleberry Finn.* Yet it manages somehow, through its humor, lyricism and distinctive, even revolutionary narrative voice, not only to survive but to transcend its author's definition of a classic: "A book which people praise and don't read." Since it was first published in this country in 1885, *Huckleberry Finn* has been read in some 65 languages and almost a thousand editions. For all its enduring popularity, Mark Twain's novel is the book many Americans love to hate and wish had never happened, but we're now as bonded to this nettlesome work as Brer Rabbit was to Tar-Baby. Like Huck, after Pap Finn "got too handy with his hick'ry," the book is "all over welts."

By now its early trials are almost as familiar as the story the novel tells. A month after publication, the trustees of the Concord (Mass.) Public Library expelled the book from its shelves. It was "trash and suitable only for the slums," they said. "It deals with a series of adventures of a very low grade of morality; it is couched in the language of a rough dialect, and all through its pages there is a systematic use of bad grammar and an employment of rough, coarse, inelegant expressions." Over the next quarter-century other libraries—in Denver, Omaha, Brooklyn and the New York State Reformatory—fell in line, claiming the book was "immoral and sacrilegious," put "wrong ideas in youngsters' heads" and set "a bad example." Within the bounds of pure literal-mindedness, the people making these judgments had a point. Son of the town drunkard, Mark Twain's hero-narrator steals, lies, consorts with swindlers and violates both the law and the prevailing social code by helping a slave to escape and recognizing him as an equal. Huck's story ridicules the work ethic, the Bible, prayer, "missionarying," preaching and pious sentiments in general—"tears and flapdoodle," "soul-butter and hogwash." Even Mark Twain's wife and daughters, the audience whose approval he most wanted for a book that came out of his deepest imperatives, acknowledged "dear old Huck" only as someone to be let in through the back door and fed in the kitchen.

It's no longer ethical and social transgressiveness that drives controversy but "racism," a mainly invisible issue in the book's earlier career. Mark Twain's characterization of Jim allegedly stereotypes black people as ignorant, superstitious, passive, indiscriminately affectionate and infantile. This ignores the fact that at crucial junctures Jim is Huck's adult guide and protector and throughout lives on a higher ethical level than anybody else in this book, including Huck.

John Wallace, a black educator who has long been on the warpath against *Huckleberry Finn,* calls it "the most grotesque example of racist trash ever given our children to read. . . . Any teacher caught trying to use that piece of trash with our children should be fired on the spot, for he or she is either racist, insensitive, naive, incompetent or all of the above." The novel figures prominently on the American Library Association's list of books most frequently challenged in schools and libraries.

Here the attack on grounds of racism and "negative stereotypes" joins a more literary sort of objection to the last quarter of the book for reducing Jim to a prop for Tom Sawyer's boyish theatrical ingenuities. Even Hemingway told readers, "The rest is just cheating." "The last 12 chapters are boring," Ms. Smiley writes, "a sure sign that an author has lost the battle between plot and theme and is just filling in the blanks." I don't disagree with this, but at the same time I'm happy to settle for any novel that, like *Huckleberry Finn,* may be only 75 percent great.

# CUMULATIVE INDEXES

# How to Use This Index

The main reference

Baum, L(yman) Frank 1856–
1919 .......................... **15**

list all author entries in this and previous volumes of *Children's Literature Review:*

The cross-references

See also CA 103; 108; DLB 22; JRDA
MAICYA; MTCW; SATA 18; TCLC 7

list all author entries in the following Gale biographical and literary sources:

*AAYA* = *Authors & Artists for Young Adults*
*AITN* = *Authors in the News*
*BLC* = *Black Literature Criticism*
*BW* = *Black Writers*
*CA* = *Contemporary Authors*
*CAAS* = *Contemporary Authors Autobiography Series*
*CABS* = *Contemporary Authors Bibliographical Series*
*CANR* = *Contemporary Authors New Revision Series*
*CAP* = *Contemporary Authors Permanent Series*
*CDALB* = *Concise Dictionary of American Literary Biography*
*CDBLB* = *Concise Dictionary of British Literary Biography*
*CLC* = *Contemporary Literary Criticism*
*CMLC* = *Classical and Medieval Literature Criticism*
*DAB* = *DISCovering Authors: British*
*DAC* = *DISCovering Authors: Canadian*
*DAM* = *DISCovering Authors: Modules*
      *DRAM*: Dramatists Module; *MST*: Most-Studied Authors Module;
      *MULT*: Multicultural Authors Module; *NOV*: Novelists Module;
      *POET*: Poets Module; *POP*: Popular Fiction and Genre Authors Module
*DC* = *Drama Criticism*
*DLB* = *Dictionary of Literary Biography*
*DLBD* = *Dictionary of Literary Biography Documentary Series*
*DLBY* = *Dictionary of Literary Biography Yearbook*
*HLC* = *Hispanic Literature Criticism*
*HW* = *Hispanic Writers*
*JRDA* = *Junior DISCovering Authors*
*LC* = *Literature Criticism from 1400 to 1800*
*MAICYA* = *Major Authors and Illustrators for Children and Young Adults*
*MTCW* = *Major 20th-Century Writers*
*NCLC* = *Nineteenth-Century Literature Criticism*
*NNAL* = *Native North American Literature*
*PC* = *Poetry Criticism*
*SAAS* = *Something about the Author Autobiography Series*
*SATA* = *Something about the Author*
*SSC* = *Short Story Criticism*
*TCLC* = *Twentieth-Century Literary Criticism*
*WLC* = *World Literature Criticism, 1500 to the Present*
*YABC* = *Yesterday's Authors of Books for Children*

# CUMULATIVE INDEX TO NATIONALITIES

**Nationality Index**

# CUMULATIVE INDEX TO TITLES

Title Index

**Title Index**

**Title Index**

**Title Index**

**Title Index**

**Title Index**

**Title Index**

Title Index

Title Index

**Title Index**

Title Index

**Title Index**

ISBN 0-7876-3225-2